NATIONAL POLICE LIBRARY

20061374

D0267323

BLACKSTONE'S GUIDE TO

The New Transfer of Undertakings Legislation

DISCARDED
NATIONAL POLICE LIBRARY

BLACKSTONE'S GUIDE TO
The New Transfer of Undertakings Legislation

Charles Wynn-Evans LL.B (Bris), B.C.L. (Oxon)
Solicitor, Partner, Dechert LLP, London

NATIONAL
POLICE
LIBRARY
X

OXFORD
UNIVERSITY PRESS

OXFORD

UNIVERSITY PRESS

Great Clarendon Street, Oxford OX2 6DP

Oxford University Press is a department of the University of Oxford.
It furthers the University's objective of excellence in research, scholarship,
and education by publishing worldwide in

Oxford New York

Auckland Cape Town Dar es Salaam Hong Kong Karachi
Kuala Lumpur Madrid Melbourne Mexico City Nairobi
New Delhi Shanghai Taipei Toronto

With offices in

Argentina Austria Brazil Chile Czech Republic France Greece
Guatemala Hungary Italy Japan Poland Portugal Singapore
South Korea Switzerland Thailand Turkey Ukraine Vietnam

Oxford is a registered trade mark of Oxford University Press
in the UK and in certain other countries

Published in the United States
by Oxford University Press Inc., New York

© Charles Wynn-Evans, 2006

The moral rights of the author have been asserted
Database right Oxford University Press (maker)

Crown copyright material is reproduced under Class Licence
Number C01P0000148 with the permission of OPSI
and the Queen's Printer for Scotland

First published 2006

All rights reserved. No part of this publication may be reproduced,
stored in a retrieval system, or transmitted, in any form or by any means,
without the prior permission in writing of Oxford University Press,
or as expressly permitted by law, or under terms agreed with the appropriate
reprographics rights organizations. Enquiries concerning reproduction
outside the scope of the above should be sent to the Rights Department,
Oxford University Press, at the address above

You must not circulate this book in any other binding or cover
and you must impose this same condition on any acquirer

British Library Cataloguing in Publication Data
Data available

Library of Congress Cataloging in Publication Data
Data available

Typeset by RefineCatch Limited, Bungay, Suffolk
Printed in Great Britain
on acid-free paper by
Biddles Limited, King's Lynn

ISBN 0–19–928905–0   978–0–19–928905–9

1 3 5 7 9 10 8 6 4 2

Acc No.   20061374

Classmark   344.012596

WYN

Foreword

This has been a massive undertaking by Charles Wynn-Evans, with no transfer out-house by him of any of his obligations to the reader to make it clear, concise, and comprehensive!

We have been awaiting the 'new' transfer of undertakings regulations now for some years, and we have them at last, accompanied by this very welcome Guide, which combines the nub of the old with the nuts and bolts of the new. To misunderstand, misapply, or simply miss TUPE has been an occupational hazard for businesses, employees, and practitioners alike. In the circumstances which formed the factual background to the recent decision in the Employment Appeal Tribunal of *Cross v British Airways* [2005] IRLR 423 (see paragraph 5.30 in the text), two very large companies and a number of trade unions all failed to appreciate for many years that they had been involved in a TUPE transfer. With this Guide on everyone's bookshelves, that will be far less likely.

Considering the job which the author had to do of rendering both readable and comprehensible his account both of the old legislation and case law and of the new Regulations, the retention of a clear structure with signposts was as important as the content, and Charles Wynn-Evans has succeeded miraculously in both respects. I believe that both now and for the foreseeable future this Guide will be the first resort of anyone involved in that long list of now familiar activities: downsizing, outsourcing, inhousing, outhousing, tendering, re-tendering, reconstructing, reorganising, regrouping, or simply closing down. If TUPE is indeed intended to have a 'Worzel Gummidge' effect (see paragraph 5.01), then this Guide has certainly made Worzel considerably more presentable and more palatable. A job well done.

Sir Michael Burton
High Court Judge, Chairman of the Central Arbitration Committee,
President of the Employment Appeal Tribunal (2002–2005)

Preface

Since 1981 the United Kingdom's transfer of undertakings legislation has been one of the most important aspects of the domestic statutory employment law regime, having immense practical, commercial, and financial significance for employers and employees in the private and public sectors in relation to issues such as outsourcing, contract retendering, and business sales. Whether considering employees' rights on an insolvency fire sale, addressing what happens to employees on an outsourcing or the retendering of a service contract, or assessing the employment-related liabilities associated with a business sale, transfer of undertakings issues are often closely scrutinised by, and affect the interests of, a variety of interested parties.

Over the past several years, the domestic and European Court of Justice (ECJ) case law on the application and interpretation of the transfer of undertakings legislation has led to an unfortunate degree of uncertainty for those employers and employees which it affects. The commercial consequences of applying an incorrect interpretation of the transfer legislation can be significant for all concerned, quite apart from the consequent potential prejudice to employees' legal rights and livelihoods. Assuming incorrectly that the transfer of undertakings legislation does not apply to a given situation can lead to the employees' employer facing penalties for failure to inform and consult employee representatives and taking responsibility for the payment of potentially avoidable redundancy and other termination costs. Also, the transferee may face unfair dismissal claims from those employees whom it did not take on. Incorrectly adopting the position that TUPE does apply in a particular scenario not only leaves an employer with termination costs (in terms of notice and redundancy entitlements) but also with potential liabilities for unfair dismissal where the employer, rather than, for example, conducting a redundancy exercise, wrongly argues that the relevant employees transfer automatically to the supposed transferee.

Following the adoption in 2001 of a new incarnation of the Acquired Rights Directive, and as part of its 'Fairness at Work' reform programme, the Government promulgated TUPE 2006 (albeit somewhat belatedly) in order to clarify, update, and amend the domestic statutory regime.

TUPE 2006 is an important restatement of the United Kingdom's transfer of undertakings legislation. Not only does it update the domestic legislation to reflect the codification by the 2001 Acquired Rights Directive of certain of the principles established in the case law on the EU and domestic transfer legislation since its inception; TUPE 2006 also makes a number of significant substantive changes to the domestic legal framework. Amongst other things, the changes made by TUPE 2006 make more likely the application of the transfer legislation to outsourcings and similar transactions, establish a limited ability for employers validly to agree with transferring employees changes to their terms of employment, require transferors to provide prescribed information to transferees about the relevant employees in advance of the TUPE transfer in question, and modify the operation of TUPE in certain insolvency situations.

The fact that TUPE historically provided no protection for the occupational pension rights of transferring employees has also been addressed by recent legislation. The combined effect of the Pensions Act 2004 and the Transfer of Employment (Pension Protection) Regulations 2005 provides a limited degree of pension protection for transferring employees who enjoyed occupational pension rights prior to transfer. This protection has important consequences for transferees in terms of transaction planning and post-transfer employment costs.

This book is intended to provide a guide to the new legislative regime for lawyers, human resources professionals, and others involved in managing the legal, commercial, and personnel aspects of situations to which TUPE applies. As TUPE 2006 not only makes substantive changes to the transfer of undertakings regime but also restates those aspects of the law which remain unchanged, this Guide summarises briefly the considerable body of existing law which is preserved by TUPE 2006. It is therefore hoped that the Guide will also be a useful introduction to the legislation as a whole for those new to the area.

This Guide seeks to provide a structured review of the provisions of TUPE 2006. After a general introduction to and overview of the changes made to the transfer legislation by TUPE 2006 in Chapter 1, Chapters 2 and 3 address the key issue of what events and transactions fall within the scope of TUPE. TUPE 2006 establishes two types of event which can now constitute a relevant transfer for the purposes of the legislation. Chapter 2 summarises what constitutes a transfer of an undertaking (which reflects the law prior to TUPE 2006) whilst Chapter 3 describes the new concept of a service provision change, which is intended to ensure comprehensive application of the transfer legislation to outsourcing, second generation contracting, and inhousing. After Chapter 4 summarises who falls within the scope of the legislation, Chapter 5 then addresses the preservation by TUPE of individual and collective rights. TUPE 2006 introduces an (albeit limited) ability validly to amend employees' terms and conditions of employment in connection with a TUPE transfer. This is addressed in Chapter 6 against the background of the previous case law prohibiting transfer-related contract changes.

After summarising the application of the legislation to transfer-related dismissals in Chapter 7, the Guide then reviews the information and consultation provisions of TUPE. Chapter 8 addresses the new obligation imposed on transferors to provide to transferees in advance of transfer prescribed employee liability information about the transferring employees. Chapter 9 summarises the largely unchanged obligations to which transferors and transferees are subject requiring them to inform and consult with appropriate representatives of the affected employees about TUPE transfers. The interaction of TUPE with other employee consultation requirements is also briefly considered.

The Guide then proceeds to a review of the operation of TUPE 2006 in certain specific contexts. Chapter 10 summarises the new regime applying in insolvency situations which, by permitting appropriate representatives of the transferring employees to agree changes to those employees' terms and conditions of employment and excusing the transferee from responsibility for certain of the transferor's debts to transferring employees, seeks to facilitate the 'rescue culture' to which the Government is committed. Chapter 11 addresses the continued exclusion of occupational pension scheme rights from the protective scope of TUPE and the separate pension protection now established for those transferring employees who enjoyed pension entitlements prior to the transfer.

Finally, Chapter 12 briefly addresses some miscellaneous and yet important issues. Some commentary is provided on the prohibition on contracting out of the legislation and the territorial aspects of the statutory regime. A very brief overview is also offered of some of the drafting and commercial points which need to be considered by those negotiating detailed contracts involving transfers of undertakings.

As Blackstone's Guides are intended to provide a concise guide to new legislation, constraints of space preclude comprehensive examination of a number of issues related to the scope and application of TUPE including the jurisprudence on what constitutes a transfer of undertaking (which is only discussed in summary form), the specific issues which arise in relation to public sector contracting, the more complex jurisdictional issues which arise in transnational transfer of undertakings situations, and the detailed drafting of commercial agreements recording TUPE transfers. Space also does not permit detailed discussion of the specific provisions of TUPE 2006 relating to its operation in Northern Ireland.

Since they are the terms deployed in TUPE, the terms 'transferor' and 'transferee' have been used throughout this book (as opposed to terms which may, in a particular context, better describe the parties involved, such as acquirer, buyer, seller etc). The term 'transferor' denotes the original owner or operator of the business or activity which is (or is potentially) the subject of the transfer of undertakings legislation and the term 'transferee' denotes the party which acquires or inherits that business or activity. All references to 'regulations' are to the regulations of TUPE 2006 and to 'Articles' are to Articles of the 2001 Acquired Rights Directive. References to 'the Directive' and 'TUPE' are respectively to the EU and domestic UK transfer legislation generally.

It should be noted that one further relevant development is anticipated. The regulations referred to in Chapter 5 with regard to the transfer of trade union recognition awarded by the Central Arbitration Committee under the statutory trade union recognition regime will clarify that aspect of the operation of the legislation. These regulations have not been promulgated as at the time of writing.

The law is stated as at 6 April 2006. Whilst all errors, infelicities, obscurities, and omissions remain entirely my own responsibility, I have numerous debts to acknowledge in the production of this book. The Guide would never have seen the light of day but for the seemingly endless efforts of my tireless secretary, Anna Brennan, to whom I am hugely indebted for her remarkable patience, perseverance, and accuracy particularly in translating my hieroglyphics. Thanks are also due to my team at Dechert for their support while the book has been in gestation. Various trainee solicitors who have passed through the Dechert employment team have provided valuable research assistance including Karen Ferries, Mike Anderson, Emma Byford, Duncan Batty, Emma Butler, and Romella Manning-Brown. I have also benefited from discussions with a number of colleagues on the ramifications of the new legislation, including in particular Nicholas Robertson of Mayer Brown Rowe & Maw LLP and Geoffrey Mead of Collyer-Bristow. OUP (and in particular Annabel Moss and Louise Kavanagh) have been a great support and cajoling help in my getting the job done approximately on time. I am also extremely grateful to Sir Michael Burton for agreeing to write the Foreword. This book is dedicated to Alex, Catherine, David, and my parents with love and thanks for their tolerance of, and support for, this project.

Charles Wynn-Evans
Dechert LLP
160 Queen Victoria Street
London
EC4V 4QQ
charles.wynn-evans@dechert.com
6 April 2006

Contents—Summary

TABLE OF CASES   xix

TABLE OF STATUTES   xxiv

TABLE OF SECONDARY LEGISLATION   xxvi

TABLE OF ABBREVIATIONS AND TERMS   xxx

1. INTRODUCTION   1

2. IDENTIFYING A RELEVANT TRANSFER   19

3. SERVICE PROVISION CHANGES   41

4. WHO TRANSFERS?   59

5. TRANSFER OF INDIVIDUAL AND COLLECTIVE OBLIGATIONS   81

6. VARIATIONS TO EMPLOYEES' CONTRACTS   99

7. TRANSFER-RELATED DISMISSALS   113

8. PROVISION OF EMPLOYEE INFORMATION   127

9. COLLECTIVE INFORMATION AND CONSULTATION   149

10. INSOLVENCY SITUATIONS   179

11. PENSIONS   195

12. MISCELLANEOUS   213

APPENDIX 1. Transfer of Undertakings (Protection of Employment) Regulations 2006   227

APPENDIX 2. Pensions Act 2004, ss 257 and 258.   245

APPENDIX 3. Transfer of Employment (Pension Protection) Regulations 2005   249

INDEX   253

Contents

TABLE OF CASES	xix
TABLE OF STATUTES	xxiv
TABLE OF SECONDARY LEGISLATION	xxvi
TABLE OF ABBREVIATIONS AND TERMS	xxx

1. **INTRODUCTION**

A. The Purpose of the Transfer Legislation   1.01

B. Share-based Transactions   1.08

C. An Overview of the New Legislation
    1. Introduction   1.12
    2. The Revised Acquired Rights Directive   1.16
    3. The New Legislation Summarised   1.18
    4. Impact Assessment   1.38
    5. Transitional Provisions   1.39

D. Public Sector Issues
    1. Public Administration   1.40
    2. TUPE 2006   1.46
    3. Government Codes of Practice   1.49
    4. Regulations under the Employment Relations Act 1999, Section 38.   1.52

2. **IDENTIFYING A RELEVANT TRANSFER**

A. The Two Statutory Definitions   2.01

B. A Transfer of an Undertaking   2.08
    1. The Components of a Transfer of an Undertaking   2.09
    2. What is a Transfer?   2.11
    3. What is an Economic Entity?   2.17
    4. One Person Undertakings   2.25
    5. Single Contract Undertakings   2.27
    6. Retention of Identity   2.32
    7. Transfer of Part of an Undertaking   2.37
    8. Changes to the Operation   2.41
    9. Break in Activities   2.45
    10. Asset Transfer   2.47

C. Labour-intensive Activities   2.60

D. Miscellaneous
1. Series of Transactions and Timing of Transfer — 2.77
2. Ships — 2.83

3. SERVICE PROVISION CHANGES

A. Introduction — 3.01

B. Definition — 3.09

C. Organised Grouping of Employees — 3.15

D. Principal Purpose — 3.20

E. One-off Service Contracts — 3.22

F. Supply of Goods — 3.31

G. Innovative Bids — 3.35

H. Professional Business Services — 3.39

I. Issues of Interpretation — 3.45

J. Conclusions — 3.59

4. WHO TRANSFERS?

A. Who Transfers?
1. Employees — 4.01
2. Employment by Transferor — 4.05
3. Assignment — 4.14
4. Temporary Assignment — 4.26
5. Contract would otherwise Terminate — 4.32
6. Pre-transfer Employment — 4.37
7. Knowledge of Transfer — 4.45

B. Electing not to Transfer
1. Introduction — 4.47
2. Objection to Transfer — 4.49
3. Changes to Working Conditions — 4.57
4. Constructive Dismissal — 4.77
5. Claims against the Transferor — 4.78

5. TRANSFER OF INDIVIDUAL AND COLLECTIVE OBLIGATIONS

A. Transfer of Individual Rights
1. General Position — 5.01
2. Employer's Liability Compulsory Insurance — 5.16
3. Specific Issues — 5.20

B. Collective Agreements
1. The Directive — 5.42
2. Transfer of Collective Agreements — 5.43

3.	Definition of Collective Agreements	5.49
4.	Legal Enforceability	5.52

C. Trade Union Recognition

1.	The Directive	5.56
2.	Transfer of Recognition	5.57
3.	Continuation of Recognition	5.61
4.	Statutory Recognition	5.66

D. Other Representative Structures — 5.67

6. VARIATIONS TO EMPLOYEES' CONTRACTS

A. Case Law Background

1.	Introduction	6.01
2.	The Case Law	6.06
3.	Practical Issues	6.16

B. Changes Permitted by TUPE 2006

1.	Reform	6.24
2.	Categories of Variation	6.26
3.	Compatibility with EU Law	6.29
4.	The ETOR Problem	6.32
5.	Pension Changes	6.41

7. TRANSFER-RELATED DISMISSALS

A. Introduction — 7.01

B. Automatic Unfair Dismissal

1.	The Principle of Automatic Unfairness	7.12
2.	Protected Persons	7.14
3.	Exceptions	7.18

C. Connection with the Transfer

1.	Sole or Principal Reason	7.22
2.	Uncertain Transactions	7.25

D. Economic, Technical or Organisational Reasons Entailing Changes in the Workforce

1.	Statutory Provisions	7.30
2.	Statutory Redundancy Payments	7.34
3.	What can be an ETOR?	7.36
4.	Whose Reason?	7.42

E. Liability and Fairness Generally — 7.43

8. PROVISION OF EMPLOYEE INFORMATION

A. Introduction

1.	The Directive	8.01
2.	Domestic Implementation	8.03

B. Employees 8.08

C. Information
1. 2005 Consultation 8.10
2. Prescribed Information 8.12
3. Employment Particulars 8.15
4. Disciplinary and Grievance Procedures 8.18
5. Claims 8.21
6. Data Protection 8.26
7. Former Employees 8.34

D. Delivery and Updating 8.37

E. Instalments 8.40

F. Indirect Provision 8.41

G. Timing 8.43

H. Remedy
1. 2005 Consultation 8.48
2. TUPE 2006 8.53
3. Principles of Award 8.56
4. Minimum Award 8.60
5. Mitigation 8.65

I. Due Diligence Exercises 8.66

J. Contracting Out 8.75

9. COLLECTIVE INFORMATION AND CONSULTATION

A. Overview 9.01

B. Affected Employees 9.06

C. Information
1. Required Information 9.09
2. Legal, Economic and Social Implications 9.11
3. Timing 9.13
4. Delivery 9.15
5. Transferee Measures 9.17

D. Consultation
1. When Consultation is Required 9.21
2. Measures 9.24
3. Whose Obligation? 9.29
4. Nature and Timing of Consultation 9.31

E. Representation of Employees
1. Appropriate Representatives 9.35
2. Electing Employee Representatives 9.44
3. Protection of Employee Representatives 9.49

F. Remedies for Breach
1. Complaint 9.65

	2. Compensation	9.72
	3. Joint and Several Liability	9.83
	4. Special Circumstances Defence	9.89
	5. Injunctions	9.95
G.	Interaction with Consultation Requirements	
	1. Collective Redundancy Consultation	9.97
	2. Other Statutory Obligations	9.99
H.	Planning for Compliance	9.110

10. INSOLVENCY SITUATIONS

A.	Introduction	10.01
B.	Bankruptcy and Analogous Insolvency Proceedings	10.09
C.	Transferor's Debts	
	1. Relevant Insolvency Proceedings	10.14
	2. Affected Employees	10.16
	3. Excluded Debts	10.17
D.	Contract Variations	
	1. Introduction	10.22
	2. Which Employees?	10.28
	3. Appropriate Representatives	10.30
	4. Agreement of Employee Representatives	10.39
	5. The Nature of Permitted Variations	10.43
	6. Issues of Interpretation	10.46
E.	Misuse of Insolvency Proceedings	10.53
F.	Hiving Down	10.54

11. PENSIONS.

A.	Overview	11.01
B.	The Pensions Exclusion	
	1. The Directive	11.06
	2. Occupational Pension Schemes	11.10
C.	*Beckmann* and *Martin*	11.17
D.	TUPE 2006 Pension Provisions	11.32
E.	PA 2004 and PPR 2005	
	1. Introduction	11.38
	2. Eligibility Requirements	11.43
	3. The Minimum Standard of Pension Provision	11.47
	4. Enforcement	11.56
	5. Consultation	11.60

12. MISCELLANEOUS

    A. Contracting Out
       1. Prohibition 12.01
       2. Compromise Agreements 12.05

    B. Territoriality
       1. Introduction 12.12
       2. TUPE 2006 .... 12.16
       3. Continental Shelf 12.23
       4. International Transfers 12.24

    C. Drafting and Commercial Points
       1. Introduction 12.33
       2. Due Diligence 12.34
       3. Warranties 12.37
       4. Indemnities 12.42
       5. Outsourcing 12.46

    D. Assertion of Statutory Rights 12.47

APPENDIX 1. Transfer of Undertakings (Protection of Employment)
              Regulations 2006 227
APPENDIX 2. Pensions Act 2004, ss 257 and 258. 245
APPENDIX 3. Transfer of Employment (Pension Protection) Regulations 2005 ... 249

INDEX 253

Table of Cases

ADI (UK) Ltd v Willer EAT/11/99 [2001] IRLR 542, CA 2.21, 2.28, 2.68, 3.60
Abels [1987] CMLR 406, ECJ 10.09
Abernethy v Mott [1974] IRLR 213, CA 7.23
Abler v Sodexho MM Catering Gesellschaft [2004] IRLR 168, ECJ 2.48
Adams v Lancashire CC and BET [1997] IRLR 436, CA 11.09
Addison & others v Denholm Ship Management (UK) Ltd [1997] IRLR 389,
    EAT 12.23
Alamo Group (Europe) Ltd v Tucker and another [2003] IRLR 266, EAT 9.05
Allen v Amalgamated Construction Co Ltd [2000] IRLR 119, ECJ 1.11
Amicus v Dynamex Friction Ltd [2005] IRLR 724, HC 9.95
Amicus v GBS Tooling Ltd (in administration) [2005] IRLR 683, EAT 9.82
Anderson v Kluwer Publishing Ltd COIT 1985 COIT 1697/249 .... 4.18
Astle v Cheshire CC (1) Omnisure Property Management (2) [2005] IRLR 12,
    EAT 2.71
Astley & others v Celtec Ltd [2002] IRLR 629, CA 2.79, 5.36
Ayse Süzen [1997] IRLR 255, ECJ 2.63–2.69, 3.46

BSG Property Services v Tuck [1996] IRLR 134, EAT 5.07, 7.42
Balfour Beatty Power Networks and another v Wilcox & others [2006] IRLR 258,
    EAT 2.58
Banking Insurance and Finance Union v Barclays Bank plc [1987] ICR 495, EAT ... 9.13
Beckmann v Dynamco Whicheloe Macfarlane Ltd [2002] IRLR 578, ECJ 11.20,
                                              11.25, 11.29–11.32, 11.37, 11.40
Bernadone v Pall Mall Services Group & others [2000] IRLR 487, CA ... 5.13, 5.16, 5.17
Berriman v Delabole Slate Ltd [1985] IRLR 305, CA 6.35, 7.38
Betts v Brintel Helicopters Ltd and KLM ERA Helicopters (UK) Ltd [1997]
    IRLR 361, HC; [1997] IRLR 45, CA 2.33, 2.65, 7.01
Birch v Sports and Leisure Management [1995] IRLR 518, EAT 2.15
Boor v Ministre de la Fonction Publique [2005] IRLR 61, ECJ 6.15
Bork International A/S v Foreningen af Arbejdsledere i Danmark [1989] IRLR 41,
    ECJ 2.12, 2.45
Botzen v Rotterdam Sche Droogdok Maatschappii BV [1985] ECR 519,
    ECJ 4.16, 4.21, 4.28
Brook Street Bureau (UK) Ltd v Dacas [2004] ICR 1437, CA 4.04
Brooks and others v Borough Care Services and CLS Care Services Ltd [1998]
    IRLR 636, EAT 1.10
Buchanan-Smith v Schleicher & Co International Ltd [1996] IRLR 547, EAT 4.19
Burke v Royal Liverpool University Hospital [1997] ICR 730, EAT 2.09

CPL Distribution v Todd [2003] IRLR 28, CA 4.23
CWW Logistics v Ronald EAT, 1/12/98 .... 2.21

Cable & Wireless plc v P Muscat [2006] EWCA Civ 220, CA 4.04
Canning v (1) Niaz (2) McLaughlin [1983] IRLR 431, EAT 7.35
Carlisle Facilities Group v Matrix Events & Security Services and others
   EAT/0380/04 .... 2.73, 3.62
Castle View Services Ltd v Howes and others [2000] SLT 696 .... 2.83
Catamaran Cruises Ltd v Williams [1994] IRLR 386, EAT 6.02
Chapman v CPS Computer Group [1987] IRLR 462, CA 5.25
Charlton v Charlton Thermosystems (Romsey) Ltd [1995] IRLR 79, EAT 2.14
Cheesman v R. Brewer Contracts Ltd [2001] IRLR 144, EAT 2.22
Clark v Nomura International plc [2000] IRLR 766, QBD 11.31
Clarks of Hove Ltd v Bakers Union [1978] ICR 1076, CA 9.91
Clifton Middle School Governing Body v Askew [2000] ICR 286, CA 1.45
Collino and Chiappero v Telecom Italia SpA [2000] IRLR 788, ECJ 2.06
Computacenter (UK) Ltd v Swanton and others EAT/0256/04 .... 3.62
Cowell v Quilter [1989] IRLR 392, CA 4.02
Crawford v Swinton Insurance Brokers Ltd [1990] IRLR 42, EAT 6.35, 7.39
Credit Suisse First Boston (Europe) Ltd v Lister [1998] IRLR 700, CA 6.22
Credit Suisse First Boston (Europe) Ltd v Padiachy [1989] IRLR 315, CA 6.22
Cross v British Airways plc [2005] IRLR 423, EAT 5.30
Curr v Marks & Spencer plc [2003] IRLR 74, CA 4.04

DJM International Ltd v Nicholas [1996] IRLR 76, EAT 5.05
D'Urso v Ercole Marelli Elettromeccanica Generale SpA [1992] IRLR 136, ECJ ... 10.14
D36 Ltd v Castro EAT/0853/03 .... 5.13, 5.36
Daddy's Dance Hall see Foreningen af Arbejdsledere i Danmark v
   Daddy's Dance Hall A/S
Dines v Initial Healthcare [1994] IRLR 336, CA 2.14
Dr Sophie Redmond Stitching v Bartol [1992] IRLR 366, ECJ 2.18
Dudley Bower Building Services Ltd v Lowe and others [2003] IRLR 260, EAT 2.26
Duncan Web Offset (Maidstone) Ltd v Cooper [1995] IRLR 633,
   EAT 4.12, 4.17, 4.25, 4.30
Dundee City Council v Arshad EAT/1204/88 .... 1.45

ECM (Vehicle Delivery Service) Ltd v Cox [1998] IRLR 416, EAT; [1999]
   IRLR 559, CA 2.33, 2.68, 3.18
Eidesund v Stavanger Catering A/S [1996] IRLR 684 .... 11.09

Fairhurst Ward Abbotts Limited v Botes Building Limited & others [2004]
   IRLR 304, CA 2.38, 3.56
Farmer v Danzas EAT 858/93 .... 2.44
Foreningen af Arbejdsledere i Danmark v Daddy's Dance Hall A/S [1988]
   IRLR 315, ECJ 2.12, 4.68, 6.06, 6.07, 6.11, 6.12, 6.19,
                                                      6.24, 6.26, 6.30, 6.31, 6.39, 10.24
Frankling v BPS Public Sector Ltd [1999] IRLR 212, EAT 11.18, 11.37

GEFCO UK Ltd v Oates (1) Car & Delivery Co Ltd EAT/0014/05 .... 2.57

Hagen v ICI Chemicals and Polymers Ltd [2002] IRLR 31, HC 5.27, 11.36

Hairsine v Kingston upon Hull CC [1992] ICR 212, EAT 9.61
Harrison Bowden v Bowden [1994] ICR 186, EAT 7.28
Hartlebury Printers Ltd, Re (in liquidation) [1992] IRLR 516, HC 9.91
Hay v George Hanson (Building Contracts) Ltd [1996] IRLR 427, EAT 4.54
Henke v Gemeinde Schierke and Verwaltungsgemeinschaft 'Brocken' [1996]
    IRLR 701, ECJ 1.44, 1.53
Hope v PGS Engineering EAT/0267/04 .... 4.56
Horkulak v Cantor Fitzgerald International [2004] IRLR 942, CA 11.31
Howard v Millrise Ltd (1) SG Printers (2) EAT/0658/04 .... 9.48

Ibex Trading Co Ltd v Walton [1994] IRLR 564, EAT 7.29
Institute of Chartered Accountants of England and Wales v Customs and Excise
    Commissioners [1997] STC 1155, CA 1.42
Institution of Professional Civil Servants v Secretary of State for Defence [1987]
    IRLR 373, HC 9.24

Jowett (Angus) & Co Ltd v National Union of Tailors and Garment Workers
    [1985] IRLR 426, EAT 5.12
Jules Dettlier Equipement v Dassy [1998] IRLR 266, ECJ 10.14

Katsikas v Konstantinidis [1993] IRLR 179, ECJ 4.50
Kelman v Care Services Ltd [1995] ICR 260, EAT 2.11
Kerry Foods Ltd v Creber [2000] IRLR 10, EAT 7.07, 9.05
Kingston v Darlows Estate Agency EAT/1038/96 .... 4.22

Lawson v Serco Ltd [2006] IRLR 289, HL 12.15
Lightway (Contractors) Ltd v Associated Holdings Ltd [2000] IRLR 247,
    CS 2.11, 2.66
Litster v Forth Dry Dock Engineering Ltd [1989] IRLR 161, HL 1.02, 1.27, 3.18,
                                                        4.38, 4.39, 4.40, 7.16, 10.55
Longden v Ferrari Ltd [1994] IRLR 157, EAT 7.27

MSF v Refuge Assurance plc [2002] IRLR 324, EAT 9.94
McCormack and others v Scottish Coal Company Ltd [2005] All ER (D) 104 .... 2.54
McMeechan v Secretary of State for Employment [1997] IRLR 353, CA 4.04
Mackie v Aberdeen City Council EATS/0095/04 .... 2.30
Martin and others v South Bank University [2004] IRLR 74, ECJ 6.09, 11.23, 11.25,
                                                              11.29–11.32, 11.40
Mathieson v United News Shops Ltd EAT/554/95 .... 2.42
Mayeur v Association Promotion de l'Information Messine (APIM) [2000]
    IRLR 783, ECJ 1.40
Meade and Baxendale v British Fuels Ltd [1996] IRLR 504, EAT; [1997]
    IRLR 505, CA; [1998] IRLR 706, HL 6.08
Merckx v Ford Motors Co Belgium SA [1996] IRLR 467, ECJ 2.14, 2.42
Michael Peters Ltd v Farnfield (1) and Michael Peters Group plc (2) [1995]
    IRLR 190, EAT 4.10
Mikkelsen [1989] ICR 330, ECJ 4.01
Ministry of Defence v Jeremiah [1979] IRLR 436, CA 9.52

Mitie Managed Services Ltd v French [2002] IRLR 521, CA 5.23
Montgomery v Johnson & Ward Ltd [2001] IRLR 269, CA 4.04
Morris Angel & Son v Hollande [1993] IRLR 169, CA 5.21

Newns v British Airways plc [1992] IRLR 575, CA 1.05
Nokes v Doncaster Amalgamated Colleries Ltd [1940] 3 All ER 549, HL 1.05
Northern General Hospital NHS Trust v Gale [1994] ICR 426 ....4.17
Numast and another v P & O Scottish Ferries and others EATS/0060/04;
    [2005] All ER (D) 27, EAT 2.51, 2.54
Ny Mølle Krø [1989] IRLR 37, ECJ 2.12

Oy Liikenne [2001] IRLR 171, ECJ 2.47, 2.48, 2.50, 2.52

P & O Trans European Ltd v Initial Transport Services Ltd [2003] IRLR 128, CA ...2.49
Perth & Kinross Council v Donaldson and others [2004] IRLR 121,
    EAT 2.24, 2.45, 10.09
Photostatic Copiers (Southern) Ltd v Okuda [1995] IRLR 11, EAT 4.46
Porter and Nanayakkara v Queen's Medical Centre [1993] IRLR 486,
    HC 2.13, 2.42, 7.37
Powerhouse Retail Ltd (1) Seeboard Retail plc (2) Midlands Electricity plc (3) v
    Burroughs and others [2006] UKHL 13, HL 5.29

R v British Coal Corporation and Secretary of State for Trade and Industry,
    ex p Price [1994] IRLR 72, CA 9.33
R v Secretary of State for Trade and Industry, ex p Unison [1996] IRLR 438 ....9.49
RCO Support Services v UNISON [2002] IRLR 401, CA 2.69
Ralton v Havering College of Further Education [2001] IRLR 738, EAT 6.13
Rask v ISS Kantineservice [1993] IRLR 133, ECJ 6.07
Rossiter v Pendragon plc and Crosby-Clarke v Air Foyle Ltd [2002] IRLR 483,
    CA 4.59, 4.64, 4.68
Rygaard v Stø Mølle Akustik A/S [1996] IRLR 51, ECJ 2.19, 2.27–2.31

St John of God (Care Services) Ltd v Brooks [1992] IRLR 546, EAT 6.02
Sanchez Hidalgo [1999] IRLR 136, ECJ 1.40, 2.14, 2.16, 2.20
Schmidt v Spar und Leihkasse der Früheven Ämter Bordesholm,
    Kiel und Cronshagen [1994] IRLR 302, ECJ 2.25, 3.52
Secretary of State for Employment v Spence [1986] IRLR 248, CA 4.39
Secretary of State for Trade & Industry v Cook [1997] IRLR 150, EAT 4.46
Securicor v Fraser Security Services Ltd [1996] IRLR 552, EAT 4.30, 4.31
Securiplan v Bademosi [2003] All ER (D) 435, EAT 4.29, 4.31
Senior Heat Treatment Ltd v Bell [1997] IRLR 614, EAT 4.55, 5.40, 6.21
Sita (GB) Ltd v Burton [1997] IRLR 501, EAT 4.80
Skillbase Services v King [2005] All ER (D) 106, CS 4.24
Smith and another v Cherry Lewis Ltd [2005] IRLR 86, EAT 9.79
Solectron Scotland Ltd v Roper [2004] IRLR 4, EAT 6.17, 6.18, 12.08
Spano v Fiat Geotech [1995] ECR I-4321 ....10.14
Spijkers v Gebroeders Benedik Abbatoir [1986] ECR 1119, ECJ 2.33, 2.34, 2.36,
                                                        2.45, 2.59, 2.61, 2.62, 2.64, 3.04

Sunley Turriff Holdings Ltd *v* Thompson [1995] IRLR 184, EAT 4.11
Susie Radin *v* GMB and others [2004] ICR 893, CA 9.79
Sweetin *v* Coral Racing [2006] IRLR 252, EAT 9.76

TGWU *v* James McKinnon, JR Haulage and others [2001] IRLR 597, EAT 9.05
Taylor *v* Connex South Eastern Ltd EAT/1243/99 .... 4.74, 6.23, 7.24
Thompson and others *v* Walton Car Delivery and BRS Automotive [1997]
    IRLR 343, EAT 12.10
Thompson *v* SCS Consulting Ltd [2001] IRLR 801, EAT 7.43
Trafford *v* Sharpe and Fisher (Building Supplies) Ltd [1994] IRLR 325, EAT 7.07
Transport and General Workers Union *v* Morgan Platts Ltd (in administration)
    EAT/0646/02 .... 9.81

Unicorn Consultancy Services *v* Westbrook [2000] IRLR 80, EAT 5.06
University of Oxford *v* Humphreys [2000] IRLR 183, CA 4.78, 4.79, 12.41, 12.42

Vigdösdottir *v* Islandspostur HF [2003] IRLR 425, ECJ 6.06

Waite *v* GCHQ [1983] 2 AC 714, HL 5.33
Walden Engineering Co Ltd *v* Warrener [1993] ICR 967, EAT 11.08
Warner *v* Adnet [1998] IRLR 394, CA 7.07
Wheeler *v* Patel [1987] IRLR 211, EAT 7.37
Whent *v* T Cartledge Ltd [1997] IRLR 153, EAT 5.08, 5.55
Whitehouse *v* Chas A Blatchford & Sons Ltd [1999] IRLR 492, CA 7.40
Wickens *v* Champion Employment [1984] ICR 365, EAT 4.04
Williams *v* Advance Cleaning Services (1) Engineering & Railway Solicitors Ltd
    (in liquidation) EAT 0838/04 .... 4.25
Wilson *v* St Helen's BC [1996] IRLR 320, EAT; [1997] IRLR 505, CA;
    [1998] IRLR 706, HL 6.08, 6.13
Wynnwith Engineering Co Ltd *v* Bennett [2002] IRLR 170, EAT 2.23

Table of Statutes

*Paragraph numbers in **bold** indicate that the text is reproduced in full*

Aliens Restriction (Amendment) Act
1919
s.5 .... 7.19
Civil Liability (Contribution) Act
1978 .... 9.86
Company Directors' Disqualification Act
1986 .... 10.53
Contracts of Employment Act 1963
Sch.1, para.10 .... 1.04
Contract (Rights of Third Parties) Act
1999 .... 12.10
Data Protection Act 1998 .... 8.27, 8.28,
8.32, 8.33, 8.42
s.2 .... 8.29
Sch.1 .... 8.32
Sch.3 .... 8.29
Disability Discrimination Act 1995 12.42
s.9 .... 12.03
Employers' Liability (Compulsory
Insurance) Act 1969 (ELCI)
s.1(1) 5.17, 5.18
s.3 .... 5.18
s.3(1)(a) 5.18
s.3(1)(b) 5.18
s.3(1)(c) 5.18
Employment Act 2002 .... 7.44
Employment Protection Act 1975 .... 9.13
Employment Relations Act 1999
(ERA 1999) 1.30
s.38 .... 1.15, 1.48. 1.52, 12.26
s.38(1) **1.53**
s.98(1) 7.32
s.98(2)(c) 7.32
s.98(4) 7.32
s.135 .... 7.32
Employment Rights Act 1996
(ERA 1996) 1.04, 7.03, 7.04, 7.10,
7.20, 10.37
s.1 .... 8.13, 8.15, 8.17

s.47(1) 9.50, 9.51
s.47(1A) 9.51
s.47(2) 9.54
s.49(1) 9.54
s.49(3) 9.54
s.49(4) 9.54
s.49(5) 9.54
s.61 .... 9.61
s.63 .... 9.61
s.63(2)–(5) 9.62
s.94 .... 5.32
s.95(1)–(2) 9.75
s.95(1)(c) 11.35
s.97 .... 9.75
s.98 .... 7.44
s.98(4) 6.02
s.102(b) 10.19
s.103 .... 9.56
s.105 .... 9.56
s.108(3)(f) 9.57
s.109 .... 5.32
s.109(2)(f) 9.57
s.120 .... 9.58
s.139 .... 9.74
s.155 .... 9.74
ss 166–170 .... 10.18
ss 182–190 .... 10.18
s.203 .... 12.01, **12.02**
s.205(1) 9.65
s.210(5) 6.21
s.212(1) 6.21
s.212(3) 6.21
s.214(2) 5.41
s.218(2) 5.38, 6.21
s.218(3) 5.39
s.218(4) 5.39
s.218(5) 5.39
s.218(6) 5.39
s.218(7) 5.39

s.218(8) 5.39
ss 220–228 .... 9.75
s.230(1) 4.02
s.230(2) 4.02
Employment Tribunals Act 1996
s.18 .... 7.21, 8.53, 9.65, 12.03, 12.11
European Communities Act 1972 ... 12.26
s.2(2) 1.15
s.2(2)(a) 1.01
Insolvency Act 1986 .... 10.53
s.388(1)(a)–(b) 10.10
s.389(2) 10.10
ss 390–398 .... 10.10
Merchant Shipping Act 1894 .... 2.84
Merchant Shipping Act 1970 .... 2.84
National Health Service and Community
Care Act 1990
s.60(7) 5.18
National Minimum Wage Act 1998
s.49(3) 12.03
Pensions Act 1993 .... 11.46
s.12A 11.54
Pensions Act 1995
s.124(1) 11.44
Pensions Act 2004 (PA 2004) 1.14,
1.20, 1.35, 1.50, 6.41, 6.42, 6.43, 9.27,
9.28, 11.04, 11.05, 11.08, 11.28
s.7 .... 11.57
s.10 .... 11.57
s.17 .... 11.57
s.239 .... **11.13**, 11.14
s.256(b) 11.59
s.257 .... 11.39, **Appendix 2**
s.257(1) 11.43
s.257(2) 11.44, 11.46
s.257(3) 11.44, 11.46
s.257(4) 11.44, 11.46
s.257(5) 11.59

s.257(7) 11.46, 11.52
s.257(8) 11.43
s.258 ..... 6.44, 11.39, 11.56, **Appendix 2**
s.258(1) 11.47, 11.56
s.258(2) 11.47, 11.53
s.258(3) 11.47
s.258(7) 11.47, 11.48
s.318(1) 11.44
Pension Schemes Act 1993 .... 11.08
s.1 .... **11.12**, 11.16
Race Relations Act 1976 .... 12.42
s.72 .... 12.03
Sex Discrimination Act 1975 .... 12.42
s.77 .... 12.03
Trade Union and Labour Relations
(Consolidation) Act 1992
(TULRCA) 7.20, 8.29, 9.34
s.146 .... 9.60
s.152 .... 9.60
s.154 .... 9.60
s.168 .... 9.63, 10.38
s.169 .... 5.66, 9.63
s.178(1) 5.49
s.178(2) 5.49, 5.50
s.178(3) 5.46
s.179 .... 5.44, 5.52
s.179(3) 5.53
s.180 .... 5.44, 5.52
s.188 .... 5.12, 6.03, 8.56, 9.08, 9.13,
9.23, 9.90, 9.97, 12.42
s.188(7) 9.92
s.237 .... 7.21
s.237(1A) 9.57
s.238(2A) 9.57
s.288 .... 12.03
Welfare Reform and Pensions Act
1999 .... 11.15
s.2 .... 11.47

Table of Secondary Legislation

Paragraph numbers in **bold** *indicate that the text is reproduced in full*

Statutory Instruments

Collective Redundancies and Transfer of
Undertakings (Protection of
Employment) (Amendment)
Regulations 1995
(SI 1995/2587) 9.04

Collective Redundancies and Transfer of
Undertakings (Protection of
Employment) (Amendment)
Regulations 1999
(SI 1999/1925) 9.04, 9.37

Employment Act 2002 (Dispute
Resolution) Regulations 2004
(SI 2004/752) 7.44, 8.13
Reg.2(1) 8.19
Reg.3(1) 8.19
Reg.6(1) 8.20
Sch.3 .... 8.20
Sch.4 .... 8.20

Employment Equality
(Religion or Belief) Regulations
2003 (SI 2003/1660) 12.42
Reg.35 .... 12.03

Employment Equality (Sexual
Orientation) Regulations 2003
(SI 2003/1661) 12.42
Reg.35 .... 12.03

Employment Rights (Increase of
Limits) Order 2005
(SI 2005/3352) 9.59, 9.75

Fixed-term Employees (Prevention of
Less Favourable Treatment)
Regulations 2002 (SI 2002/2034)
Reg.10 .... 12.03

Information and Consultation of
Employees Regulations 2004 (ICE)
(SI 2004/3426) 5.68, 9.99, 9.111
Reg.9 .... 12.03
Reg.20(1)(a)–(c) 9.100, 9.105

Reg.20(2) 9.101
Reg.20(4)(d) 9.101
Reg.20(5) 9.105

Occupational Pension Schemes
(Contracting-out) Regulations 1996
(SI 1996/1172) 11.54

Occupational and Personal Pension
Schemes (Consultation by
Employers and Miscellaneous
Amendment) Regulations 2006
(SI 2006/349) 11.60

Part-time Workers (Prevention of Less
Favourable Treatment) Regulations
2000 (SI 2000/1551)
Reg.9 .... 12.03

Transfer of Employment (Pension
Protection) Regulations 2005 (PPR)
(SI 2005/649) 1.14, 1.20, 1.35,
1.50, 6.41, 6.44, 9.27, 9.28, 11.04,
Appendix 3
Reg.2(1) 11.55
Reg.2(2) 11.55
Reg.3(1)–(3) 11.52

Transfer of Undertakings (Protection of
Employment) Regulations
1981(TUPE) (SI 1981/1794) 1.01,
1.10, 1.12, 2.02, 6.05,
9.04, 9.20, 10.55
Reg.2(2) 2.83
Reg.3(2) 2.14
Reg.3(4) 2.77
Reg.4(1) 10.54
Reg.5 .... 5.34, 5.43, 5.45, 5.49, 5.51
Reg.5(1) 4.06, 4.15, 4.32, 4.33, 4.39
Reg.5(2) 5.34
Reg.5(4) 5.40
Reg.5(4A) 4.49, 4.78
Reg.5(4B) 4.49, 4.78
Reg.5(5) **4.57**, 4.59, 4.73, 11.36

Reg.7 .... 11.01, 11.09, 11.18, 11.32
Reg.8 .... 7.22, 12.14
Reg.8(1) 7.06
Reg.8(2) 7.06
Reg.8(3) 7.14
Reg.8(4) 7.19
Reg.9 .... 5.57
Reg.10 .... 1.39, 9.04, 9.100, 12.14
Reg.10(2)(d) 9.20
Reg.10A 1.39
Reg.11 .... 9.04, 9.77, 9.100, 12.14
Reg.12 .... 6.24, 9.100, 12.08, 12.09
Reg.13(1) 12.14
Reg.13(2) 12.14
Transfer of Undertakings (Protection of
    Employment) Regulations 2006
    (TUPE) (SI 2006/246) .... **Appendix 1**
Reg.2(1) 2.03, 3.01, 3.14, 3.52, 4.02,
                4.07, 4.09, 4.28, 5.46
Reg.2(2) 9.39
Reg.2(3) 12.16
Reg.3 .... 2.02, 3.14
Reg.3(1)(a) 2.06, 2.09, 2.11, 2.15,
    2.16, 2.18, 2.23, 2.24, 2.25, 2.31, 2.32,
    2.35, 2.37, 2.38, 2.41, 2.45, 2.60, 2.69,
    2.72, 2.76, 2.77, 3.01, 3.11, 3.17, 3.19,
        3.25, 3.42, 3.47, 3.51, 3.55, 4.13,
    10.05, 11.32, 12.16, 12.18, 12.27
Reg.3(1)(b) 2.06, 2.15, 2.31, 2.59,
    2.60, 2.72, 2.75, 2.77, 3.01, 3.09, 3.11,
    3.14–3.22, 3.27–3.30, 3.34, 3.35, 3.37,
    3.43, 3.45, 3.47, 3.51, 3.55–3.62, 4.13,
    4.36, 10.05, 11.32, 12.16, 12.18, 12.27
Reg.3(1)(b)(i) 3.09
Reg.3(1)(b)(ii) 2.15, 3.09
Reg.3(1)(b)(iii) 3.09
Reg.3(2) 3.61
Reg.3(3)(a)(i) 3.10, 3.14, 3.18
Reg.3(3)(a)(ii) 2.31, 3.10, 3.14,
                            3.22–3.26
Reg.3(3)(b) 3.14
Reg.3(3)(b)(i) 3.31
Reg.3(4)(a) 1.41, 2.06
Reg.3(4)(b) 12.19, 12.20
Reg.3(5) 1.41, 1.43, 1.45
Reg.3(6)(a) 2.82, 3.12
Reg.3(6)(b) 2.10, 3.12
Reg.3(7) 2.84

Reg.4 .... 4.35, 5.03, 5.55, 7.14, 7.44,
    8.11, 10.09, 10.13, 10.17, 10.21,
                11.32, 11.60
Reg.4(1) 4.05, 4.06, 4.13, 4.15,
    4.35, 5.20, 5.43, 8.09, 9.06, 12.46
Reg.4(2) **5.02**, 5.03, 5.11, 5.34
Reg.4(2)(a) **5.25**, 5.36, 7.44
Reg.4(3) **4.37**, 4.38, 4.42, 7.17,
                7.44, 8.35
Reg.4(4) 4.75, 5.22, 6.25, 6.30,
    6.37, 6.39, 6.43, 10.24, 10.27,
                10.45, 12.07
Reg.4(4)(a) 6.26, 6.32
Reg.4(4)(b) 6.26, 6.32
Reg.4(5) 4.75, 5.22, 6.25, 6.30,
    6.37, 6.39, 6.43, 10.24, 10.27,
                10.45, 12.07
Reg.4(5)(a) 6.26, 6.32
Reg.4(5)(b) 6.26, 6.32, 10.45
Reg.4(6) 5.11
Reg.4(7) 4.33, 4.49–4.53, 4.75,
                4.78, 5.40
Reg.4(8) 4.33, 4.49, 4.75, 4.78
Reg.4(9) 4.47, 4.58–4.79, 5.61, 8.24,
                10.51, 11.36, 12.42
Reg.4(10) 4.47, 4.65, 4.67, 4.79,
                7.13, 10.51
Reg.4(11) 4.77, 8.24
Reg.5 .... 8.13, 11.32, 11.60
Reg.6 .... 5.56, 5.61, 5.67
Reg.6(1) **5.56**, 5.57, 5.63
Reg.6(2) **5.58**, 5.64
Reg.7 .... 7.05, 7.08, 7.10, 7.11, 7.14,
    7.15, 7.22, 7.23, 10.09, 10.13
Reg.7(1) 7.03, **7.12**, 7.17, 7.18, 7.20,
                7.26, 7.43, 7.44, 10.16
Reg.7(1)(a) 7.05
Reg.7(1)(b) 7.05
Reg.7(2) 7.05, **7.31**, 7.44
Reg.7(3) 7.32
Reg.7(3)(a) 7.44
Reg.7(3)(b) 7.09, 7.34, 7.44
Reg.7(4) 7.14
Reg.7(5) 7.18
Reg.7(6) 7.18, **7.20**
Reg.8 .... 10.05, 10.17
Reg.8(1)–(6) 10.14
Reg.8(2) 10.16, 10.19

Reg.8(2)(a)–(b) 10.16
Reg.8(3) 10.19
Reg.8(4) 10.17, 10.18
Reg.8(5) 10.17
Reg.8(6) 10.14
Reg.8(7) 10.09, 10.11–10.14
Reg.9 .... 10.05, 10.22, 10.26, 10.29,
10.32, 10.39, 10.42, 10.51
Reg.9(2) **10.30**
Reg.9(2)(b)(i) 10.35
Reg.9(3) 10.34
Reg.9(4) 10.38
Reg.9(5) 10.40
Reg.9(6) 10.43, 10.51
Reg.9(7) 10.25, 10.40
Reg.10 .... 5.10, 6.43, 8.11, 8.14, 9.27,
11.11, 11.32, 11.60
Reg.10(1) 11.01, 11.32, **11.33**
Reg.10(1)(b) 5.28
Reg.10(3) **11.35**
Reg.11 .... 8.07, 8.11, 8.13, 8.15, 8.16,
8.19–11.47, 8.52, 8.57–8.75,
12.30, 12.46
Reg.11(1) 8.09
Reg.11(2) 8.13, 8.17, 8.28, 8.30,
8.35, 8.59. 8.69
Reg.11(2)(a)–(e) 8.03
Reg.11(2)(a) 8.13, 8.26
Reg.11(2)(b) 8.13
Reg.11(2)(c) 8.14
Reg.11(2)(d) 8.14
Reg.11(2)(d)(i) 8.13, 8.22
Reg.11(2)(d)(ii) 8.13, 8.21, 8.23
Reg. 11(2)(e) 8.13
Reg.11(7)(a) 8.40
Reg.11(7)(b) 8.41
Reg.11(4) **8.34**
Reg.11(5) 8.61
Reg.12 .... 8.07, 8.53, 8.65
Reg.12(4)(b) 8.58
Reg.12(5) 8.62
Reg.12(6) 8.65
Reg.13 .... 1.39, 5.64, 9.01, 9.06, 9.13,
9.22, 9.34, 9.35, 9.39, 9.41, 9.65, 9.71,
9.76, 9.86, 9.87, 9.95, 9.107, 10.13,
10.34, 10.49, 11.60, 12.11, 12.30,
12.41, 12.42, 12.46
Reg.13(1) 8.62, 9.06, 10.34

Reg.13(2) 9.02, 9.09, 9.11, 9.13,
9.23, 9.48, 9.89
Reg.13(2)(a) 9.10
Reg.13(2)(b) 9.11
Reg.13(2)(d) 9.20, 9.30
Reg.13(3) 9.35, 9.44, 9.89
Reg.13(3)(b)(i) 9.44
Reg.13(4) 9.18, 9.20, 9.88, 9.89
Reg.13(5) 9.15, 9.89
Reg.13(6) 9.02, 9.21, 9.23, 9.31, 9.89
Reg.13(7) 9.31, 9.89
Reg.13(8) 9.43
Reg.13(9) 9.89
Reg.13(11) 9.48
Reg.13(12) 9.92
Regs 13–15 .... 8.56, 10.31
Reg.14 .... 9.01, 9.36, 9.41, 9.44, 9.65
Reg.14(1) 9.35, 9.45
Reg.15 .... 9.01, 9.65
Reg.15(1) 9.65
Reg.15(2) 9.67
Reg.15(3) 9.42, 9.68
Reg.15(4) 9.69
Reg.15(5) 9.19
Reg.15(7) 9.70
Reg.15(8) 9.72
Reg.15(8)(a) 9.83
Reg.15(9) 9.83
Reg.15(11) 9.83
Reg.15(12) 9.71
Reg.15(15) 9.02
Reg.16 .... 8.56
Reg.16(1) 12.32
Reg.16(2) 9.65
Reg.16(3) 9.73
Reg.16(4) 9.73, 9.74
Reg.17 .... 5.18
Reg.17(1)(a) 5.19
Reg.17(1)(b) 5.19
Reg.17(2) 5.18, 5.19
Reg.18 .... 6.24, **12.01**, 12.11
Reg.20(1) 1.39
Reg.21(1)(a) 1.39
Reg.21(1)(b) 1.39
Reg.21(2)(a) 1.39
Reg.21(2)(b) 1.39
Reg.21(3) 1.39
Reg.21(4) 1.39

Transfer of Undertakings
(Protection of Employment)
(Transfer to OFCOM) Regulations
2003 (SI 2003/2715) 1.53
Transfer of Undertakings
(Protection of Employment)
(Rent Officer Service) Regulations
1999 (SI 1999/2511) 1.53
Transnational Information and
Consultation of Employees
Regulations 1999
(SI 1999/3323) 9.108
Reg.41 .... 12.03
Working Time Regulations 1998
(SI 1998/1833) Reg.35 .... 12.03,
12.42

European Legislation

Directives
Dir.77/187/EEC OJ L/061 Acquired
Rights Directive
(ARD 1977) 1.21, 2.07, 2.18
Art.1(1) 4.16
Art.3(3) 11.06

Dir.98/50/EC OJ L201/88 Acquired
Rights Directive
(ARD 1998) 1.01, 1.04, 1.16
Dir.2001/23/EC OJ L82/16 Acquired
Rights Directive
(ARD 2001) 1.01, 1.04, 1.16,
1.21, 1.44, 3.07, 6.05, 9.04, 11.10
Art.1(b) 2.04
Art.2.1(a) 4.08
Art.2.1(b) 4.08
Art.2.1(d) 4.01
Art.2.2 .... 4.01
Art.3 .... 5.43
Art.3.1 .... 8.49, 9.86
Art.3.2 .... 8.01, **8.02**, 8.03
Art.3.3 .... **5.42**
Art.4 .... 11.01, **11.06**
Art.4.1 .... 6.29, 7.02
Art.4.2 .... 4.47, 4.48, **4.58**, 4.59, 6.15
Art.5.1 .... 10.02, 10.07, 10.11
Art.5.2 .... 10.03, 10.07, 10.12,
10.14, 10.22
Art.6.1 .... 5.56, 5.57
Art.7.4 .... 9.92

Table of Abbreviations and Terms

ARD 1977	Acquired Rights Directive
	Council Directive 77/187/EEC OJ L/061
ARD 1998	Acquired Rights Directive
	Council Directive 98/50/EC OJ L 201/88
ARD 2001	Acquired Rights Directive
	Council Directive 2001/23/EC OJ L 82/16
CA	Court of Appeal
CAC	Central Arbitration Committee
CS	Court of Session
Consultation Response	*TUPE, Draft Revised Regulations, Government Response to the Public Consultation*, Department of Trade and Industry, February 2006
DPA 1998	Data Protection Act 1998
DTI	Department of Trade and Industry
DTI Guidance	*Employment Rights on the Transfer of an Undertaking, A Guide to the 2006 TUPE Regulations for Employees, Employers and Representatives*, Employment Relations Directorate, Department of Trade and Industry, January 2006
EAT	Employment Appeal Tribunal
ECJ	European Court of Justice
ELCI 1969	Employers' Liability (Compulsory Insurance) Act 1969
ERA 1996	Employment Rights Act 1996
ERA 1999	Employment Relations Act 1999
ET	Employment Tribunal
ETOR	an economic, technical or organisational reason entailing changes in the workforce
EWC	European Works Council
HL	House of Lords
IA 1986	Insolvency Act 1986
ICE	Information and Consultation of Employees Regulations 2004 SI 2004/3426
PSA 1993	Pension Schemes Act 1993
PA 2004	Pensions Act 2004
PPR 2005	Transfer of Employment (Pension Protection) Regulations 2005 SI 2005/649
PRP	profit-related pay
TEC	Training and Enterprise Council

TULRCA 1992	Trade Union and Labour Relations (Consolidation) Act 1992
TUPE 2006	Transfer of Undertakings (Protection of Employment) Regulations 2006 SI 2006/246
TUPE 1981	Transfer of Undertakings (Protection of Employment) Regulations 1981 SI 1981/1974
TURERA 1993	Trade Union Reform and Employment Rights Act 1993
2001 Consultation	*Transfer of Undertakings (Protection of Employment) Regulations 1981, Government Proposals for Reform, Detailed Background Paper*, Employment Relations Directorate, Department of Trade and Industry, September 2001, URN 01/1158
2004 Regulations	Employment Act 2002 (Dispute Resolution) Regulations 2004 SI 2004/752.
2005 Consultation	*TUPE, Draft Revised Regulations, Public Consultation Document*, Employment Relations Directorate, Department of Trade and Industry, March 2005, URN 05/926

1

INTRODUCTION

A. The Purpose of the Transfer Legislation	1.01
B. Share-based Transactions	1.08
C. An Overview of the New Legislation	1.12
D. Public Sector Issues	1.40

A. THE PURPOSE OF THE TRANSFER LEGISLATION

The Transfer of Undertakings (Protection of Employment) Regulations **1.01** (TUPE), which address the rights of employees and the obligations and responsibilities of employers in respect of the wide range of transactions and events which fall within their scope, derive constitutionally from the European Union (EU). The United Kingdom is required to implement into its domestic law the principles established by the Acquired Rights Directive (ARD) which, to quote its longer title, relates to 'the approximation of the laws of the Member States relating to the safeguarding of employees' rights in the event of transfers of undertakings, businesses or parts of businesses'.[1]

The EU law basis of the transfer of undertakings legislation is the reason that **1.02** so much of the relevant case law guidance has been provided by the European Court of Justice (ECJ) when addressing the proper application and interpretation of the domestic legislation of the Member States. Cases such as *Litster v Forth Dry Dock & Engineering Ltd*[2] demonstrate the readiness of the domestic courts and tribunals to apply (and the necessity of their applying) a purposive interpretation to the domestic legislation in order to ensure compliance with the Directive and its objectives.

The range of transactions and events to which the transfer of undertakings **1.03** legislation can apply is wide. Examples include:

---

[1] TUPE 1981 was originally introduced, as a statutory instrument rather than primary legislation, pursuant to European Communities Act 1972, s 2(2)(a) in order to implement ARD 1977 into domestic law.

[2] [1989] IRLR 161, HL.

1

- the sale of the whole or part of the assets and undertaking of a business, whether by the owner or operator of the business, or, in an insolvency situation, by administrators or administrative receivers;

- an internal group reorganisation pursuant to which assets and activities are transferred between different companies in a group (which may be desirable for a variety of reasons such as tax planning, organisational convenience or as a precursor to a sale of a corporate entity);

- the outsourcing of a specific business activity or business support function such as information technology support and administration, payroll management, or the manufacture of components;

- the award of a contract to an external service provider for the provision of services such as security, catering, cleaning, refuse collection, and property management;

- the re-tendering of outsourced services leading to the award of a contract to a replacement service provider ('second generation contracting') or its being brought back in-house ('in-housing').

1.04   In implementing the ARD into domestic law, supplemented by provisions relating to the preservation of continuity of employment for statutory purposes,[3] TUPE establishes a legal regime for the protection of employees' employment and related entitlements when the ownership of or responsibility for the operation of the business in which they work transfers from their employer to a third party.

1.05   A central objective of the transfer of undertakings legislation in the domestic context is to reverse the consequences for employees at common law of a disposal or other transfer by their employer of the business in which they work. Since the employment contract is a contract personally to provide services, it cannot at common law transfer to a new owner or operator of the relevant business without the consent of that new owner/operator.[4] Transfer to a third party of the business in which an employee works therefore leads at common law to a dismissal of the employee by the pre-transfer employer.

1.06   Against this background, the mischiefs which the transfer of undertakings legislation seeks to address are that, as a consequence of a transfer of the business in which he or she works, an affected employee:

- is left with no entitlement to continued employment in the business in which he or she was employed prior to the transfer in question;

---

[3] Originally contained in the Contracts of Employment Act 1963, Sch 1, para 10, the relevant provisions are now set out in ERA 1996, Pt I, Chapter XIV. See Chap 5, para 5.36 et seq for further discussion.

[4] See *Nokes v Doncaster Amalgamated Colleries Ltd* [1940] 3 All ER 549, HL. See also *Newns v British Airways plc* [1992] IRLR 575, CA (at para 11): 'It is . . . basic to contract law that a contract of employment cannot be transferred without the consent of both parties to it. But that is the common law position before the intervention of statute.'

- has no right to be employed on his or her previous contractual terms (even if the new owner/operator is willing to engage the employee);
- has no entitlement to any information about or consultation in relation to the transfer and its consequences.

In establishing a regime of protection for employees in relation to business **1.07** transfers and implementing the requirements of EU law, TUPE has three principal effects:

- the employment contracts of those employees working in the relevant undertaking automatically pass to the transferee of the undertaking along with associated liabilities, rights, and powers (save for certain categories of pension entitlement);
- unless legitimate 'economic, technical or organisational' reasons provide a justification, neither the pre- nor the post-transfer employer may dismiss the relevant employees without unfair dismissal consequences;
- both the pre- and post-transfer employers are required to provide prescribed information to 'appropriate representatives' of the employees who are affected by a transfer about the impending transfer and, where action is anticipated in connection with the transfer (by way, for example, of dismissals and changes to terms and conditions), to consult with those representatives about those anticipated steps.

B. SHARE-BASED TRANSACTIONS

Whilst it is a trite point to anyone familiar even in outline with the operation of **1.08** TUPE, it is essential to appreciate at the outset that the legislation does not apply to transfers of shares. TUPE does not apply to transactions solely comprising the transfer (whether by sale or otherwise) of all or part of the share capital of a corporate entity.

In a share-based transaction, in contrast to a business sale, the ownership of **1.09** all or part of the share capital of the employer changes but the contracts of employment of the relevant employees are unaffected. As the change of ownership is share-related, there is no change of employer. The employees engaged in the company's business remain employed by the relevant company (or other group company). This is the case regardless of whether the company in question is a private or public company.

An example of this point in operation is *Brooks and Others v Borough Care* **1.10** *Services and CLS Care Services Ltd*,[5] where TUPE 1981 was held not to apply to

---

[5] [1998] IRLR 636, EAT.

a transfer of a company limited by guarantee. The argument was rejected that TUPE should have applied to an arrangement structured around the transfer of ownership of a company in order to evade the application of the transfer of undertakings legislation.

1.11   It can, however, be dangerous entirely to discount the transfer legislation from consideration merely on the basis that the transaction in question is primarily share based. It may be that a transfer of an undertaking falling within the scope of the legislation is a necessary precursor to, or is part of, a primarily share-based corporate transaction. A TUPE transfer may occur effectively in parallel with a share-based transaction to which TUPE does not apply. For example, a group reorganisation which entails a transfer or transfers falling within the scope of TUPE may be implemented in order to transfer the requisite assets and business activities to the particular corporate entity whose shares are the subject of a sale transaction.[6] Alternatively, a function which has been outsourced (externally or to other group companies) by a corporate entity being disposed of may be brought back in-house by the new owner when it acquires the shares of the target company. Another scenario to which TUPE may apply is where an internal group reorganisation is effected by a purchaser after acquisition of the shares of a target company. It is therefore important to be alert to the potential for a TUPE transfer to arise in conjunction or connection with a share-based transaction to which TUPE does not apply.

C. AN OVERVIEW OF THE NEW LEGISLATION

1. Introduction

1.12   Proposals to amend and update TUPE 1981 were a considerable time in their gestation and implementation. The Government's 'Fairness at Work' White Paper in 1998 confirmed the intention to reform TUPE 1981. As the Government put it:

> As business becomes more open and competitive the pressures on businesses to trim down through redundancies, more flexible contracting out arrangements or to develop through merger and acquisition will intensify . . . The existing provisions have been widely criticised and the Government intends to amend them. Employers will in future have clearer obligations to inform and consult recognised trade unions or, in their absence, independent employee representatives. Where businesses are transferred the law will strike the right balance between safeguarding employees' existing rights and enabling businesses to adapt to changing circumstances.[7]

---

[6] An example is *Allen v Amalgamated Construction Co Ltd* [2000] IRLR 119, ECJ, where a transfer of business between group companies was confirmed as falling within the scope of the transfer of undertakings legislation.

[7] Cm 3968, May 1998.

ARD 1998 and ARD 2001 amended the provisions of the Directive so that 1.13 Member States had new alternatives open to them in terms of the domestic legislation which they could adopt. This provided further impetus to and opportunity for reform of TUPE 1981.

Although in the 2001 Consultation[8] it was anticipated that a 'new TUPE' 1.14 would be laid before Parliament in the summer of 2002, it was March 2005 before revised draft regulations were issued for consultation.[9] Implementation slipped from the initially targeted 1 October 2005 to enable consideration of the representations received as part of the consultation process on the initial draft of what was to become TUPE 2006. The final version of TUPE 2006 was made on 6 February 2006, laid before Parliament on 7 February 2006 and came into force with effect from 6 April 2006. Guidance on the new regulations was issued by the DTI[10] as was some useful commentary on the results of the consultation process which was conducted in relation to the new regulations.[11] Neither of those documents are of legal force but they both provide some useful insights into the intention behind the drafting of certain aspects of the amended legislation. In the meantime, the Pensions Act 2004 and the Transfer of Employment (Pension Protection) Regulations 2005 introduced, with effect from 6 April 2005, minimum required levels of pension protection for those transferring employees who enjoyed pension entitlements in their pre-transfer employment.

TUPE 2006 was introduced pursuant to the Employment Relations Act 1999 1.15 (ERA 1999), s 38[12] as well as the European Communities Act 1972, s 2(2), reflecting the fact that in certain respects (such as the new concept of a service provision change) the new legislation provides greater protection for employees than the Directive requires.

2. The Revised Acquired Rights Directive

As was noted in the 2001 Consultation,[13] the Government made it a social 1.16 affairs priority for the United Kingdom Presidency of the EU in 1998 to secure the revision of ARD 1977. The twin objectives of this process were, first, to clarify the application of the legislation by reference to jurisprudence of the ECJ

---

[8] *Transfer of Undertakings (Protection of Employment) Regulations 1981, Government Proposals for Reform, Detailed Background Paper*, Employment Relations Directorate, Department of Trade and Industry, September 2001, URN 01/1158.

[9] *TUPE, Draft Revised Regulations, Public Consultation Document*, Employment Relations Directorate, Department of Trade and Industry, March 2005, URN 05/926.

[10] *Employment Rights on the Transfer of an Undertaking, A Guide to the 2006 TUPE Regulations for Employees, Employers and Representatives*, Employment Relations Directorate, Department of Trade and Industry, January 2006.

[11] *TUPE, Draft Revised Regulations, Government Response to the Public Consultation*, Department of Trade and Industry, February 2006.

[12] Whose effect is in essence to permit regulations to be implemented to extend the protection of TUPE beyond the strict scope of the Directive. See also para 1.52.

[13] Para 9.

and, second, to give the Member States increased flexibility in tailoring their national implementing legislation to domestic circumstances. As a result of this process, ARD 1998 was adopted,[14] which was consolidated with ARD 1977 by the adoption of ARD 2001.[15]

1.17 The principal amendments to ARD 1977 made as a result of this process were the introduction of the following options for Member States in their implementing legislation:

- trade union or appropriate representative of the employees can be permitted by domestic legislation to negotiate changes to the terms and conditions of employment of the transferring employees in order to save jobs on the transfer of the undertaking of an insolvent employer;[16]

- it can be provided by domestic legislation that, in order to assist the preservation of jobs on the transfer of an insolvent company's undertaking, certain of the transferor's outstanding debts to its employees do not pass to the transferee;[17]

- the transferor can be required by domestic legislation to provide to the transferee prescribed information about the transferor's rights, powers, duties, and liabilities to the transferring employees of which the transferor is or should be aware.[18]

3. The New Legislation Summarised

1.18 The Government considered TUPE to be based on the positive principle of combining flexibility for business with fairness for employees.[19] The objective of the reform process which led to TUPE 2006 was to ensure that the transfer of undertakings legislation should operate effectively for all concerned including employers, employees, contractors, and local authorities who use it as a framework for contracting.[20]

1.19 As the DTI put it:

Failure to introduce the revised Regulations would mean that their shortcomings remained unaddressed, contrary to the Government's commitment to review and where necessary reform outdated and deficient regulation that imposes undue burdens on business [and] would mean that the valuable new flexibilities in the revised Directive, successfully negotiated by the UK in 1998, were not taken advantage of.[21]

1.20 The approach in formulating TUPE 2006 was not to amend TUPE 1981 unless the intention was to bring about a specific substantive change or where amendments were considered to be useful in order to reduce or eliminate confusion,

---

[14] Council Directive 98/50/EC OJ L 201/88.   [15] Council Directive 2001/23/EC OJ L 82/16.
[16] Art 5(2)(b).   [17] Art 5(2)(a).   [18] Art 3(2).   [19] 2001 Consultation para 12.
[20] 2005 Consultation para 13.
[21] 2005 Consultation Partial Impact Assessment para 8.

address case law conflicts, or deliver 'increased user-friendliness'.[22] The principal respects in which TUPE 2006, together with the pension-related provisions of the Pensions Act (PA) 2004 and the Transfer of Employment (Pension Protection) Regulations (PPR) 2005, made changes to the statutory regime can be summarised as follows.

(a) *New Definition of a Relevant Transfer*

TUPE 2006 adopts twin definitions of what constitutes a 'relevant transfer'. The first type of relevant transfer is the 'transfer of an undertaking, business or part of an undertaking to another employer ... where there is a transfer of an economic entity which retains its identity'. This reflects the definition of a transfer of an undertaking which was adopted in ARD 2001 as a distillation of the jurisprudence on the issue in relation to ARD 1977. **1.21**

The second type of relevant transfer is the concept introduced by TUPE 2006 of a 'service provision change' which ensures the application of the transfer legislation to outsourcing, re-tendering, and in-housing of services. Where there is an 'organised grouping of employees ... which has as its principal purpose [the] carrying out of the activities concerned on behalf of the client', the award (other than on a one-off and short duration basis) of a contract for the provision of services (as opposed to goods) will fall within the scope of the transfer legislation. This concept was introduced to ensure certainty and, for contractors, a 'level playing field'[23] given the uncertainty as to the application of TUPE 1981 to contract awards where the relevant activity is labour intensive. **1.22**

Purchasing of services from a contractor on a one-off short duration basis without the intention to enter into an ongoing relationship will not fall within the scope of this concept of a service provision change for the purpose of TUPE 2006 unless a series of short-term one-off contracts is entered into in order to avoid its application. Also, where the arrangement is wholly or mainly for the supply of goods, the service provision change concept does not apply. **1.23**

(b) *Transfer of Employment Contracts and Liabilities*

TUPE 2006 restates the legal position with regard to the transfer of employment contracts and their associated rights, obligations, and liabilities but makes no substantive changes to the general operation of the legislation (other than in relation to employers who are exempt from the requirement to maintain employers' liability compulsory insurance). The formulation adopted was described as 'an updated provision that is designed to incorporate well-established developments in case law since the Regulations were first introduced, and to reflect more closely what the Government considers to be the correct interpretation of the Directive in this regard'.[24] **1.24**

---

[22] 2005 Consultation para 10.   [23] Ibid para 18.

[24] Ibid para 37.

(c) *Employers' Liability Insurance*

1.25 In the private sector, it has been established by case law that, as a consequence of TUPE, the benefit of the transferor's employer's liability insurance cover transfers with the employees to the transferee. To provide protection for employees in this regard in relation to transfers out of the public sector, TUPE 2006 provides that, where the transferor does not have a statutory obligation to maintain employers' liability insurance, the transferor and transferee are jointly and severally liable for any employers' liability claim which a transferring employee may have arising from employment by the transferor prior to the transfer.

(d) *Who Transfers*

1.26 TUPE 2006 updates the identification by the legislation of who transfers from the transferor to the transferee on a relevant transfer. An employee falls within the scope of TUPE 2006 if he or she is 'employed by the transferor and assigned to the organised grouping of resources or employees that is subject to the relevant transfer'. Assignment is now given a specific definition as 'assigned other than on a temporary basis'.

(e) *Transfer-related Dismissals*

1.27 TUPE 2006 codifies into the legislation the principle established by the House of Lords in *Litster v Forth Dry Dock Engineering Co Ltd*[25] in order to ensure that the legislation provides protection for those dismissed before and in connection with a relevant transfer. Employees protected by TUPE include not just those employed immediately before the transfer but also those who would have been so employed but for a transfer-related automatically unfair dismissal. To remove some previous uncertainty, TUPE 2006 also clarifies both that a dismissal which is effected because of or in relation to a relevant transfer can still potentially be fair if an economic, technical, or organisational reason entailing changes in the workforce (ETOR) applies, and that an employee dismissed by reason of an ETOR can claim a statutory redundancy payment if the eligibility requirements relating to that entitlement are satisfied.

(f) *Changes to Terms and Conditions of Employment*

1.28 The case law in relation to TUPE 1981 established that a change to an employee's terms of employment which is by reason of or connected to a TUPE transfer is not valid even if the employee freely consents to the variation. Where an ETOR exists to justify a proposed change to employees' terms or conditions of employment, TUPE 2006 enables such a transfer-related change to be implemented validly, subject to the variation otherwise being contractually binding. It is also expressly made clear that an otherwise valid change to employees' terms

---

[25] [1989] IRLR 161, HL.

and conditions is not invalidated by TUPE 2006 if the reason for the change is unconnected with the transfer.

(g) *Liability for Failure to Inform and Consult*

Following TUPE 2006, the liabilities which arise for failure to comply with the requirements imposed under TUPE to provide information to and to consult with employee representatives are borne jointly and severally by transferor and transferee, removing the prior case law uncertainty in this regard as to whether the transferee could inherit that liability. **1.29**

(h) *Trade Union Recognition*

New regulations (which have not been promulgated at the time of writing) will confirm that any award of statutory trade union recognition pursuant to the ERA 1999 is inherited by the transferee on a TUPE transfer. This provision will extend to any current recognition application as well as to declarations of recognition already made by the Central Arbitration Committee (CAC). **1.30**

(i) *Notification of Employee Liability Information*

TUPE 2006 introduced a new obligation on the transferor to provide to the transferee specified 'employee liability information' relating to matters such as the age and identities of the transferring employees, their employment particulars, disciplinary and grievance issues, applicable collective agreements, and actual and potential claims on the part of the transferring employees. This information must be provided by no later than 14 days before the transfer. There is a 'special circumstances' defence in respect of a failure to comply with the obligation timeously but the required information must in any event be provided as soon as reasonably practicable. If any of the information changes after it has been provided, then an appropriate update must be supplied by the transferor to the transferee. **1.31**

The requirement imposed by TUPE 2006 with regard to employee liability information is satisfied if a third party provides the requisite information to the transferee on the transferor's behalf. For example, therefore, on a re-tendering the relevant employee liability information may be provided by the client rather than the outgoing contractor. The required information can be provided in instalments. The remedy for failure to comply with this obligation is determined by the Employment Tribunal (ET) on a complaint by the transferee and is based on loss. Unless the ET considers it just and equitable to award a lesser sum, the minimum compensation award in respect of a breach of this obligation is £500 per employee in respect of whom the transferor has failed to comply with its employee liability information obligations. **1.32**

(j) *Insolvency*

TUPE 2006 modifies the application of the legislation in the insolvency context. In certain types of insolvency proceedings, the transferee does not inherit liability **1.33** for certain of the transferor's debts to its employees which can be claimed from the National Insolvency Fund. Appropriate representatives of the transferring employees can also, in certain types of insolvency proceedings and subject to certain procedural safeguards, agree on behalf of the relevant employees variations to their terms and conditions of employment which are designed to safeguard employment opportunities.

(k) *Territoriality*

1.34 The provision in TUPE 1981 excluding employees working abroad from its scope was removed by TUPE 2006. Whether an employee working abroad is able to bring a claim under TUPE 2006 now depends on the principles of international law. TUPE 2006 does nonetheless contain some specific provisions concerning the location of the undertakings and activities to which it applies.

(l) *Occupational Pensions*

1.35 As a result of the combined effect of PA 2004 and PPR 2005, transferees are now required to provide a specific minimum level of pension provision in respect of those transferring employees who were active, eligible, or contingently eligible members of occupational pension schemes operated by the transferor during their pre-transfer employment. The transferee is able to determine the nature of the pension arrangement which it will offer post-transfer (ie money purchase, defined benefit, or stakeholder). The pension provision put in place must in any event comply with certain minimum standards.

1.36 In relation to a defined contribution or stakeholder scheme the employer must match the employee's contributions up to a maximum of 6 per cent of remuneration. In relation to a defined benefit scheme, unless the statutory 'reference scheme' test is met, the requirements of the legislation are that either the value of the benefits provided must be at least 6 per cent of pensionable pay per year or the scheme must provide for the employer to make contributions which match the employee's contributions up to a maximum of 6 per cent of basic pay.

1.37 TUPE 2006 also makes clear that a proposal by the transferee to provide transferring employees with a less generous level of pension post-transfer than that provided by the transferor prior to the transfer does not constitute constructive dismissal on the part of the transferor (as was previously considered, at least theoretically, possible).

4. Impact Assessment

1.38 Whilst the impact of the changes made by TUPE 2006 will vary from case to case depending on the factual and commercial circumstances, it did not go unacknowledged by the Government that its amendments to the transfer of undertakings legislation would have costs consequences for the economy. Constraints of space do not permit detailed discussion of the assumptions made and statistics relied upon in the regulatory impact assessment[26] conducted by the Department of Trade and Industry (DTI) in relation to the introduction of TUPE 2006. However, the following points are worth noting:

- it was assumed that TUPE 2006 would create no additional implementation costs to companies who 'would in any case be referring to lawyers on what they can and cannot do so would incur the costs with or without the changes in the Regulations';[27]

- the introduction of the concept of a service provision change (which ensures more comprehensive application of the legislation to outsourcings, contract awards etc) was anticipated to facilitate employee retention on changes of service provider and therefore to lead to a 70 per cent reduction in the number of associated redundancies, entailing a saving to business of between £6.5 million and £14.5 million each year in redundancy payments;[28]

- a reduction in TUPE-related ET claims was anticipated as a result of the increased certainty as to the application of the legislation delivered by TUPE 2006 (offset to an extent by increased litigation arising from its broadened scope). The number of ET claims related to TUPE was anticipated to reduce by between 10 and 20 per cent, leading to savings to employers of up to £1.6 million and to Government of £0.5 million per year;[29]

- the costs associated with the information and consultation obligations imposed by TUPE were anticipated to increase as a result of the expansion of its scope—the increased costs were estimated as between £0.3 to £0.6 million each year for all businesses;[30]

- the anticipated cost to transferees of the legislation being more likely to apply by virtue of the changes introduced by TUPE 2006 (such that employees have to be engaged on their existing terms) was estimated to be between £17 million and £39 million per year;[31]

- the annual cost of the requirement introduced by TUPE 2006 that transferors provide specified employee liability information to the transferee in advance of the transfer was estimated to be £0.125 million;[32]

- the clarification of the operation of the legislation in relation to transfer-related dismissals was considered likely to reduce the number of related ET disputes, thereby reducing costs to employers by £0.2 million per year;[33]

- the benefits of an increased ability validly to make transfer-related changes to employees' contracts of employment were considered to be 'significant, but . . . unquantifiable';[34]

---

[26] *Revision of the Transfer of Undertakings (Protection of Employment) Regulations 1981, Draft Final Regulatory Impact Assessment*, Employment Relations Directorate, Department of Trade and Industry, January 2006.

[27] Ibid para 20.   [28] Ibid paras 35–37.   [29] Ibid paras 38–41.   [30] Ibid para 43.
[31] Ibid para 42.   [32] Ibid para 53.   [33] Ibid paras 54–57.   [34] Ibid paras 58–60.

- consultation revealed no particular concerns from small firms;[35]
- the insolvency-related costs to the Government of the new regime (excepting from transfer to the transferee of certain debts owed by the transferor to the transferring employees, for which the State is responsible) were estimated at £6.6 million per annum on the basis of an estimated 12 per cent increase in government payments;[36]
- the benefit to employers of the ability to agree permitted variations to employees' terms and conditions in certain types of insolvency situation was estimated to be £3 million per annum.[37]

5. Transitional Provisions

1.39 Subject to regulation 21, TUPE 1981 is revoked by regulation 20(1). Regulation 21 sets out various transitional provisions relating to the introduction of TUPE 2006, the principal aspects of which to note are as follows:

- TUPE 1981 applied to a relevant transfer (or other event deemed by another enactment to be a relevant transfer for its purposes) that took place before 6 April 2006;[38]
- TUPE 2006 applies to a relevant transfer (or other event deemed by another enactment to be a relevant transfer for its purposes) that took or takes place on or after 6 April 2006;[39]
- the duty to provide employee liability information established by TUPE 2006 did not arise in respect of a relevant transfer taking place on or before 19 April 2006.[40] This provision allows for the required minimum 14 days pre-notification period to run from the date when TUPE 2006 came into force and not to predate its commencement;
- any steps taken by a transferor or transferee to comply with the requirements of TUPE 1981 in respect of collective information and consultation[41] are deemed to satisfy the corresponding requirements in TUPE 2006[42] 'insofar as that action would have discharged those obligations had the action taken place on or before 6 April 2006'.[43] Parties to a TUPE transfer do not have to restart their collective information and consultation processes afresh just because the new legislation has come into force, and can rely on their actions prior to 6 April 2006 in satisfying their obligations in relation to a transfer occurring on or after that date;
- the provisions of TUPE 2006 relating to collective information and consultation[44] do not apply to a service provision change (which is not also a transfer

---

[35] Ibid para 80.   [36] Ibid para 64.   [37] Ibid para 72.
[38] Regulation 21(2)(a) and (b).   [39] Regulation 21(1)(a) and (b).   [40] Regulation 21(4).
[41] TUPE 1981, regulations 10 and 10A.   [42] Regulation 13.   [43] Regulation 21(3).
[44] Regulation 13.

of an undertaking for these purposes) that took place on or before 4 May 2006.[45] Accordingly, in respect of pure service provision changes which do not also satisfy the traditional concept of a transfer of an undertaking, nearly one month's grace was given from the commencement of TUPE 2006 to allow for appropriate collective information and consultation to be arranged. Such service provisions changes evaded the otherwise applicable information and consultation obligations if effected in the period from 6 April 2006 to 4 May 2006.

D. PUBLIC SECTOR ISSUES

1. Public Administration

(a) *Transfers In and Out of the Public Sector*
Transfers to and from the public sector can fall within the scope of the Directive and TUPE 2006. By way of example, in *Sanchez Hidalgo*[46] the contracting out of home-help services by a local authority fell within the scope of the Directive. That the transfer of undertakings legislation can also apply where a public authority assumes responsibilities for a particular function previously conducted in the private sector was demonstrated by *Mayeur v Association Promotion de l'Information Messine (APIM)*.[47] The Directive applied where a tourist information function conducted by a private non-profit-making organisation was taken over by a public authority. **1.40**

That said, there are two principal limitations to the applicability of the transfer legislation to transactions, contracts, and other arrangements in the public sector context. First, regulation 3(4)(a) makes clear that TUPE applies to public (as well as private) undertakings 'engaged in economic activities whether or not they are operating for gain'. A public sector activity may fall outside the scope of the legislation because it does not constitute an economic activity. Second, TUPE may not apply because of the specific exclusion from its scope by regulation 3(5) of internal public sector reorganisations. **1.41**

(b) *Economic Activity*
The question may therefore arise of what constitutes an economic activity. In the absence from the transfer of undertakings case law of specific guidance as to the meaning of what constitutes an economic activity, the case of *Institute of Chartered Accountants of England & Wales v Customs and Excise Commissioners*[48] is of assistance. In that decision, Beldam LJ commented that: **1.42**

[t]he concept of an economic activity is an activity which typically is performed for consideration and is connected with economic life in some way or other. It is not an essential characteristic that it should be carried on with a view to profit or for commercial

---

[45] Regulation 21(5).   [46] [1999] IRLR 136, ECJ.   [47] [2000] IRLR 783, ECJ.
[48] [1997] STC 1115, CA.

13

reasons but it must be an activity which is analogous to the activities so carried on. An activity which consists in the performance of a public service to which the idea of commercial exploitation with a view to profit or gain is alien is not of an economic nature particularly where the activity is one typically of a public authority.[49]

The operations of the Institute of Chartered Accountants were considered to be a regulatory public service and therefore not to constitute an economic activity.

(c) *The Public Sector 'Exclusion Zone'*

1.43 Regulation 3(5) provides that an administrative reorganisation of public administrative authorities or the transfer of administrative functions between public administrative authorities is not a relevant transfer for the purposes of TUPE 2006.[50]

1.44 The exception from the scope of TUPE 2006 of administrative reorganisations of public administrative authorities and transfers of administrative functions between public administrative authorities effectively establishes an exclusion zone with regard to transfers internal to the public sector of administrative functions and administrative reorganisations. The ECJ decision which confirmed that this was the proper analysis of the effect of the Directive (and which principle was specifically incorporated into ARD 2001) was *Henke v Gemeinde Schierke and Verwaltungsgemeinschaft 'Brocken'*.[51] Administrative tasks relating to the exercise of public authority were considered to be outside the scope of the Directive, which focuses on concepts of business and enterprise.

1.45 This exclusion zone appears, however, to be of potentially limited application in domestic law. In *Clifton Middle School Governing Body v Askew*[52] the scope of TUPE in this context was considered. A middle school was transferred between governing bodies and it was found that a state-funded school could be an economic entity even if it were non-profit making. In contrast, in *Dundee City Council v Arshad*,[53] the transfer of undertakings legislation was held not to apply to a situation where a local government reorganisation led to the transfer of a residential home from one regional council to three new unitary authorities. In an admittedly very brief judgement, the *Henke* decision was considered not to preclude the transfer of economic activities within local government from being within the scope of TUPE. *Arshad* was viewed by the DTI[54] as indicating that only a relatively limited range of situations involving the transfer of entities pursuing non-economic objectives within the public sector is excluded by what is now regulation 3(5).

---

[49] At page 1116 para c.
[50] This reflects Art 1(c) and the position under TUPE 1981.
[51] [1996] IRLR 701, ECJ.   [52] [2000] ICR 286, CA.   [53] EAT/1204/88.
[54] 2001 Consultation para 19.

2. TUPE 2006

In the 2001 Consultation the DTI considered whether reform of the legislation in **1.46** relation to its application to the public sector was appropriate. It was concluded that the case law was such that the scope of the exclusion from the coverage of the legislation of transfers within public administration was unclear. The DTI's policy was that employees in public sector organisations should be treated no less favourably than those in private sector organisations when they are part of an 'organised grouping of resources' that is transferred between employers.[55]

The possibility was considered of specifically applying the domestic legisla- **1.47** tion to administrative reorganisations of public administrative authorities and the transfer of administrative functions between public administrative author- ities. However, in view of the uncertainty of the meaning of those terms and the difficulty of framing a general definition of the public sector, specific legislative coverage was not considered to be the most appropriate way in which to achieve the policy objective of the protection of public sector employees affected by situations which in a non-public context would constitute or be similar to a transfer of an undertaking falling within the scope of TUPE.

The Government concluded that it should continue to apply its guidance and **1.48** statements of practice on staff transfers in the public sector, and to ensure that, where considered necessary, 'TUPE-equivalent protections' are afforded to affected employees either by specific legislation or by regulations made under ERA 1999, s 38. Accordingly, therefore, whilst the transfer legislation can clearly apply to transfers of private sector activities into the public sector and vice versa (provided that they constitute economic activities and otherwise satisfy the requirements of what constitutes a relevant transfer), purely internal public sector transfers, especially where they relate to functions which do not constitute economic activities, will remain outside the scope of the legislation and are to be dealt with in accordance with Government practice and policy.

3. Government Codes of Practice

Two significant challenges to the protection of public sector employees' rights in **1.49** the transfer of undertakings context have been perceived as the exclusion from the liabilities which are inherited by a transferee of occupational pension scheme rights (a particularly pertinent issue in contracting-out situations) and the inapplicability of the transfer of undertakings legislation to transfers/ reorganisations within the public sector. Various government guidance sets out the Government's expectations concerning how these issues should be addressed with regard to transfers internal to the public sector and external contracting out.

---

[55] Ibid.

1.50   The introduction in TUPE 2006 of the concept of a service provision change removes much of the doubt over whether the transfer legislation applies to contracting out, contract re-tendering, and in-housing. That said, the Government's statements of practice do have practical relevance and importance both in relation to purely intra-public sector transfers and in terms of what employment conditions the public sector, in its capacity as a contracting party, will expect first and subsequent generation contractors to undertake to provide for employees—both those who transfer to the private sector on a relevant transfer and also employees subsequently recruited by the private sector contractor. The Government's policy on pensions in this context augments, and potentially improves upon, the basic level of pension provision required by PA 2004 and PPR 2005.

1.51   The principal guidance (detailed treatment of which is outside the scope of this Guide) comprises:

- Staff Transfers in the Public Sector (2000);[56]
- Staff Transfers from Central Government—A Fair Deal for Staff Pensions (1999);[57]
- Code of Practice on Workforce Matters in Local Authority Service Contracts (2003);[58]
- Code of Practice on Workforce Matters in Public Sector Service Contracts (2005).[59]

4. Regulations under the Employment Relations Act 1999, Section 38

1.52   As the 2001 Consultation noted,[60] protection for employees falling outside the scope of TUPE on the basis that the relevant activities and their transfer are within the public sector can be provided pursuant to regulations made under ERA 1999, s 38.

1.53   ERA 1999, s 38 empowers the Secretary of State to make provision by statutory instrument, subject to the negative resolution procedure, for employees to be given the same or similar treatment in specified circumstances falling outside the scope of the EU transfer legislation to that which they are given under the domestic legislation.[61] The Secretary of State can therefore confer 'TUPE-

---

[56] http://www.hm-treasury.gov.uk./media/7BB/E3/staff_transfers_145.pdf

[57] http://www.hm-treasury.gov.uk./media/7BB/E3/staff_transfers_145.pdf

[58] http://www.odpm.gov.uk/stellent/groups/odpm_localgov/documents/page/odpm_locgov_609121.pdf

[59] http://archive.cabinetoffice.gov.uk/workforce_reform/code_of_practice/index.asp

[60] Paras 18–23.

[61] ERA 1996, s 38 provides as follows:

(1) This section applies where regulations under section 2(2) of the European Communities Act 1972 (general implementation of Treaties) make provision for the purpose of implementing, or for a purpose concerning, a Community obligation of the United Kingdom which relates to the treatment of employees on the transfer of an undertaking or business or part of an undertaking or business.

equivalent' protection on employees affected by public sector transfers which fall outside the scope of the transfer legislation on the basis of the *Henke* decision. Examples of regulations to this effect include the Transfer of Undertakings (Protection of Employment) (Rent Officer Service) Regulations 1999[62] and the Transfer of Undertakings (Protection of Employment) (Transfer to OFCOM) Regulations 2003.[63]

---

(2) The Secretary of State may by regulations make the same or similar provision in relation to the treatment of employees in circumstances other than those to which the Community obligation applies (including circumstances in which there is no transfer, or no transfer to which the Community obligation applies).

(3) Regulations under this section shall be subject to annulment in pursuance of a resolution of either House of Parliament.

[62] SI 1999/2511.   [63] SI 2003/2715.

2
IDENTIFYING A RELEVANT TRANSFER

A. The Two Statutory Definitions	2.01
B. A Transfer of an Undertaking	2.08
C. Labour-intensive Activities	2.60
D. Miscellaneous	2.77

A. THE TWO STATUTORY DEFINITIONS

In the 2005 Consultation it was noted[1] that: 2.01

The Government considers that, ideally, everyone should know where they stand when a business sale or reorganisation, or a contracting-out or similar exercise, takes place, so that employers can plan effectively in a climate of fair competition and affected employees are protected as a matter of course.

It was with this objective of clarity in mind that regulation 3 was drafted. The   2.02
new formulation of what constitutes a relevant transfer clarifies and expands the events and transactions to which the Transfer of Undertakings (Protection of Employment Regulations (TUPE) apply.

There are now two types of event which fall within the scope of TUPE—a   2.03
'transfer of an undertaking'[2] and a 'service provision change'.[3] These concepts operate as alternatives and therefore both need to be considered when addressing whether TUPE 2006 applies to a given situation. If either a transfer of an undertaking or a service provision change occurs, then there is a 'relevant transfer'[4] for the purposes of TUPE 2006 and the panoply of rights and obligations established by the legislation is triggered.

---

[1] Para 15.   [2] This 'traditional' definition reflects the position under TUPE 1981.
[3] Discussed in detail in Chapter 3.
[4] Regulation 2(1) defines a 'relevant transfer' as 'a transfer or a service provision change to which [TUPE 2006 applies] in accordance with regulation 3'.

2.04　　Mirroring the provisions of the Acquired Rights Directive (ARD) 2001,[5] a transfer of an undertaking is defined by regulation 3(1)(a) as 'a transfer of an undertaking, business or part of an undertaking or business situated immediately before the transfer in the United Kingdom to another employer where there is a transfer of an economic entity which retains its identity'.

2.05　　The principal effect of the new concept of a service provision change is to apply the transfer of undertakings legislation to situations where a client outsources or re-tenders the provision of services or brings a service contract in-house. There must be an organised group of employees principally dedicated to that contract or activity prior to the transfer for there to be a service provision change. The contract award must be on an ongoing rather than a one-off and short term basis and not relate to the supply of goods.

2.06　　Regulation 3(4)(a) provides that, regardless of whether regulation 3(1)(a) or regulation 3(1)(b) is being considered, TUPE 2006 applies to 'public and private undertakings engaged in economic activities whether or not they are operating for gain'. Provided that it constitutes an economic activity, the relevant activity need not be conducted on a commercial basis in order to fall within the scope of TUPE 2006.[6]

2.07　　The previous case law in relation to the issue of what constituted a transfer of an undertaking for the purposes of ARD 1977 and TUPE 1981 needs to be considered when addressing both definitions of a relevant transfer deployed in TUPE 2006 not only because it is still relevant to the application of regulation 3(1)(a) but also because it demonstrates the rationale for the introduction of the concept of a service provision change under regulation 3(1)(b).

B. A TRANSFER OF AN UNDERTAKING

2.08　Regulation 3(1)(a) provides that TUPE 2006 applies to:

a transfer of an undertaking, business or part of an undertaking or business situated

---

[5] Article 1(b) states that '. . . there is a transfer within the meaning of this Directive where there is a transfer of an economic entity which retains its identity, meaning an organised grouping of resources which has the objective of pursuing an economic activity, whether or not that activity is central or ancillary'. A separate definition of an 'economic entity' is provided in regulation 3(3), consistent with the terms of ARD 2001—see para 2.17 *et seq* below.

[6] See Chap 1, para 1.42 for discussion of what constitutes economic activities. See also, by way of example, *Collino and Chiappero v Telecom Italia SpA* [2000] IRLR 788, ECJ where the Directive was held to apply to the transfer of a concession in respect of telecommunications activities from state-owned to private sector responsibility—there was a transfer of an economic entity regardless of whether or not the relevant activities were carried on for profit prior to the putative transfer. As the DTI Guidance put it at p 7: 'The Regulations can apply regardless of the size of the transferred business: so the Regulations equally apply to the transfer of a large business with thousands of employees or of a very small one (such as a shop, pub or garage). The Regulations also apply equally to public or private sector undertakings and whether or not the business operates for gain, such as a charity.'

immediately before the transfer in the United Kingdom to another person where there is a transfer of an economic entity which retains its identity.

1. The Components of a Transfer of an Undertaking

The regulation 3(1)(a) definition of a transfer of an undertaking comprises the following components: **2.09**

- there must be a transfer;
- that transfer must be of an undertaking, business, or part thereof;
- the undertaking, business, or part transferred must be situated in the United Kingdom immediately before the transfer;[7]
- the transfer must be to another employer;[8]
- there must be a transfer of an 'economic entity';
- the economic entity transferred must retain its identity.

Regulation 3(6)(b) makes clear that there may be a relevant transfer 'whether or   **2.10** not any property is transferred to the transferee by the transferor'. The absence of any transfer of assets is not therefore of itself a determining factor (although the issue of asset transfer can be relevant where the relevant activities are asset reliant).[9]

2. What is a Transfer?

The process of determining whether an undertaking has been transferred for the   **2.11** purposes of what is now regulation 3(1)(a) is an employment test rather than a corporate, property, or conveyancing test.[10] A transfer arises where a change of responsibility for or of management of the relevant undertaking occurs. While far from being a decisive factor, the parties' view as to the application of the legislation can be taken into account.[11]

As was made clear by the European Court of Justice (ECJ) in *Daddy's Dance*   **2.12**

---

[7] See Chap 12 for a discussion of some of the territoriality aspects of TUPE 2006.

[8] An example of this requirement in practice is *Burke v Royal Liverpool University Hospital* [1997] ICR 730, EAT where TUPE did not apply in circumstances where an in-house bid was successful in a council's tendering process and so the operation continued to be operated by the same legal person—the employer of the staff affected remained the same (ie the Council).

[9] See para 2.47 *et seq* below.

[10] As the EAT stated in *Kelman v Care Services Ltd* [1995] ICR 260, EAT (at para 268A), 'the theme running through all the recent cases is the necessity of viewing the situation from an employment perspective, not from a perspective conditioned by principles of property, company or insolvency law'.

[11] See *Lightways (Contractors) Ltd v Associated Holdings Ltd* [2000] IRLR 247, CS where a contractor won a contract as a result of a tender in which it stated its view that TUPE would apply—a 'declared intention' that TUPE would apply was a relevant factor in the assessment of whether there was a relevant transfer.

Hall,[12] the transfer legislation 'applies as soon as there is a change resulting from a conventional sale or from a merger of the natural or legal person responsible for operating the undertaking . . . and it is of no importance to know whether the ownership of the undertaking is transferred'.[13]

2.13 As *Porter and Nanayakkara v Queen's Medical Centre*[14] indicated, in circumstances where the ultimate responsibility for provision of paediatric services remained with the relevant health authority but the relevant provider was changed, TUPE applies when there is a change in the person responsible for operating the undertaking. In *Porter* the change was to the actual provision of the relevant services rather than to the responsibility for arranging and ensuring their provision.

2.14 There need be no formal legal agreement[15] for there to be a transfer of an undertaking nor indeed any legal relationship between transferor and transferee.[16] *Merckx*[17] demonstrates this latter point—an economic entity comprising a Ford car dealership transferred within the scope of the legislation when the dealership was awarded by Ford to a new contractor. A further example is *Charlton v Charlton Thermosystems (Romsey) Ltd*[18] where TUPE applied, despite the lack of any formal transfer, where the directors of a dissolved company continued its trade.

2.15 While the test is one of responsibility, the existence of a transfer of an undertaking falling within regulation 3(1)(a) will not necessarily be prejudiced by some degree of retention of control over the relevant operation by the purported transferor. In *Birch v Sports and Leisure Management*,[19] a council retained some control over contracted-out sports facilities but TUPE nevertheless applied.

2.16 While the concept of a service provision change introduced by regulation 3(1)(b) specifically addresses the replacement of one contractor by another in relation to services,[20] regulation 3(1)(a) contains no equivalent provision in its definition of a transfer of an undertaking specifically addressing the replacement of a supplier. That said, there is no doubt that there can be a transfer of an

---

[12] *Foreningen af Arbejdsledere i Danmark v Daddy's Dance Hall A/S* [1988] IRLR 315, ECJ (at para 9).

[13] This principle has been reiterated in a number of decisions such as *Ny Mølle Krø* [1989] IRLR 37, ECJ and *Bork International A/S* [1989] IRLR 41, ECJ.

[14] [1993] IRLR 486, HC.

[15] TUPE 2006 does not contain an equivalent to TUPE 1981, regulation 3(2) which provided that TUPE 1981 applied 'whether the transfer is effected by sale or by some disposition or by operation of law'. It is presumed that such a provision was not considered necessary when TUPE 2006 was drafted as the point is so clearly established by the case law.

[16] *Dines v Initial Healthcare* [1994] IRLR 336, CA first demonstrated in the domestic case law that on a re-tendering TUPE 1981 could apply to transfer staff from an outgoing to an incoming contractor (between whom there was no contractual relationship). In *Sanchez Hildalgo* [1999] IRLR 136, ECJ it was stated (at para 23) that 'there is no need, in order for the Directive to be applicable, for there to be any direct contractual relationship between the transferor and the transferee'.

[17] *Merckx v Ford Motors Co Belgium SA* [1996] IRLR 467, ECJ.   [18] [1995] IRLR 79, EAT.

[19] [1995] IRLR 518, EAT.   [20] Regulation 3(1)(b)(ii).

undertaking where an operation is transferred between contractors at the behest of the ultimate client.[21] Despite some case law uncertainty, the preferred view as to the operation of what is now regulation 3(1)(a) in this context is that there is one transfer between outgoing and incoming contractor rather than a two-stage transfer of the undertaking from the incumbent contractor to the client and then on to the new contractor.

3. What is an Economic Entity?

A transfer of an undertaking for the purposes of regulation 3(1)(a) must entail the transfer of an economic entity. Regulation 3(2) defines an economic entity for the purposes of identifying a transfer of an undertaking falling within regulation 3(1)(a) as 'an organised grouping of resources which has the objective of pursuing an economic activity, whether or not that activity is central or ancillary'.   **2.17**

The key points to note in relation to this definition of an economic entity are as follows: **2.18**

- the objective of the entity must be the pursuit of an economic activity. As already noted,[22] in this context it is worth recalling that TUPE can apply to non-commercial activities.[23] The nature of the activity must be economic even if not pursued for commercial purposes;

- the activity in question need not be the primary purpose of the organisation in question. Thus, IT, security, catering, cleaning, payroll, back office, and other functions may be ancillary to an organisation's primary objectives or raison d'être but can nonetheless of themselves constitute an economic entity for the purposes of regulation 3(1)(a);

- the entity must be constituted by an 'organised group of resources'—this requirement derives from the ECJ case law in relation to the Directive and reflects Article 1(b).

Satisfaction of the requirement that there be an organised group of resources entails a stable structure which renders the relevant function more than a mere activity. Autonomy and stability of the operation in question are crucial. As the Advocate General commented in *Rygaard*,[24] '[i]t will be for the National Court to examine, inter alia, whether the activity transferred in the given case is autonomous from an organisational point of view in the sense that persons and possibly materials have been allocated for its completion'.   **2.19**

---

[21] See *Sanchez Hidalgo* [1999] IRLR 136, ECJ.   [22] See para 2.06 above.
[23] See also *Dr Sophie Redmond Stichting v Bartol* [1992] IRLR 366, ECJ which applied ARD 1977 to the transfer of a subsidy by a local authority from one charitable foundation to another. The Trade Union Reform and Employment Rights Act (TURERA) 1993, s 33 removed from TUPE 1981 the exclusion of non-commercial ventures from its scope.
[24] *Rygaard v Stø Mølle Akustik A/S* [1996] IRLR 51, ECJ (at para 978).

2.20   In relation to an activity which is asset reliant, the transfer of assets can be relevant in determining whether there has been a relevant transfer.[25] However, it is clear from *Sanchez Hildalgo*,[26] in the context of the prior question of identifying whether an economic entity exists, that '[w]hilst such an entity must be sufficiently structured and autonomous, it will not necessarily have significant assets, material or immaterial. Indeed, in certain sectors, such as cleaning and surveillance, these assets are often reduced to their most basic and the activity is essentially based on manpower. Thus, an organised grouping of wage earners who are specifically and permanently assigned to a common task may, in the absence of other factors of production, amount to an economic entity'.

2.21   By way of a further useful gloss, Burton J, in *ADI v Willer*,[27] described the use of the expression 'distinct cost centre'[28] as 'notwithstanding the resort to modern jargon, . . . a helpful thought process'.

2.22   In this context, it is also worth bearing in mind the succinct summary provided by Lindsay P in *Cheesman v R. Brewer Contracts Ltd*[29] of the ECJ and domestic case law as to whether there is an economic entity for the purposes of TUPE:

i.   There needs to be a stable economic entity whose activity is not limited to performing one specific works contract, an organised grouping of persons and of assets enabling (or facilitating) the exercise of an economic entity which pursues a specific objective.

ii.   In order to be such an undertaking it must be sufficiently structured and autonomous but will not necessarily have sufficient assets, tangible or intangible.

iii. In certain sectors such as cleaning and surveillance the assets are often reduced to their most basic and the activity is essentially based on manpower.

iv.   An organised grouping of wage earners who are specifically and permanently assigned to a common task may, in the absence of other factors of production, amount to an economic entity.

v.   An activity of itself is not an entity; the identity of an entity emerges from other factors such as its workforce, management staff, the way in which its work is organised, its operating methods and, where appropriate, the operational resources available to it.

2.23   *Wynnwith Engineering Co Ltd v Bennett*[30] is a further example of the requirement of stability and structure for there to be an economic entity for the purposes of what is now regulation 3(1)(a) in a given situation. A group of employees who had ceased employment by way of voluntary early retirement were re-engaged by the employer. The employees were subsequently required to transfer their employment from the original employer to a third-party employment agency. This transfer of the employment of the relevant employees from the original employer to the employment agency was held to fall outside the scope of TUPE. The employees in question were not devoted to a specific common activity but

---

[25] See para 2.47 *et seq* below.   [26] [1999] IRLR 136, ECJ (at para 26).
[27] EAT/11/99 (at para 10).
[28] Which had been utilised by the ET in *CWW Logistics v Ronald* EAT, 1/12/98.
[29] [2001] IRLR 144, EAT (at para 10).   [30] [2002] IRLR 170, EAT.

were deployed across various parts of the original employer's business. They did not constitute an economic entity merely on the basis that they were treated in the same way in employment terms.

Perth & Kinross Council v Donaldson and Others[31] also demonstrates the **2.24** importance of stability in the relevant operation for it to fall within the scope of what is now regulation 3(1)(a). *Inter alia*, the Employment Appeal Tribunal (EAT) held that there was no stable economic entity capable of transfer to a council, after the insolvency of a housing maintenance contractor, when the council took the relevant activities in-house. In circumstances where the relevant work was handed out on an ad hoc basis, the contractor had no contractual entitlement to work and the operation could be terminated at any time, there was no stable economic entity.

4. One Person Undertakings

Schmidt[32] indicates that an activity conducted by one person can constitute an **2.25** economic entity for the purposes of the Directive and therefore, by extension, TUPE. In that case, a cleaning contract performed by one employee was outsourced by a bank and the Directive was held by the ECJ to apply. The *Schmidt* decision is particularly important to the issue[33] of the extent to which transfers of labour-intensive activities without assets can fall within the scope of the transfer of undertakings legislation. That said, for there to be a transfer of undertaking for the purposes of the Directive and regulation 3(1)(a), not only must there be an economic entity in existence pre-transfer but the multifactorial assessment based on the *Spijkers* principles[34] must also indicate that the putative economic entity retains its identity post-transfer.

A further example of the fact that single person undertakings can fall within **2.26** the scope of TUPE is *Dudley Bower Building Services Ltd v Lowe and Others*[35] in which a reactive maintenance programme was substantially performed by one employee. The EAT considered that there was no reason in principle why work performed by a single employee could not form a stable economic entity. Structure and autonomy were seen as key factors. As the EAT put it, while there might not be an economic entity for these purposes where an activity consists of a cleaning lady and her mop, there could be such an entity where a single employee conducts a complex and sophisticated task requiring planning, specification, and costings. The question was viewed as one of fact and degree with relevant factors including the organisation of work, any operational resources deployed, and the operating methods utilised.

---

[31] [2004] IRLR 121, EAT.
[32] *Schmidt v Spar und Leihkasse der Früheven Ämter Bordesholm, Kiel und Cronshagen* [1994] IRLR 302, ECJ.
[33] See para 2.60 *et seq* below for further discussion. [34] See para 2.32 *et seq* below.
[35] [2003] IRLR 260, EAT.

5. Single Contract Undertakings

2.27 A particular activity can be so limited in its scope or duration that it is not sufficiently stable to constitute an undertaking capable of transfer within the scope of the Directive. The ECJ decision establishing this potential exception from the scope of the Directive and therefore TUPE is *Rygaard*,[36] a case which concerned the award of a contract to complete some building works. The work had already started before the contract award was made. The ECJ concluded that the contract for completion of the relevant building works did not constitute the stable economic entity required for there to be a transfer of an undertaking for the purposes of the Directive because the relevant activity was limited to performing the completion of one specific works contract.

2.28 *Argyll Training Ltd v Sinclair*[37] considered the application of *Rygaard* in the domestic context and took a narrow view of the scope of the argument that single contracts can lack the autonomy and stability to fall within the scope of TUPE. The EAT considered that there was no basis for automatically excluding what were described as single contract undertakings from the potential application of TUPE. It was not accepted that single contracts necessarily lack the autonomy and stability to come within the scope of the transfer legislation.

2.29 *Rygaard* therefore appears to be of relatively narrow scope in terms of its application in practice. A useful indicator of the nature of the exclusion from the scope of TUPE and the Directive of contracts of the kind addressed in *Rygaard* is Burton J's description of the scenario in that case as 'the transfer of the fag-end, or run-off, of a particular construction sub-contract'.[38]

2.30 A related decision is *Mackie v Aberdeen City Council*[39] where the employee's role had been to set up an operational smart card system for one of her employer's clients. When the client of the employee's original employer offered employment to her in a role involving administration of the relevant system, the new employer treated the transfer of employment as falling within TUPE. Nonetheless the original employer's contract was considered to be for a fixed price for a fixed task and defined product, and therefore as a one-off contract on termination of which nothing was left to transfer. Accordingly, TUPE did not apply to the change of the employee's employer, despite the new employer's view of the position at the relevant time. TUPE did not apply and the employee's continuity of employment for statutory purposes was not preserved on the change of employer.

2.31 The transfer of contracts for the provision of services in respect of single specific events or tasks of short-term duration is specifically excluded from the concept of a service provision change introduced by TUPE 2006.[40] Accordingly, an approach similar to that adopted in *Rygaard* is effectively now codified into

---

[36] [1996] IRLR 51, ECJ.   [37] [2000] IRLR 630, EAT.
[38] *ADI v Willer* EAT/11/99 (at para 8).   [39] EATS/0095/04.
[40] Regulation 3(3)(ii). See Chap 3, para 3.22 *et seq*.

domestic law as part of the test of whether there is a service provision change for the purposes of regulation 3(1)(b). Regulation 3(1)(a) does not, however, specifically address the issue. Accordingly, *Rygaard* and the associated case law remain relevant to the issue of whether there is a transfer of undertaking for the purposes of regulation 3(1)(a). There appears to be no general rule preventing single contract undertakings from being the subject of a regulation 3(1)(a) transfer of an undertaking where the relevant transaction entails the transfer of more than just performance of the 'fag end' of the contract.

6. Retention of Identity

That the economic entity transferred should retain its identity on transfer is a **2.32** crucial requirement of the traditional definition of a transfer of an undertaking set out in regulation 3(1)(a). As reformulated by TUPE 2006, the definition of a transfer of undertaking expressly entails the relevant economic entity retaining its identity.

The leading case on retention of identity is *Spijkers*[41] which stated the relevant **2.33** test to be 'whether the business was disposed of as a going concern, as would be indicated inter alia by the fact that its operation was either continued or resumed'.[42] The ECJ made it clear that in this assessment it is necessary to consider all the factual circumstances relating to the transaction in question. The '*Spijkers* factors' adumbrated by the ECJ set out the range of issues to be considered in the factual determination of whether the Directive (and by extension TUPE) apply to a given situation. Similarity of pre- and post-transfer activities is only one of these factors, being variously described as 'necessary but not sufficient'[43] and 'relevant but not critical'.[44]

The following '*Spijkers* factors' were articulated by the ECJ as potentially **2.34** relevant:

- the type of undertaking or business concerned;
- whether tangible assets, such as buildings and movable property, are transferred;
- whether or not the majority of the employees assigned to the undertaking are taken over by the new employer;
- whether or not the customers of the business are transferred;
- the degree of similarity between the activities carried on before and after the transfer;
- the period, if any, for which the activities of the undertaking are suspended in connection with the alleged transfer.

---

[41] *Spijkers v Gebroeders Benedik Abbatoir* [1986] ECR 1119, ECJ.   [42] At para 15.
[43] Per Morrison J in *ECM v Cox* [1998] IRLR 416, EAT (at para 21).
[44] Per Kennedy LJ in *Betts v Brintel* [1997] IRLR 361, CA (at para 43).

2.35 These factors remain the cornerstone of the assessment of whether particular circumstances constitute a transfer of an undertaking for the purposes of regulation 3(1)(a) (which expressly records the requirement that the economic entity retain its identity but gives no further express guidance on the application of that requirement).

2.36 The *Spijkers* factors were described by the ECJ[45] as 'merely single factors in the overall assessment' to be conducted by the relevant court in its factual appraisal. As the analysis of the case law which follows indicates, a distinction has often been drawn in applying the *Spijkers* test between asset-reliant and labour-intensive activities. Absence of asset transfer in relation to an asset-reliant activity could be a contra-indication of the relevant economic entity retaining its identity and there being a TUPE transfer, as could, in relation to a labour-intensive activity, the putative transferee not taking on the relevant staff. However, the dichotomy often deployed in the cases between asset-reliant and labour-intensive activities is only a gloss on the central test of retention of identity which rests on the 'multifactorial' *Spijkers* considerations.

7. Transfer of Part of an Undertaking

2.37 Regulation 3(1)(a) can apply to the transfer of part of an undertaking as much as to the transfer of the whole undertaking. In determining whether the transfer of part of an undertaking falls within the scope of regulation 3(1)(a), it still remains essential for the part undertaking transferred to retain (or acquire) identity and stability on transfer.

2.38 The application of what is now regulation 3(1)(a) to transfers of parts of undertakings was considered in *Fairhurst Ward Abbotts Limited v Botes Building Limited & Others*.[46] A contract for the carrying out of maintenance works and alterations to domestic residences for a three-year period was contracted out by a London Borough Council. On re-tendering, the original contract area was divided into two separate areas. The ET found that the area which had been awarded to Fairhurst Ward Abbotts did not constitute a discrete economic entity prior to the end of the original contract. However, on award of a contract to the new contractor, there was nonetheless a relevant transfer for the purposes of TUPE 1981.

2.39 The EAT agreed with this finding. It held that there could be a transfer of part of an undertaking falling within the scope of TUPE even if that part was not a separate economic entity prior to the transfer (ie in this case the re-tendering). The EAT made clear that this was not a rule of general application and that a relevant transfer will not necessarily occur in every case where an undertaking is split into parts on re-tendering. It was acknowledged that there could be circumstances in which there was a sufficiently high degree of fragmentation of the

---

[45] At para 13.   [46] [2004] IRLR 304, CA.

original economic entity that TUPE did not apply. In such circumstances what would have emerged would neither be recognisably the same entity nor sufficiently stable an economic entity for the transaction to constitute a transfer of an undertaking for the purposes of TUPE. The Court of Appeal rejected an appeal against the EAT's decision.

It is uncontroversial that the transfer legislation should apply to a re-tendering **2.40** involving the division of a contract of this nature where the functional activities remain the same (although geographically divided). However, the question still remains as to which (if any) employees would transfer to the two contractors taking over the relevant areas, given that only those assigned to the relevant undertaking transfer. Moreover, a division of activities themselves (as opposed to a division of their geographical scope) may further prejudice the application of the legislation on the basis that the undertaking consequently does not retain its identity.

8. Changes to the Operation

One difficult issue to be considered in determining whether regulation 3(1)(a) **2.41** applies to a specific set of circumstances is the weight to be given, in the assessment of whether an economic entity retains its identity, to changes to the relevant operation in the period after transfer. If, for example, the transferee changes the location or methods of work of the undertaking or integrates it with its own existing operations, can it be argued that the TUPE does not apply on the basis that the undertaking does not retain its identity by virtue of the pre- and post-transfer activities being different? TUPE 2006 provides no specific guidance beyond the regulation 3(1)(a) definition already described (which centres on an economic entity retaining its identity). The previous case law is therefore relevant.

In *Porter and Nanayakkara v Queen's Medical Centre*,[47] the location of the **2.42** provision of paediatric services changed when a new provider was appointed. The way in which the services were to be provided also changed. Neither factor precluded TUPE 1981 from applying. The EAT recognised that an economic entity could retain its identity even though its location might change and its mode of delivery might evolve (as was acknowledged as inevitable in the medical context).[48]

Another example is *Mathieson v United News Shops Ltd.*[49] A hospital shop's **2.43** replacement by an operation which stocked a far wider variety of items did not fall within the scope of TUPE because the undertaking had changed so much that it did not retain its identity.

That the economic entity transferred may be absorbed into the transferee's **2.44**

---

[47] [1993] IRLR 486, EAT.
[48] See also *Merckx v Ford Motors Co Belgium SA* [1996] IRLR 467, ECJ.
[49] EAT/554/95.

existing operations does not of itself preclude TUPE from applying. Otherwise, the legislation could be too easily avoided by virtue of the integration which is the natural consequence of many business acquisitions. In *Farmer v Danzas*,[50] the integration of the transferor's business with the transferee's existing operations (by removing its trading name) was held not to preclude the operation of TUPE not least because, immediately after the transfer but before the integration took place, the economic entity retained its identity.

9. Break in Activities

2.45 A suspension of the relevant activities at or around the point of a putative transfer is one of the potentially relevant *Spijkers* factors and one which is still applicable in relation to regulation 3(1)(a). The particular facts will of course be crucial but various cases have demonstrated that an interruption to the relevant activity will not necessarily avoid there being a transfer of an undertaking.[51] The ET or court will look at why the suspension occurred and whether that had any impact on the retention (or otherwise) by the relevant operation of its identity.

2.46 In appropriate circumstances, it may be concluded that there was nothing left to transfer at the relevant time. This was the case in *Perth Kinross Council v Donaldson and Others*,[52] where the relevant housing contractor's work had come to an end at the time of the putative transfer when the awarding council took the work back in-house after the contractor's insolvency and an intervening ad hoc arrangement. There was no relevant transfer because there was nothing left to transfer.

10. Asset Transfer

2.47 The application of the transfer legislation to situations where the relevant activity is 'labour-intensive' and needs few or no assets to be operated is considered below.[53] But what if assets are a key component of the activity and are not transferred? This was the case in *Oy Liikenne*[54] where, on transfer of a contract to supply bus services, a majority of the relevant employees but none of the buses used to fulfil the relevant services transferred to the new contractor. There was held to be no transfer of an undertaking for the purposes of the Directive in the absence of the transfer of those assets which contributed significantly to the operation and conduct of the relevant activity. The ECJ considered that bus transport could not be regarded as an activity based on manpower in view of the

---

[50] EAT 858/93.

[51] For example, *P Bork International A/S v Foreningen af Arbejdsledere i Danmark* [1989] IRLR 41, ECJ where the owner of a leased undertaking repossessed it after forfeiture of the lease and then sold the undertaking to a third party which resumed operation of the business after a period of closure. The Directive was held to apply.

[52] [2004] IRLR 121, EAT.   [53] See para 2.60 *et seq.*   [54] [2001] IRLR 171, ECJ.

need for assets to conduct the relevant operation. Accordingly, in the absence of asset transfer, the transfer of employees was not of itself sufficient to establish the application of the Directive.

By contrast, in *Abler v Sodexho MM Catering Gessellschaft*,[55] none of the **2.48** relevant staff were taken on by a contractor which replaced an incumbent operator in relation to a catering contract which was viewed as asset reliant. The equipment upon which the performance of the relevant contract was dependent remained the property of the client hospital throughout. Since the relevant function was asset reliant, the transfer (or not) of employees was not of itself a decisive factor. Even though the new contractor did not acquire moveable assets, it used a variety of assets provided by the relevant hospital. The Directive was held to apply. It was also relevant, as a factor indicating the existence of a transfer falling within the scope of the Directive, that the new contractor provided its service to the same group of customers (hospital patients) as the old contractor. The better view, therefore, is that *Oy Liikenne* does not establish an absolute principle that the transfer legislation cannot apply to the transfer of an asset-reliant activity where the relevant assets do not change hands. The test is one of fact in all the circumstances and asset transfer is just one of the *Spijkers* factors.

This point is further demonstrated by *P&O Trans European Ltd v Initial* **2.49** *Transport Services Ltd.*[56] Shell operated petroleum delivery activities by way of a combination of an in-house function and the use of P&O and Initial as external contractors. Shell awarded a comprehensive contract to P&O which was treated as a transfer for TUPE purposes. Initial contended that the transfer legislation also applied to the service which it provided to Shell and that therefore four administrative staff who worked on that service should have transferred to P&O. Against this interpretation stood the facts that the relevant activity was asset reliant, P&O took none of Initial's vehicles, and there was no transfer of assets.

Oy Liikenne was viewed by the Court of Appeal as reconfirming the factors to **2.50** be considered in the assessment of the application of the transfer legislation. The ECJ was not considered to have established a principle that, in relation to asset-intensive activities, the lack of transfer of significant assets would indicate that there was not a relevant transfer. The ET was held to have been entitled to conclude that TUPE applied in these circumstances, having applied the appropriate multifactorial test. Particularly relevant matters were the fact that all the other employees involved in the operation transferred, that the core service remained the same, and that there was a dedicated workforce of which the relevant administrators were a part.

In *Numast and another v P&O Scottish Ferries & others*,[57] the EAT considered **2.51** *Oy Liikenne* in the context of the re-tendering of a ferry service from Scotland

---

[55] [2004] IRLR 168, ECJ.   [56] [2003] IRLR 128, CA.
[57] EATS/0060/04; [2005] All ER (D) 27, EAT.

to the Northern Isles. None of the outgoing contractors' ships were acquired by the new contractor due to health and safety requirements which required new vessels. The vast majority of seafaring staff did, however, transfer. Workshop maintenance staff did not transfer as this work was subcontracted by the new contractor.

2.52 The EAT held that the ET had been entitled to find there to have been a relevant transfer and that both the seafarers and maintenance staff had been employed in the undertaking (or parts thereof) transferred. *Oy Liikenne* was again viewed as not laying down a principle that 'in all cases of asset intensive industries the absence of a transfer to a significant extent of such assets would always lead to the conclusion that no transfer had taken place'.[58] On the basis of the multifactorial test, the ET's decision was safe, based as it was on the strong correlation between the premises and piers used by the transferor and transferee (which constituted the significant asset transfer absent in *Oy Liikenne*), the transfer of the intangible asset of the applicable government subsidy, the transfer of 90 per cent of the transferor's seafarers, the transfer of customers, and the high degree of similarity between the pre- and post-transfer activities. *Oy Liikenne* was therefore easily distinguished.

2.53 As the EAT put it,[59] '[i]n an asset-intensive industry the fact that assets were not transferred will be a circumstance to be taken into account. But the whole of the transaction has to be looked at in order to see whether one particular factor is decisive'.

2.54 The approach adopted in *Numast* was echoed in *McCormack and Others v Scottish Coal Company Ltd*,[60] a decision which largely addressed the adequacy of the ET and EAT's reasoning but which also considered the weight to be given to the transfer or otherwise of assets. The majority of the relevant employees became employed by the putative transferee/respondent when it took over certain coal-mining activities and the relevant activities essentially remained the same. The ET finding that TUPE 1981 applied was challenged on the basis that it failed to follow the ECJ guidance with regard to the transfer of plant or lack thereof.

2.55 Whilst it was held by the Court of Session that the position with regard to assets was inadequately explored and analysed by the ET, some useful observations were made with regard to the issue of asset transfer. With regard to the relevance of plant, it was made clear that the issue is contextual rather than the crucial determining factor:

It does not necessarily flow from use, even intensive use, of plant by an entity that the plant employed before transfer is definitive of the identity of the entity.[61]

2.56 With regard to the approach to be adopted overall, the view was that, following *Oy Liikenne*:

---

[58] At para 28. [59] Ibid. [60] [2005] All ER (D) 104. [61] At para 30.

In assessing the degree of importance to be given to plant, and the transfer or non-transfer of it as part of the transaction, the national court must have regard to all the circumstances and must take into account the type of undertaking or business transferred, having regard in particular to the sector of activity in which it operates. That requires a close examination of the wider industry context, and the activities of the predecessor entity within that context. It is in the light of that enquiry that the national court must determine what are the essential and indispensable elements required in order for the economic entity to carry on operating and establish whether these elements have been taken over by [the] transferee.[62]

GEFCO UK Ltd v Oates (1) Car & Delivery Co Ltd[63] addressed similar ground **2.57** where a contract for car transportation was held to fall within the scope of TUPE despite the lack of transfer of any tangible or intangible assets. Acknowledging that similarity of pre- and post-transfer activities was insufficient on its own to establish a TUPE transfer, continuity of customers enabled the ET properly to find that TUPE applied.

These decisions are a useful reminder that, while the categorisation of an **2.58** undertaking as asset reliant or labour intensive can be of assistance in applying the *Spijkers* criteria, they do present a potentially false dichotomy. That concrete rules cannot and should not be based on a distinction between asset-reliant and labour-intensive activities was noted by Langstaff J in *Balfour Beatty Power Networks and another v Wilcox & others*:[64]

It seems to us that . . . the factual assessment of the importance of the balance between the significance of equipment, plant, premises, goodwill, tangible and intangible assets, and the question whether the identity of the labour force is a significant part of the undertaking, will necessarily vary. If one were to regard it as a spectrum, then if at one end of the spectrum were activities which would be regarded as almost entirely labour-intensive (the example used in argument was cleaning) and at the other an undertaking which was almost completely reliant upon heavy plant, machinery and premises (such perhaps as heavy manufacturing requiring no skilled labour input), there would be a sliding scale between them in which the relevant importance of the number and skills of the workforce engaged would necessarily vary.

It can therefore be seen from the jurisprudence that the multifactorial approach **2.59** should still be followed in relation to asset-reliant activities. While usage of assets may be a factor to take into account, the absence of their transfer will not necessarily be fatal to the application of TUPE. Bearing in mind the primacy of the multifactorial approach of *Spijkers*, some short commentary is now provided on the approach adopted in the cases prior to TUPE 2006 in relation to activities considered not to be asset reliant but to be labour intensive and which contributed to the introduction of the concept of a service provision change in regulation 3(1)(b).

---

[62] At para 32.   [63] EAT/0014/05.   [64] [2006] IRLR 258, EAT (at para 25).

C. LABOUR-INTENSIVE ACTIVITIES

2.60 Before the concept of a service provision change introduced by regulation 3(1)(b) is analysed in detail in Chapter 3, it is worth considering, very much in brief summary, the case law in relation to the application to labour-intensive activities of the traditional test of a transfer of an undertaking (now contained, suitably updated, in regulation 3(1)(a)). This review will put into context the introduction of the regulation 3(1)(b) concept of a service provision change which aims to make the application of a transfer of undertakings legislation more predictable in the areas of contracting out, re-tendering and in-housing of labour-intensive activities.

2.61 The *Spijkers* principles, as interpreted by the subsequent case law and effectively enshrined into UK law by TUPE 2006, have caused considerable difficulty and uncertainty in cases where the relevant activities are 'labour intensive'. This is a term used to describe activities (such as security and cleaning) which do not require particular assets to pass over for the activities to be capable of being carried on by a new contractor.

2.62 The problem with which the courts and tribunals have grappled can be described as follows. In relation to labour-intensive activities, the alleged transferee might well not take on the transferor's employees. Employees might not transfer on the assumption or contention that the transfer legislation does not apply or indeed with the deliberate intention of evading its application. There might well be no assets required to transfer from transferor to putative transferee. Two of the *Spijkers* factors indicating the transfer of an economic entity retaining its identity—transfer of assets and transfer of employees—would therefore then not be made out, thereby raising doubt as to the application of the legislation and rendering its application less likely. If the transfer legislation could be avoided in this way, the parties could potentially have the ability to influence whether the legislation would apply to a given scenario in circumstances where they were able to determine between themselves whether assets and employees needed to or did transfer. Allowing the parties such a potential influence over the application of the legislation would undermine its employment protection objectives.

2.63 In *Ayse Süzen*,[65] the ECJ indicated that more was required for the Directive to apply than merely the transfer from one contractor to another of a service contract. Transfer of a service contract without more would not suffice. As the ECJ put it:[66]

> The mere fact that the service provided by the old and the new awardees of a contract is similar does not therefore support the conclusion that an economic entity has been transferred. An entity cannot be reduced to the activity entrusted to it. Its identity also

---

[65] [1997] IRLR 255, ECJ.   [66] At para 15.

emerges from other factors, such as its workforce; its management staff; the way in which its work is organised; its operating methods, or indeed, where appropriate, the operational resources available to it.

Acknowledging the *Spijkers* principles and that each case must be assessed on **2.64** its own facts, the ECJ considered in *Ayse Süzen* that a transfer of significant tangible or intangible assets or a major part of the relevant employees in terms of numbers or skills would be necessary for the Directive to apply.

Betts v Brintel Helicopters Ltd and KLM ERA Helicopters (UK) Ltd[67] con- **2.65** cerned an operation which did entail the use both of assets and equipment. Nonetheless, it applied *Ayse Süzen* in finding that all that was transferred in relation to the re-tendering of a contract to provide helicopter services was the right to land on and utilise the facilities of oil rigs. With no staff or equipment transferred, TUPE was held not to apply.

The concern which arose from *Ayse Süzen* was that it would enable parties to **2.66** avoid the application of TUPE to labour-intensive activities by electing not to transfer the relevant employees. This concern was assuaged to an extent by the fact that a relevant transfer can take place when the major part of the relevant employees in terms of skills (as opposed to numbers) transfers. In *Lightway (Contractors) Ltd v Associated Holdings Ltd*,[68] a minority of the relevant staff were taken on by the transferee but there was nonetheless a relevant transfer since those that transferred were mostly skilled.

Subsequent case law has also considered the motive of the parties in order **2.67** to ensure that TUPE's objectives are not frustrated in relation to labour-intensive activities by employers exploiting the focus in *Ayse Süzen* on whether employees actually transfer. It is accepted that the alleged transferee's motives can be relevant to determining whether or not the transfer legislation applies.

In *ECM (Vehicle Delivery Service) Ltd v Cox*[69] the Court of Appeal con- **2.68** sidered that it was proper for the ET, in relation to the transfer of a contract for vehicle delivery where no assets were transferred and no employees taken on, to consider whether the transferee refused to take on the employees with a view to avoiding TUPE. That this approach was legitimate in appropriate circumstances was also endorsed by the Court of Appeal in *ADI (UK) Ltd v Willer*.[70]

A further decision providing guidance on the application of TUPE (by virtue **2.69** of what is now regulation 3(1)(a)) to labour-intensive activities is *RCO Support Services v UNISON*.[71] The Court of Appeal's summary of the proper approach to be adopted by ETs in assessing whether a given scenario constitutes a transfer of an undertaking was as follows:

- in relation to a labour-intensive function, following *Ayse Süzen*, whether transfers of a major part of the workforce (in terms of numbers and skills) will be an important factor;

---

[67] [1997] IRLR 311, CA. [68] [2000] IRLR 247, CS. [69] [1999] IRLR 559, CA.
[70] [2001] IRLR 542, CA. [71] [2002] IRLR 401, CA.

- given that a multifactorial approach must be adopted, the lack of transfer of employees will not necessarily debar TUPE from applying;
- the motive of the employer in not taking on staff can be relevant.

2.70 In *RCO*, the transferee was willing to employ the relevant cleaning staff on a contracting out but not on their pre-transfer terms of employment as would be preserved by TUPE. This, as well as the specialist nature of the relevant cleaning services, supported the conclusion that TUPE applied.

2.71 *Astle v Cheshire County Council (1) Omnisure Property Management (2)*[72] is an example of how motive remains a potentially challenging factor in assessing whether TUPE applies to circumstances where the parties have genuine commercial reasons for implementing arrangements which they appreciate may have the collateral consequence of precluding the application of TUPE. The EAT's analysis was as follows. Whilst there must be more than a transfer of an activity for TUPE to apply and the reason for employees not transferring can be relevant, an intention to evade the application of TUPE of itself is not relevant unless there would have been a TUPE transfer had the employees actually transferred. If there would have been a TUPE transfer had employees been taken on by the transferee, TUPE will apply where employees are not taken on by the transferee in order to seek to avoid the application of the legislation.

2.72 In *Astle* the council in question established a panel of consultants to replace a supplier of outsourced architectural services which had been terminated for performance reasons. The local authority viewed this structure as a way to 'thwart' TUPE so that the relevant employees would not pass back to the council. Ultimately the way in which the relevant panel was appointed was varied due to advice that TUPE might apply. The council did take over the relevant service for a short period after the incumbent contractor had been terminated. Despite this, TUPE was held not to apply on the basis that the panel system, which caused the operation not to retain its identity post-transfer, was found to have been implemented for genuine commercial reasons rather than the purposes of TUPE avoidance. This decision has been criticised on the basis that it can be viewed as providing too much scope to organisations engaged in the outsourcing of functions to structure their arrangements in a way which evades what is now regulation 3(1)(a). Regulation 3(1)(b), discussed in Chapter 3, is far less easy to avoid by such structuring.

2.73 The issue of the motive of the transferee in not taking on the transferor's staff falls into particularly sharp relief where the unsatisfactory performance of the relevant staff has led to the putative relevant transfer in the first place. The EAT addressed this scenario in *Carlisle Facilities Group v Matrix Events & Security Services and others*.[73] Sea France decided for a variety of reasons, including the poor performance of the staff of its contractor, Carlisle, which provided guarding services, that it wished to replace Carlisle by a new contractor, Matrix.

---

[72] [2005] IRLR 12, EAT.   [73] EAT/0380/04.

Whilst the relevant activities remained similar, none of the relevant employees transferred from Carlisle to Matrix.

The ET determined that, whilst the security guards comprised an undertaking 2.74 for the purposes of TUPE, the lack of any transfer of employees or assets and the fact that there was no intention on the part of Matrix to evade TUPE by not taking on Carlisle's staff led to the conclusion that TUPE did not apply.

An appeal against this decision failed. The ET was entitled to find that the 2.75 decision not to take on the Carlisle staff was not motivated by an intention to evade TUPE but to comply with the ultimate client's wishes with regard to the staffing of the contract. Accordingly, the non-transfer of employees was properly taken into account as indicating that there was no relevant transfer in these circumstances. It should be noted that this is an example of a case which would be decided differently under TUPE 2006 as the facts appear potentially to fall squarely within the concept of a service provision change under regulation 3(1)(b).

It should also be noted in passing and contradistinction that the service 2.76 provision change concept adopted in regulation 3(1)(b) entails different considerations of motive to those which apply in relation to regulation 3(1)(a). What matters for the purposes of regulation 3(1)(b) is the pre-transfer existence of an organised grouping of employees and a switch in the conduct of activities (relating to the provision of services rather than goods) where the intention is to create a relationship which is not one-off and of short duration. Motive is only relevant to the intended nature of the relationship between supplier and recipient of services. The parties' motivation in relation to their decisions as to transfer (or otherwise) of employees is irrelevant to the issue of whether particular circumstances give rise to a service provision change falling within the scope of TUPE.

D. MISCELLANEOUS

1. Series of Transactions and Timing of Transfer

A relevant transfer, whether by way of a transfer of an undertaking under 2.77 regulation 3(1)(a) or a service provision for the purposes of regulation 3(1)(b), can occur as a result of the combination of a number of transactions which are linked and entered into by a variety of parties. Regulation 3(6)(a)[74] provides that a relevant transfer may be effected by a series of two or more transactions. A variety of connected transactions or a series of sequential transactions may have the cumulative effect of constituting a relevant transfer. This provision ensures the application of the legislation even if a complex series of transactions implements the actual transfer.

---

[74] Which restates TUPE 1981, regulation 3(4).

2.78   The timing of a transfer is of course of importance for a variety of reasons. In particular, it determines when the transferee commences employment obligations, by reference to what date the parties should provide the required information to appropriate employee representatives, when consultation with those representatives (if required) should commence, and the timeframe for the provision by the transferor to the transferee of the required employee liability information. The key point is that, regardless of the structure which the parties may adopt in any commercial documentation, what matters is when management or responsibility for the operation changes.

2.79   *Astley & Others v Celtec Ltd*[75] addressed a situation where a transfer of an undertaking was initially found to have occurred over a considerable period of time. Training and Enterprise Councils (TECs) were established to take over the management of training and enterprise facilities from the Department of Employment. The relevant organisations were staffed by seconded civil servants. At the end of a three-year secondment period, the relevant staff were given the choice of returning to the Department of Employment for redeployment or resigning from the civil service and taking up employment with the relevant TEC.

2.80   The Court of Appeal held that the ET was justified in concluding that the Directive preserved the continuity of employment for statutory purposes of those employees who transferred to a TEC on the basis that they were employed in the relevant undertaking by the transferor (the Department of Employment) 'at the time of transfer'. The wording of the Directive was considered to be sufficiently wide to embrace a transfer of an undertaking which takes place over a period of time. Once it was accepted that an undertaking can be transferred over a period of time, it was a matter of fact to establish the precise timing of the transfer.

2.81   Accordingly, the Court of Appeal considered that the ET was entitled to find as it did. There was a relevant transfer commencing when the TEC started business—the transfer took place over a period of years until the last secondments from the Civil Service ended. Each time a seconded employee became directly employed by the TEC, there was another part transfer immediately before which the employee was employed by the transferor such that the employee's employment and associated rights passed to the transferee under TUPE. The ET saw no reason in principle why such a very long period should not be found to constitute the transfer when that was the plan from the outset.

2.82   The flexibility of this approach to the timing and occasion of a transfer appears no longer to be tenable in the light of the subsequent ECJ decision in the same litigation.[76] The ECJ found that the date of transfer for the purposes of the Directive is the particular moment when responsibility as employer for carrying on the business of the undertaking transferred moves from the

---

[75] [2002] IRLR 629, CA.   [76] [2005] IRLR 647, ECJ.

transferor to the transferee. The ECJ considered that the Directive intended to create certainty by reference to its protection applying at the date of transfer. This suggested that the workers who are to benefit from the Directive's protection should be identified at a particular moment in time. The date of a transfer was therefore 'the date on which responsibility as employer for carrying on the business of the unit transferred moves from the transferor to the transferee'.[77] Little guidance was actually provided as to how to deal with complex issues such as that which arose in the particular case and the specific issue will require further consideration by the domestic courts particularly with regard to how this analysis interacts with the provision of regulation 3(6)(a) which envisages a transfer over a period of time by virtue of a series of transactions.

2. Ships

As the 2005 Consultation noted,[78] TUPE 2006 does not contain a provision equivalent to TUPE 1981, regulation 2(2) which provided that a transfer of a ship without more did not constitute a relevant transfer. The reason for the absence of such a provision is the Government's view that the TUPE 1981 provision was 'declaratory only' and added nothing of substance to the operation of the legislation. Only if a ship, even with its crew, were sold as part of a business would the legislation apply.[79]   **2.83**

Regulation 3(7) makes specific provision to deal with the situation where ships[80] registered in the United Kingdom cease to be so. The right of seamen to be discharged from the relevant ship's crew when it ceases to be registered in the United Kingdom[81] is not affected by the fact that such a change in registration may take place in connection with a transaction which otherwise falls within TUPE.   **2.84**

---

[77] At para 44.   [78] Para 13.

[79] As para 13 of the 2005 Consultation noted, this interpretation was confirmed by the Court of Session in *Castle View Services Ltd v Howes and others* (29.2.00 Inner House).

[80] Within the meaning of the Merchant Shipping Act 1894.

[81] Conferred by Merchant Shipping Act 1970.

3

SERVICE PROVISION CHANGES

A. Introduction	3.01
B. Definition	3.09
C. Organised Grouping of Employees	3.15
D. Principal Purpose	3.20
E. One-off Service Contracts	3.22
F. Supply of Goods	3.31
G. Innovative Bids	3.35
H. Professional Business Services	3.39
I. Issues of Interpretation	3.45
J. Conclusions	3.59

A. INTRODUCTION

In order in part to address the uncertainty which had arisen from the European **3.01** Court of Justice (ECJ) and domestic jurisprudence in relation to the application of the Transfer of Undertakings (Protection of Employment) Regulations (TUPE) to the transfer of labour-intensive activities, regulation 3(1)(b) establishes a new concept of a service provision change which constitutes a relevant transfer[1] for the purposes of TUPE. This new definition of what can constitute a relevant transfer is supplementary to the traditional concept of a transfer of an undertaking maintained by regulation 3(1)(a).

A service provision change occurs on a change (other than on a one-off short- **3.02** term basis or in relation to the supply of goods) to the identity of the person who has the conduct of activities to which an organised grouping of employees has principally been dedicated for a particular client. According to the Department of Trade and Industry (DTI) Guidance,[2] '[s]ervice provision changes concern relationships between contractors and the clients who hire their services'.

---

[1] Pursuant to regulation 2(1).   [2] At page 9.

The Consultation Response[3] indicated that the term 'describes situations where a contract to provide a business service to a client is let, re-let or ended by bringing it in house'.

3.03   This additional and alternative concept of a relevant transfer is intended to ensure that the transfer legislation applies to outsourcing, in-housing, and the re-tendering of contracts from one contractor to another. As the DTI put it,[4] in the absence of further ECJ jurisprudence to resolve what it saw as the case law conflict with regard to the application of the transfer legislation to labour-intensive activities, it was considered to be a 'moot point' to what extent the Directive and TUPE 1981 already applied to such problem cases. The objective of the new formulation is to ensure that the comprehensive application of TUPE in such cases will reduce insecurity and help to 'take the fear out of transfer' by smoothing the transfer process, thereby improving workplace relationships and partnership and promoting business flexibility.[5]

3.04   The 2001 Consultation acknowledged that the introduction of this concept of a service provision change would be a significant extension of the scope of TUPE.[6] It can be argued cogently that (in analytical if not necessarily practical terms) the service provision change concept goes beyond the Directive's requirements in terms of employee protection. Basing the application of the legislation on the dedication of staff to an activity which is taken over by a new operator is to the effective exclusion of the other factors to be considered when following the *Spijkers* approach.

3.05   One attraction of this new formulation was perceived to be the improved predictability of the application of TUPE. This was anticipated as creating a 'level playing field'[7] for contractors competing for contracts to provide services. In the light of the obligation on the transferor to notify the transferee of pre-scribed employee information,[8] the more predictable application of TUPE in these circumstances could therefore be catered for and dealt with adequately by those affected. The desirability of the introduction of the new concept was not, it has to be said, accepted unanimously—the Engineering Employers' Federation argued that the introduction of the service provision change concept would 'create inflexibility in contract provision and reduce competition and innovation at the same time as creating new areas of legal uncertainty'.[9]

3.06   That the comprehensive application of TUPE to contracting out, re-tendering and in-housing would create a level playing field was also seen as promoting competition in line with, for example, the Government's best value framework

---

[3] At para 2.1.   [4] 2005 Consultation Annex D para 3.

[5] 2005 Consultation Annex D, para 7.

[6] Para 28. Notwithstanding this, the Consultation Response, in defending the decision to adopt the service provision change concept, stated (at para 2.5) that '[m]any service provision changes are also in fact business transfers and are thus already covered by TUPE'.

[7] 2005 Consultation para 18.

[8] Although watered down from what was first proposed—see Chap 8.

[9] Consultation Response para 2.5.

for local authority services. An expanded and clarified TUPE was expected to remove a significant disincentive for potential bidders (and particularly smaller firms) from becoming involved in service contracting.[10] The service provision change concept would also assist in ensuring that the principles set out in the Government's statement of practice on staff transfers in the public sector were fully observed within local government and the non-central government public sector.

The 2001 Consultation also noted that excluding the application of the new **3.07** concept from arrangements which were 'one-off' task-specific contracts would ensure that the legislation did not go beyond the scope of the Acquired Rights Directive (ARD) 2001 in terms of the stability and focus of the activity.[11] The view was also taken that employees providing the kind of 'commodity services' which were perceived as being purchased on such a one-off basis are less likely to be at risk of redundancy as a result of the awarding of contracts for the supply of such services. They were therefore less likely to be in need of statutory employment protection by TUPE. These employees would be likely to remain part of the workforce of the provider of such commodity services which would presumably deploy such staff to its remaining variety of clients and customers. A degree of stability as between client and supplier is required to attract the application of employment protection for the employees affected by a contract award by way of there being a service provision change.

The Government considered the possibility of introducing a specific exemp- **3.08** tion[12] in respect of services of a professional nature such as legal, banking, accountancy, and consultancy services but this was ultimately rejected. The service provision change concept therefore applies equally to the professional services sector.

B. DEFINITION

For the purposes of regulation 3(1)(b), a service provision change arises in the **3.09** following situations:

- 'activities cease to be carried out by a person ("a client") on his own behalf and are carried out instead by another person on the client's behalf ("a contractor")'.[13] This essentially covers outsourcing;

- 'activities cease to be carried out by a contractor on a client's behalf (whether or not those activities had previously been carried out by the client on its own behalf) and are carried out instead by another person ("a subsequent

---

[10] 2001 Consultation para 29.   [11] 2001 Consultation para 30.
[12] Ibid para 33. See para 3.39 *et seq* below for further discussion.   [13] Regulation 3(1)(b)(i).

contractor") on the client's behalf.[14] This essentially covers a re-tendering or contractor change;

- 'activities cease to be carried out by a contractor or a subsequent contractor on a client's behalf (whether or not those activities had previously been carried out by the client on its own behalf) and are carried out instead by the client on his own behalf'.[15] This essentially covers in-housing.

3.10 The activities in question must, however, also be of the requisite stability and structure before transfer. Accordingly, immediately before the service provision change:

- there must be an 'organised grouping of employees situated in Great Britain which has as its principal purpose the carrying out of the activities concerned on behalf of the client';[16]
- the client must also intend 'that the activities will, following the service provision change, be carried out by the transferee other than in connection with a single specific event or task of short term duration'.[17]

3.11 Essential elements of the application of regulation 3(1)(b) are therefore the existence immediately prior to the putative transfer of an organised grouping of employees, its dedication to one client, and the change of service provider. The transfer of assets or employees, so integral to the test of whether there is a transfer of an undertaking for the purposes of regulation 3(1)(a), is not relevant to the test of whether there is a service provision change. Nor are the motives of a putative transferee in not taking employees on post-transfer or any break in activities apparently to be considered, again in contrast to the approach of regulation 3(1)(a).

3.12 It is submitted that, despite the fact that there is no express statement to that effect, the new concept of a service provision change under regulation 3(1)(b) will apply regardless of whether the transfer is voluntary or involuntary and of whether there is any contractual relationship between the parties. This would be consistent with the approach in relation to what is now regulation 3(1)(a) and is central to ensuring the application of the legislation. As is the case with regulation 3(1)(a), regulation 3(6) confirms that no property need transfer for there to be a service provision change which constitutes a relevant transfer[18] and that a service provision change can be effected by a series of two or more transactions.[19]

3.13 Two key elements of regulation 3(1)(b)—the reference to 'service' in the descriptive term 'service provision change' and the concept of 'activities'—are not specifically defined in TUPE. The drafting approach was not to define these aspects of regulation 3(1)(b) but rather to exclude specific matters from its scope.

---

[14] Regulation 3(1)(b)(ii). [15] Regulation 3(1)(b)(iii). [16] Regulation 3(3)(a)(i).
[17] Regulation 3(3)(a)(ii). [18] Regulation 3(6)(b). [19] Regulation 3(6)(a).

Accordingly, the service provision change concept does not apply to one-off contracts of short duration.[20] Also, a service provision change only arises where the relevant activities 'do not consist wholly or mainly of the supply of goods for the client's use'.[21]

Concern had been expressed by some commentators in relation to the draft of **3.14** what became TUPE 2006 that regulation 3(1)(b) might not cover the sub-contracting of activities by a client's contractor or changes of subcontractor. This concern was addressed by the inclusion in regulation 2(1) of the specific provision that 'references to "contractor" in regulation 3 shall include a sub-contractor'. As the DTI indicated in the Consultation Response,[22] the Government 'decided to make it explicit (rather than implicit) that sub-contractors are in the same position as contractors when activities are performed by them'. Transactions involving awards and re-tendering of subcontracts will therefore be equally susceptible to the application of TUPE as contract awards by the ultimate client. The key question about the application of the regulation 3(1)(b) concept of a service provision change in relation to subcontractors will be whether the requisite organised grouping of employees dedicated to a particular client exists prior to the putative service provision change.

C. ORGANISED GROUPING OF EMPLOYEES

In order for there to be a service provision change within regulation 3(1)(b), the **3.15** relevant activity must, before the service provision change, be conducted by an 'organised grouping of employees situated in Great Britain which has as its principal purpose the carrying out of the activities concerned on behalf of the client'.[23] As the 2005 Consultation indicated,[24] this requirement confines the application of the concept of a service provision change to situations where the incumbent service provider (which includes the client where a service is being contracted out) operates the relevant activities by way of an identifiable team of employees which is essentially dedicated to meeting one particular client's needs.

Where there is no identifiable group of employees assigned to a function or **3.16** contract conducted for a particular client, a service provision change for the purposes of TUPE 2006 will not arise on the award or reassignment of the contract. Accordingly, adopting the example used by the 2005 Consultation,[25] courier services provided by various different couriers on an ad hoc basis to various clients would not fall within regulation 3(1)(b) but a permanently assigned team of couriers working for a particular client would transfer should a replacement contractor be appointed by that client.

---

[20] Regulation 3(3)(a)(ii). See para 3.22 *et seq* below.
[21] Regulation 3(3)(b). See para 3.31 *et seq* below.
[22] Para 27.   [23] Regulation 3(3)(a)(i).   [24] Para 22.   [25] Ibid.

3.17   The requirement that there be an organised grouping of employees not only ensures that the relevant activities are sufficiently structured, stable, and identifiable that they can sensibly fall within the general scope of the legislation. It also renders the concept workable in terms of which employees should transfer on a change of contractor in relation to service provision. As the DTI Guidance noted,[26] 'it would be unclear which employees should transfer in the event of a change of contractor, if there was no such grouping'. Presumably, in applying regulation 3(1)(b), some evidence of the relevant employees being organised will be required, whether by reporting structure, division, or otherwise. It is not sufficient for employees just to be dedicated to a particular client. By analogy with the requirement in relation to regulation 3(1)(a) that there be an organised grouping of resources which entails a degree of stability, structure, or autonomy,[27] there must be some connection between the employees in question to constitute the required organised grouping.

3.18   The test of whether there is an organised grouping of employees adequate to satisfy regulation 3(1)(b) is applied immediately before the change.[28] That said, purposive arguments analogous to those deployed in *Litster*[29] and *ECM*[30] will surely be capable of being deployed by employees seeking to establish that they are protected by TUPE in relation to a service provision change. The Courts and Employment Tribunals (ETs) may well find that TUPE applies where, for example, a client disbands a dedicated group of staff in advance of an out-sourcing deliberately in order to seek to avoid the application of regulation 3(1)(b).

3.19   The requirement that there be an organised grouping of employees only applies to the pre-transfer activities under consideration. If the activities, as they are carried on by the transferee after a putative service provision change, are not conducted by an organised and dedicated group of employees this does not avoid the application of regulation 3(1)(b). As the Consultation Response indicated,[31] '[t]here is no implied requirement for [the relevant] activities to be carried out by the transferee in an identical manner'. The regulation 3(1)(b) formulation, lacking as it does the requirement of retention of identity which applies in relation to the transfer of an economic entity for the purposes of regulation 3(1)(a), applies TUPE regardless of how the transferee chooses to service the relevant contract. Assuming that there is no economic, technical, or organisational reason entailing changes in the workforce (ETOR) justifying pre-transfer dismissal, the legal consequence of regulation 3(1)(b) being structured in this way is effectively to allocate liability for any consequent termination costs in relation to service provision changes to the transferee (subject of course to any commercial agreement between the parties). Nonetheless, if activities are divided between suppliers post-transfer, problems may arise with regard

---

[26] At page 9.   [27] See 2.19 *et seq.*   [28] Regulation 3(3)(a)(i).
[29] [1989] IRLR 161, HL.   [30] [1999] IRLR 559, CA. See 2.68.   [31] Para 2.7.

to identifying whether and to whom employees transfer on the basis of the assignment test.[32]

D. PRINCIPAL PURPOSE

Even if there is an organised grouping of employees, their principal purpose **3.20** must be to carry out the relevant activities for the particular client if regulation 3(1)(b) is to apply to a given scenario. An established team of staff providing services to a variety of clients or customers will fall outside the scope of the concept of a service provision change. It is on this basis that many simple service contracts will fall outside the scope of the legislation such as, for example, where a contractor's cleaners work for various clients.

That said, the test is that the organised grouping must have the principal **3.21** (rather than exclusive) purpose of carrying out the relevant activities on behalf of the client. There will no doubt be considerable debate about the test to be applied in establishing what is a group of employees' principal purpose. Percentage tests as to the amount of time spent by a group of employees on a relevant client's business or the revenue which is attributable to a client may well be evidentially important but may not be determinative of what should be, it is submitted, a test to be determined by reference to all the circumstances. The issue should be treated as a matter of fact for the ET. No doubt the principles used in determining whether employees are assigned to the undertaking transferred[33] will be useful in this context by way of analogy.

E. ONE-OFF SERVICE CONTRACTS

Regulation 3(3)(a)(ii) excludes from the scope of a service provision change for **3.22** the purpose of regulation 3(1)(b) situations where a client obtains services from a contractor on a one-off and short-term basis as opposed to entering into an ongoing relationship with that contractor. The 2005 Consultation anticipated that, where a one-off contract is awarded, it is unlikely that the transfer legislation would apply in any event in such circumstances. The basis for this view was the view that an organised grouping of employees with the principal purpose of meeting the particular client's needs would be unlikely to exist prior to the relevant contract award.[34] However, in situations where the nature of the project in question entails the establishment of a team of employees, the Government considered that it was appropriate to provide this express exception in order clearly to exclude from the scope of the legislation contracts for single specific events or tasks.

---

[32] See Chap 4, para 4.14 *et seq.*   [33] Ibid.   [34] 2005 Consultation para 24.

3.23 Moreover, the Government's intention[35] was that, even if a client engages a particular contractor on a number of separate occasions to provide one-off services, the exclusion established by regulation 3(3)(a)(ii) should still apply provided that the series of engagements is 'coincidental or fortuitous' and the client has no intention of establishing an ongoing relationship with the contractor. It is for that reason that the client's intention is specifically referred to as an essential requirement for there to be a service provision change in regulation 3(3)(a)(ii)—'the client intends that the activities will, following the service provision change be carried out by the transferee other than in connection with a single specific event or task of short-term duration'. An ongoing stable relationship is intended to be caught by the service provision change concept. One-off unrelated and short-term contract awards are not.

3.24 The DTI Guidance explained this principle as follows:

> the Regulations should not be expected to apply where a client engaged a contractor to organise a single conference on its behalf, even though the contractor had established an organised grouping of staff—e.g. a 'project team'—to carry out the activities involved in fulfilling that task. Thus, were the client subsequently to hold a second conference using a different contractor, the members of the first project team would not be required to transfer to the second contractor.[36]

3.25 There was initial concern, when the first draft of what became TUPE 2006 was published, that the service provision change concept would not apply to large projects, which might otherwise be expected to attract the application of the legislation, simply because they were 'one-off'. Unless regulation 3(1)(a) applied in any event, very significant but one-off service contracts would then fall outside the scope of TUPE due to their specific exclusion from the scope of regulation 3(1)(b) by virtue of regulation 3(3)(a)(ii) as originally drafted. The employment protection objectives of the legislation would not necessarily be best served by the blanket exclusion of single specific events and tasks from the scope of the regulation 3(1)(b) service provision change.

3.26 This point was addressed by the addition of the words 'of short-term duration' to regulation 3(3)(a)(ii). As noted in the Consultation Response,[37] the original wording was accepted not to have been sufficiently precise, as was the scope for litigation over whether a particular contract concerned a specific, overarching task or a series of inter-linked tasks. The Government therefore determined that it should make clear that the exemption applies to tasks or events of short-term duration.

3.27 The DTI Guidance explained the requirement that a one-off service contract must also be of short-term duration to fall outside the scope of regulation 3(1)(b) as follows:[38]

---

[35] Ibid para 25.   [36] At p 10.   [37] At para 2.13.   [38] On p 10.

To illustrate the point take the example of two hypothetic [*sic*] contracts concerning the security of an Olympic Games or some other major sporting event. The first contract concerns the provision of security advice to the event organisers and covers a period of several years running up to the event; the other concerns the hiring of security staff to protect athletes during the period of the event itself. Both contracts have a one-off character in the sense that they both concern the holding of a specific event. However, the first contract runs for a significantly longer period than the second; therefore, the first would be covered by the TUPE Regulations (if the other qualifying conditions are satisfied) but the second would not.

Whether a contract relates to a single specific event or task of short-term dur- **3.28** ation will be determined as a matter of fact and evidence. Despite the inclusion of the requirement that an excluded one-off contract be 'of short duration', it may not always be the case that ETs will find it easy to assess a client's intention with regard to the award of an initial contract which employees seek to argue falls outside the exclusion of one-off short-term contracts from the scope of regulation 3(1)(b). It is unlikely that specific evidence will often be obtained of an intention to establish an ongoing business relationship with the relevant contractor in such circumstances, let alone an intention to structure the parties' commercial arrangements by way of ostensibly one-off contracts to seek to avoid regulation 3(1)(b). An anti-avoidance mechanism based on intention may be difficult to apply in practice at the time when it is most needed to be effective in order to protect employees (ie at the point of the initial contract award). Being able to establish that an initial contract was not one-off by reference to sub-sequent contract awards will presumably come too late to provide protection to employees whose employment did not transfer to the initial contractor because at the time it was considered that the one-off contract exclusion applied.

The same challenge will arise in determining whether successive contracts are **3.29** fortuitous and therefore that each still relates to a 'single specific event or task of short term duration'. Conversely, as a contractor relationship develops over time, the risk increases of retrospective claims (perhaps directed particularly at issues of continuity of employment for statutory purposes) that TUPE applied to the original contract awards or extensions.

This ongoing risk was acknowledged in the Consultation Response which **3.30** noted the possibility of misuse of the exemption of contracts of short-term duration from the scope of regulation 3(1)(b) by parties 'deliberately break[ing] up longer term contracts into a series of smaller contracts of a short-term duration'.[39] The Government felt confident that the ET would be able to deal with such issues, being 'accustomed to assessing the motivation of parties when considering cases put before it'.[40]

---

[39] At para 2.13.   [40] Ibid.

F. SUPPLY OF GOODS

3.31 Regulation 3(3)(b)(i) excludes from the scope of the concept of a service provision change situations where the contractor's engagement by the client is wholly or mainly for the supply of goods for the client's use. The example given in the 2005 Consultation[41] is where a client engages a contractor to supply sandwiches and drinks to a canteen for the client to sell on to its own staff. If the contract were for the running of the canteen, then its award to a new contractor could well constitute a relevant transfer by virtue of being a traditional transfer of an undertaking or as a service provision change, provided that the applicable conditions were satisfied.[42] In that case, the main activities involved in the contract would be to deal with managing facilities, serving customers, washing crockery etc. In contrast, the supply of food and drink would be ancillary to these main activities and the goods would not be for direct sale—a contract simply for supply of such goods would not constitute a service provision change for these purposes.

3.32 Whilst the distinction between a contract to run a canteen and a contract simply to supply food to a canteen is superficially straightforward, the application of this exception of what can be termed 'goods-only supply contracts' from the concept of a service provision change may not always be simple, especially where a team of staff is dedicated to the supply of goods to a client.

3.33 Disputes about the extent of this exception may well centre on the fact-sensitive issue of whether a contract is 'wholly or mainly' for the supply of goods for the client's use or constitutes a broader service-based relationship which is not caught by the exception. An example of a difficult case would be where machinery or equipment is supplied (a supply of goods) but that machinery or equipment requires maintenance or technical support (which is more than just supply of goods).

3.34 It should be noted that, in the initial draft of what became TUPE 2006, the 'procurement' of goods was also excluded from the scope of the service provision change concept. The reference to 'procurement' was deleted from the final version of TUPE 2006, not least as it might have meant that the outsourcing of a client's procurement department would have fallen outside the scope of regulation 3(1)(b), 'an effect which the Government did not want to achieve as such departments clearly provide a service function'.[43]

---

[41] Para 26.

[42] An example of there being a transfer of undertaking in such circumstances is *Abler*—see Chap 2, para 2.48.

[43] Consultation Response at para 2.7.

G. INNOVATIVE BIDS

In formulating its reforms to TUPE, the possibility was considered by the 3.35
Government of providing expressly that regulation 3(1)(b) should not apply
where the relevant service is to be provided in a new or innovative manner.[44] It
was ultimately concluded that such an exemption would not be included in
TUPE 2006.

The rationale for this decision was as follows. If new methods of working 3.36
(such as computerisation) are introduced as part of a service provision change,
the employees engaged in the relevant activities might be redundant as regards
the relevant activities as carried on by the transferee if they do not have the
relevant skills. To apply TUPE in these circumstances, thereby transferring
responsibility for the relevant employees to the new service provider, was considered to be in line with the employment protection objectives of the legislation—it would maximise the possibility of those employees who do not have the
relevant skills retaining their jobs by having the opportunity to be retrained or
reallocated elsewhere in the new contractor's business. A transferee inheriting
employees (or liability for them) in such circumstances would, not least in order
to minimise the risk of unfair dismissal claims and liability for termination
payments, seek alternative positions for those employees or provide training in
order to avoid or reduce termination costs associated with the transfer and
related technological or other changes.

Moreover, a level playing field would be created in relation to re-tendering 3.37
exercises thereby increasing 'certainty and confidence for all concerned'.[45] It can
certainly be argued that the exclusion of innovative bids from the scope of
regulation 3(1)(b) would have encouraged structuring of transactions to avoid
the application of regulation 3(1)(b).

The decision not to exclude innovative bids from the scope of the concept of 3.38
service provision changes reinforces the point that it may well be difficult to
argue, in the context of service provision changes, that there is no relevant
transfer even if there is a significant change in the mode of delivery of the
relevant activities at or around the time of the change of operator. This effectively allocates to the transferee termination costs associated with the transfer
arising as a consequence of efficiencies, improvements to service delivery, and
new methods of contract performance. The parties may of course seek in their
commercial arrangements to allocate liabilities between themselves by way of
indemnities for employment termination costs or the pricing of a contract.

---

[44] 2005 Consultation paras 27 and 28.　　[45] Ibid.

H. PROFESSIONAL BUSINESS SERVICES

3.39 During the course of formulating its reforms to TUPE, the Government received representations from some employers' organisations that 'white collar' professional business services should be exempted from the scope of the service provision change provisions.[46] The argument in favour of this proposed exemption[47] was principally that professionally qualified employees 'by virtue of having skills that are generally highly sought after by employers' are less in need of additional legal protection than those engaged in routine manual work. In practice changes of provider in relation to professional services such as accountancy, legal advice, and software design were considered rarely to give rise to difficulties for the relevant employees.

3.40 The opposing view[48] argued that a professional services exemption should not be created for a variety of reasons including its perceived lack of regular practical relevance, the inappropriateness of distinguishing between white collar and blue collar workers in terms of the application of employment protection legislation, and the legal and practical difficulties of drawing a distinction between professional business services and other types of services. With regard to that latter point, the Government considered[49] establishing a professional business services exception by reference to either a 'generic description' of such services or, as was its preference (if the proposal were to proceed), a list of specified services meriting exceptional treatment by reference to their distinctive features.

3.41 It was also noted[50] that a professional business services exemption would only apply to the private sector since the relevant provisions relating to transfers out of the public sector contain no such limitation. Presumably, although the 2005 Consultation did not say so expressly, such a distinction would have been difficult to justify.

3.42 In any event the likelihood of a business services exemption having practical relevance was considered to be low. It would only apply[51] in cases of a change of an ongoing arrangement to which an organised grouping of employees was dedicated pre-transfer and the award of the relevant contract did not also constitute a traditional transfer of an undertaking pursuant to regulation 3(1)(a). Cases in which there would not be a traditional transfer of an undertaking but the other requirements of a service provision change would be satisfied were considered likely to be rare.[52]

3.43 The DTI also took the view that banks, solicitors, and accountants would rarely in practice service their major clients by way of dedicated teams which

---

[46] 2005 Consultation para 30.   [47] Ibid para 31.   [48] Ibid para 32.

[49] Ibid paras 35 and 36.   [50] Ibid para 32(e).   [51] 2005 Consultation para 33.

[52] Ibid para 34. A comment which is somewhat at odds with the view expressed at para 28 of the 2001 Consultation (see n 6 above) that the introduction of the service provision charge concept would represent a significant extension of the legislation.

would fall within the scope of regulation 3(1)(b) in the absence of a business services exemption, especially in the context of what were styled 'high street' providers of services. It was considered that any team of staff which is devoted to a particular client will normally carry out tasks for a number of clients even if this is done on an 'irregular or ad hoc basis'. Analytically as opposed to empirically, it can be argued that this argument is flawed—irregular or ad hoc work for other clients by the relevant team will not necessarily disapply regulation 3(1)(b) (whose application is parasitic upon the fact-sensitive test of the relevant organised grouping of employees having the principal, rather than exclusive, purpose of servicing a particular client).

Ultimately the Government decided not to proceed with the proposal for a **3.44** business services exemption in the light of what were described as the strong arguments against the exclusion and the fact that most consultees considered that these disadvantages outweighed the potential benefits.[53] It is therefore clear that a dedicated team of staff in, for example, an accountancy or solicitors' firm principally devoted to one client's requirements can constitute an organised grouping of employees for the purposes of regulation 3(1)(b) and therefore could fall to transfer to a new firm under TUPE if the client switches its instructions or retainer on an ongoing basis. This new regime may lead employers in the professions (and elsewhere) to arrange staffing to ensure that employees do not work exclusively for a single client if they wish to avoid TUPE issues to arise on the loss of that client's retainer. Similarly, an incoming provider of professional services may need to be considering TUPE issues from an early stage.

I. ISSUES OF INTERPRETATION

Regulation 3(1)(b) is more straightforward to apply than regulation 3(1)(a). **3.45** Where a contract is awarded and the requirements of regulation 3(1)(b) are satisfied, lack of asset transfer, retention of identity, and the transferee's motives in not taking on employees are not relevant considerations. That said, the formulation of regulation 3(1)(b) is not without its difficulties.

The concept of a service provision change for the purposes of regulation **3.46** 3(1)(b) is (and is intended to be) of wider scope than the regulation 3(1)(a) concept of a transfer of an undertaking. As *Ayse Süzen*[54] noted, a transfer of an undertaking for the purposes of the legislation (what is now regulation 3(1)(a)) does not arise on transfer of a mere activity—more is required. By contrast, a service provision change requires only the transfer of an activity (albeit one which does not relate to the supply of goods, to which an organised grouping of employees has principally been dedicated and which is not transferred on a one-off short-term basis). Whether a group of employees is organised and is

---

[53] Consultation Response para 2.12.   [54] [1997] IRLR 255, ECJ.

principally dedicated to a client's requirements are inherently fact-specific issues and no further guidance is provided as to the nature or duration of the required organisation of the relevant employees or indeed how ETs are to assess their principal purpose. No doubt judicial guidance on the consideration of these issues will emerge in due course.

3.47 Regulation 3(1)(b) and its supplementary provisions do not expressly require that the activities which are the subject of a service provision change retain their identity on transfer. This is in contrast to the definition of an economic entity for the purposes of a regulation 3(1)(a) transfer of an undertaking which does so. No specific definitions of the concepts of services or activities are provided in TUPE 2006 from which guidance in this regard could usefully be gleaned. Leaving aside the exceptions in respect of one-off short-term contracts and the supply of goods, the test of a service provision change is based only on there being a dedicated organised grouping of employees servicing the relevant function and there being a change to the identity of the person performing or providing the activities.

3.48 Contractors will find it difficult to avoid the application of regulation 3(1)(b) on the basis of a change to the nature of the service delivery unless ETs and courts can be persuaded that retention of identity is to some degree implicit in the requirement that the relevant pre-transfer activities must be conducted by the transferee. An incoming contractor seeking to avoid TUPE would have to argue that the activities have changed drastically so that they are not the same as the pre-transfer activities and that therefore regulation 3(1)(b) does not apply because the transferee is not conducting the activities which the transferor did. Such an argument would be consistent with the approach adopted in relation to the traditional test of a transfer of an undertaking but faces a number of difficulties.

3.49 First, the express requirement of retention of identity contained in regulation 3(1)(a) is absent from the definition of a service provision change in regulation 3(1)(b). Second, the Government's decision not to exclude innovative bids from the scope of regulation 3(1)(b) indicates that changes to the mode of operation or delivery of the relevant activities do not take the contract award in question outside the scope of regulation 3(1)(b). Third, the Consultation Response set out the Government's view that '[t]here is no implied requirement for ... activities to be carried out by the transferee in an identical manner'.[55]

3.50 Against this background, interpreting the service provision change concept to require a strict requirement of retention of identity of the relevant activities post-transfer would, whilst attractive from the employer's perspective, place a considerable strain on the formulation of regulation 3(1)(b). Only in extreme cases would it appear possible to argue that regulation 3(1)(b) does not apply to a contract award on the basis that what the new contractor is to do is so different

---

[55] At para 2.7.

to the pre-transfer operation that it will not be carrying out the activities concerned after the transfer. In any event further legislative or judicial guidance will be required before arguments along these lines can be run with confidence.

It will also be interesting to see in what circumstances an interruption or temporary cessation of activities will disapply regulation 3(1)(b) or will not do so. The jurisprudence on what is now regulation 3(1)(a) may be prayed in aid but can be argued not to be strictly relevant to this domestic, rather than EU, concept of a service provision change.[56] **3.51**

The concept deployed to denote the stability of the relevant activities (an 'organised grouping of employees') refers to plural employees. This might have been taken to imply that, in contrast to *Schmidt*,[57] the transfer of a single person activity, even though dedicated to a single client, would not constitute a service provision change. Regulation 2(1), however, makes clear that this is not the case, providing that 'references to "organised grouping of employees" shall include a single employee'.[58] To have provided otherwise would have led to the arguably anomalous position that a single person undertaking would fall within regulation 3(1)(a) but a service activity conducted by one person would not be covered by regulation 3(1)(b). **3.52**

As the Consultation Response put it,[59] '[s]ome contractual services—for example, the cleaning of a relatively small office—are sometimes undertaken by just one person, and the Government accepts it would be unfair to deny rights to such individuals simply because they are single employee units'. **3.53**

The DTI Guidance echoed this point:[60] 'it should be noted that a "grouping of employees" can constitute just one person, as may happen, say, when the cleaning of a small business premises is undertaken by a single person employed by a contractor'. **3.54**

A similar point of interpretation arises in relation to the division of activities between a number of contractors where prior to the contract award there is an organised grouping of employers dedicated to a particular client. This is not explicitly covered by regulation 3(1)(b) which refers only to a singular contractor. To interpret regulation 3(1)(b) as potentially inapplicable where a number of transferees take over activities previously conducted by an organised grouping of employees would be inappropriate (and inconsistent with regulation 3(1)(a)'s clear application to transfers of parts of undertakings). Functional or geographical division of activities on a contract award is not difficult to envisage even in relation to the example of courier services cited in the 2005 Consultation as demonstrating how regulation 3(1)(b) will operate.[61] **3.55**

While the DTI did not expressly state that it considered there still to be a service provision change where pre-transfer activities are divided on a contract **3.56**

---

[56] Chap 2, para 2.45 *et seq.*   [57] [1994] IRLR 302, ECJ.

[58] This provision was not included in the original draft of what became TUPE 2006 but was added to remove the uncertainty which would otherwise have resulted.

[59] At para 2.8.   [60] At p 10.   [61] See para 3.16 above.

award, that view was implicit in the position adopted in the Consultation Response. In defending its use of the term 'activities' in formulating regulation 3(1)(b),[62] the Government indicated that it considered that the approach adopted in *Fairhurst Ward Abbotts v Botes Building Limited and others*[63] in relation to transfers of undertakings[64] was equally applicable to service provision changes. Whilst not argued in detail, it seems that the DTI's view was that, if on a traditional transfer a separate economic entity can emerge for the first time, there is no reason why divided activities cannot lead to service provision changes to the various contractors who take over different parts of the pre-transfer activities carried on by the relevant organised grouping of employees.[65]

3.57   The DTI Guidance more directly indicates that this is the correct interpretation, stating[66] that the service provision change concept

> would also potentially cover situations where just some of those activities in the original service contract are re-tendered and awarded to a new contractor, or where the original service contract is split up until two or more components, each of which is assigned to a different contractor. In each of these cases, the key test is whether an organised grouping has as its principal purpose the carrying out of the activities that are transferred.

3.58   It will also be important in applying regulation 3(1)(b) to identify precisely the activities in question and their scope to ascertain if the exclusion of the supply of goods from the scope of regulation 3(1)(b) applies. A function may have elements which are goods related and some which are service related. Given that the test of the exclusion in regulation 3(3)(b) is that the activities should not 'wholly or mainly' consist of the supply of goods, key factual issues will include identifying the nature of the services, whether they are separable from the supply of goods (functionally and in terms of whether there is an organised grouping of employees principally conducting them), and whether, if not entirely separable, the function is wholly, mainly, or only partially related to the supply of goods.

J. CONCLUSIONS

3.59   One view is that the adoption of the regulation 3(1)(b) definition of a service provision change will have a significant impact on contracting out, contracting in, and re-tendering of contracts.[67] Regulation 3(1)(b) ensures that, if an organised team of employees is established in relation to the servicing of a particular client's or customer's requirements for services, as distinct from goods, and a contract in respect of these requirements is awarded on more than a one-off

---

[62]   As opposed to other concepts which consultees had suggested such as 'function' or 'service' (see Consultation Response para 2.6).

[63]   [2004] IRLR 304, CA—see Chap 2, para 2.38 *et seq.*

[64]   For the purposes of what is now regulation 3(1)(a).

[65]   See Consultation Response para 2.7.   [66]   At p 10.   [67]   See para 3.04 above.

short-term basis, TUPE will apply. Cases such as *Ayse Süzen* will no longer be capable of being relied upon to contend that TUPE does not apply in relation to the transfer of a labour-intensive contract falling within the scope of regulation 3(1)(b).

The alternative view is that the introduction of the concept of the service **3.60** provision change will be of limited impact. The basis for this view is the contention that the traditional test of a transfer of an undertaking under regulation 3(1)(a) will be satisfied in relation to most, if not all, situations which the service provision change concept is intended to address and is likely to cover, a point which the Government itself recognised.[68] This is particularly apparent when one considers decisions such as *ADI (UK) Ltd v Willer*[69] where the transfer of security services fell within the scope of TUPE despite the lack of any transfer of assets or staff.

The principal consequence of the introduction of this new regime is the **3.61** removal of the, if nothing else perceived, uncertainty and unpredictability which the jurisprudence on TUPE 1981 produced. In situations where no or few resources are needed for the relevant activity,[70] where the transferee does not take on affected staff or where the method of delivery of the service changes, the new definition will be particularly relevant.

An example of a recent decision which might well be decided differently under **3.62** regulation 3(1)(b) is *Computacenter (UK) Ltd v Swanton and others*.[71] A dedicated team of employees were engaged in servicing a subcontract from IBM repairing Lloyds TSB computers. This arrangement constituted an economic entity in the view of the ET. The subcontract was awarded to a new subcontractor and no staff transferred. The ET found that there was no relevant transfer on the basis of the lack of any transfer of assets or employees, the lack of any relationship between the two subcontractors, and the fact that the arrangements had not been structured deliberately to avoid TUPE. The EAT rejected an appeal. Given the presence of the key factors of a dedicated team of employees and the transfer of the relevant activities between contractors, the ET might well, had it been required to consider regulation 3(1)(b), have found there to be a service provision change, despite the fact that the requirements of what is now regulation 3(1)(a) were not satisfied.

---

[68] 2005 Consultation para 18. 'In most cases, service provision changes fall within the scope of the Directive and of the existing Regulations in any event.'

[69] [2001] IRLR 542, CA.

[70] Regulation 3(2) defines an economic entity for the purpose of identifying a transfer of an undertaking within the meaning of regulation 3(1)(a) by reference to 'an organised grouping of resources'.

[71] EAT/0256/04. *Carlisle Facilities Group v Matrix Events & Security Services* discussed in Chap 2 at para 2.73 is another example of a situation to which regulation 3(1)(b) could apply but what is now regulation 3(1)(a) did not.

4

WHO TRANSFERS?

| A. Who Transfers? | 4.01 |
| B. Electing not to Transfer | 4.47 |

A. WHO TRANSFERS?

1. Employees

The Directive's protection only extends to employees. As recorded by Article **4.01**
2.1(d), for these purposes the concept of an employee covers 'any person who, in
the Member State concerned, is protected as an employee under national
employment law'.[1] Moreover, as Article 2.2 provides, the Directive is 'without
prejudice to national law as regards the definition of contract of employment or
employment relationship'.

Consistent with the Directive, the Transfer of Undertakings (Protection of **4.02**
Employment) Regulations (TUPE) 2006 operate to transfer to the transferee
the employment of, or to render the transferee responsible for liabilities in
respect of, only those who satisfy the technical requirements of status as an
employee. For these purposes, regulation 2(1) defines an employee as 'any individual who works for another person whether under a contract of service or
apprenticeship or otherwise but does not include anyone who provides services
under a contract for services and references to a person's employer shall be
construed accordingly'.[2]

---

[1] See also *Mikkelsen* [1989] ICR 330, ECJ.

[2] This is not the same wording as that deployed in the Employment Rights Act 1996 (ERA 1996),
s 230(1) where it is provided that the term 'employee' means an individual who has entered into or
works under (or, where the employment has ceased, worked under) a contract of employment.
Under ERA 1996, s 230(2) 'contract of employment' means 'a contract of service or apprenticeship,
whether express or implied, and (if it is express) whether oral or in writing'. Despite their different
drafting, there seems to be no difference in substance or practice in the interpretation of the two
formulations. See also *Cowell v Quilter* [1989] IRLR 392, CA which held that an equity partner is not
an employee for these purposes on the basis that his or her contract is 'for services' rather than 'of
service'.

4.03   Those who fall within the employment law concept of 'workers' or who are independent contractors providing services in the course of a profession or occupation therefore fall outside the protections provided by TUPE. The engagement of such non-employees therefore does not automatically transfer to the transferee as a consequence of a TUPE transfer nor is the panoply of other transfer-related obligations triggered in respect of such persons (such as the transferor's obligation to provide employee liability information to the transferee, the obligation to provide information to and consult with employee representatives and so on). A transferee who wishes to engage workers or independent contractors who fall outside the scope of the transfer of undertakings legislation must conduct separate discussions with those parties effectively in order to agree the novation of their contracts.

4.04   The complexity and unpredictability of the issue of what constitutes employment status for the purposes of UK employment law (a detailed treatment of which issue is outside the scope of this work) renders the application of TUPE uncertain in difficult cases of status categorisation. The various decisions, often potentially conflicting, with regard to the status of agency workers present particular problems and therefore the position of such individuals needs to be considered carefully.[3] Whether those on career breaks remain employed and therefore capable of transfer to the transferee on a relevant transfer may also be problematic.[4]

2. Employment by Transferor

4.05   Regulation 4(1) provides that the relevant employees' contracts of employment shall have effect after the transfer as if originally made between the individual and the transferee. This implements the requirement of Article 3.1 that '[t]he transferor's rights and obligations arising from a contract of employment or from an employment relationship existing on the date of a transfer shall, by reason of such transfer, be transferred to the transferee'.

4.06   The relevant category of employee whose contract of employment transfers to the transferee as a consequence of a relevant transfer is described in regulation 4(1)[5] as 'any person employed by the transferor'. The issue which can arise as a result of this formulation derives from the fact that the transferor may not

---

[3] Relevant cases include *Wickens v Champion Employment* [1984] ICR 365, EAT; *McMeechan v Secretary of State for Employment* [1997] IRLR 353, CA; *Montgomery v Johnson & Ward Limited* [2001] IRLR 269, CA; *Brook Street Bureau (UK) Limited v Dacas* [2004] ICR 1437, CA. The latest decision in this regard at the time of writing, *Cable & Wireless plc v P Muscat* [2006] EWCA Civ 220, CA, demonstrated particularly acutely the relevance of this issue in the TUPE context. A telecommunications specialist who was engaged through an employment agency was held to have been the employee of the end-user client after the acquisition, by way of a TUPE transfer, of a company by which he had originally been engaged as an employee and subsequently a contractor.

[4] See *Curr v Marks & Spencer plc* [2003] IRLR 74, CA.

[5] As it was in TUPE 1981, regulation 5(1).

actually be the employer of the employees who work in the business or activity which is potentially the subject of a relevant transfer.

The definition of 'relevant transfer' in regulation 2(1) provides that **4.07** 'transferor' is a term to be construed in connection with the relevant transfer. The concept of the transferor in domestic law is generally considered to denote the owner/operator of the relevant operation which disposes or divests itself of that operation (as opposed to the potentially separate actual employer of the relevant employees). In the context of a service provision change, the transferor is expressly stated to be the person 'who carried out the activities prior to the service provision change' and the transferee to be 'the person who carries out the activities as a result of the service provision change'.[6] No more specific definition is provided.

By contrast, the wording of the Directive is more focused on the employees' **4.08** employer than the party which transfers the relevant undertaking or conducts the relevant activities prior to a relevant transfer. Article 2.1(a) defines the transferor as 'any natural or legal person who, by reason of a transfer . . ., ceases to be the employer in respect of the undertaking, business or part of the undertaking or business'.[7] The Directive therefore identifies those employees whose employment transfers from transferor to transferee by reference to the effect of the transfer on the identity of the relevant employees' employer rather than employment by the transferor (as TUPE does).

The reference in regulation 4(1) to its applying to those employed by the **4.09** transferor raises the issue of how TUPE operates in circumstances where the transferor of the business (in terms of the party transferring or disposing of the undertaking in question or awarding a contract capable of constituting a service provision change) is not the company or other legal person which actually employs the employees who work in the relevant business or on the relevant activities. In group situations, the relevant employees may be employed by a central management services company and will therefore not formally be employed by the transferor. Therefore, on a literal interpretation of TUPE 2006, they would not fall within its scope so as to transfer to the transferee. This would hardly be the intention of the legislation in terms of its employment protection purposes. Despite the fact that this formulation is potentially unsatisfactory in terms of the objectives of the legislation, TUPE 2006 did not change the legislative framework. Regard therefore needs to be had to the previous case law in relation to this issue.

In *Michael Peters Limited v Farnfield (1) and Michael Peters Group plc* **4.10** *(2)*,[8] the Employment Appeal Tribunal (EAT) overturned the finding of the

---

[6] Regulation 2(1).

[7] Article 2.1(b) defines 'transferee' as 'any natural or legal person who, by reason of a transfer . . . becomes the employer in respect of the undertaking, business, or part of the undertaking or business'.

[8] [1995] IRLR 190, EAT.

industrial tribunal (as it then was) that the chief executive of a group who was employed by its parent company could argue that he was protected by TUPE 1981 when the business of four of its subsidiaries were sold. Quite apart from the point that the employee was found not to have been wholly or mainly assigned to the undertakings disposed of, the industrial tribunal had been wrong to pierce the corporate veil and to conclude that the business of the subsidiaries was the business of the parent company so that the parent company was the transferor and the employee therefore fell within the scope of TUPE.

4.11   By way of contrast, in *Sunley Turriff Holdings Limited v Thompson*,[9] the EAT upheld a decision to take the 'exceptional step' of lifting the veil of incorporation. Even though the contracting party in respect of the sale of the business was a group company by which the employee in question was not employed, TUPE was held to apply to transfer the employee's employment to the transferee. Part of the business disposed of was that of his employer. He devoted some of his time to the remainder. It was found that what was transferred was in reality not only the undertaking of a group company by which the employee was not employed but also a substantial part of the undertaking of his actual employer, thereby bringing his employment within the scope of TUPE.

4.12   In *Duncan Web Offset (Maidstone) Limited v Cooper*[10] the important comment was made that '[i]ndustrial tribunals will be astute to ensure that the provisions of the regulations are not evaded by devices such as service companies, or by complicated group structures which conceal the true position'.[11] The EAT raised the possibility that, in a group context, a service company could in appropriate circumstances be viewed as employing the relevant employees on behalf of and as agent for the operating company for whom the employees in reality performed their services. Rather more speculatively, it is submitted, the EAT also raised the possibility that the Employment Tribunal (ET) might, in its assessment of the factual matrix, regard the service company employing the employees as effectively a party to the transfer (thereby becoming a/the transferor), even if it were not a signatory to any commercial agreement recording the arrangements.

4.13   It is therefore clear that, whilst regulation 4(1) maintains the requirement that an employee be employed by the transferor in order for his or her contract of employment to transfer to the transferee on a relevant transfer, the ET will, where possible, construe the relevant arrangements in a way which will ensure that the objectives of the legislation are met, in terms of protecting those working in businesses which are transferred. This approach will presumably apply equally to service provision changes for the purposes of regulation 3(1)(b) as to transfers of undertakings for the purposes of regulation 3(1)(a). Whilst little may hang in practice on the issue, it is perhaps regrettable that TUPE 2006 did not address this issue directly.

---

[9] [1995] IRLR 633, EAT.   [10] [1995] IRLR 184, EAT.   [11] At para 16.

3. Assignment

To reflect the fact that there are now twin definitions of a relevant transfer (ie a **4.14** transfer of an undertaking and a service provision change), the definition contained in TUPE 2006 of those employees employed by the transferor whose contracts of employment transfer to the transferee was updated from that contained in TUPE 1981.

Regulation 4(1) provides for the transfer of a contract of employment 'of any **4.15** person employed by the transferor and assigned to the organised grouping of resources or employees that is subject to the relevant transfer'. As the 2005 Consultation noted,[12] TUPE 2006 expanded upon the equivalent provision in TUPE 1981[13] which had simply made reference to 'any person employed by the transferor in the undertaking or part transferred'. The additional wording included in regulation 4(1) incorporates by reference the assignment test established by the European Court of Justice (ECJ) case law and which, as the 2005 Consultation noted,[14] is a question of fact in each case.

This assignment test was articulated in *Botzen v Rotterdam Sche Droogdok* **4.16** *Maatschappij BV*.[15] The ECJ established the principle that the employees who transfer under the legislation are those who are assigned to the relevant part of the undertaking or business. The ECJ held that '[a]n employment relationship is essentially characterised by the link existing between the employee and the part of the undertaking or business to which he is assigned to carry out his duties. In order to decide whether the rights and obligations under an employment relationship are transferred under Directive No 77/187 by reason of a transfer within the meaning of Article 1(1) thereof, it is therefore sufficient to establish to which part of the undertaking or business the employee was assigned'.[16]

By way of a gloss on this test, *Northern General Hospital NHS Trust v Gale*[17] **4.17** advanced a 'human stock' approach based around integration into the relevant business. In *Duncan Web Offset*[18] the EAT indicated that a variety of factors should be borne in mind by the ET in assessing whether employees are assigned to the undertaking (or activities) including the relative amounts of time spent in different classes of a business, the value given to each part of the business, the terms of the employee's contract, and the apportionment of the costs related to the employee's employment.

A percentage test of involvement in the relevant undertaking (or activities), it **4.18** is submitted, cannot be elevated to primacy in the test of assignment although such an approach was applied in *Anderson v Kluwer Publishing Limited*.[19] In that case the employee in question was found to be assigned to the undertaking transferred when he dedicated 80 per cent of his time to it.

The issue of assignment was also addressed by the EAT in *Buchanan-Smith* **4.19**

---

[12] Paras 38–41.   [13] TUPE 1981, regulation 5(1).   [14] Para 39.
[15] [1985] ECR 519, ECJ.   [16] At para 15.   [17] [1994] ICR 426, CA.
[18] [1995] IRLR 184, EAT.   [19] COIT 15068/85.

v Schleicher & Co International Limited.[20] The employee in question was a director and company secretary dealing with both some of the transferor's shredding machine sales and its service business. The service side of the business was disposed of and the sales function ceased. The employee transferred to the acquirer of the service business and argued that this transfer of employment fell within the scope of TUPE, thereby preserving the employee's continuity of employment for statutory purposes.

4.20   The EAT noted that '[t]he test for whether a person is employed in an undertaking or part is simply: was he assigned to that undertaking or part? That is a question of fact to be determined by considering all the relevant circumstances'.[21]

4.21   Allowing an appeal against the ET's decision that the employee was not assigned to the service side of the business transferred, the EAT found that, since at the time of transfer one part of the business in which she worked was to cease, the employee was assigned to the (remaining) transferred sales operation. An employee could be assigned to one of two undertakings operated by an employer even if he or she is engaged to some extent in the other. Whilst exclusivity was not required for the *Botzen* test of assignment to be satisfied, some small degree of involvement in an undertaking or work for its benefit would in contrast not suffice for assignment to be established.

4.22   *Kingston v Darlows Estate Agency*[22] also demonstrates the application of the assignment test. The Court of Appeal rejected an appeal against an ET decision that two senior estate agent employees who had respectively managerial and administrative responsibilities covering the relevant organisation's Wales and West region as a whole were not assigned to a particular part of the undertaking. When a number of Welsh branches were sold to a transferee, the two employees in question did not transfer as they were not assigned to the particular part of the business transferred.

4.23   In *CPL Distribution v Todd*,[23] the employee in question worked as personal assistant to a manager who had responsibility for a contract to distribute coal (to which contract most of her typing related) but who also had other responsibilities. The personal assistant was found (on the basis of her overall, rather than just typing, duties) not be assigned to the coal distribution part of the employer's undertaking which was transferred.

4.24   *Skillbase Services Ltd v King*[24] concerned a council housing maintenance contract which constituted about 80 per cent of the work carried on by the relevant contractor's Grangemouth depot of which Mr King was the branch manager. When the contract was brought back in-house, TUPE applied but both the ET and EAT held that Mr King was not wholly or predominantly employed in the undertaking transferred. The basis for this decision, which the Court of Session found to be sound, was that Mr King was not involved directly in the daily

---

[20] [1996] IRLR 547, EAT.   [21] At para 21.   [22] [1995] IRLR 623, CA.
[23] [2003] IRLR 28, CA.   [24] [2005] All ER (D) 106, CS.

operational aspects of the contract, did not have regular contact with the client council and managed the other functions conducted at the depot for which he was responsible. The proper approach had been applied, which was to consider a wide range of circumstances. Relevant considerations could include the amount of time spent in the relevant business, the terms of the employee's contract, and the allocation within the business of the costs of the employee's employment.

A further useful example of the assignment test is *Williams v Advance Cleaning* **4.25** *Services (1) Engineering & Railway Solicitors Ltd (In liquidation)*[25] where between 60 and 70 per cent of a manager's work related to one particular contract but he was not assigned to that part-undertaking when it was awarded elsewhere—his job related to several contracts and not just the one lost by the transferor. The useful observations were made by the EAT that 'it is not sufficient for an employee to show that he was substantially involved in the part transferred—he has to show that he was effectively assigned to the part transferred'[26] and that the potential factors set out in *Duncan Web Offset* were 'neither an exhaustive list nor a mandatory one that a tribunal has to recite and consider item by item'.[27]

4. Temporary Assignment

One of the issues which will concern a transferee in relation to a TUPE transfer **4.26** is the quality of the workforce which it will inherit. If the test of assignment is applied as a snapshot at the point of transfer, then a transferee will be exposed to the risk that the transferor may, in the period prior to a TUPE transfer, seek to redeploy staff within its organisation in order to assign to the transferring undertaking or activities, and therefore to pass to the transferee, employees of lower skills and experience than would otherwise have transferred.

Conversely, if an employee works in an operation for a short period on, for **4.27** example, a one-off project basis, it can be argued that he or she does not form part of the human stock of the undertaking or activities in question and should therefore not fall within the scope of TUPE on the basis of the fortuitous occurrence of a TUPE transfer during the duration of that temporary engagement.

Commercial agreement, identifying the transferring employees, and seeking to **4.28** control the degree to which a workforce can be varied in the run up to transfer, is the preferable solution to these issues. As noted above, TUPE 2006 introduced the concept of assignment into the legislation expressly for the first time, thereby codifying the *Botzen* principle. Regulation 2(1) also specifically addresses the issue of temporary involvement in the relevant undertaking or activities by providing, by way of a specific definition, that for these purposes assignment means that the relevant employee is 'assigned other than on a temporary basis'.

The 2005 Consultation noted that this qualification, excluding those who are **4.29**

---

[25] EAT 0838/04.   [26] At para 15.   [27] At para 13.

temporarily assigned to an undertaking or activities from the scope of TUPE, reflects the EAT decision in *Securiplan v Bademosi*.[28] A security guard had been temporarily transferred from his regular place of work to work at a magistrates' court for a period of one year. He was found not to have been assigned to the magistrates' court for the purposes of TUPE on the basis that the assignment was temporary (which thereby took his position outside the scope of the *Botzen* principle).

4.30   *Duncan Web Offset*[29] made the point that the terms of the relevant employees' contracts can be taken into account in determining the assignment issue. However, this is just one factor. In *Securicor v Fraser Security Services Limited*[30] the relevant employees had mobility clauses in their contracts pursuant to which the employer could require them to work at any of its branches. Nonetheless, the fact that there was a mobility clause did not mean that for the purposes of TUPE, assessing the circumstances as a whole, the employees in question were not assigned to the relevant site at which they had been working for two years prior to the relevant transfer.

4.31   There may be difficult distinctions to be drawn in practice between temporary redeployments and specific consecutive assignments as part of an overall contractual engagement. The substance of the matter will need to be addressed carefully by the ET as a matter of fact as is evidenced by the contrasting results in the *Securicor* and *Securiplan* cases. The Department of Trade and Industry (DTI) Guidance makes the point[31] that '[w]hether an assignment is "temporary" will depend on a number of factors, such as the length of time the employee has been there and whether a date has been set by the transferor for his return or re-assignment to another part of the business or undertaking'. Nonetheless, the amendment to the statutory formulation introduced by TUPE 2006 sheds little additional light on the resolution in practice of this fact-sensitive assignment issue.

5. Contract would otherwise Terminate

4.32   TUPE 1981, regulation 5(1) identified the employees whose employment transferred to the transferee on a relevant transfer as those employed under a contract 'which would otherwise have been terminated by the transfer'. The rationale for that wording was presumably the fact that at common law a transfer of the business in which an employee works constitutes a termination by the employer of that employee's contract of employment. The objective of the transfer legislation is to address that very consequence in order to protect the employment of those employees whose employment would terminate at common law on a transfer of an undertaking.

---

[28] [2003] All ER (D) 435, EAT (discussed at 2005 Consultation para 40).
[29] [1995] IRLR 184, EAT.   [30] [1996] IRLR 552, EAT.   [31] At p 13.

The reference to transferring employees being those whose contracts would 4.33
otherwise terminate as a result of the transfer was omitted from the initial draft
of what became TUPE 2006. The language which was removed was viewed as
adding nothing of value.[32] Moreover, the wording of TUPE 1981, regulation
5(1) was seen as presenting a potential and unintended loophole. If a transferor
determined that it would retain employees who might otherwise fall within the
scope of TUPE, then their employment would not terminate by reason of the
transfer because the transferor was content to and did continue to employ them.
Accordingly, since they would not terminate as a consequence of the transfer,
the contracts of those employees could be argued not to transfer automatically
to the transferee (as is the objective of the transfer legislation). This could be to
the prejudice of the employees (who might wish to be able to transfer with
the relevant undertaking and activities) and indeed the transferee (who might
well wish to inherit the employees central to the operation of the relevant
undertaking or activities).

The omission from TUPE 2006 of the TUPE 1981 formulation would 4.34
have removed this possibility. Retention by the transferor of employees who
would otherwise transfer to the transferee would then have been a matter of
the employees in question exercising their right to refuse to transfer[33] and reaching a separate agreement with the transferor in relation to their continued
employment by it.

Despite having adopted such a firm view, as a result of its consultation about 4.35
the amendments to be made by what became TUPE 2006, the Government
concluded that it would not dispense with the requirement that an employee
falling within the scope of regulation 4 be one whose contract would terminate
as a result of the transfer.[34] Although the proviso in question had been omitted
from the initial draft of the new legislation on grounds that it was unnecessary
and encouraged the transferor to pick and choose which employees to transfer, it
was retained presumably to meet the wishes of those respondents to the 2005
Consultation who favoured the retention of the relevant wording in order to
provide some scope for them to retain employees who would otherwise transfer.[35] Given the existing ability on the part of employees to object to transfer and
agree their retention by the transferor, the Government's change of heart on
this point is arguably unnecessary and misconceived and likely to preserve
uncertainty about the ability of the transferor unilaterally to decide which
employees potentially within the scope of TUPE actually should transfer to the
transferee.

That said, the retention of this formulation makes it easier for it to be 4.36

---

[32] 2005 Consultation para 42.

[33] Pursuant to regulations 4(7) and 4(8). See para 4.47 *et seq* below.

[34] Although slightly rephrased as regulation 4(1) refers to a contract which would otherwise 'be terminated' rather than 'have been terminated'.

[35] See Consultation Response para 3.7.

argued that secondments do not trigger the application of TUPE in relation to the transfer of employees to work for the organisation to which they are seconded. Otherwise the transfer of conduct of their activities could constitute a regulation 3(1)(b) service provision change (assuming that the secondment did not fall within the exception from that concept of one-off short-duration arrangements).

6. Pre-transfer Employment

4.37 Regulation 4(3) further refines the process of the identification of the employees whose contract of employment and associated liabilities transfer to the transferee. It provides that:

> any reference ... to a person employed by the transferor and assigned to the organised grouping of resources or employees that is subject to a relevant transfer, is a reference to a person so employed immediately before the transfer or [who] would have been so employed if he had not been dismissed in the circumstances described in regulation 7(1) including, where the transfer is effected by a series of two or more transactions, a person so employed and assigned or who would have been so employed and assigned immediately before any of those transactions.

4.38 As the 2005 Consultation noted,[36] regulation 4(3) updates TUPE 1981 to reflect the decision in *Litster v Forth Dry Dock & Engineering Co. Ltd.*[37] This ensures that the transferee inherits liabilities in respect of those who would have transferred to it pursuant to TUPE had they not been dismissed prior to transfer for a transfer-related reason.

4.39 Prior to *Litster*, it had been considered that employees needed to be employed up until or until just before the point of transfer in order for their employment to transfer under TUPE 1981.[38] On this basis dismissal prior to a relevant transfer would deny employees the protection of TUPE because they would not then be employed immediately before transfer. This was a serious limitation on the protective scope of TUPE.

4.40 In *Litster*, the House of Lords applied a purposive interpretation to the requirement that an employee be employed by the transferor 'immediately before the transfer' in order to fulfil the protective purposes of the legislation. Dismissal effected before the transfer and solely because of it could not be effective to avoid transfer to the transferee of liabilities in respect of that automatically unfair dismissal. Regulation 4(3) encapsulates that principle.

4.41 Accordingly, if there is no economic, technical or organisational reason

---

[36] Para 43.   [37] [1989] IRLR 621, HL. See also Chap 7, para 7.14.

[38] *Secretary of State for Employment v Spence* [1986] IRLR 248, CA. This decision was based on the formulation of TUPE 1981, regulation 5(1) which referred only to employment 'immediately before' the transfer.

entailing changes in the workforce (ETOR) justifying dismissal,[39] then a dismissal connected with a transfer, even if it results in the employee ceasing to be employed some time before the transfer, does not preclude the transferee from inheriting liability for that dismissal under TUPE. Regulation 4(3) operates in such circumstances to transfer the employee's contract to the transferee and the provisions with regard to transfer-related dismissals then come into play.[40]

Regulation 4(3) also clarifies that a series of transactions, pursuant to which, **4.42** for example, the relevant undertaking passes through various hands over a period of time, does not disqualify employees employed in the relevant undertaking or activities at the outset of the relevant series of transactions from the protection of the legislation.

Some respondents to the 2005 Consultation had been concerned that regula- **4.43** tion 4(3) would have the unintended effect of transferring to the transferee the actual employment or contracts of employees dismissed prior to transfer.[41] The Government rejected this concern (which was also raised in relation to regulation 7) on the basis in part that domestic law does not render a transfer-related dismissal a nullity. Accordingly, all that can transfer to the transferee are the liabilities associated with a pre-transfer dismissal as opposed to the employee's (terminated) contract. Whilst this analysis is uncontroversial as a matter of principle, the matter could have been made clearer by way of express provision.

It is worth noting in passing that an employee who remains employed by the **4.44** transferor as at the point of a TUPE transfer but is serving out a period of notice (served by either the employer or employee) still transfers to the transferee. Similarly, an employee of the transferor who is absent from work at the time of transfer (for example, by reason of sickness absence, maternity leave, or an extended career break) will still fall to transfer to the transferee by virtue of TUPE.

7. Knowledge of Transfer

There is no express requirement imposed by TUPE on the transferor or the **4.45** transferee to notify the relevant employees on an individual basis of the fact of their impending or actual transfer to the transferee either generally or in order for the transfer of their employment to the transferee to be effective. There is nonetheless a collective obligation to provide information to and consult with appropriate representatives of the affected employees in advance of a TUPE transfer.[42] Individual notification is effectively achieved in practice by way of compliance with collective obligations. TUPE 2006 made no amendment in this regard to the position obtaining under TUPE 1981.

---

[39] See Chap 7 for further discussion of the inheritance by the transferee of liability for pre-transfer dismissals.

[40] Regulation 7.   [41] See Consultation Response para 3.9.   [42] See Chap 9.

4.46   In *Photostatic Copiers (Southern) Limited v Okuda*,[43] it was suggested that TUPE could not operate to transfer an employee's employment to the transferee unless the employee was informed of the transfer and of the identity of the transferee. This approach has been rejected and was subsequently not followed in cases such as *Secretary of State for Trade & Industry v Cook*.[44] As Morison J put it in *Cook*, '. . . if the employee needs to know, in advance, the identity of the transferee before the contract is transferred, unscrupulous employers would simply refuse to disclose what was happening'.[45]

B. ELECTING NOT TO TRANSFER

1. Introduction

4.47 TUPE 2006 updates and materially amends the provisions of the transfer legislation relating to the ability of an employee who would otherwise transfer to the transferee to elect not to do so. In particular, the 2005 Consultation[46] noted that TUPE 2006 was intended to make clearer the United Kingdom's full implementation of Article 4.2.[47]

4.48   By way of its implementation of Article 4.2 and its preservation of the ability of employees to object to transfer and to claim constructive dismissal, TUPE 2006 provides three routes by which an employee can elect not to transfer to the transferee:

- an objection to the transfer—which leads to no claim against transferor or transferee;
- resignation in response to a substantial change in working conditions to the employee's material detriment. This does not lead to a breach of contract claim against the employer (or indeed the employee) but does enable the employee to bring an unfair dismissal claim;
- resignation without notice in response to a repudiatory breach of contract. This entitles the employee to treat himself or herself as constructively dismissed, and therefore potentially to bring wrongful and unfair dismissal claims.

2. Objection to Transfer

4.49 Regulations 4(7) and 4(8) restate the right to object to transfer provided by TUPE 1981, regulations 5(4A) and 5(4B). Regulation 4(7) provides that the employee's contract of employment and its associated rights, powers, duties, and liabilities do not transfer to the transferee if the employee 'informs the

---

[43] [1995] IRLR 11, EAT.   [44] [1997] IRLR 150, EAT.   [45] At para 12.
[46] Para 46.   [47] By virtue of regulations 4(9) and 4(10).

transferor or the transferee that he objects to becoming employed by the transferee'. Regulation 4(8) provides that, where an employee objects to his or her employment transferring to the transferee as a result of a relevant transfer in accordance with regulation 4(7), the relevant transfer operates to terminate the employee's contract of employment with the transferor and that, in such circumstances, the employee shall 'not be treated, for any purpose, as having been dismissed by the transferor'.

This right to object to transfer, if exercised, therefore operates to avoid the **4.50** automatic transfer of employment from transferor to transferee of an employee assigned to the relevant undertaking or grouping of employees. This right to object to transfer was established by the ECJ in *Katsikas v Konstantinidis*.[48] The fact that exercise of the right to object to transfer leads to the employee not being treated for any purpose as having been dismissed by the transferor[49] leaves the employee with no claim against either transferor or transferee in relation to the termination of his or her employment, absent a claim under regulation 4(9) or regulation 4(11) (discussed below). Regulations 4(7) and 4(8) therefore provide a simple statutory right to opt out of transferring to the transferee and to leave the business without notice, compensation, or any claim against transferor or transferee.

It is important to note that exercise of the right to object under regulation 4(7) **4.51** simply operates to terminate the employee's employment. It does not provide a statutory ability to remain with the transferor. In terms of the correct legal analysis (as opposed to what happens in practice), an agreement to remain with the transferor needs to be agreed, coupled with an objection, if both transferor and employee wish the employee not to transfer automatically to the transferee. This is the structure adopted in the Retention of Employment Model deployed in relation to certain National Health Service (NHS) Private Finance Initiative Projects.

The termination of employment occasioned by an objection to transfer under **4.52** regulation 4(7) does not of itself free the employee from any restrictive covenants to which he or she may be contractually subject following the termination of employment. However, a number of points should be noted. First, the transferee will have acquired the relevant business but will not have inherited the employee and the contractual benefit of any relevant covenants. The transferee will therefore have no contractual privity with regard to the employee entitling it to enforce the relevant restrictive covenants against an employee whom it never employed. Second, the transferor no longer has a legitimate business interest to protect (to the extent that it has disposed of the business to which the employee's restrictive covenants apply) upon which it would to a greater or lesser extent have to base a contention that the restrictive covenants are enforceable. Any restrictive covenants contained in the employee's contract of employment may

---

[48] [1993] IRLR 179, ECJ.   [49] Regulation 4(8).

therefore be difficult to enforce against the employee by either transferor or transferee.

4.53   Third, an objection to transfer pursuant to regulation 4(7) does not need to be justified or reasonable to be valid. Exercising the statutory right to object to transfer therefore enables employees to depart ignoring the notice period which they would otherwise be required to serve in order lawfully to terminate employment. An event as apparently anodyne as an internal group reorganisation may provide employees with an opportunity to exercise the right to object to transfer in order to be able to leave immediately. This possibility can be particularly relevant if at the particular time employees wish to join a competitor.

4.54   Certain particular points are worth noting in relation to the statutory right to refuse to transfer. In *Hay v George Hanson (Building Contracts) Limited*,[50] it was held that the objection must be communicated to the transferor or transferee before the transfer by way of an actual refusal but that this communication can be by word or deed. Simply to complain about the transfer is not sufficient to avoid the automatic transfer of the employee's employment. That said, it is submitted that it cannot be correct that an obligation must be communicated before the transfer. This would disable an employee who only learned of the transfer on or after the occurrence of the event itself from relying on this right. *Hay* also makes the point that TUPE does not require the employer to inform the employee of the 'draconian' consequences of his or her objection (which situation the EAT viewed as 'singularly unfortunate'[51] and which TUPE 2006 left unchanged).

4.55   Second, the objection must be real. In *Senior Heat Treatment Limited v Bell*,[52] employees completed forms stating that they did not wish to transfer employment to the transferee but wished to receive details of the redundancy payments available to them. Having received the relevant redundancy payments on termination of their employment with the transferor, the individuals took up employment with the transferee pretty much immediately thereafter. Despite the fact that the individuals had completed a form which specifically stated that they did not wish to transfer, the fact that they did start employment with the transferee immediately after the transfer was considered to be inconsistent with an objection to transfer for the purposes of TUPE.

4.56   The importance for transferors of understanding the potential consequences of an employee's exercise of his or her right to object to transfer is demonstrated by *Hope v PGS Engineering*.[53] The employee notified the transferee of the business in which he worked that he did not wish to transfer to its employment. Had that action been treated as the exercise of the right to object to transfer, the employee would have had no claim as the termination of his employment would not have constituted a dismissal.[54] However, the transferor placed the employee

---

[50] [1996] IRLR 427, EAT.   [51] At para 9.
[52] [1997] IRLR 614, EAT. Also discussed at 5.40.   [53] EAT/0267/04.
[54] Per TUPE 1981, reg 5(4B); now regulation 4(8).

on garden leave for his notice period after his objection. The employee's employment therefore came to an end by virtue of the dismissal effected by expiry of the notice period as opposed to the exercise of the right of objection. Being transfer-related, the dismissal was automatically unfair. Because the employee objected to transfer, the liability for this dismissal remained with the transferor.[55]

3. Changes to Working Conditions

(a) *TUPE 1981*

TUPE 1981, regulation 5(5) provided that its provisions with regard to automatic transfer of employment and the right to object to transfer[56] were: **4.57**

... without prejudice to any right of an employee arising apart from these Regulations to terminate his contract of employment without notice if a substantial change is made in his working conditions to his detriment; but no such right shall arise by reason only that, under that paragraph, the identity of his employer changes unless the employee shows that, in all the circumstances, the change is a significant one and is to his detriment.

TUPE 1981, regulation 5(5) and its successor, regulation 4(9), are based on Article 4.2 which states that: **4.58**

If the contract of employment or the employment relationship is terminated because the transfer involves a substantial change in working conditions to the detriment of the employee, the employer shall be regarded as having been responsible for termination of the contract of employment or the employment relationship.

In *Rossiter v Pendragon plc and Crosby-Clarke v Air Foyle Limited*,[57] it was made clear by the Court of Appeal that TUPE 1981, regulation 5(5) only permitted an employee to bring a constructive dismissal claim in the context of a TUPE transfer where the traditional common law test of a repudiatory breach of contract by the employer was satisfied. A change to working conditions, even if detrimental, was not sufficient to give rise to a constructive dismissal claim unless there were a fundamental breach of contract. The Court of Appeal in *Rossiter* considered it unlikely that Article 4.2 could create a new form of constructive dismissal based on a threshold lower than repudiatory breach of contract. Accordingly, it was held that TUPE 1981, regulation 5(5) was not intended to create a right to claim constructive dismissal, based on detrimental changes to working conditions which did not constitute a repudiatory breach of contract, in addition to and distinct from the right to claim constructive dismissal arising in relation to a repudiatory breach of contract. Regulation 5(5) could entitle an employee to elect not to transfer to the transferee but not to have a consequent claim in the absence of a constructive dismissal on orthodox principles.   **4.59**

---

[55] Per TUPE 1981, reg 5(4A); now regulation 4(7).
[56] TUPE 1981 regulations 5(1) and 5(4A) respectively.   [57] [2002] IRLR 483, CA.

(b) *Regulation 4(9)*

4.60 *Rossiter* has now effectively been reversed by virtue of the restatement by regulation 4(9) of the right on the part of an employee to terminate his or her employment in response to a substantial change to working conditions to the employee's detriment.

4.61 Regulation 4(9) provides that where a relevant transfer:

involves or would involve a substantial change in working conditions to the material detriment of a person whose contract of employment is or would be transferred under paragraph 1(1), such an employee may treat the contract of employment as having been terminated, and the employee shall be treated for any purpose as having been dismissed with notice by the employer.

4.62 In terms of what constitutes a 'substantial change in working conditions to the material detriment' of the relevant employee, the DTI Guidance states[58] that

[t]his will be a matter for the courts and the tribunals to determine in the light of the circumstances of each case. What might be a trivial change in one setting might constitute a substantial change in another. However, a major relocation of the workplace which makes it difficult or much more expensive for an employee to transfer, or the withdrawal of a right to a tenured post, is likely to fall within this definition.

4.63 It is important to note the inclusion of the word 'material'. The introduction of the materiality of the detriment into the drafting of regulation 4(9) was made as a result of the consultation process over what became TUPE 2006. It makes the test a more difficult one to satisfy, meaning that changes which do not impact materially on the particular employee do not entitle the employee to exercise regulation 4(9) and accordingly, as noted below, to be able to bring an unfair dismissal claim. That said, as materiality is not a concept referred to in the equivalent wording in the Directive, its efficacy in TUPE 2006 is open to question.

4.64 Regulation 4(9) creates a claim of constructive dismissal separate to the traditional test based on repudiatory breach of contract. This analysis accords with the wording of regulation 4(9) when compared with that of TUPE 1981, regulation 5(5). TUPE 1981, regulation 5(5) described the employee's response to a substantial detrimental change to working conditions as a right 'to terminate his contract of employment without notice'. It was this right to terminate which *Rossiter* viewed as not founding a separate constructive dismissal claim. Regulation 4(9), however, expressly provides that the employee is to be 'treated for any purpose as having been dismissed with notice by the employer'. Whereas TUPE 1981, regulation 5(5) provided a right to terminate, regulation 4(9) expressly determines there to be a dismissal in these circumstances.

4.65 Notwithstanding the fact that regulation 4(9) deems there to be a dismissal when the employee exercises the right which it provides, regulation 4(9) denies the employee a wrongful dismissal claim against the employer. Regulation 4(10)

---

[58] At p 20.

provides that '[n]o damages shall be payable by an employer as a result of a dismissal falling within [regulation 4(9)] in respect of any failure by the employer to pay wages to an employee in respect of a notice period which the employee has failed to work'. This is a different formulation from the first draft of what was to become TUPE 2006 which deemed the dismissal resulting from the exercise of the regulation 4(9) right to be 'with notice', thereby denying a damages claim in respect of the notice period. Regulation 4(9) as reformulated does not deny the employee his or her right to payment should the employee work his or her notice period.

In the 2005 Consultation,[59] the formulation that the deemed dismissal created **4.66** by regulation 4(9) would not lead to a contractual claim in respect of the employee's notice period was justified by the Government's view that it was not 'right for an employer to be penalised for failing to give notice of termination in a situation where the employment contract was terminated in [such] circumstances'. Quite why that was considered to be the case was not articulated. There is no obvious reason why an unfair dismissal claim can ensue when the regulation 4(9) right is exercised but not a wrongful dismissal claim.

Since regulation 4(9) deems there to be a dismissal when an employee exer- **4.67** cises the right which it provides, an unfair dismissal claim can be founded on an employee's election to terminate his or her employment pursuant to regulation 4(9). That traditional constructive dismissal is specifically and separately referred to in regulation 4(11) only reinforces the view that regulation 4(9) creates, in the TUPE context, a separate form of constructive dismissal claim based on a less demanding test than the traditional constructive dismissal claim.

This effective recreation of a TUPE-specific form of constructive dismissal **4.68** can be argued to go further than EU law requires when one considers the statement in *Daddy's Dance Hall* that '[t]he benefit of the Directive, therefore, can only be invoked to ensure that the worker concerned is protected in his relations with the new employer in the same way as he was in his relations with the original employee pursuant to the laws of the Member State concerned'.[60] This statement indicates, it can be argued, that the domestic test of constructive dismissal should apply rather than a wider one based on the wording of the Directive (as was effectively the analysis of the Court of Appeal in *Rossiter*).

(c) *Consequences*

Regulation 4(9) therefore potentially provides employees affected by a relevant **4.69** transfer with rights of action additional to the simple right to object to transfer if their position is prejudiced, even if a change made by the new employer falls short of a repudiatory breach of contract. As the 2005 Consultation put it, a substantial change of working conditions to the detriment of an employee 'may not be sufficiently serious to amount to repudiatory breach of contract by the

---

[59] Para 46.   [60] [1988] IRLR 315, ECJ at para 979.

employer, entitling the employee to resign and claim constructive dismissal'.[61] For example, the transferee may act entirely lawfully (ie without breach of contract) by relying on an express contractual power to vary bonus or benefit arrangements or to relocate staff. However, if this results in a substantial change to the employee's material detriment, regulation 4(9) will be engaged.

4.70 That exercise of the right afforded by regulation 4(9) leads to an unfair dismissal claim is supported by the answer in the DTI Guidance[62] to the question of whether it is unlawful for the transferee to make such substantial changes in working conditions and whether it is automatically unfair when an employee resigns because such a change has taken place. The DTI Guidance indicates that:

> The Regulations merely classify such resignations as 'dismissals'. This can assist the employee if he subsequently complains of unfair dismissal because he does not need to prove he was 'dismissed'. However, to determine whether the dismissal was unfair, the tribunal will still need to satisfy itself that the employer had acted unreasonably, and there is no presumption that it is unreasonable for the employer to make changes. Also, because the statutory dismissal procedures do not apply in these circumstances, any failure by the employer to follow those procedures does not make the 'dismissal' automatically unfair.

4.71 However, the issue of the fairness of the dismissal may not be so open. *Ex hypothesi*, the dismissal deemed to occur on exercise of the right conferred by regulation 4(9) will be transfer-related and therefore automatically unfair for the purposes of regulation 7(1) unless saved by the existence of an ETOR and the dismissal not being otherwise unfair. It is not entirely clear how ETs are to address the detailed issue of fairness in this context—presumably to have any chance of defending a claim the employer will need to show that the reason for the change to working conditions which led to the objection to transfer being exercised was an ETOR, which may be problematic, not least as this entails a change in the workforce.

4.72 Again the termination appears capable of being immediate in effect, providing a potential exit route similar to that provided by regulation 4(7), albeit one which is potentially available some time later than the time of transfer depending upon when the relevant changes arise.

(d) *Other Points*

4.73 Certain aspects of TUPE 1981, regulation 5(5) are not carried over into regulation 4(9). First, although it is implicit in the provision that the employee's employment is terminated with immediate effect by the employer if the employee terminates his or her employment on that basis, regulation 4(9) does not expressly state that the employee can in such circumstances terminate his

---

[61] Para 46.   [62] On p 20.

employment without notice. Second, there is no equivalent of the proviso to TUPE 1981, regulation 5(5). This provided that the right to terminate employment in response to a substantial detrimental change to working conditions did not arise by reason only that the identity of the employer would change, unless the employee could show that in all the circumstances the change of employer was a significant change and was to his or her detriment. Arguably that wording was always otiose. Whether the change to the identity of the employer consequent upon a TUPE transfer can lead to regulation 4(9) being engaged will presumably be dependent on evidence as to the consequent detriment (which, importantly, must be to working conditions) and its materiality.

There appears to be no temporal limitation to the application of regulation 4(9). Presumably, if a change to working conditions is transfer related, regulation 4(9) applies regardless of the timing of the change and therefore what matters is the connection of the change in working conditions with the transfer rather than when the change occurs.[63] Presumably, it is also necessary to show the causal link between a change to working conditions and the relevant transfer. Regulation 4(9) requires that it be the case that the transfer 'involves or would involve' such a change to working conditions, anticipating that regulation 4(9) can be relied upon either before or after a relevant transfer. There is no express requirement that the transfer be the sole or principal reason for the changes to working conditions.[64] Nonetheless there must presumably be a clear link between the two for regulation 4(9) to be engaged.   **4.74**

The ability to terminate employment based on a substantial and materially detrimental change to working conditions presumably (although it is not stated expressly) does not apply where contractual variations are agreed by the employee in connection with the transfer under regulations 4(4) and 4(5). Likewise, since regulation 4(9) is stated expressly to be subject to regulation 9, an affected employee cannot invoke regulation 4(9) in relation to a permitted variation agreed in an insolvency situation by appropriate representatives. As with regulations 4(7) and 4(8), depending on when the employee becomes aware of the transfer or when the detrimental change occurs, presumably it is not a requirement that the exercise of the right under regulation 4(9) to treat the contract of employment as terminated be exercised or communicated prior to the transfer. Otherwise, the right conferred by regulation 4(9) would be unworkable where the employee, for whatever reason, learns about the transfer or the detrimental change is made after the event.   **4.75**

---

[63] See *Taylor v Connex South Eastern Limited* discussed in Chap 7 at para 7.24 for an example of an event being transfer-related two years after the transfer itself.

[64] In contrast to the categorisation of transfer-related variations adopted in regulations 4(4) and 4(5) (see Chap 6, para 6.26 *et seq*) and of transfer-related dismissals in regulation 7 (see Chap 7, para 7.5), both of which link the relevant event to the transfer by its being the sole or principal reason for the contract change or dismissal as the case may be.

(e) *Substantial and Material*

4.76 Concern that employees could exercise the right provided by regulation 4(9) on the basis of trivial concerns is met by two elements of the provision—that the change be substantial and its detrimental effect be material. Lack of case law or other guidance renders these limitations on the scope of regulation 4(9) unpredictable but can be assumed to present significant hurdles for employees to overcome, even if not as strict a test as establishing the repudiatory breach of contract required for the constructive dismissal claim preserved by regulation 4(11).

4. Constructive Dismissal

4.77 Regulation 4(11) states that the 'automatic transfer' provisions[65] of and the rights to object to transfer[66] provided by TUPE 2006 are 'without prejudice to any right of an employee arising apart from these Regulations to terminate his contract of employment without notice in acceptance of a repudiatory breach of contract by his employer'. This preserves the ability of an employee to claim constructive dismissal by reason of the transferor's or transferee's fundamental breach of contract on the basis of the traditional test of a repudiatory breach of contract.

5. Claims Against the Transferor

4.78 Nothing in TUPE 2006 addresses or operates to overrule the principle established in *University of Oxford v Humphreys*.[67] An employee terminated his contract in advance of a relevant transfer because the terms of employment which the transferee intended to impose upon him would have been significantly to his detriment. The Court of Appeal held that the right to object to transfer[68] was entirely separate from the free-standing right to terminate employment without notice in response to a substantial detrimental change to working conditions.[69] The Court of Appeal's analysis was that the (common law) constructive dismissal claim which was being made by the employee prior to transfer could only lie against the employer at the relevant time ie the transferor. Moreover, TUPE 1981, regulation 5(4A) specifically stated that, as a consequence of an objection of the kind under consideration, no 'rights, powers, duties or liabilities' would transfer to the transferee under TUPE (as an exception to the general principle of transfer of employment-related liabilities). The remedy against the transferor was specifically stated not to transfer to the transferee.

4.79 TUPE 2006 does nothing to remove liability from the transferor in such

---

[65] Regulation 4(1).   [66] Regulations 4(7), 4(8), 4(9) and 4(10).
[67] [2000] IRLR 183, CA.
[68] Under TUPE 1981, regulations 5(4A) and 5(4B); now regulations 4(7) and 4(8).
[69] TUPE 1981, regulation 5(5); now, as amended, regulation 4(9).

circumstances (where it is arguably the transferee which creates the problem). Regulation 4(7) repeats the provisions of TUPE 1981 considered by *Humphreys*. This interpretation is supported by the rejection by the Government of suggestions during the consultation process that references in regulation 4(9) should be to the transferor or transferee depending on the timing: 'an employee can use draft Regulation 4(9) and 4(10) to seek redress against the transferor or the transferee, depending on the identity of his employer at the material time'.[70] It therefore is still the case (however counterintuitive it may seem) that an employee can object to transfer on the grounds of an anticipatory constructive dismissal on the part of (or even arguably an anticipatory change to his or her employment terms to be implemented by) the transferee and yet have an unfair dismissal claim against the transferor rather than the transferee. This reinforces the need for transferors where possible to seek appropriate indemnities from transferees to protect themselves against the financial consequences of such claims.

In contrast, in *Sita (GB) Limited v Burton*,[71] the transferee's conduct towards **4.80** the employees prior to transfer was not found capable of leading to a constructive dismissal. As the relevant issues arose prior to transfer when the employees were employed by the transferor, the transferee's conduct could not lead to a breach of a contract to which the transferee was not yet party nor did it create a breach of trust and confidence in the transferor as the employer at the material time. Being based on an alleged breach of the implied duty to maintain trust and confidence rather than the right to object to transfer or a substantial change to working conditions to their detriment, the employees' claims failed.

---

[70] Consultation Response para 3.11.   [71] [1997] IRLR 501, EAT.

5

TRANSFER OF INDIVIDUAL AND COLLECTIVE OBLIGATIONS

A. Transfer of Individual Rights	5.01
B. Collective Agreements	5.42
C. Trade Union Recognition	5.56
D. Other Representative Structures	5.67

A. TRANSFER OF INDIVIDUAL RIGHTS

1. General Position

(a) *Introduction*

Subject to the Transfer of Undertakings (Protection of Employment) Regula-   **5.01**
tions (TUPE) 2006's specific provisions relating to insolvency situations,[1]
employees' rights to object to their transfer to the transferee[2] and the exclusion
of criminal liabilities and occupational pension rights from those liabilities
which the transferee inherits,[3] the transferee effectively sits in the shoes of
the transferor following the relevant transfer as regards the employment of
the employees, including responsibilities for the past acts and omissions of the
transferor. Subject to these important exceptions, on a relevant transfer the
transferor ceases to be responsible for any employment obligations in respect of
the transferring employees—these all transfer to the transferee. TUPE has been
described as having a 'Worzel Gummidge' effect whereby '[t]he head is swapped
but the body (the business) continues'.[4]

More specifically, the operation of TUPE attaches to the relevant employees'   **5.02**
contracts of employment. Regulation 4(2) provides that:

---

[1] Regulations 8 and 9—see Chap 10.   [2] Regulations 4(7)–(10)—see Chap 4.
[3] Regulations 4(6) and 10—see paras 5.10–12 below and Chap 11.
[4] David Pollard 'Pensions and TUPE' (2005) 34 ILJ 127.

(a) all the transferor's rights, powers, duties and liabilities under or in connection with any such contract shall be transferred by virtue of this regulation to the transferee; and

(b) any act or omission before the transfer is completed, of or in relation to the transferor in respect of that contract or a person assigned to that organised grouping of resources or employees shall be deemed to have been an act or omission of or in relation to the transferee.

5.03   The 2005 Consultation described regulation 4 as 'an updated provision that is designed to incorporate well-established developments in case law since the Regulations were first introduced, and to reflect more closely what the Government considers to be the correct interpretation of the Directive in this regard'.[5] That regulation 4(2) attracted no substantive comment in the 2005 Consultation is consistent with this analysis and therefore in analysing its effect resort must be had to the previous case law (which is now summarised in brief outline).

5.04   One amendment made to the draft regulations in this regard following the 2005 Consultation was the specific clarification that the transferee inherits any 'act or omission' of the transferor as distinct from anything done by it (as was the formulation in TUPE 1981 and the first draft of what became TUPE 2006). This change was made 'for completeness'.[6]

(b) *What is Transferred?*

5.05   The transferee is liable for everything the transferor has done in relation to the transferring employees (save where TUPE 2006 expressly provides otherwise) in terms of 'powers, rights, duties and liabilities'. The matters for which the transferee becomes responsible are those which arise 'under or in relation to' the relevant contract and therefore go wider than the contract of employment's strict terms to cover all the appurtenances of employment status. Accordingly, the transferee becomes responsible for the consequences of the transferor's conduct whether in connection to failure to pay wages, acts of discrimination, or otherwise. That the transferee is liable for pre-transfer actions of the transferor is particularly acutely demonstrated by *DJM International Limited v Nicholas*.[7] An act of discrimination against an employee on the part of the transferor was inherited by the transferee even though that claim related to a contract which had expired prior to the employment the termination of which led to the proceedings in question.

5.06   *Unicorn Consultancy Services v Westbrook*[8] demonstrates that the transferee can inherit rights which employees had against the transferor and which crystallised prior to transfer. In that case, the transferor operated a profit-related pay (PRP) scheme in respect of employees whose employment transferred to a new contractor pursuant to TUPE. The transferor failed to make to the employees payments due under the PRP scheme when they fell due shortly before the

[5] 2005 Consultation para 37.   [6] Consultation Response para 3.8.
[7] [1996] IRLR 76, EAT.   [8] [2000] IRLR 80, EAT.

relevant transfer. The Employment Appeal Tribunal (EAT) held that the liability to make the relevant PRP payments transferred under the legislation to the transferee. This was the case even though the liability arose prior to transfer.

The transferee will (unless it reverses the decision) be bound by any decision **5.07** by the transferor to terminate an employee's employment on notice and by the reason for it. In *BSG v Tuck*[9] the transferor and transferee incorrectly concluded that TUPE did not apply to the transfer of a local authority activity. The transferee inherited the relevant employees who had been given notices of termination by the transferor which had not expired as at the date of the transfer. As the actions of the transferor were deemed by TUPE to be those of the transferee, the transferee was bound by the transferor's (redundancy) reason for dismissal. That reason for dismissal, being incorrectly predicated on TUPE not applying, was untenable. Consequently the dismissals were unfair.

Whent v T Cartledge Ltd[10] demonstrates that collectively bargained employ- **5.08** ment terms may be inherited by the transferee. The employee, having become employed on a relevant transfer by the transferee, could still rely on the fact that contractually his terms of employment were to be determined by reference to a collective agreement to which the transferor was a party but the transferee was not.

The contractual status of rights to which transferring employees claim to be **5.09** entitled may nonetheless be open to debate. Whilst express entitlements to specific termination payments (for example by way of enhanced redundancy entitlements) will clearly be inherited by the transferee, the position may be less than clear where the entitlement is claimed by reference to a custom and practice alleged to render the entitlement contractual. Changes to matters which do not have the status of contractual entitlements may nonetheless be relevant to the ability of a transferring employee to terminate his or her employment by reason of a substantial change to his or her working conditions to his or her material detriment.[11]

(c) *What is Not Transferred?*

The transferee does not inherit responsibility for occupational pension entitle- **5.10** ments falling within the subject matter of the 'pensions exclusion' (ie old age, invalidity, and survivors' benefits under occupational pension schemes).[12]

Criminal liabilities are also excluded from the scope of the transferee's **5.11** inheritance but the transfer does not remove the transferor's responsibility for the relevant offence. Regulation 4(6)[13] provides that regulation 4(2) 'shall not transfer or otherwise affect the liability of any person to be prosecuted for,

---

[9] [1996] IRLR 134, EAT.   [10] [1997] IRLR 153, EAT.
[11] Pursuant to regulation 4(9). See Chap 4, para 4.57 *et seq.*
[12] Regulation 10—see Chap 11.
[13] Which again attracted no comment in the 2005 Consultation and maintains the previous position.

convicted of and sentenced for any offence'. Therefore, whilst a transferee may inherit contractual and tortious liabilities in respect, for example, of a pre-transfer breach of the transferor's health and safety responsibilities to the transferring employees, it will not inherit any liability to prosecution if the default committed by the transferor also constituted a criminal offence. The transferor will remain liable for the criminal offence.

5.12   *Jowett (Angus) & Co Ltd v National Union of Tailors and Garment Workers*[14] confirmed that liability for failure to comply with the obligation to consult with a recognised trade union or employee representatives in relation to a redundancy situation required by the Trade Union and Labour Relations (Consolidation) Act (TULRCA) 1992, s 188 does not transfer to the transferee. The possibility was raised in the 2005 Consultation of making liability for such a protective award joint and several on the transferor and transferee where the relevant redundancies were transfer related.[15] As the consultation process produced no consensus on the issue, the position was not changed by TUPE 2006.[16]

(d) *Summary*

5.13   To summarise, the following pre-transfer liabilities therefore pass to transferees under TUPE:

- liability for breaches of contract arising prior to transfer (such as failure to make a pay rise or pay a bonus);
- liability in respect of statutory employment claims;
- liability in tort (for example an employee's claim for personal injuries);[17]
- continuous employment for statutory purposes;[18]
- the transferor's compulsory employers' liability insurance.[19]

5.14   The following liabilities do not transfer:

- criminal liability;
- liabilities relating to occupational pension scheme benefits for old age, invalidity, or survivors;
- failure to comply with TULRCA, s 188.

5.15   What the transferee inherits in terms of collective agreements and liabilities for failure to comply with TUPE's obligations to inform and consult appropriate representatives is addressed separately.[20]

---

[14] [1985] IRLR 426, EAT.   [15] 2005 Consultation para 85.
[16] Consultation Response para 7.8.
[17] Cf *Bernadone v Pall Mall Services Group & others* [2000] IRLR 487, CA which decision the 2005 Consultation described (at para 86) as according with 'the Government's own view of the legal position under the Directive and the Regulations'.
[18] *D36 Ltd v Castro* EAT/0853/03. See para 5.36 below.   [19] See para 5.16 below.
[20] See, respectively, para 5.42 *et seq* and Chap 9.

2. Employers' Liability Compulsory Insurance

In *Bernadone v Pall Mall Services Group & Others*,[21] the Court of Appeal held **5.16** that liabilities to employees for personal injury or disease arising from their employment by the transferor prior to a TUPE transfer are automatically inherited by the transferee. This was unsurprising. Rather more intriguingly, given the common law concept of privity of contract, the Court of Appeal also held that the benefit of any compulsory employers' liability insurance taken out by the transferor similarly passes to the transferee on a transfer. The result of this transfer of the benefit of the transferor's arrangements means that the transferee may (subject to the terms of the insurance cover itself) rely on the transferor's pre-transfer insurance cover as against the transferor's insurer to meet any liabilities incurred pre-transfer but for which it becomes responsible by virtue of the operation of TUPE. This is the case even though it was not a party to that insurance contract.

The *Bernadone* decision affects private sector employers which have the statu- **5.17** tory obligation to arrange appropriate employers' liability insurance.[22] The Government considered the position established by *Bernadone* in relation to transfers between private sector employers to be satisfactory[23]—'the transfer of the benefit of the insurance cover bought by the transferor ensures that the transferee can comply with [employers' liability compulsory insurance] requirements in relation to liabilities incurred pre-transfer'.[24]

In the context of transfers from the public sector to the private sector, the **5.18** Government considered the situation to be unsatisfactory. Public sector employers are generally not covered by, or are exempt from, the requirement to put employers' liability insurance cover in place.[25] As had been flagged in the 2001 Consultation,[26] TUPE 2006 expressly deals with this issue. Since in such circum-

---

[21] [2000] IRLR 487, CA.

[22] The Employers' Liability (Compulsory Insurance) Act (ELCI) 1969, s 1(1) provides that: '[e]xcept as otherwise provided by this Act, every employer carrying on any business in Great Britain shall insure, and maintain insurance, under one or more approved policies with an authorised insurer or insurers against liability for bodily injury or disease sustained by his employees, and arising out of and in the course of their employment in Great Britain in that business, but except in so far as regulations otherwise provide not including injury or disease suffered or contracted outside Great Britain'.

[23] 2005 Consultation para 87.   [24] Ibid.

[25] ELCI 1969, s 3 provides exemptions pursuant to which the legislation does not require any insurance to be effected by certain specified authorities, any body corporate established by or under any enactment for the carrying on of any industry or part of an industry, or of any undertaking, under national ownership or control and any employer exempted by regulations. Examples of specified authorities for the purposes of this exemption include health service bodies as defined in s 60(7) of the National Health Service and Community Care Act 1990, National Health Service trusts established under Part 1 of that Act, the Common Council of the City of London, district and county councils, the councils of London boroughs, the London Fire and Emergency Planning Authority, and any police authority.

[26] Paras 112–115.

stances no insurance is in place prior to the relevant transfer the benefit of which can transfer to the transferee, regulation 17(2) renders the transferor and the transferee jointly and severally liable for liabilities to employees where compulsory insurance does not apply.[27]

5.19   This joint and several liability arises 'on completion of a relevant transfer'[28] in respect of the prescribed category of liability but only where the transferor is not required or is exempted from the requirement to effect employers' liability insurance.[29] A transferee entering into a TUPE transaction with a public sector employer may therefore wish in such circumstances to seek an indemnity from the transferor in respect of such pre-transfer liabilities.

3. Specific Issues

5.20   Regulation 4(1) puts the transferee in the shoes of the transferor for contractual purposes. Practical difficulties may, however, arise in relation to the continuation of benefits and other matters as a consequence of the change to the identity of the employee's employer. TUPE 2006 added nothing to clarify these potential difficulties so regard must be had to the previous case law.

(a) Restrictive Covenants

5.21   The concerns which may arise in relation to restrictive covenants in the contracts of employment of the transferring employees are demonstrated by *Morris Angel & Son Limited v Hollande*.[30] The relevant restrictive covenants precluded the employee in question from soliciting or doing business with customers who had dealt with the transferor in the previous year. The employee was dismissed immediately after a relevant transfer. When the transferee sought to enforce the restrictive covenants against the employee, at first instance the covenant was construed as having effectively been amended (by virtue of the TUPE transfer) so that references to the transferor were replaced by references to the transferee. Accordingly, the covenant's provisions identifying the protected category of customers whom the employee should not approach or deal with was

---

[27] Article 3(1) permits such a provision (as noted in the 2005 Consultation at para 88). Regulation 17 provides that:

'(1) Paragraph (2) applies where:
    (a) by virtue of section 3(1)(a) or (b) of the Employers' Liability (Compulsory Insurance) Act 1969 ("the Act"), the transferor is not required by that Act to effect any insurance; or
    (b) by virtue of section 3(1)(c) of the 1969 Act, the transferor is exempted from the requirement of that Act to effect insurance.
(2) Where this paragraph applies, on completion of a relevant transfer the transferor and the transferee shall be jointly and severally liable in respect of any liability referred to in section 1(1) of the 1969 Act, in so far as such liability relates to the employee's employment with the transferor.'

[28] Regulation 17(2).

[29] Regulation 17(1)(a) and (b) by reference to the Employers' Liability (Compulsory Insurance) Act 1969 s 3(1)(a), (b), (c).

[30] [1993] IRLR 169, CA.

construed as referring to any person who had done business with the transferee in the previous year. So construed, since during the previous year the employee had been engaged by and the relevant business conducted by the transferor, rather than the transferee, no person fell within the scope of the covenant. However, the Court of Appeal permitted a purposive interpretation which enabled enforcement of the covenant on the basis that it should be construed as referring to those who dealt with the undertaking (as opposed to the transferor or transferee) in the year prior to the termination of the employee's employment.

(b) *Bonuses and Benefits*

Bonus schemes and other benefit arrangements may also cause difficulties in terms of post-transfer replication. If a transferee acquires part of an undertaking, it may find it difficult precisely to replicate benefits which are specific to the transferor's group (such as group travel, health, and concessionary purchase arrangements). Moreover, the criteria applying, for example, to a bonus scheme operated by the transferor may be entirely irrelevant to the business of the transferee (as opposed to that of the transferor) and yet may form terms of the contract of employment by which the transferee is bound pursuant to regulation 4(1). Subject to the ability to agree changes to employees' terms and conditions of employment provided by regulations 4(4) and 4(5), a continuing concern is the fact that the literal application of TUPE operates to transfer all contractual obligations to the transferee regardless of the fact that, as a consequence of the change to the identity of the employer, the transferring entitlements might be rendered inappropriate or meaningless. **5.22**

Mitie Managed Services Limited v French[31] addressed the extent to which a transferee could be required to replicate a profit-sharing or bonus arrangement which was operated by the transferor and therefore which was tailored to its particular circumstances rather than those of the transferee. A number of employees participated in a profit-sharing scheme operated by the transferor prior to their transfer to the transferee. The employees argued that they remained contractually entitled to participate in the scheme operated by the transferor after the transfer even though they were no longer employed by that company. The EAT rejected this claim and also considered that it would be impossible, unjust, and absurd to require the transferee to be held to exact replication of a scheme based on the performance of the transferor. A test of 'substantial equivalence' was adopted. In such circumstances, employees are entitled to 'a scheme of substantial equivalence but one which is free from unjust, absurd or impossible features'.[32] **5.23**

It is therefore clear that transferees may to some extent be able to modify the entitlements of transferring employees which cannot exactly be replicated in **5.24**

---

[31] [2002] IRLR 521, CA.   [32] At para 16.

their organisations, provided that the employees are not thereby prejudiced. Whilst the substantial equivalence concept assists a transferee deal with a benefit which it cannot replicate in the context of its business, that principle does not appear capable of permitting replacement on an equivalence basis of benefits which can be continued but that the transferor would like to vary in some way. Given that *French* addressed the specific circumstance where benefits cannot be practicably or sensibly replicated, it is submitted that the substantial equivalence test is limited to the sort of hard cases which it was designed to address.

(c) *Share Options*

5.25 Unless an ongoing contractual entitlement to receive further benefits can be established, it is strongly arguable that share option rights granted to transferring employees prior to a relevant transfer are not inherited by the transferee. One argument in support of this analysis is that the share option arrangement is a separate contract additional to the employment contract and therefore not an obligation which transfers to the transferee 'under or in connection' with the relevant employee's employment contract in accordance with regulation 4(2)(a).[33] This argument (which faces the difficulty that share option grants are often parasitic and conditional upon employment) is arguably bolstered by the fact that share option schemes often state (in order to seek to exclude their benefits from the scope of a wrongful damages claim by the relevant employee if dismissed in breach of contract) that they and entitlements awarded under them form no part of the employees' contracts of employment.

5.26 More compellingly, a share option can often be construed as a historic entitlement whose own terms determine what happens on the occurrence of a relevant transfer. The relevant share option scheme rules may trigger the ability to exercise the option on the employee leaving the employment of the grantor of the option or its group (as will be the consequence of a relevant transfer other than by way of an internal group reorganisation). In such circumstances, the relevant scheme rules will often require exercise of the share option during a specified period following termination of employment, failing which the option will lapse. The benefit of the option in such circumstances is 'self-determining' and delivered in accordance with its original terms. Requiring the transferee to replicate the benefit would lead to a (counterintuitive) windfall for the relevant employees, who would be able both to exercise their options under the express rules applying to their entitlements as against the transferor and to demand replacement share option entitlements from the transferee. The position, however, would be different in relation to a contractually binding obligation to continue regular option grants by which the transferee could, subject to its terms, be bound and in relation to which the 'substantial equivalence' test described above might well come into play.

---

[33] See *Chapman v CPS Computer Group* [1987] IRLR 462, CA.

(d) Misrepresentation and Pensions Claims

In *Hagen v ICI Chemicals and Polymers Ltd*,[34] Elias J held that employees could **5.27** bring claims of negligent misstatement against a transferor which had inaccurately indicated that the post-transfer pension arrangements which the transferee would operate would be broadly comparable to their pre-transfer entitlements. The employees had suffered a detriment as a result of this misrepresentation. In the light of their bargaining position, it was held that the employees would have been able to secure more advantageous pension entitlements with the transferee had they been aware of the true position.

As the subject matter of the transferor's misrepresentations was the applicable **5.28** occupational pension arrangements, Elias J held that the liability for the relevant representations remained with the transferor.[35] This does, however, raise the spectre of transferees becoming liable for a transferor's pre-transfer (and non-contractual) representations outside the pensions context in cases where detrimental reliance on the representations by affected employees can be established. Protection against such liabilities can only be obtained by the transferee by an appropriate contractual indemnity.

In a similar vein, *Powerhouse Retail Ltd (1) Seeboard Retail plc (2) Midlands* **5.29** *Electricity plc (3) v Burroughs and others*[36] makes a useful point about equal pay claims in the pensions context. The time limit of six months for making a claim based on an equality clause in respect of a transferor's pension scheme ran from the date of transfer (ie termination of employment with the transferor) rather than the termination of employment with the transferee.

(e) Retirement and Unfair Dismissal

Whilst perhaps on unusual facts, *Cross v British Airways plc*[37] made, *inter alia,* **5.30** the points, first, that the rights of transferring employees are preserved by TUPE regardless of the understanding of the parties at the time of the relevant transaction and, second, that statutory employment rights are to be applied at the time when the employees seek their enforcement and the occurrence of a TUPE transfer has no bearing on the application of those rights.

British Airways had a contractual retirement age of 55 from 1971. Employees **5.31** of British Caledonian, which merged with British Airways in 1988, enjoyed a retirement age of 60. TUPE was not considered by the parties to apply to the merger of the two companies at the time of the relevant transaction. Nonetheless, the Employment Tribunal (ET) concluded that the merger did constitute a relevant transfer. Accordingly, despite their having accepted British Airways'

---

[34] [2002] IRLR 31, HC.
[35] Under TUPE 2006, the position remains the same—regulation 10(1)(b) extends the exclusion of occupational pension scheme rights from those entitlements under a contract of employment or collective agreement which the transferee inherits to 'rights, powers, duties and liabilities' in that connection.
[36] [2006] UKHL 3, HL.   [37] [2005] IRLR 423, EAT.

employment terms (including a contractual retirement age of 55) in 1988 and British Airways paying substantial monies to fund full pension entitlements at 55, the employees retained their contractual retirement age of 60 by virtue of TUPE's preservation of their contractual rights.[38]

5.32   The issue then arose as to the effect of TUPE on 'normal retirement age' for statutory purposes. Contending that 55 was its normal retirement age, British Airways argued that, even if the British Caledonian contractual retirement age of 60 were preserved by TUPE, the dismissal of the relevant employees could not lead to unfair dismissal claims on the basis of the provisions of the Employment Rights Act 1996 (ERA 1996), s 109. ERA 1996, s 109 disapplies the right in ERA 1996, s 94 to claim unfair dismissal where an employee has attained normal retirement age on or before the effective date of termination of employment. Normal retirement age for these purposes is the normal retiring age for an employee holding the position held by the employee or, if there is none, 65.

5.33   Despite finding that the normal retiring age of 55 was well known throughout the business, the ET concluded that the former British Caledonian staff had a normal retirement age of 60. On appeal, the EAT found 55 to be the normal retirement age based on the proper test.[39]

5.34   Against this, the employees had argued that to permit a new normal retirement age for statutory purposes coming into effect post-transfer would contravene the provisions of TUPE 1981 regulation 5(2)[40] which transferred all rights, powers, duties, and liabilities in relation to the transferring employees to the transferee. This provision was argued to preserve the pre-transfer normal retirement age for statutory (including unfair dismissal) purposes as well as contractually. The ET agreed, holding that the right to claim unfair dismissal was a right, power, duty, or liability within the scope of TUPE 1981, regulation 5 for the protective purposes of TUPE and the Directive.

5.35   The EAT rejected the argument that TUPE rendered impermissible an altered normal retirement age for statutory purposes introduced after a relevant transfer. The statutory unfair dismissal jurisdiction should be applied to the facts pertaining at the time of dismissal (rather than by reference to the position obtaining at some earlier point in time such as the employee becoming employed by the dismissing employer as a consequence of a TUPE transfer). It is therefore clear that TUPE does not preserve employees' statutory (as distinct from contractual) rights in aspic as they are as at the point of transfer. Statutory

---

[38] The principle established in *Wilson* meant that any purported or alleged consent to the variation of retirement age was invalid—see Chap 6.

[39] Which is 'to ascertain what would be the reasonable expectation or understanding of the employees holding that position at the relevant time' per Lord Fraser in *Waite v GCHQ* [1983] 2 AC 714, HL.

[40] Now regulation 4(2).

entitlements must be determined by reference to the relevant legislation at the particular time when an issue of eligibility or otherwise arises.

(f) Continuity of Employment

Regulation 4(2)(a) preserves on a relevant transfer 'all the transferor's rights, **5.36** powers, duties and liabilities under or in connection with any [transferred] contract of employment' and thereby preserves the continuity of employment of the transferring employees for statutory purposes. The EAT confirmed this in *D36 Limited v Castro*[41] (which approved the conclusion reached with the agreement of the parties by the Court of Appeal in *Astley v Celtec*).[42]

ERA 1996, s 218(2) addresses the issue more directly providing that: **5.37**

If a trade or business, or an undertaking (whether or not established by or under an Act), is transferred from one person or another:
(a) the period of employment of an employee in the trade or business or undertaking at the time of the transfer counts as a period of employment with the transferee; and
(b) the transfer does not break the continuity of the period of employment.

Whilst it can be debated whether jurisprudence relating to the European Union **5.38** (EU) law-derived TUPE can be relevant to the purely domestic statutory continuity of employment provisions, it is strongly arguable that the TUPE case law is relevant to establishing whether ERA 1996, s 218(2) applies to a particular scenario.

Other express provisions governing the preservation of continuity of **5.39** employment in circumstances which could, depending upon the circumstances, constitute or which are similar to a TUPE transfer are ERA 1996, s 218(3) (change of employer as a result of an Act of Parliament); s 218(4) (transfer of employment to personal representatives on death of the employer); s 218(5) (change in the composition of a partnership); s 218(6) (transfer of employment between associated employers); s 218(7) (local education transfers); and s 218(8), (9) (transfer of employees between health service employers).

Senior Heat Treatment v Bell[43] demonstrates the operation of the statutory **5.40** provisions with regard to continuity of employment in slightly unusual circumstances. The relevant employees opted to object to transfer and received redundancy payments. Their signing new contracts and becoming employed by the transferee pretty much immediately thereafter meant not only that they did not object validly to the transfer of their employment to the transferee under what was then TUPE 1981, regulation 5(4).[44]

Also, their receipt of a redundancy payment did not operate to break their **5.41** continuity of employment as provided for by ERA 1996, s 214(2). As the employees were neither dismissed (nor for that matter redundant) because their employment transferred to the transferee under TUPE, the payment they

---

[41] EAT/0853/03.   [42] [2002] IRLR 629, CA.   [43] [1997] IRLR 614, EAT.
[44] Now regulation 4(7).

received was not a statutory redundancy payment. ERA 1996, s 214(2) therefore did not apply to break continuity of employment for statutory purposes. On termination of employment with the transferee, employment with both the transferor and transferee applied to entitle the employees to a statutory redundancy payment taking into account pre-transfer employment. The employees therefore received payment twice in respect of their pre-transfer employment.

B. COLLECTIVE AGREEMENTS

1. The Directive

5.42 Article 3.3 provides that:

> [f]ollowing the transfer, the transferee shall continue to observe the terms and conditions agreed in any collective agreement on the same terms applicable to the transferor under that agreement, until the date of termination or expiry of the collective agreement or the entry into force or application of another collective agreement. Member States may limit the period for observing such terms and conditions with the proviso that it shall not be less than one year.

This provision is translated into domestic law by regulation 5 which addresses the inheritance by the transferee of the collective agreements with recognised trade unions by which the transferor was bound prior to transfer.

2. Transfer of Collective Agreements

5.43 The effect of regulation 5 is that on a relevant transfer the transferee inherits any collective agreement made by or on behalf of the transferor with a trade union which is recognised by the transferor in respect of any employee whose contract transfers to the transferee pursuant to regulation 4(1). TUPE 2006 does not take advantage of the ability in Article 3 to limit the period for which a transferee is required to observe the terms and conditions of a collective agreement relating to the transferring employees. As noted above, the minimum obligation, if this option had been taken up, would have been to require the collective agreement to be complied with for one year post-transfer.

5.44 Regulation 5(a) (which does not change the substantive position under TUPE 1981) provides that:

> [w]here at the time of a relevant transfer there exists a collective agreement made by or on behalf of the transferor with a trade union recognised by the transferor in respect of any employee whose contract of employment is preserved by regulation 4(1) above, then—
> (a) without prejudice to sections 179 and 180 of the 1992 Act (collective agreements presumed to be unenforceable in specified circumstances) that agreement, in its application in relation to the employee, shall, after the transfer, have effect as if made by or on behalf of the transferee with that trade union, and accordingly anything done under or in connection with it, in its application in relation to the employee by or in

relation to the transferor before the transfer, shall, after the transfer, be deemed to
have been done by or in relation to the transferee; and

(b) any order made in respect of that agreement, in its application in relation to the
employee, shall, after the transfer, have effect as if the transferee were a party to the
agreement.

Accordingly, in the same way that employment contracts transfer under TUPE   5.45
to the transferee with all associated rights, powers, duties, obligations, and liabilities, collective agreements satisfying the relevant requirements and which are
applicable to the transferring employees (or some of them) transfer to the transferee. Also, any order made in respect of the collective agreement shall, after the
transfer, have effect as if the transferee were a party to the agreement.[45]

The principal elements of the application of regulation 5 are: 5.46

• there must have been an agreement made by or on behalf of the transferor;
• the agreement must have been with a recognised trade union;[46]
• the agreement must satisfy the statutory test of what constitutes a collective
agreement;
• the agreement must have been in existence at the time of transfer;
• whether the agreement was legally enforceable is irrelevant.

The transferee is not bound by an agreement reached with a trade union which is   5.47
not recognised by the transferor. That a collective agreement made 'on behalf of'
the transferor falls within the scope of regulation 5 extends its protection to
industry-wide collective agreements agreed by employers' organisations (on
behalf of their member organisations) and recognised trade unions to which the
transferor may not be a direct party.

The relevant collective agreement must also have been in place at the time of   5.48
the relevant transfer. This raises the possibility, subject to the potential industrial relations consequences, of the agreement being terminated prior to the
relevant transfer in order to avoid transfer to the transferee. This would be a
potentially bold strategy for the transferor and transferee to adopt since they
will presumably at the time potentially be in dialogue with the relevant trade
union or unions in compliance with their collective information and consultation obligations pursuant to regulation 13. Termination of trade union agreement to evade the effect of regulation 5 is therefore perhaps less than practicable
(especially if such termination is precluded by virtue of the currency of an
award of statutory recognition).

---

[45] Regulation 5(b).
[46] Pursuant to regulation 2(1) 'recognised' has the meaning given to it by TULRCA 1992, s 178(3)
ie 'recognition of the union by an employer or two or more associated employers, to any extent, for
the purpose of collective bargaining'.

3. Definition of Collective Agreements

5.49 The term 'collective agreement' for these purposes[47] bears the same meaning in regulation 5 as ascribed by TULRCA 1992, s 178(1), ie 'any agreement or arrangement by or on behalf of one or more trade unions and one or more employers or employers' associations and relating to one or more of the matters mentioned in TULRCA, Section 178(2)'. Unless an agreement with a recognised trade union constitutes a collective agreement for these purposes, it does not fall to transfer to the transferee under regulation 5.

5.50 The matters prescribed by TULRCA 1992, s 178(2), to at least one of which a putative collective agreement must relate for it to satisfy the statutory test for these purposes, are:

- terms and conditions of employment or the physical conditions in which legal workers are required to work;
- engagement or non-engagement or termination or suspension of employment or the duties of employment of one or more workers;
- allocation of work or the duties of employment as between workers or groups of workers;
- matters of discipline;
- the membership or non-membership of the trade union on the part of a worker;
- facilities for officials of trade unions;
- machinery for negotiation or consultation, and other procedures, relating to any of the foregoing matters including the recognition by employers or employees' associations of the right of a trade union to represent workers in any such negotiation or consultation or in the carrying out of such procedures.

5.51 Only if one of the above matters is addressed will an agreement qualify as a collective agreement for the purposes of regulation 5 and so be susceptible to transfer to the transferee as a consequence of a relevant transfer.

4. Legal Enforceability

5.52 A collective agreement made with a recognised trade union is inherited by the transferee regardless of whether the collective agreement in question is legally enforceable and regardless of whether its provisions have been incorporated into individual employees' contracts of employment. The fact of transfer does not of itself render the relevant collective agreement any more or less legally enforceable. Regulation 5(a) provides for the transfer of a (qualifying)

---

[47] Pursuant to regulation 2(1).

collective agreement 'without prejudice to sections 179 and 180 of the 1992 [TULRCA] Act (collective agreements pursuant to be enforceable in certain circumstances) . . .'.

TULRCA 1992, s 179(1) and (2) provides that a collective agreement entered into before 1 December 1971 or after 15 September 1974 is presumed not to be legally enforceable. Pursuant to TULRCA 1992, s 179(3), if a written collective agreement contains an express statement that the parties intend the agreement to be a legally enforceable contract, then this presumption is displaced.   **5.53**

It might be argued that, if a collective agreement is not legally enforceable and therefore can effectively be ignored by the transferee in contractual (if not industrial relations) terms, regulation 5 provides little meaningful protection for a recognised trade union or its members in relation to a relevant transfer. However, the provision does have the benefit of subjecting the transferee to the collective agreements by which the transferor was bound, breach or termination of which by the transferee could lead to lawful industrial action (subject to applicable requirements being satisfied).   **5.54**

If particular terms of a collective agreement have already been incorporated into the terms of an individual's contract of employment, no reliance need be placed by an affected employee (as opposed to the relevant trade unions) on regulation 5. As a contractual entitlement, the relevant terms are enforceable against the transferee by the individual by virtue of regulation 4. An example is *Whent*[48] in which after a transfer employees could, as against the transferee, insist on an ongoing basis on their pre-transfer entitlement to rely on terms negotiated by the relevant National Joint Council (the relevant collective agreement in question), even though after the transfer the transferee had terminated the union's recognition and did not participate in the National Joint Council negotiation process.   **5.55**

C. TRADE UNION RECOGNITION

1. The Directive

Article 6.1 (which regulation 6 implements into domestic law) provides that: **5.56**

[if] the undertaking, business or part of an undertaking or business [subject to a transfer] preserves its autonomy, the status and function of the representatives or of the representation of the employees affected by the transfer shall be preserved on the same terms and conditions and subject to the same conditions as existed by virtue of law, regulation, administrative provision or agreement, provided that the conditions necessary for the constitution of the employees' representation are fulfilled.

---

[48] [1997] IRLR 153, EAT.

2. Transfer of Recognition

5.57 As the 2005 Consultation noted,[49] in implementing the principle of Article 6.1 into domestic law, regulation 6 replicates TUPE 1981, regulation 9 in relation to the effect of a relevant transfer on trade union recognition.[50] Regulation 6 only applies where, after a relevant transfer, the organised grouping of resources or employees which is transferred to the transferee maintains an identity distinct from the remainder of the transferee's undertaking. Whether the relevant transfer occurs by way of a transfer of an undertaking within regulation 3(1)(a) or a service provision change within regulation 3(1)(b), the crucial requirement is that the pre-transfer grouping must maintain an identity distinct from the remainder of the transferee's operation.[51]

5.58 Assuming that the requisite distinct identity of the relevant grouping of resources or employees is maintained, regulation 6(2) provides that:

[w]here before such a transfer an independent trade union is recognised to any extent by the transferor in respect of employees of any description who in consequence of the transfer become employees of the transferee, then, after the transfer—
(a) the trade union shall be deemed to have been recognised by the transferee to the same extent in respect of employees of that description so employed; and
(b) any agreement for recognition may be varied or rescinded accordingly.

5.59 Accordingly, only if the relevant trade union is independent and recognised by the transferor in respect of transferring staff can recognition transfer to the transferee automatically under TUPE 2006. Recognition will only be continued on the same basis as it applied pre-transfer (ie in respect of the relevant employees and substantive issues with regard to which the trade union was recognised). The union will not acquire recognition rights in respect of any wider category of employees or a wider scope of collective bargaining rights simply by virtue of the transfer.

5.60 It should also be noted that there is no requirement as to the scope of pre-transfer recognition for regulation 6 to apply. The pre-transfer recognition does not have to be comprehensive in its scope or substance. There is no minimum threshold of recognition. All that is required by regulation 6(2) is recognition 'to any extent'.

3. Continuation of Recognition

5.61 No special transfer-related protection is provided with regard to the continuation of recognition. Since regulation 6(2)(b) expressly states that a transferring

---

[49] Para 48.

[50] With all that entails in terms of rights such as the right to provision of information for collective bargaining purposes and the right to be provided with information concerning, and to be consulted about, redundancy exercises and further TUPE transfers.

[51] Regulation 6(1).

collective agreement can be varied or rescinded, the relevant trade union's rights to continued recognition are only those which were enjoyed pre-transfer. This lack of protection for continued recognition raises the possibility of, in appropriate circumstances, the removal of recognition entitling an employee to resign and make a claim based on the ability established by regulation 4(9) for a transferring employee to terminate his or her employment in response to a substantial change to his or her working conditions to his or her material detriment.

These provisions are of no value to employees or trade unions in circumstances where the relevant undertaking transferred is integrated into the transferee's business and loses its identity. Absent agreement with the transferee, the trade union in those circumstances would not retain recognition in respect of the transferred employees whom it represented pre-transfer. This is a potentially significant limitation on the operation of regulation 6 where transferring operations are integrated into the transferee's existing activities. The transferring employees will retain their employment terms but potentially not the recognised status of their trade union. **5.62**

In the consultation process conducted prior to the implementation of TUPE 2006, the Government did raise the possibility of addressing the issue of the protection of trade union recognition post-transfer where the transferring operations or activities are integrated into the transferee's operations and lose their autonomy or identity. In the 2001 Consultation,[52] the Government welcomed views as to whether additional measures might usefully be introduced in the United Kingdom in order to address this situation and to reflect further the obligation in Article 6(1): **5.63**

[if] the undertaking, business or part of an undertaking does not preserve its autonomy . . . [to] take the necessary measures to ensure that the employees transferred who were represented before the transfer continue to be properly represented during the period necessary for the reconstitution or reappointment of the representation of employees in accordance with national law or practice.

However, no additional provisions in this regard were enacted. Arguably TUPE 2006 does not adequately implement Article 6 in this regard. The obligation to provide information to and consult with appropriate representatives under regulation 13 provides a degree of ongoing representation for transferring employees. However, the domestic legislation does not offer any specific transitional or other protection in respect of recognition arrangements (as opposed to the effects of the transfer more generally) where integration of the transferring undertaking or group of employees into the transferee's organisation disapplies the statutory preservation of recognition by regulation 6(2). The regulation 13 consultation obligations are limited in their value as they are engaged only in relation to transfer-related measures. They cannot impose any greater obligation **5.64**

---

[52] Para 107.

than consultation about the measure of potential cessation or variation of the scope of recognition of the trade union or unions recognised by the transferor.

5.65   If recognition is lost because the organised grouping of resources or employees does not retain an identity distinct from the remainder of the transferee's undertaking by virtue of a process of post-transfer integration, recognition could then only be reinstated by way of industrial relations pressure or the statutory recognition process. In either case, attempts to re-establish recognition would be conducted by reference to the transferee's wider workforce with all that entails in terms of timing and the feasibility of a recognition claim (in terms, for example, of levels of trade union support and the relevant workforce constituency being different).

3. Statutory Recognition

5.66   It is clear, even absent specific regulations, that the concept of recognition in TUPE is wide enough to cover recognition awarded under the statutory procedures as much as it does voluntarily agreed recognition. Nonetheless, regulations are planned in due course pursuant to TULRCA 1992, s 169(b) to ensure that declarations made by the Central Arbitration Committee (CAC) and outstanding applications made to the CAC under the statutory trade union recognition procedure are preserved in the event of a change in the identity of the employer including by reason of a relevant transfer. It was considered appropriate[53] to implement such measures 'to make explicit' the transfer of CAC declarations of trade union recognition.

D. OTHER REPRESENTATIVE STRUCTURES

5.67   Unless they fall within the scope of trade union recognition or the specific definition of collective agreements, other employee consultative or representative arrangements relating to the transferring employees, such as consultation fora and staff consultative committees, do not fall within the scope of regulation 6. Accordingly, such arrangements are therefore arguably not required by TUPE to be complied with by the transferee unless necessary or appropriate for industrial relations or human resource management reasons.

5.68   The lack of express provision in TUPE 2006 catering for the consequences of a TUPE transfer for other statutory representative structures, and most particularly on information and consultation arrangements put in place to comply with the Information and Consultation of Employees Regulations 2004 (ICE) and European Works Councils. Essentially, it appears that such arrangements can only be continued or re-established post-transfer by reference to the transferee's operations.

---

[53] 2001 Consultation para 105 *et seq*. See also 2005 Consultation para 48.

6

VARIATIONS TO EMPLOYEES' CONTRACTS

A. Case Law Background	6.01
B. Changes Permitted by TUPE 2006	6.24

A. CASE LAW BACKGROUND

1. Introduction

One of the most controversial aspects of the transfer of undertakings legislation **6.01** is the extent to which it confers mandatory protection on the terms and conditions of employment of transferring employees. This negatives any consent which those employees might give (whether explicitly or by conduct) to any changes to those terms in connection with the transfer in question. Whilst the precise scope of this protection is open to some debate, the Transfer of Undertakings (Protection of Employment) Regulations (TUPE) 2006 seek in the domestic context to establish a framework for some degree of valid transfer-related contract variation to be permissible.

In situations where TUPE does not apply, employers may in the normal **6.02** course of events seek to vary the terms and conditions of the employment of their employees in a number of ways. To avoid the risk of constructive dismissal or a refusal to accept a unilaterally imposed change to terms and conditions, agreement may be sought to a change. In more extreme circumstances, where employees will not agree to changes which an employer wishes to introduce, the employer may seek to serve notice of termination on the relevant employees coupled with an offer of re-engagement on the revised terms. This of course risks a refusal of the offer of continued employment and consequent unfair dismissal claims. In such circumstances, an unfair dismissal claim can be defended if the employer can demonstrate a sufficient business reason for needing to implement the change and has conducted itself in a way which the tribunal accepts constituted fair dismissal for the purposes of the Employment

Rights Act 1996 (ERA 1996), s 98(4). A variety of factors are taken into account in assessing the fairness of such a dismissal.[1]

6.03   It should also be noted that dismissals or proposed dismissals connected with an exercise seeking to change employees' terms and conditions of employment can trigger the application of the collective redundancy information and consultation obligations prescribed by the Trade Union and Labour Relations (Consolidation) Act (TULRCA) 1992, s 188.

6.04   Since TUPE is intended to protect employees' rights on the occurrence of a transfer of an undertaking, it might be assumed, in the context of changes to employees' terms and conditions of employment, that it would be sufficient for the law simply to extend to employees in a transfer situation the same protection which applies in the absence of a relevant transfer. On this analysis, for an employer unilaterally to impose contract changes which the employee does not accept (either by agreement or waiver) would (as is uncontroversial) constitute a breach of contract but employees could also freely agree to the amendment of their terms.

6.05   The development of the case law in relation to the Directive and TUPE 1981 has indicated that this is not the case and that, in the transfer of undertakings context, employees enjoy inderogable mandatory protections. Whilst a change to an employee's contract which is entirely unconnected with a relevant transfer will be valid (subject to the more general points about contractual validity and constructive dismissal), a transfer-related change has been held not to be effective even where the employee consents to the variation. In the context of TUPE transfers, particularly in relation to insolvency situations where the viability of a particular transaction may to an extent depend on changing employees' terms, this principle has been viewed from the commercial perspective as a significant obstacle. The principle that transfer-related changes cannot be agreed makes more difficult transactions whose feasibility may depend to a material extent on reductions in employment costs or harmonisation of the terms of employment of the transferring employees with those of the transferee's existing workforce, and may hamper the avoidance of dismissals by way of variations to the employees' contracts.

2. The Case Law

6.06   The principle that an employee may not waive the rights established by the Directive was established in *Daddy's Dance Hall*.[2] In this case, the provision in question

---

[1] Relevant cases on this issue, detailed treatment of which falls outside the scope of this work, include *St. John of God (Care Services) Limited v Brooks* [1992] IRLR 546, EAT and *Catamaran Cruises Limited v Williams* [1994] IRLR 386, EAT.

[2] [1988] IRLR 315, ECJ. See also *Vigdösdottir v Islandspostur HF* [2003] IRLR 425, ECJ.

was a new notice period applying for a probationary period which was agreed in relation to a transfer. The European Court of Justice (ECJ) stated[3] that:

[t]he benefit of the Directive, therefore, can only be invoked to ensure that the worker concerned is protected in his relations with the new employer in the same way as he was in his relations with the original employer, pursuant to the laws of the Member States concerned. Consequently, insofar as national law allows, apart from a transfer of undertaking, an alteration in the employment relationship in a way which is unfavourable to workers, in particular as regards their protection against dismissal, such alteration is not excluded purely because the undertaking has been the subject of a transfer . . . In the present case, as the second lessee had been substituted for the first lessee pursuant to Article 3(1) of the Directive in respect of rights and obligations arising from the employment relationship, this relationship could be altered with regard to the second lessee within the same limits as for the first lessee, on the understanding that in no case can the transfer of the undertaking itself constitute the reason for this alteration.

The proviso to the last part of that statement is crucial. Employee protection in   6.07
this context requires that the transfer itself cannot be the reason for a contract change. To that (potentially very significant) extent the traditional common law ability of parties to vary their contractual relations is removed. What is particularly challenging for those unfamiliar with the operation of the transfer legislation is the fact that this protection of employees' contractual rights is mandatory and inderogable. It was made clear in *Daddy's Dance Hall* that an employee cannot waive the rights conferred on him or her even if the disadvantages of a particular change are offset by other advantages such that he or she is in no worse position overall. That the transfer itself may never constitute the reason for a change to employees' terms and conditions of employment was again confirmed in *Rask*.[4]

These principles first made their way into the domestic case law of the United   6.08
Kingdom in *Wilson v St. Helen's Borough Council*[5] together with the closely associated case *Meade and Baxendale v British Fuels Limited*.[6] In *Wilson*, management of the operation of a care home transferred from a county council to a borough council and the transferring employees agreed to being employed on the borough council's inferior terms. Some time later, the employees sought to rely on their old terms of employment as against the transferee. In *Meade* employees were dismissed and re-engaged on new terms in connection with a relevant transfer and similarly sought to rely on the terms they had enjoyed prior to transfer.

Whilst this litigation covered a variety of issues and legal analyses during   6.09
its various iterations, the principles established can be summarised as follows. If an employer agrees changes to terms and conditions of employment with employees by reason of a relevant transfer then, even if these changes are agreed

---

[3] At paras 17 and 18.   [4] *Rask v ISS Kantineservice* [1993] IRLR 133, ECJ.
[5] [1996] IRLR 320, EAT; [1997] IRLR 505, CA; [1998] IRLR 706, HL.
[6] [1996] IRLR 541, EAT; [1997] IRLR 505, CA; [1998] IRLR 706, HL.

by the employees, they are invalid. The invalidity of transfer-related changes to employees' contracts of employment was reiterated in *Martin v South Bank University*[7] where it was held that acceptance by transferring employees of new terms of employment harmonising their terms with those of the transferee's existing staff was invalid.

6.10 However, if an employee is dismissed and re-engaged on new terms, even though this course of action is adopted to achieve the same result as a simple agreement, the new terms agreed in respect of the employee's re-engagement are valid in the context of the transfer of undertakings legislation (although an unfair dismissal claim may result from the dismissal). The dismissal is not, as had been argued, a nullity.

6.11 The principal analytical difficulty arising from this line of case law (and one which TUPE 2006 seeks in part to address) is the degree of causal link or connection (between the transfer in question and the contract changes which are sought to be challenged) which is required for the amendments to be invalid. As noted above, in *Daddy's Dance Hall* the ECJ indicated that changes permitted by national law would be valid 'provided that the transfer of the undertaking itself may never constitute the reason for the amendment'. Where the transfer is not the reason for contract changes because they are prompted by some other economic or organisational reason they will be valid; by contrast, transfer-related changes can still be invalid even if agreed some time after the transfer. What has not been addressed with sufficient clarity in the case law is the degree of the connection between the relevant transfer and the contract changes which will render such amendments invalid.

6.12 There is an argument that contract changes should only be invalid if the transfer is the only or sole reason for them and that accordingly post-transfer changes for which there are other reasons (which may be nonetheless to a greater or lesser extent transfer related) should be permitted. *Daddy's Dance Hall* concerned changes at the point of (rather than after) transfer and which therefore fell foul of the prohibition of transfer-related changes. A contract change at the time of transfer for no other reason would be invalid as an attempt to contract out of the protection of the Directive. An example would be dismissals effected to enhance the saleability of the relevant operation. However, once the employee has transferred to the transferee with his or her employment rights intact, it can be argued that the purpose of the Directive has been achieved (in terms of the protection of employment and contractual rights on transfer). The relevant employees have not been prejudiced by the fact of transfer. A post-transfer change to the employees' contracts (even if it is transfer related because it would not have occurred had there not been a transfer) may not solely be by reason of the transfer if there are other reasons for it. The parties should (it is then argued) be free to agree subsequent contract changes, subject to the usual protections of

---

[7] [2004] IRLR 74, ECJ.

domestic law. This would be consonant with the (limited) function of the Directive which, as *Daddy's Dance Hall* confirms, is to ensure protection of the employee as against the transferee to the same extent as applied in respect of the transferor. It also accords with the important proviso that the transfer itself can never constitute the reason for a valid contract change.

However, the case law does not easily admit of such a straightforward (and, **6.13** from the perspective of the traditional common law approach, sensible) analysis to the effect that the transferee should remain free after transfer to agree contract changes with the relevant employees in the same way as would have been permissible pre-transfer. Nor does the jurisprudence provide clear guidance on the nature of the connection between the transfer and the contract change which will invalidate the amendment. While Lord Slynn in *Wilson* referred to contract changes being invalid if 'due to the transfer and no other reason' and the Employment Appeal Tribunal (EAT) in *Ralton v Havering College of Further Education*[8] described such invalidity arising where the transfer is the 'sole cause', the ECJ's decision in *Martin* does not evince such a strict test in determining whether an otherwise permissible contractual change is invalid by virtue of its connection with a relevant transfer.

In *Martin*, the Advocate General's view was that a contract change would be **6.14** valid if the reason or at least the main reason for the change was not the transfer. Various factors could be taken into account in this assessment including the proximity of the change to the transfer and whether the change was part of a process of harmonisation of employees' terms of employment. The ECJ ultimately held that offering less favourable terms was precluded by the Directive. Relatively little assistance was provided with regard to the causal link between the transfer and the potentially invalid term other than to indicate that a process of harmonisation of the terms of employment of the transferring employees with those of the transferee's existing employees would be connected with the transfer and therefore invalid. A material connection with the transfer appears to be sufficient to invalidate the contract changes (as opposed to the transfer being the sole reason for them) regardless of the fact that there might be other reasons for their introduction.

Mention should also be made in passing of *Boor v Ministre de la Fonction* **6.15** *Publique*.[9] On transfer from a private sector to public sector employer the relevant employee's salary was reduced in order to comply with applicable legislation but in apparent conflict with the *Daddy's Dance Hall* principle against transfer-related changes to employees' contracts, whether or not voluntary. Whilst it is a decision probably limited to its particular statutory context, the ECJ indicated that the Directive did not preclude the application of national legislation to reduce an employee's salary in such circumstances. The salary reduction was not invalidated by the Directive but the relevant employees were

---

[8] [2001] IRLR 738, EAT.   [9] [2005] IRLR 61, ECJ.

nonetheless left with the ability to terminate employment on grounds of a substantial change in working conditions to their detriment pursuant to Article 4.2.

3. Practical Issues

(a) *Retrospective Claims*

6.16 That transfer-related changes to employees' contracts of employment can be invalidated by TUPE even where implemented with the agreement of the employee in question is particularly problematic for transferees who wish to agree transfer-related variations. The fact that the employee's consent is effectively negated by the change being transfer related enables an employee to bring retrospective claims in respect of benefits which have ostensibly been freely and voluntarily bargained away. Where a contract change can be treated as invalid, employees can bring breach of contract claims in respect of the preceding six years. Claims can extend over a potentially longer period by way of a claim in respect of unlawful deductions from wages based on a series of deductions (such as payments of reduced salary).

(b) *Compromise Agreements and Contracting Out*

6.17 Some employers have sought to address the issue of the inability of employees to agree valid changes to their contracts of employment in relation to a relevant transfer by employees being terminated and re-engaged. As noted above, the new terms are valid but the initial dismissal can lead to an unfair dismissal claim. Statutory compromise agreements have on occasion been used to waive any consequent unfair dismissal and other statutory claims. That this approach is of doubtful efficacy has not specifically been addressed in the case law. However, the decision in *Solectron Scotland Limited v Roper*[10] suggests that it may well be.

6.18 In *Solectron*, compromise agreements entered into by employees on termination of their employment settling all claims, including a dispute about the validity of certain contractual changes made in relation to a TUPE transfer were valid, notwithstanding the contracting out provisions of the transfer legislation. What the employees were doing by entering into the compromise agreements in question was to compromise disputes with regard to their entitlements on the termination of their employment. The employer was not seeking to vary the employees' contracts as the employees were being made redundant.

6.19 As there was no change in terms and conditions for the future, because the relevant contracts came to an end, the compromise agreements did not arise solely or even mainly by reason of the transfer. Accordingly, the prohibition of transfer-related changes established by *Daddy's Dance Hall* and the related cases was not breached. The implication of this decision is that compromise agreements entered into as part of an arrangement implementing changes to

---

[10] [2004] IRLR 4, EAT.

employees' terms as a result of or in connection with a relevant transfer may fall foul of the prohibition on transfer-related changes and therefore be ineffective.

More specifically, in relation at least to transfer-related changes agreed at the **6.20** point of transfer, arrangements of this sort would also potentially fall foul of the prohibition of contracting out from the effect of TUPE provided by regulation 18.[11]

(c) *Continuity of Employment*

Even if the use of a compromise agreement to waive unfair dismissal claims in **6.21** connection with a dismissal and re-engagement on new terms were valid, it would not be effective to break continuity of employment for the purposes of statutory employment rights.[12] Continuity for these purposes may well be preserved on the basis of ERA 1996, s 218(2) where the cessation of employment and re-engagement arise at the point of transfer. Even where the dismissal precedes and the re-engagement occurs subsequent to a TUPE transfer, continuity may be preserved, especially in the light of the presumption of continuity established by ERA 1996, s 210(5), on the basis of there not being a week in which the employee's relations with his employer were not governed by a contract of employment[13] or of there being effectively an agreed cessation of work.[14]

(d) *Restrictive Covenants*

The consequences of the rule invalidating transfer-related contract changes can **6.22** be significant and can go wider than the financial issues described above. Not only can employees who agree to salary reductions subsequently bring proceedings to recover the amounts they had agreed to forgo; other terms agreed in connection with a relevant transfer as part of the process of the transferring employees joining the transferee can be ignored. An example is *Credit Suisse First Boston (Europe) Limited v Lister*.[15] The employee in question had received significant financial benefits under retention arrangements put in place in connection with a transfer which also imposed new restrictive covenants upon him. He was found not to be bound by those new restrictive covenants as their introduction was related to the relevant transfer.

(e) *Distancing the Change from the Transfer*

Regardless of the jurisprudential difficulties described above, establishing that **6.23** a change to the terms of employment of a transferring employment is not

---

[11] See Chap 12.

[12] See Chap 4, para 4.55 and Chap 5, para 5.40 for discussion of *Senior Heat Treatment v Bell* [1997] IRLR 614, EAT which related to the effect on continuity of employment for statutory purposes of the making of redundancy payments when the employees' employment transferred to the transferee for the purposes of TUPE.

[13] ERA 1996, s 212(1).   [14] ERA 1996 s 212(3).

[15] [1998] IRLR 700, CA; see also *Credit Suisse First Boston (Europe) Limited v Padiachy* [1989] IRLR 315, CA.

transfer related may often be difficult in the absence of clear evidence that the change would have been introduced regardless of whether the employer at the relevant time was the transferor or transferee or that the change is prompted by separate economic or other developments. A decision demonstrating that a proposed contractual variation (and related dismissal) could be transfer-related some considerable time after the transfer in question is *Taylor v Connex South Eastern Limited*.[16] As the Department of Trade and Industry (DTI) Guidance put it:[17]

[t]here is likely to come a time when the link with the transfer can be treated as no longer effective. However, this must be assessed in the light of all the circumstances of the individual case, and will vary from case to case. There is no 'rule of thumb' used by the courts or specified in the Regulations to define a period of time after which it is safe to assume that the transfer did not impact directly or indirectly on the employer's actions.

B. CHANGES PERMITTED BY TUPE 2006

1. Reform

6.24 In the 2001 Consultation, the Government made clear[18] that it believed that the approach of the ECJ in *Daddy's Dance Hall* was in line with the employment protection aims of the Directive and the principle that employees cannot contract out of the rights afforded to them.[19] In the light, however, of the uncertainty in the domestic case law as to the circumstances in which a change in terms and conditions can validly be made, the Government proposed to 'improve the operation of the regulations by making clear that they do not preclude transfer-related changes to terms and conditions that are made for an ETO reason—that is, an economic, technical or organisational reason entailing changes in the workforce'.[20] Accordingly, the validity of such changes would then depend only on the normal contractual principles applying in circumstances other than a transfer of an undertaking.

6.25 Regulations 4(4) and 4(5) implement the Government's decision to update and clarify the effect of TUPE in this context and to seek to establish some flexibility in relation to transfer-related changes to terms and conditions of employment. Despite reference in the 2005 Consultation[21] to the possibility of valid contractual variations being agreed between the parties or their representatives, contract changes pursuant to regulations 4(4) and 4(5) can only be validly agreed by the employees themselves and not by a trade union or elected employee representatives on their behalf.[22]

---

[16] EAT/1243/99. See Chap 7, para 7.24 for detailed discussion.   [17] At p 18.
[18] Para 78.   [19] TUPE 1981, regulation 12 (now, as redrafted, regulation 18).
[20] Para 83.   [21] Para 44.
[22] In contrast to the permitted variations introduced in the insolvency context by regulation 9 which can only be agreed by recognised trade unions or elected employee representatives.

2. Categories of Variation

Three categories of contractual variation are established by TUPE 2006, the **6.26** key element of the application of which is the 'sole or principal reason' for the relevant change:

- variations for which the sole or principal reason is 'the transfer itself'[23] or 'a reason connected with the transfer that is not an economic, technical or organisational reason entailing changes in the workforce'.[24] Such variations are void and ineffective regardless of the employee's consent. This provision reflects the principle established in *Daddy's Dance Hall*;

- variations for which the sole or principal reason is unconnected with the transfer.[25] These are valid, since *Daddy's Dance Hall* does not apply to them, subject to the normal rules of contractual variation. To adopt the example given in the DTI Guidance,[26] '[a] reason unconnected with a transfer could include the sudden loss of an expected order by a manufacturing company or a general upturn in demand for a particular service or a change in a key exchange rate';

- variations for which the sole or principal reason is 'a reason connected with the transfer that is an economic, technical or organisational reason entailing changes in the workforce'.[27] It is this third category of variation which is intended to increase employers' ability to make valid transfer-related contract changes.

The DTI Guidance[28] addressed the issue of the difference between an action that **6.27** is by reason of the transfer itself and an action which is for a reason which 'is connected with' the transfer and indicated that:

[w]here an employer changes terms and conditions simply because of the transfer and there are no extenuating circumstances linked to the reason for that decision, then such a change is prompted by reason of the transfer itself. However, where the reason for the change is prompted by a knock-on effect of the transfer—say, the need to re-qualify staff to use the different machinery used by the transferee—then the reason is 'connected to the transfer'.

Regulation 4(5) provides that employees are not prevented from agreeing **6.28** variations falling within the latter two categories. This preserves the need for variations to be valid under the applicable contractual principles.

3. Compatibility with EU Law

It was acknowledged in the 2005 Consultation[29] that the Acquired Rights **6.29** Directive (ARD) 2001 contains no specific provision allowing for variations to

---

[23] Regulation 4(4)(a).   [24] Regulation 4(4)(b).   [25] Regulation 4(5)(b).
[26] At p 17.   [27] Regulation 4(5)(a).   [28] At p 16.   [29] Para 45.

employees' terms and conditions of employment to be potentially effective where the sole or principal reason for them is a transfer-related ETOR (an economic, technical or organisational reason entailing changes in the work-force). Nonetheless in terms of compatibility with EU law, the Government based its argument that these new provisions are legitimate on Article 4.1, which permits dismissals on the basis of an ETOR. The Government's view was that it was illogical for ARD 2001 to permit employers to dismiss employees on the basis of an ETOR but for them not to be able (perhaps as an alternative to dismissal) to agree changes to terms and conditions for the very same category of reason. Otherwise, there would be what was described as a 'perverse incentive' for employers to dismiss employees and then offer to re-engage them (with potential loss of continuity) or to recruit new staff on different terms and conditions. This would be contrary to the employment protection aims of the legislation and was considered not to have been the intention of the Directive.

6.30   In the light of the *Daddy's Dance Hall* principle that the employee cannot agree to a waiver of his or her rights where the change is transfer related, the compatibility with the Directive of this ability to agree contract changes occasioned by an ETOR is questionable, despite the undoubted commercial sense and logic behind the Government's analysis from an employer's perspective and the points made about the internal consistency of the legislation. The possibility therefore remains of employees retrospectively challenging changes to which they have agreed pursuant to regulations 4(4) and 4(5) by reference to *Daddy's Dance Hall*. Their argument would be that TUPE 2006 is ultra vires the Directive because it seeks to permit what *Daddy's Dance Hall* prohibits by legitimising transfer-related contract changes.

6.31   A different view can be taken if one accepts the more limited interpretation of the Directive and *Daddy's Dance Hall* described above (which requires preservation of terms on transfer but which permits subsequent consensual agreement). Expressly rendering void not just contract changes which are solely by reason of a relevant transfer but also those which are transfer related and not by reason of an ETOR, regulation 4(4) provides more extensive protection to employees than this interpretation would require.

4. The ETOR Problem

6.32   Quite apart from their legitimacy in terms of compatibility with the Directive, regulations 4(4) and 4(5) present significant interpretational problems. The qualitative connection (or otherwise) between the reason for the contract variation and the relevant transfer is crucial. If there is no connection between the contract change and the relevant transfer then the change is not invalid.[30] A contract change is invalid if the sole or principal reason for the variation is the

---

[30] Regulation 4(5)(b).

transfer itself.[31] If the contract change is transfer related but the reason for it is not an ETOR, the amendment remains invalid.[32] If there is an ETOR justifying the change, then it will not be invalid.[33] The reason for the contract change in question and the nature of that reason are therefore central to whether it can validly be agreed.

Accordingly, if an employer wishes to make changes to an employee's terms and conditions of employment and this is prompted by or connected causally with the transfer, then the employer needs to jump two hurdles. The employer needs to demonstrate that the amendment is valid in general contractual terms. Also, it also needs to demonstrate that the reason for the change is an ETOR. **6.33**

Establishing that the reason for proposed contract amendments is an ETOR may be a significant challenge for an employer which seeks to implement what, absent a relevant transfer, would otherwise be valid changes to terms and conditions of employment. It is easy to conceive of situations where economic, technical or organisational reasons may exist for changes to employees' contracts of employment. For example, changes may need to be made to salary, overtime, or commission levels and other working practices to reflect commercial challenges facing the business in question. Technical changes may require amendments to terms of contract as to working methods. Relocation, integration, and restructuring can provide organisational reasons for changes. **6.34**

An ETOR for these purposes, however, does not validate a contract change which is connected with or related to the transfer unless it entails changes in the workforce. This requirement of a change to the workforce is a central component of the definition of an ETOR.[34] *Berriman v Delabole Slate Limited*[35] makes clear that, for the purposes of TUPE, an economic, technical or organisational reason must also entail a change in the workforce. In that case, no change occurred to the workforce as there were no dismissals and no reduction of the number of staff. There was simply a change to the employees' terms and conditions. It was considered that the concept of a change in the workforce required either a change in the numbers involved or, possibly, a change in their job functions which did not result in any overall reduction in numbers. This principle was subsequently followed in cases such as *Crawford v Swinton Insurance Brokers Ltd*,[36] where there was a significant change to the employee's job function which constituted an ETOR. **6.35**

Justifying changes to the contracts of employment of transferring employees by reference to changes to the workforce (construed as it is by reference to changes in workforce numbers or functions) may therefore be challenging. A transferee may need to reduce salaries or benefits and to reduce headcount in order to make viable an undertaking which it is contemplating acquiring. Subject to appropriate implementation, there will be in such circumstances an **6.36**

---

[31] Regulation 4(4)(a).   [32] Regulation 4(4)(b).   [33] Regulation 4(5)(a).
[34] Also discussed at Chap 7, para 7.38.   [35] [1985] IRLR 305, CA.
[36] [1990] IRLR 42, EAT.

ETOR which can validate the contract changes as well as provide a defence to unfair dismissal claims. But what if the contract changes which are agreed (as they may often be intended to) enable the employer to avoid entirely the very dismissals and/or changes to the workforce which regulations 4(4) and 4(5) require in order to render permissible the changes proposed to the contracts of those employees who remain? The changes then appear to be impermissible despite the consequences for the workforce overall being less severe.

6.37   It therefore appears that the provisions of regulations 4(4) and 4(5) introduced by TUPE 2006, which were presented as increasing the ability of employers to make changes to employees' terms and conditions of employment in connection with a transfer, are potentially severely limited in their practical value. Cost-saving measures which do not accompany or entail changes in job numbers or functions will not validate transfer-related changes, however justified they might be in economic, technical, or organisational terms, because the definition of an ETOR will not be satisfied—there is no associated change in the workforce. Only if the changes are associated with changes in workforce numbers or functions will the changes be valid and effective in accordance with regulations 4(4) and 4(5).

6.38   Whilst superficially attractive, the ETOR requirement renders the new provisions of dubious value and reliability. Employers may lack confidence in utilising regulations 4(4) and 4(5) in the light of the analytical and other issues which arise from the reliance of TUPE 2006 in this regard on the ETOR concept. The DTI Guidance asked the question of whether this freedom to vary contracts permits the transferee employer to harmonise the terms and conditions of the transferred workers to those of the equivalent grades and types of employees which it already employs and provided precisely the answer which employers would wish not to hear:

No. According to the way the courts have interpreted the Acquired Rights Directive, the desire to achieve 'harmonisation' is by reason of the transfer itself. It cannot therefore constitute 'an ETO reason connected with a transfer entailing changes in the workforce'.[37]

6.39   A framework which permitted contract changes effected post-transfer by reason of an economic, technical or organisational reason (ie omitting the requirement of a change in the workforce) would have been more straightforward. It would also, arguably still have been consistent with the Directive on the basis of the narrower interpretation of the scope of the *Daddy's Dance Hall* principle described above. Such a formulation would, however, have been even more questionable in EU law terms than the solution regulations 4(4) and 4(5) seek to provide.

6.40   The Government made its position clear in the Consultation Response.[38] It saw great merit in permitting agreement to vary terms to achieve greater harmonisation as long as the employees were left no worse off overall. It recognised

---

[37] At p 17.   [38] Paras 3.4–3.7.

the damaging cost and human resources consequences of groups of employees being on different sets of terms and conditions. With regret the Government effectively concluded that it could go no further than regulations 4(4) and 4(5) whilst (in its view) ensuring compatibility with the Directive. Only after amendment of the Directive, which the Government supports and will pursue, would any greater ability to harmonise terms be permissible.

5. Pension Changes

Changes to occupational pension scheme arrangements fall outside the scope of **6.41** the issues discussed in this chapter both with regard to the invalidity in principle of transfer-related changes and the limited ability introduced by TUPE 2006 to make valid transfer-related amendments to the terms and conditions of employment of transferring employees. This is a consequence of regulation 10 which excludes occupational pension scheme benefits from the entitlements preserved on a relevant transfer. Transferring employees are entitled to insist on the levels of pension provision required by the combined effect of the Pensions Act (PA) 2004 and the Transfer of Employment (Pension Protection) Regulations (PPR) 2005 as against the transferee but only if they enjoyed or were (actually or contingently) eligible to participate in an occupational pension scheme operated by the transferor.

Since occupational pension scheme entitlements (as strictly construed by the **6.42** case law) do not survive a relevant transfer, a transferee's changes to pre-transfer pension arrangements do not constitute changes to employees' contracts which require employee consent or fall within the scope of regulation 4. This is the case even if compliance with the pension protection regime established by PA 2004 and PPR 2005 involves the introduction of a materially inferior level of pension provision. The transferee therefore has, subject to PA 2004 and PPR 2005, considerable scope to amend occupational pension provision without employees' consent and without concern about those pension changes subsequently being found to be invalid, provided that the relevant pension arrangements are not preserved by TUPE because they fall outside the scope of the pensions exclusion.

The pensions exclusion extends only to the limited category of old age, **6.43** invalidity, and survivors' benefits falling within its scope. Other benefits provided under occupational pension schemes (such as, potentially, early retirement and redundancy entitlements), as well as pension arrangements which do not fall within the scope of the pensions exclusion (such as contributions to employees' personal pension arrangements), cannot be varied with the impunity which, subject to PA 2004 and PPR 2005, regulation 10 affords to transferees. Changes to such pension benefits as do transfer to the transferee under regulation 4 because they do not fall within the scope of regulation 10 will (outside the scope of the specific insolvency provisions of TUPE) fall to be covered by the regime established by regulations 4(4) and 4(5) and therefore, if transfer related, will need to be justified by an ETOR if they are to be valid and effective.

6.44   In this context, it is also worth noting that PA 2004, s 258(b) permits transfer-related changes to the pension benefits required to be provided by PA 2004 and PPR 2005. Such changes can validly be agreed post-transfer subject to the normal contractual rules. No further requirements need to be satisfied.

7

TRANSFER-RELATED DISMISSALS

A. Introduction	7.01
B. Automatic Unfair Dismissal	7.12
C. Connection with the Transfer	7.22
D. Economic, Technical or Organisational Reasons Entailing Changes in the Workforce	7.30
E. Liability and Fairness Generally	7.43

A. INTRODUCTION

A crucial element of the protection which the Directive and the Transfer of 7.01 Undertakings (Protection of Employment) Regulations (TUPE) 2006 provide for employees affected by an event or transaction falling within their scope is the remedy available if the transferee fails to honour its obligation to continue the employment of the relevant employees or if either the transferor or the transferee effects dismissals which are connected with the transfer. The remedy in the domestic law of the United Kingdom (in addition to any wrongful dismissal damages available) is an unfair dismissal claim.[1]

Article 4.1 provides that 'the transfer of an undertaking, business or part of 7.02 the undertaking or business shall not in itself constitute grounds for dismissal by the transferor or the transferee. This provision shall not stand in the way of dismissals that may take place for economic, technical or organisational reasons entailing changes in the workforce'.

Regulation 7(1) implements this principle, establishing the protection provided to employees dismissed in connection with a relevant transfer by deeming an offending dismissal automatically unfair for the purposes of the Employment

---

[1] That an injunction cannot be sought to restrain dismissals alleged to be transfer related was confirmed in *Betts v Brintel Helicopters Ltd and another* [1997] IRLR 361, HC. Detailed discussion of the unfair dismissal regime falls outside the scope of this work.

Rights Act 1996 (ERA 1996), Part X.[2] TUPE does not itself provide the remedy for an impermissible transfer-related dismissal—it creates a specific category of automatically unfair dismissal for the purposes of the domestic unfair dismissal jurisdiction.

7.04 A crucial element of the operation of the protection of employees against unjustifiable transfer-related dismissals is the concept of an 'economic, technical or organisational reason entailing a change in the workforce' (ETOR). Where an ETOR exists in respect of a dismissal which is nonetheless transfer related, the dismissal is not automatically unfair but is tested for its fairness in the normal way under ERA 1996. The concept of an ETOR, which applies only where there are legitimate reasons for a dismissal based upon the running of the relevant business, therefore provides the gateway for the avoidance of the automatic unfairness of an otherwise transfer-related dismissal.

7.05 That a transfer-related dismissal is in principle automatically unfair save where an ETOR justifies the dismissal was always the position under TUPE 1981. However, in an attempt to clarify the operation of TUPE in this context, regulation 7 establishes four different categories of dismissal:

- dismissals for which the sole or principal reason for the dismissal is the transfer itself.[3] An example would be dismissal of employees to facilitate sale of the business in which they work;

- dismissals for which the sole or principal reason is a reason connected with the transfer that is not an ETOR.[4] An example would be dismissals resulting from a transfer-related contract harmonisation exercise not entailing a change in the workforce (and therefore not fulfilling the requirements of an ETOR);

- dismissals for which the sole or principal reason is not the transfer itself but is a reason connected with the transfer that is an ETOR of either the transferor or transferee before the transfer.[5] An example would be dismissals by reason of a genuine redundancy situation arising from the acquisition of a business and a consequent rationalisation conducted by the transferee;

- dismissals for which the sole or principal reason is unconnected with the transfer.[6] An example would be dismissals consequent upon a relocation which would have been necessary regardless of the change in ownership of the business.

---

[2] '. . . that employee shall be treated for the purposes of Part X of the 1996 Act (unfair dismissal) as unfairly dismissed . . .' This formulation incorporates by reference the eligibility requirement of one year's service under ERA 1996. This limitation on the eligibility of employees to claim the protection against transfer-related dismissal established by TUPE is permissible as a result of Article 4(1) which permits Member States to provide that the protection against dismissal provided by that Article 'shall not apply to certain specific categories of employees who are not covered by the laws and practice of the Member States in respect of protection against dismissal'.

[3] Regulation 7(1)(a).   [4] Regulation 7(1)(b).   [5] Regulation 7(2).

[6] This is an implicit category not expressly recorded by TUPE 2006.

This categorisation in part seeks to address a concern which had arisen in relation to TUPE 1981. TUPE 1981, regulation 8(1) deemed transfer-related dismissals automatically unfair.[7] TUPE 1981, regulation 8(2) then proceeded to disapply TUPE 1981, regulation 8(1) and to apply the usual test of unfair dismissal where there was an ETOR justifying the dismissal.[8] **7.06**

Some decisions had indicated that this structure meant that, once a dismissal was found to be transfer related, the Employment Tribunal (ET) could not then consider whether an ETOR excepted the dismissal from automatic unfairness.[9] This analysis was generally considered to be unsound but regulation 7 makes the position clear. **7.07**

The categorisation of dismissals adopted in regulation 7 is based on the Government's view of the 'correct interpretation of the Directive's requirements in this regard'[10] and 'mirrors the approach taken in draft Regulation 4 in relation to changes to terms and conditions'.[11] **7.08**

Other than with regard to this new structure and the change made by regulation 7(3)(b) with regard to redundancy payments,[12] the remainder of regulation 7 was considered to 'essentially mirror provisions of the existing Regulation 8 [of TUPE 1981], with some minor drafting changes, and . . . not [to] call for detailed comment'.[13] **7.09**

To summarise, therefore: **7.10**

- dismissals for which the reason is a relevant transfer or which are connected with a relevant transfer but for which there is no ETOR justifying the dismissal are automatically unfair;

- if a dismissal is transfer related but is nonetheless for an ETOR, then the dismissal is potentially unfair subject to the normal test of unfair dismissal pursuant to ERA 1996;

- where a dismissal is not in any way connected with a transfer, then TUPE's prohibition on transfer-related dismissals does not engage and the fairness of dismissal will again be assessed under the normal principles of unfair

---

[7] 'Where either before or after a relevant transfer, any employee of the transferor or transferee is dismissed, that employee shall be treated . . . as unfairly dismissed if the transfer or a reason connected with it is the reason or principal reason for his dismissal.'

[8] 'Where an economic, technical or organisational reason entailing changes in the workforce of either the transferor or the transferee before or after a relevant transfer is the reason or principal reason for dismissing an employee:

(a) paragraph (1) above shall not apply to his dismissal; but

(b) without prejudice to the . . . test of fair dismissal . . . the dismissal shall . . . be regarded as having been for a substantial reason of a kind such as to justify the dismissal of an employee holding the position which that employee held.'

[9] See *Trafford v Sharpe and Fisher (Building Supplies) Ltd* [1994] IRLR 325, EAT; *Warner v Adnet* [1998] IRLR 394, CA; *Kerry Foods Ltd v Creber* [2000] IRLR 10, EAT. Also 2001 Consultation para 75.

[10] 2005 Consultation para 51.   [11] Ibid.   [12] See para 7.34 below.

[13] 2005 Consultation para 53.

dismissal. Even if contemporaneous with a relevant transfer, a dismissal based on misconduct, capability, or redundancy entirely unconnected with the transfer falls to be assessed under the usual unfair dismissal principles rather than regulation 7.

7.11 The law remains otherwise unchanged and a brief summary is now offered of the operative provisions of regulation 7 and the case law under TUPE 1981 which remains relevant.

B. AUTOMATIC UNFAIR DISMISSAL

1. The Principle of Automatic Unfairness

7.12 Regulation 7(1) provides as follows:

Where either before or after a relevant transfer, any employee of the transferor or trans-feree is dismissed, that employee shall be treated for the purposes of Part X of the 1996 [ERA] (unfair dismissal) as unfairly dismissed if the sole or principal reason for his dismissal is—

(a) the transfer itself; or

(b) a reason connected with the transfer that is not an economic, technical or organisa-tional reason entailing changes in the workforce.

7.13 Accordingly, those who are eligible to claim unfair dismissal[14] are in principle able to claim automatic unfair dismissal where they can show that a transfer-connected reason is the reason for dismissal and no ETOR applies to 'save' the dismissal from automatic unfairness. It is clear that regulation 7 extends to cases of constructive dismissal as well as express dismissal, not least by virtue of the fact that regulation 4(11) expressly records the right of an employee to terminate his or her employment on grounds of repudiatory breach of contract.

2. Protected Persons

7.14 It is important to note that regulation 7 applies to protect employees who are dismissed in connection with a relevant transfer regardless of whether their employment is such that it should transfer to the transferee under regulation 4. Non-transferring employees dismissed by reason of the transfer can still claim automatic unfair dismissal under regulation 7. The basis for this is regula-tion 7(4) which provides that regulation 7 applies 'irrespective of whether the employee in question is assigned to the organised grouping of resources or employees that is, or will be, transferred'.[15]

---

[14] By virtue of being employees and having completed the relevant qualifying period of (currently) one year's service.

[15] This provision replicates TUPE 1981, regulation 8(3) updated to reflect the twin definitions of a relevant transfer and the incorporation of assignment into the statutory language.

Accordingly, if employees of the transferor whose employment does not fall 7.15
to transfer to the transferee pursuant to TUPE (because they are not assigned to
the relevant undertaking or the organised grouping of employees which is the
subject of a service provision change) or if existing employees of the transferee
are dismissed for a reason connected with the transfer, then those employees will
be able to claim automatic unfair dismissal under regulation 7. The consequent
unfair dismissal claim lies against the actual employer (the transferor or transferee, as the case may be). An employee whose employment should not transfer
under TUPE to the transferee because he or she does not fall within the scope of
the legislation can hardly bring a claim against the transferee if dismissed by the
transferor even if that reason is connected with the transfer.[16]

TUPE 2006 also expressly recorded in the legislation the decision in *Litster v* 7.16
Forth Dry Dock & Engineering Co. Ltd,[17] which ensured that the protection of
the legislation extends beyond those whose employment actually transfers to the
transferee by virtue of regulation 4. Accordingly, TUPE's protections apply
to those who should have so transferred but were dismissed prior to the transfer (other than where an ETOR applies) such that they were not employed
immediately before the transfer so as to be within the scope of TUPE.

This protection is effected by regulation 4(3) which defines those employees 7.17
whose contracts and associated liabilities transfer to the transferee on a relevant
transfer as those employed immediately before the transfer or who would have
been so employed if they had not been unfairly dismissed in the circumstances
described in regulation 7(1).[18] As noted above, in the absence of an ETOR,
regulation 7(1) deems transfer-related dismissals automatically unfair whether
they are effected before or after a relevant transfer. The combination of these
two provisions ensures that an employee whose employment is dismissed by
reason of the transfer, even if that occurs some time before the transfer occurs,
can claim automatic unfair dismissal under regulation 7(1) and can pursue that
claim against the transferee pursuant to regulation 4(3) provided that no ETOR
applied to his or her detriment.

3. Exceptions

Two particular exceptions to regulation 7 are contained in regulations 7(5) 7.18
and 7(6).

First, regulation 7(5)[19] provides that the deeming of a dismissal automatically 7.19
unfair by regulation 7(1):

shall not apply in relation to the dismissal of any employee which was required by reason

---

[16] Regulation 4(3) only operates to transfer to the transferee liabilities in respect of those assigned
to the relevant undertaking or organised grouping of employees. See para 7.43 *et seq* below.
[17] [1989] IRLR 161, HL.   [18] See Chap 4, para 4.37 *et seq*.
[19] Which repeats verbatim TUPE 1981, regulation 8(4).

of the application of section 5 of the Aliens Restriction (Amendment) Act 1919 to his employment.[20]

7.20 Second, regulation 7(6) provides that regulation 7(1):

shall not apply in relation to a dismissal of an employee if the application of section 94 of the 1996 [Employment Rights] Act to the dismissal of the employee is excluded by or under any provision of the 1996 [Employment Rights] Act, the 1996 [Employment] Tribunals Act or [the Trade Union and Labour Relations (Consolidation) Act (TULRCA)] 1992.

7.21 Consequently, employees cannot rely on regulation 7(1) in support of a claim of automatically unfair dismissal if, for example, a claim for unfair dismissal cannot be made because:

- the employee has not satisfied the requirement of continuous service imposed by ERA 1996, s 94 (of currently one year);
- an unfair dismissal claim is barred by virtue of his or her having been engaged in unlawful industrial action as provided by TULRCA 1992, s 237 *et seq*;
- conciliation has taken place under the Employment Tribunals Act 1996, s 18.

C. CONNECTION WITH THE TRANSFER

1. Sole or Principal Reason

7.22 While regulation 7 adopts a different structure from that of TUPE 1981, regulation 8 (based around its categorisation of the different reasons there may be for dismissals), the essential test of connection between dismissal and transfer remains the same. A dismissal will be automatically unfair where the 'sole or principal' reason for the transfer is 'the transfer itself' or 'a reason connected with the transfer' that is not an ETOR.

7.23 Whether the transfer or a connected reason is the 'sole or principal' reason for the dismissal will be a matter of fact. However, where the reason for dismissal is not directly the transfer the employer does not necessarily escape from the protective scope of the legislation—regulation 7 will still apply where the reason is 'connected with the transfer'. As the Court of Appeal put it in *Abernethy v Mott*,[21] 'a reason for dismissal is a set of facts known to the employer or beliefs held by him which cause him to dismiss the employee'. Connecting that reason for dismissal with the transfer need not necessarily be based on the employer appreciating or considering that its knowledge of facts or beliefs which cause the decision to dismiss has anything to do with the transfer. Factual or causal connection can be established independently of the employer's view of whether

---

[20] Space precludes a detailed examination of this maritime-related provision.
[21] [1974] IRLR 213, CA (at para 13).

the transfer was anything to do with the dismissal. There is no time limit upon the period during which dismissal can be deemed to be transfer related and therefore automatically unfair. A dismissal may be transfer related even if occurring some considerable time after the transfer itself.

That the crucial issue is whether the sole or principal reason for an employee's **7.24** dismissal is 'connected with' (as distinct from caused by) the transfer is demonstrated, particularly notably in terms of timing, by *Taylor v Connex South Eastern Ltd*[22] in which the employee was dismissed two years after a relevant transfer. Nonetheless, the dismissal was held to be transfer related. The employee was dismissed for refusing to accept a new contract removing contractual holiday and redundancy entitlements which he had enjoyed with his previous employer. That the majority of staff accepted the changes was of no relevance—the reasonableness of either party's position is not relevant to the process of identifying the causative reason for the dismissal. In this case the ET legitimately found the reason for the dismissal to have been the relevant transfer, without which the contractual changes would not have been demanded. By contrast, in *Warner v Adnet*,[23] the reason for dismissals effected by receivers was the attempt to continue to trade rather than the transfer in question. Accordingly, the dismissals were not transfer related.

2. Uncertain Transactions

With regard to the issue of establishing the connection of a dismissal with the **7.25** transfer, problems can arise where a transfer is not finalised and indeed the identity of any potential transferee is not yet settled as at the point of dismissal. This can be a particularly acute problem in the context of receiverships and administrations, not least as employees will often seek to bring claims against a solvent transferee rather than an insolvent transferor.

Dismissals may be effected to make the relevant business more attractive **7.26** (which would point towards the dismissals being transfer related). They may, however, be required to preserve the viability of the business (pointing towards the dismissal being for an ETOR). The situation is further complicated if at the time of dismissal a specific potential acquirer is not in the course of negotiations with the eventual transferor or there are a number of parties interested in acquiring the business. The cases in this area demonstrate that establishing whether a dismissal is connected with a particular transfer and therefore falls within the scope of regulation 7(1) can be a complex matter, albeit one to be resolved by the ET as a question of fact.

In *Longden v Ferrari Limited*,[24] a redundancy exercise was conducted prior to **7.27** a relevant transfer. It was concluded that the dismissals in question were not connected with the transfer in circumstances where a potential acquirer of the

---

[22] EAT/1243/99.   [23] [1998] IRLR 394, CA.   [24] [1994] IRLR 157, EAT.

relevant business had simply indicated which employees it wished be retained. Despite the purchaser's indications of who should be dismissed (which, importantly, were not requested or required to be complied with), the financial problems of the relevant business were held to have led to the dismissals rather than a request by the transferee.

7.28 By way of contrast, in *Harrison Bowden v Bowden*,[25] connection of the dismissal in question with the transfer was established, rendering the dismissal automatically unfair, even though no specific transferee had been identified at the time of dismissal. The dismissals could be transfer related even in the absence of an identifiable specific transferee at the time of dismissal and claims made against the actual eventual transferee were then possible. The Employment Appeal Tribunal (EAT) considered that the reference in the legislation to the transfer in this context was to a transfer which takes place but that it was not required that the transferee has been identified at or before the moment of dismissal.

7.29 In *Ibex Trading Co. Ltd v Walton*,[26] employees were dismissed before any approach had been made to the administrator of the relevant business with regard to its disposal. As a transfer was a mere 'twinkle in the eye' at the point of dismissal, liability did not pass to the ultimate transferee. The approach adopted in *Harrison Bowden* was rejected—to fall within the scope of TUPE's protection, a dismissal needed to be connected with *the* transfer as distinct from *a possible* transfer.

D. ECONOMIC, TECHNICAL OR ORGANISATIONAL REASONS ENTAILING CHANGES IN THE WORKFORCE

1. Statutory Provisions

7.30 The automatic unfairness which flows from a dismissal being by reason of a relevant transfer or for a reason connected with it is avoided where the employer can establish an 'economic, technical or organisational reason entailing changes in the workforce' (ETOR) for the dismissal.

7.31 Regulation 7(2) is the operative provision in this regard and applies:

where the sole or principal reason for the dismissal is a reason connected with the transfer that is an economic, technical or organisational reason entailing changes in the workforce of either the transferor or the transferee before or after a relevant transfer.

7.32 Regulation 7(3) then sets out the effect of an ETOR (ie the avoidance of automatic unfairness of the dismissal and the application of the normal test of unfair dismissal):

Where paragraph [7](2) applies—

---

[25] [1994] ICR 186, EAT.   [26] [1994] IRLR 564, EAT.

(a) paragraph [7](1) shall not apply;
(b) without prejudice to the application of section 98(4) of the 1996 [Employment Rights] Act (test of fair dismissal), the dismissal shall, for the purposes of sections 98(1) and 135 of that Act (reason for dismissal), be regarded as having been for redundancy where section 98(2)(c) of that Act applies, or otherwise for a substantial reason of a kind such as to justify the dismissal of an employee holding the position which that employee held.

Accordingly, where an ETOR applies in relation to a particular transfer-related dismissal, there is a potentially fair reason for dismissal for the purposes of ERA 1996, s 98(4). The dismissal therefore falls to be tested for its fairness on the usual principles of unfair dismissal law.   **7.33**

2. Statutory Redundancy Payments

Regulation 7(3)(b) specifically confirms that a transfer-related dismissal which is for an ETOR can also, for statutory purposes, be by reason of redundancy, thereby entitling the dismissed employee (if otherwise eligible) to a statutory redundancy payment.[27] The predecessor provision in TUPE 1981, regulation 8(2)(b) deemed a transfer-related dismissal which was by reason of an ETOR to be for 'a substantial reason of a kind such as to justify the dismissal of an employee holding the position which that employee held' as distinct from being by reason of redundancy. This potentially led to a paradoxical position. The employer could avoid automatic unfairness of a transfer-related dismissal if it could demonstrate that the dismissal was by reason of redundancy (clearly an economic reason satisfying the concept of an ETOR). However, that employee would not be entitled to a statutory redundancy payment because the reason for the dismissal was deemed by TUPE 1981 to be for a reason other than redundancy. Since dismissal by reason of redundancy is a prerequisite of entitlement to the statutory redundancy payment, the drafting of TUPE 1981 potentially denied dismissed employees payments which would have been expected to be due given the nature of the reason for dismissal.   **7.34**

The inclusion in TUPE 2006 of the wording in regulation 7(3)(b), which effectively confirms that a transfer-related dismissal by reason of an ETOR can also be by reason of redundancy where applicable, was seen as correcting a 'longstanding error'.[28] Where the relevant statutory test is satisfied, an employee who is dismissed by reason of an ETOR which is redundancy can claim the statutory redundancy payment (as well as potentially unfair dismissal by reason of unfair selection for redundancy).   **7.35**

---

[27] See para 7.32 above.
[28] 2005 Consultation para 52 referring to *Canning v (1) Niaz (2) McLaughlin* [1983] IRLR 431, EAT.

3. What can be an ETOR?

7.36   The concept of an ETOR remains otherwise unchanged by TUPE 2006 and therefore the previous case law still needs to be considered. As the Department of Trade and Industry (DTI) Guidance put it:[29]

> there is no statutory definition of [the] term, but it is likely to include:
> (a) a reason relating to the profitability or market performance of the transferee's business (ie an economic reason);
> (b) a reason relating to the nature of the equipment or production processes which the transferee operates (ie a technical reason); or
> (c) a reason relating to the management or organisational structure of the transferee's business (ie an organisational reason).

7.37   *Wheeler v Patel*[30] established that the concept of an economic reason for dismissal can relate only to the conduct of the relevant business rather than wider issues such as the wish of the transferee to sell the business (which otherwise could be used to legitimate dismissals simply to facilitate sale). A technical reason might arise from changes in processes, technologies, etc. In terms of what can constitute an organisational reason entailing changes in the workforce, *Porter and Nanayakkara v Queens Medical Centre*[31] indicates that changes to job functions can fall within the concept of an ETOR. In this particular case, an entirely new organisation was introduced with regard to the provision of paediatric services.

7.38   It is not, however, sufficient just to show an economic, technical or organisational reason in order to avoid a transfer-related dismissal being automatically unfair. The economic, technical or organisational reason must also entail a change in the workforce. As *Berriman v Delabole State Limited*[32] demonstrated, where there is no change in the workforce but simply changes to terms and conditions of employment, then an ETOR is not established. In this particular case, a (constructive) dismissal relating to changes to rates of remuneration was not associated with any change to the workforce as the same number of employees remained employed. There was therefore no change to the workforce as required for there to be an ETOR and, accordingly, since the constructive dismissal was transfer related, it was automatically unfair.

7.39   For the ETOR defence to automatic unfairness of a transfer-related dismissal to apply, there must be a change in the numbers of the workforce or possibly a change in their job functions as a result of the economic, technical, or organisational justification for the dismissal. An example of where a change in job functions was, even in the absence of a change in workforce numbers, found to constitute an ETOR is *Crawford v Swinton Insurance Brokers Limited*.[33] In connection with a relevant transfer, the role of the employee in question was changed from being that of a secretary to being an insurance saleswoman. In

---

[29] At p 17.   [30] [1987] IRLR 211, EAT.   [31] [1993] IRLR 486, HC.
[32] [1985] IRLR 305, CA.   [33] [1990] IRLR 42, EAT.

relation to her constructive and unfair dismissal claims, the EAT acknowledged that a change in job function could satisfy the concept of an ETOR without there being a change in the identity or numbers of the workforce.

Whitehouse v Chas A Blatchford & Sons Ltd[34] provides an interesting illustration of what can constitute an ETOR and the need to establish the connection of the reason for dismissal with the running of the relevant operation for the ETOR 'defence' successfully to be relied upon. The transferee of a contract to supply prosthetic appliances to a hospital body had been informed during a re-tendering process (in which it was successful) that the award of the contract was conditional upon staffing costs being lowered by the number of technicians being reduced by one. The employee selected for redundancy complained that his dismissal was automatically unfair but the ET held that the dismissal was for an ETOR on the basis that a redundancy was inevitable. **7.40**

The Court of Appeal upheld the ET's decision. The argument was rejected that there was no difference between a dismissal designed to facilitate the sale of a business and a dismissal to secure a contract. While the relevant transfer was in this case the occasion for the reduction in staff numbers, it was held not to be the cause or reason for it. The requirement for fewer technicians was directly connected with the provision of the relevant services and therefore could constitute an ETOR. **7.41**

4. Whose Reason?

BSG Property Services v Tuck[35] makes the important point that the relevant reason for dismissal to be assessed for its potential unfairness (whether automatic or otherwise) is that of the employer who dismisses the employee or employees in question. The transferee inherited employees at the point of transfer who were serving out notice of termination of employment which had prior to transfer been served by the transferor on the erroneous assumption that TUPE did not apply in the particular circumstances and therefore the employees were redundant. The transferee was bound by the reason the transferor had for making redundancies. **7.42**

E. LIABILITY AND FAIRNESS GENERALLY

In respect of pre-transfer dismissals, the transferee only becomes liable for unfair dismissal liabilities pursuant to TUPE where the dismissal is automatically unfair under regulation 7(1). *Thompson v SCS Consulting Limited*[36] neatly encapsulates the key issues of the connection with the transfer of the dismissal, **7.43**

---

[34] [1999] IRLR 492, CA.   [35] [1996] IRLR 134, EAT.   [36] [2001] IRLR 801, EAT.

whether there is an ETOR and with whom the liability for termination costs rests. Mr Thompson was dismissed some 11 hours before a transfer agreed by receivers. His dismissal, at the behest of the transferee, was held to be for an ETOR, in that the dismissal was decided upon as part of a reduction to the size of the workforce of an overstaffed, inefficient, and insolvent business. This was held not to be a case of collusion between transferor and transferee to effect dismissal in order to secure a sale or enhance the sale price. Accordingly, even though it was transfer related, the dismissal was not automatically unfair and liability for the dismissal, even if unfair on normal principles, remained with the transferor. Under TUPE 2006, the position would be exactly the same.

7.44   By way of conclusion, the scheme of the legislation with regard to transfer-related dismissals can be summarised as follows:

- regulation 4 is the operative provision which transfers to the transferee the employment contracts (and associated liabilities) of employees falling within the scope of TUPE;

- regulation 4(3) extends regulation 4 not just to those employed as at the point of transfer but also those who would have been so employed had they 'not been unfairly dismissed in the circumstances described in regulation 7(1)';

- regulation 4(2)(a) transfers to the transferee all the liabilities of the transferor in respect of the employees covered by regulation 4(3);

- if an employee is transfer before the transfer and the dismissal is automatically unfair under regulation 7(1) (because the transfer or a connected reason is the sole or principal reason for the transfer and there is no ETOR), regulations 4(2)(a) and (b) render the transferee liable for that automatically unfair dismissal and any liabilities created by the transferor whilst it employed the employee;

- if the transferee does inherit liability under the combination of regulations 7(1), 4(2), and 4(3), it inherits not only unfair dismissal liability but also potentially other liabilities arising prior to transfer such as for unpaid wages and wrongful dismissal;

- if an employee is dismissed for a transfer-related reason but there is an ETOR for that dismissal satisfying regulation 7(2), then the dismissal is not automatically unfair for the purposes of regulation 7(1);

- where regulation 7(2) applies to a pre-transfer dismissal by virtue of there being an ETOR, then since regulation 4(2) only transfers to the transferee liabilities relating to dismissals which are automatically unfair for the purposes of regulation 7(1), liability for the dismissal, and any consequent unfairness, rests with the transferor;

- regulation 7(3)(a) provides that, where there is an ETOR, regulation 7(1) does not apply (so as to render the dismissal automatically unfair). However, pursuant to regulation 7(3)(b), this avoidance of automatic unfair dismissal is without prejudice to the ability of an eligible employee to claim unfair dismissal under the normal unfair dismissal principles by virtue either of being substantively or procedurally unfair. The dismissal, being for an ETOR, is deemed to be for a potentially fair reason of the purposes of ERA 1996, s 98;

- accordingly, provided that it can establish there to be an ETOR which avoids a transfer-related dismissal being automatically unfair, an employer will be deemed to have dismissed the employee for the potentially fair reason of either redundancy (if the statutory criteria in that regard are satisfied) or a substantial reason justifying dismissal;

- at that stage of the analysis, the ET adjudicating an unfair dismissal claim will have to have regard to the principles of whether the dismissal was substantively and procedurally fair in terms, for example, of whether it falls within the range of reasonable responses test and whether the employer complied with the statutory dismissal procedure requirements introduced by the Employment Act 2002 and the Employment Act 2002 (Dispute Resolution) Regulations 2004 (SI 2004/752).

8

PROVISION OF EMPLOYEE INFORMATION

A.	Introduction	8.01
B.	Employees	8.08
C.	Information	8.10
D.	Delivery and Updating	8.37
E.	Instalments	8.40
F.	Indirect Provision	8.41
G.	Timing	8.43
H.	Remedy	8.48
I.	Due Diligence Exercises	8.66
J.	Contracting Out	8.75

A. INTRODUCTION

1. The Directive

8.01 Article 3.2 introduced an option for Member States enabling them to introduce into their domestic legislation implementing the Directive provisions requiring the transferor to notify the transferee of all rights and obligations in relation to the employees whose employment is to transfer to the transferee on a transfer of undertaking insofar as those matters are (or ought to be) known to the transferor at the time of the transfer. This obligation operates independently from the other protections provided by the Directive so failure to comply does not affect the transfer of employees and associated rights otherwise effected by the legislation.

8.02 Specifically, Article 3.2 provides that:

Member States may adopt appropriate measures to ensure that the transferor notifies the transferee of all the rights and obligations which will be transferred to the transferee under this Article [3], so far as those rights are or ought to have been known to the transferor at the time of transfer. A failure by the transferor to notify the transferee of any such right or obligation shall not affect the transfer of that right or obligation and the rights of any employees against the transferee and/or transferor in respect of that right or obligation.

The Transfer of Undertakings (Protection of Employment) Regulations (TUPE) 2006 adopt this option but on a far more specific basis than the language of Article 4.2 permits and indeed by way of more precisely confined requirement than was initially proposed in the 2005 Consultation.

2. Domestic Implementation

8.03 In the 2001 Consultation, the Government confirmed its intention to take advantage of the option provided by Article 3.2. The benefit of an obligation on the transferor to provide what TUPE 2006 defines as 'employee liability information'[1] was considered to be that transferees would be entitled to full and accurate information about the liabilities which they would inherit as a result of a TUPE transfer and therefore would be 'well placed to meet them'.[2] This obligation would ensure transparency and avoid what was described as 'sharp practice'[3] such as where, just before transfer, terms and conditions of employment or the composition of the workforce assigned to the particular undertaking or activities are varied to the disadvantage of the transferee.

8.04 It has to be questioned whether this particular objective could ever be achieved by the obligation merely to provide information to the transferee about the transferring employees, however widely or narrowly defined the information to be disclosed might be. An obligation to provide information does not of itself prevent the mischiefs in question being committed. If complied with, it simply alerts the transferee to any such development. Amendment to the employment situation at a late stage simply triggers the obligation to update the original notification of employee liability information.

8.05 The obligation to notify the transferee of employee liability information was also perceived as promoting competitiveness. Smaller businesses with lesser bargaining power were considered to be less able than others to negotiate contractual safeguards with regard to employee information, which disadvantage this new notification obligation would remedy. Again, this is arguably optimistic. The notification obligation will no doubt make it more likely that transferees will be given by transferors the information which they need to operate the employment contracts of those employees whom they inherit as a consequence of a relevant transfer. However, it may well be unlikely to have an effect on the relative bargaining strengths of the parties in relation to the negotiation of warranties, indemnities, and contract pricing not least in light of the fact that

---

[1] Regulation 11(2)(a)–(e). [2] 2001 Consultation para 69; 2005 Consultation para 80.
[3] 2005 Consultation para 80.

the obligation is only required to be complied with 14 days prior to the transfer itself as opposed to the (potentially far earlier) time at which the contract binding the parties into the relevant contract is entered into.

Not least since the obligation imposed on the transferor to provide employee **8.06** liability information to the transferee was watered down considerably from the initial proposals set out in the 2005 Consultation, regulation 11 will arguably do little to remove the need for transferees to seek detailed due diligence, backed by appropriate warranties and indemnities, in the process of negotiation of a transfer. Its assistance to a transferee who commercially cannot secure such protections will be limited. Nonetheless, in the absence of comprehensive contractual protection, disclosure in accordance with regulation 11 will assist not just logistically in ensuring that the transferee knows what terms and conditions it needs to continue but also evidentially in relation to any dispute with employees concerning their contractual entitlements. It will not, however, necessarily give adequate commercial protection. While considerable substantive detail must be provided, the information required to be disclosed is not comprehensive enough for the purposes of many due diligence exercises.

Regulations 11 and 12 set out the requirements and applicable conditions of **8.07** the obligation to provide employee information in detail. It should be appreciated that these are obligations triggered by the fact of an impending relevant transfer. No request from the transferee is required for the obligation to provide employee liability information to arise.

B. EMPLOYEES

The obligation imposed upon the transferor to provide information to the trans- **8.08** feree relates only to those who are, for legal purposes, employees. Those who are, for the purposes of employment law, workers or those who are genuinely in business on their own account (by way of the provision, for example, of consultancy services) do not constitute employees and do not transfer to the transferee under TUPE 2006. Consistent with that, details about their terms of engagement, associated liabilities and the like do not fall within the scope of the obligation imposed on the transferor to provide employee liability information to the transferee. That said, particularly in view of the ongoing uncertainty concerning the issue of what constitutes employee status, not least in the context of agency workers, ensuring compliance with regulation 11 may on occasion be far from straightforward in terms of assessing in respect of which individuals information needs to be collated and disclosed to the transferee.

Regulation 11(1) provides that the employees about whom the relevant infor- **8.09** mation must be supplied by the transferor to the transferee are those who are 'assigned to the organised grouping of resources or employees that is the subject of a relevant transfer'. Care therefore needs to be taken to ensure that the proper (ie transferring) group of employees is identified for the purposes of complying with the obligation to provide the employee liability requisite information. The wording adopted in regulation 11(1) mirrors the wording used to identify those employees who transfer.[4] The assessment of which employees are the subject of the obligation to provide employee liability information needs to be conducted on the basis of the guiding principle of assignment (other than on a temporary basis) to the relevant undertaking or organised grouping of employees.[5]

C. INFORMATION

1. 2005 Consultation

8.10 In the draft of the new TUPE provided as part of the 2005 Consultation, draft regulation 11(1) defined the 'employee liability information' which the transferor is required to notify to the transferee as:

[i]nformation which is or ought to be known to the transferor as to the transferor's rights, powers, duties and liabilities under or in connection with any contract of employment of any employee who is assigned to the organised grouping of resources or employees that is the subject of a relevant transfer.

8.11 The information to be notified by the transferor to the transferee under the draft of regulation 11 was not limited to those liabilities which actually transfer to the transferee under regulation 4. Accordingly, the transferor would have been required to notify the transferee of all liabilities existing prior to transfer relating to the transferring employees, of which it knew or ought to have known, including those liabilities which the transferee would not inherit (such as criminal liabilities[6] and those occupational pension rights excluded from transfer[7]).

2. Prescribed Information

8.12 The formulation adopted in TUPE 2006 with regard to the identification of the requisite employee liability information was far more precise than that suggested in the initial draft. A variety of precise matters, which are not (save in the case of potential claims) calibrated by reference to the employer's actual or imputed knowledge, must be disclosed.

8.13 Regulation 11(2) prescribes the employee information to be disclosed by the transferor to the transferee which is to be disclosed in respect of the relevant employees as:

- the identity and age of the employee;[8]
- those particulars of employment that an employer is obliged to give to an employee pursuant to the Employment Rights Act 1996 (ERA 1996), s1;[9]

---

[4] Regulation 4(1).   [5] See Chap 4, para 4.14 *et seq*.   [6] Pursuant to regulation 4(6).
[7] Pursuant to regulation 10.   [8] Regulation 11(2)(a).   [9] Regulation 11(2)(b).

- information of any:
  - disciplinary procedure taken against the employee,[10]
  - grievance procedure taken by the employee,[11]
  within the previous two years in circumstances where the Employment Act 2002 (Dispute Resolution) Regulations 2004 (the 2004 Regulations)[12] apply;
- information of any court or tribunal case, claim, or action:
  - brought by an employee against the transferor, within the previous two years,[13]
  - that the transferor has reasonable grounds to believe that an employee may bring against the transferee, arising out of the employee's employment with the transferor;[14]
- information of any collective agreement which will have effect after the transfer, in its application in relation to the employee, pursuant to regulation 5(a).[15] Accordingly, only collective agreements which fall to transfer to the transferee in respect of the transferring employees pursuant to regulation 5 need to be disclosed in accordance with the requirements of regulation 11.

The formulation adopted in TUPE 2006 will result in the regulation 11 obligation operating somewhat differently to the requirements of the initial draft which based the obligation on rights, powers, duties, and liabilities owed to the transferring employees regardless of whether those rights, powers, duties, and liabilities transferred to the transferor. Regulation 11 as finally implemented does not cover criminal liabilities so these need not be disclosed by the transferor in respect of the transferring employees, even if foreseeable, because they do not entail claims against the transferor or transferee by the employee as required by regulation 11(2)(d). The fact that the items within the scope of the obligation to provide written particulars of employment must be disclosed means that occupational pension entitlements must be notified even though they do not, in principle, transfer to the transferee pursuant to regulation 10. Claims in respect of accrued pension rights presumably need not be disclosed if (as is likely save in cases of claims based on the *Beckmann/Martin* cases) the transferor can conclude that, by virtue of regulation 10, no claim in that regard can be brought against the transferee. **8.14**

3. Employment Particulars

Rather than define the contractual entitlements of transferring employees by reference to generic concepts of remuneration, benefits, entitlements, and liabilities, the contractual aspects of the transferor's relationship with the assigned employees must be disclosed to the transferee by reference to those written particulars of employment which an employer is obliged to provide to an **8.15**

---

[10] Regulation 11(2)(c)(i).   [11] Regulation 11(2)(c)(ii).   [12] SI 2004/752.
[13] Regulation 11(2)(d)(i).   [14] Regulation 11(2)(d)(ii).   [15] Regulation 11(2)(e).

employee pursuant to ERA 1996, s 1. That no such, or incomplete, particulars have been provided to the relevant employee by the transferor is presumably irrelevant as the reference to the ERA 1996, s 1 obligation is deployed to identify the types of information to be disclosed in order to comply with regulation 11.

8.16   If written particulars have been provided (in a contract or formal statement), the transferor will need to ensure that up-to-date and comprehensive details are provided. If no such particulars have been provided to the employees, they will need to be compiled for the purposes of complying with regulation 11.

8.17   The written particulars which are listed in ERA 1996, s 1 and are therefore the items which fall within the scope of the employee liability information to be disclosed pursuant to regulation 11(2) are:

- the names of the employer and employee;[16]
- the date when the employment began;[17]
- the date on which the employee's period of continuous employment began (taking into account any employment with a previous employer which counts towards that period);[18]
- the scale or rate of remuneration or the method of calculating remuneration;[19]
- the intervals at which remuneration is paid (that is, weekly, monthly, or other specified intervals);[20]
- any terms and conditions relating to hours of work (including any terms and conditions relating to normal working hours);[21]
- any terms and conditions relating to any of the following:
  - entitlement to holidays, including public holidays, and holiday pay (the particulars given being sufficient to enable the employee's entitlement, including any entitlement to accrued holiday pay on the termination of employment, to be precisely calculated),
  - incapacity for work due to sickness or injury, including any provision for sick pay,
  - pensions and pension schemes;[22]
- the length of notice which the employee is obliged to give and entitled to receive to terminate his contract of employment;[23]
- the title of the job which the employee is employed to do or a brief description of the work for which he is employed;[24]
- where the employment is not intended to be permanent, the period for which it is expected to continue or, if it is for a fixed term, the date when it is to end;[25]

---

[16] ERA 1996, s 1(3).   [17] Ibid.   [18] Ibid.   [19] ERA 1996, s 1(4)(a).
[20] ERA 1996, s 1(4)(b).   [21] ERA 1996, s 1(4)(c).   [22] ERA 1996, s 1(4)(d).
[23] ERA 1996, s 1(4)(e).   [24] ERA 1996, s 1(4)(f).   [25] ERA 1996, s 1(4)(g).

- either the place of work or, where the employee is required or permitted to work at various places, an indication of that and of the address of the employer;[26]
- any collective agreements which directly affect terms and conditions of the employment including, where the employer is not a party, the persons by whom they were made;[27]
- where the employee is required to work outside the United Kingdom for a period of more than one month:
  - the period for which he is to work outside the United Kingdom,
  - the currency in which remuneration is to be paid while he is working outside the United Kingdom,
  - any additional remuneration payable to him, and any benefits to be provided to or in respect of him, by reason of his being required to work outside the United Kingdom,
  - any terms and conditions relating to his return to the United Kingdom.[28]

4. Disciplinary and Grievance Procedures

The requirement to disclose information about disciplinary and grievance procedures conducted in relation to the transferring employees is confined to those matters to which the 2004 Regulations apply. Accordingly, informal warnings and grievances, as well as procedures which were not commenced with dismissal as a potential result, are not covered. No substantive guidance is given as to the detail of the information which is to be provided about disciplinary and grievance procedures which fall within the scope of the regulation 11 obligation. **8.18**

Whilst discussion of their detailed rules is outside the scope of this work, the 2004 Regulations apply (and consequently action within the relevant timeframe needs to be disclosed pursuant to regulation 11) where the employer 'contemplates dismissing or taking relevant disciplinary action against the employee'.[29] For these purposes, 'relevant disciplinary action' means 'action, short of dismissal, which the employer asserts to be based wholly or mainly on the employee's conduct or capability, other than suspension on full pay or the issuing of warnings (whether oral or written)'.[30] Accordingly, the disclosure which needs to be made pursuant to regulation 11 does not need to extend to suspensions or issues which could only ever lead to warning (ie dismissal was not a potential result of the procedure when commenced). **8.19**

In terms of grievances, the dispute resolution regulations apply 'in relation to any grievance about action by the employer that could form the basis of a **8.20**

---

[26] ERA 1996, s 1(4)(h).   [27] ERA 1996, s 1(4)(j).
[28] ERA 1996, s 1(4)(k) (subject to ERA 1996, s 1(5)).
[29] 2004 Regulations, regulation 3(1).   [30] 2004 Regulations, regulation 2(1).

complaint by an employee to an employment tribunal under [one of the relevant jurisdictions]'.[31]

5. Claims

8.21 The initial draft of regulation 11 made no express reference to potential as opposed to actual claims. Regulation 11(2)(d)(ii) does so although again no substantive guidance is given as to the detail of the information to be provided about claims falling within the scope of regulation 11.

8.22 It should not be problematic for a transferor to comply with the obligation to provide information about court or tribunal claims or actions brought against the transferor in the period of two years prior to the relevant transfer in respect of the transferring employees.[32] Presumably (but TUPE 2006 does not expressly address the point) if a transferring employee is not employed by the transferor but still falls to transfer to the transferee by virtue of TUPE in accordance with the applicable jurisprudence,[33] the obligation applies *mutatis mutandis*.

8.23 The second limb of the requirement to provide claims information—to provide information effectively about potential claims—is less straightforward.[34] What constitutes 'reasonable grounds' for belief of the likelihood of a claim being brought is a necessarily fact-sensitive and open textured concept. Also, regulation 11(2)(d)(ii) could have identified the disclosable claims as those which the transferring employees potentially have against the transferor and which the transferee would inherit under TUPE. It did not do so—while to be disclosable a claim or potential claim must arise from the employee's employment with the transferor, it must also be the case that the transferor reasonably believes that the claim may be brought against the transferee.

8.24 The formulation adopted in regulation 11(2)(d)(ii) with regard to potential claims can therefore be interpreted to cover not just claims which the transferee inherits as a result of the acts or omissions by the transferor in respect of the transferring employees' pre-transfer employment. Regulation 11(2)(d)(ii) potentially requires the transferor to inform the transferee of claims which the transferring employees might make against the transferee arising out of the transferee's pre-transfer conduct. If an employee is in a position, as a result of the transferee's actions, where he or she is able to exercise the right to terminate employment in response to changes to working conditions[35] or to claim constructive dismissal[36] and this possibility comes to the (reasonable) attention of the transferor, it arguably falls within the scope of regulation 11(2)(d)(iii), which is not limited to claims created by or lying only against the transferor. So construed, regulation 11 would require the transferor to inform the transferee of the

---

[31] 2004 Regulations, regulation 6(1). The relevant jurisdictions are set out in Schedules 3 and 4 of the 2004 Regulations.

[32] Regulation 11(2)(d)(i).   [33] See Chap 4.   [34] Regulation 11(2)(d)(ii).

[35] Regulation 4(9).   [36] Regulation 4(11).

claims to which it was potentially exposing itself. It is not clear that this was the intention behind the formulation adopted in regulation 11(2)(d)(iii). This analysis would only be incorrect if the reference to the relevant claim arising from the employee's employment with the transferor excludes the transferee's pre-transfer behaviour from consideration. It is to be hoped that this analysis is to be preferred.

The Department of Trade and Industry (DTI) Guidance[37] provided some **8.25** further guidance on the issue of assessing when a potential claim can fall within the scope of regulation 11(2)(d)(ii). In answer to the question of how the transferor can decide whether it is reasonable to believe that a legal action could occur, it was stated that:

[t]his is a matter of judgment and depends on the characteristics of each case. So, where an incident seems trifling—say, where an employee slipped at work but did not take any time off as a result—then there is little reason to suppose that a claim for personal injury damages would result. In contrast, if a fall at work led to hospitalisation over a long period or where a union representative raised the incident as a health and safety concern, then the transferor should inform the transferee accordingly.

6. Data Protection

It is expressly provided that the age and identity of every relevant employee must **8.26** be provided as part of the employee liability information which the transferor is required to deliver to the transferee.[38]

In order to avoid breach of the provisions of the Data Protection Act (DPA) **8.27** 1998 with regard to the processing of 'personal data', transferors had, prior to TUPE 2006, widely adopted the practice of only supplying anonymised information as part of due diligence processes. The DPA 1998 requires, if the processing of personal data such as employees' names is to be lawful, either consent of the data subject (in this context a transferring employee) or a legal obligation to effect the processing. Delivery of employees' names to a third party transferee clearly constitutes 'processing' for the purposes of DPA 1998 and therefore, prior to TUPE 2006, was only permissible with employee consent (as there would be no legal obligation to disclose personal data as part of pre-contract negotiations).

Since the requirement to provide the required employee liability information **8.28** is legally binding pursuant to regulation 11, there is no breach of the data protection legislation in providing personal and personalised details about transferring employees to the transferee in advance of their transfer from the transferor to the transferee provided that the information falls within the scope of regulation 11(2). DPA 1998, Schedule 2, paragraph 3 provides that processing of personal data (which transfer to a third party of employee names constitutes)

---

[37] At p 24.   [38] Regulation 11(2)(a).

is permitted where the processing is 'necessary for compliance with any legal obligation to which the data controller is subject, other than an obligation imposed by contract'.[39]

8.29 That regulation 11 imposes a legally binding obligation also ensures that disclosure to the transferee by the transferor of 'sensitive personal data'[40] about transferring employees is not in breach of DPA 1998, again provided that it falls within the scope of regulation 11(2). DPA 1998, Schedule 3 paragraph 2(1) provides that one of the conditions permitting the processing of sensitive personal data is that '[t]he processing is necessary for the purposes of exercising or performing any right or obligation which is conferred or imposed by law on the data controller in connection with employment'. Information relating, for example, to a potential employment claim the central facts of which related to an employee's sexual orientation appear able to be disclosed pursuant to regulation 11 (and would need to be so disclosed to ensure compliance) without any breach of the DPA 1998.

8.30 Nonetheless, careful consideration may still need to be given to whether disclosure of information containing personal data can be given without being anonymised during a pre-contract due diligence process. Only if information falls within the scope of regulation 11(2) will the DPA 1998 condition (for permissible data processing) of compliance with a legal obligation be satisfied. The supply of information wider than that specified in regulation 11(2) will still be covered by the relevant DPA restrictions.

8.31 The introduction of the obligation to notify the transferee of employee liability information and the express confirmation that it extends to employee identities serves as a useful reminder of the need in any event in pre-contract negotiations for appropriate confidentiality obligations to be agreed between potential parties to a relevant transfer.

8.32 The other protections prescribed by DPA 1998 (in terms of the data protection principles set out in its Schedule 1) will still need to be considered when complying with the obligation to provide employee liability information with regard to all 'personal' aspects of the information disclosed and not just

---

[39] In this context the transferor is the data controller and the legal obligation is that imposed by regulation 11(2).

[40] DPA 1998, s 2 defines sensitive personal data as 'personal data consisting of information as to:

(a) the racial or ethnic origin of the data subject,
(b) his political opinions,
(c) his religious beliefs or other beliefs of a similar nature,
(d) whether he is a member of a trade union (within the meaning of the Trade and Labour Relations (Consolidation) Act 1992),
(e) his physical or mental health or condition,
(f) his sexual life,
(g) the commission or alleged commission by him of any offence, or
(h) any proceedings for any offence committed or alleged to have been committed by him, the disposal of such proceedings or the sentence of any court in such proceedings.'

employee names. Examples of the applicable data protection principles which may be particularly relevant in this context are that:

- personal data shall be accurate and, where necessary, kept up to date;[41]

- appropriate technical and organisational measures shall be taken against unauthorised or unlawful processing of personal data and against accidental loss or destruction of, or damage to, personal data;[42]

- personal data shall not be transferred to a country or territory outside the European Economic Area unless that country or territory ensures an adequate level of protection for the rights and freedoms of data subjects in relation to the processing of personal data.[43]

After a relevant transfer the data protection concerns described above with regard **8.33** to the extent of permissible disclosure cease to apply. Since regulation 4(2)(a) transfers to the transferee 'all the transferor's rights, powers, duties and liabilities', it would seem that at that point the transferee can legitimately be entitled to information about those whom it now employs, subject of course to the ongoing protections generally provided by DPA 1998 in relation to personal data and sensitive personal data.

7. Former Employees

Regulation 11(4) provides that: **8.34**

[t]he duty to provide employee liability information . . . shall include a duty to provide employee liability information of any person who would have been employed by the transferor and assigned to the organised grouping of resources or employees that is the subject of a relevant transfer immediately before the transfer if he had not been dismissed in the circumstances described in regulation 7(1), including, where the transfer is effected by a series of two or more transactions, a person so employed and assigned or who would have been so employed and assigned immediately before any of those transactions.

Accordingly, if an employee is dismissed prior to the transfer in circumstances **8.35** where there is no economic, technical or organisational reason entailing changes in the workforce (ETOR) avoiding automatic unfair dismissal,[44] that employee falls within the scope of the obligation imposed upon the transferor to provide the prescribed employee liability information in accordance with regulation 11(2). Careful consideration of the nature of pre-transfer dismissals will be needed to ensure appropriate notification to the transferee in order to comply with regulation 11.

In any event in order to defend themselves against allegations of breach **8.36** of regulation 11, transferors will need to consider implementing proactive

---

[41] DPA 1998, Sch 1, principle 4.   [42] DPA 1998, Sch 1, principle 7.
[43] DPA 1998, Sch 1, principle 8.
[44] In which case, per regulation 4(3), liability for the dismissal does not transfer to the transferee.

due diligence processes to show they have sought to identify all employee liability information within the scope of the obligations imposed by regulation 11 and to seek specific information and confirmation from relevant managers and/or departments.

D. DELIVERY AND UPDATING

8.37 The transferor is obliged to notify the transferee of the requisite employee liability information either in writing[45] or 'by making it available to him in a readily accessible form'.[46] Presumably, whilst a written report may be required as to matters of which there is no documentary record, provision of copy documentation (such as contracts, handbooks, benefit scheme documentation, Employment Tribunal (ET) documentation etc) or access to an electronic data room will suffice where appropriate as part of the process of complying with regulation 11. As the DTI Guidance put it:[47]

> The information must be provided in writing or in other forms which are accessible to the transferee. So, it may be possible for the transferor to send the information as computer data files as long as the transferee can access that information, or provide access to the transferor's data storage. Likewise, in cases where a very small number of employees are transferring and small amounts of information may be involved, it might be acceptable to provide the information by telephone. However, it would be a good practice for the transferor to consult the transferee first to discuss the methods which he can use.

8.38 If there is 'any change in the employee liability information', then the transferor must notify the transferee in writing of the change.[48] The transferor therefore needs to ensure that its systems are such that, and that the management of the transfer process is conducted on the basis that, the employee liability information disclosed about employees, salary, and other remuneration, details of claims made and so on, is reviewed and updated on a regular basis in order to ensure at all times that up-to-date information has been provided.

8.39 This aspect of regulation 11 is particularly important in a detailed tendering process where bidders may have been provided with outline employee information at the outset in order to assist them with formulating their bids. It is not sufficient for the transferor to assume that it has discharged its obligations simply by providing what does constitute full disclosure as at the outset of a negotiation or contracting process but which subsequently becomes incomplete or inaccurate.

---

[45] Regulation 11(1)(a).   [46] Regulation 11(1)(b).   [47] At page 23.
[48] Regulation 11(5).

138

E. INSTALMENTS

The employee liability information required to be notified to the transferee may **8.40** be delivered 'in more than one instalment'.[49] The transferor will wish to keep a clear record of what information was provided when in order to be able to deal with any subsequent argument about the adequacy of compliance by the transferor with regulation 11. That said, it is clear that provision of employee liability information from a variety of sources (for example, through the due diligence process handled by lawyers for the commercial parties in the course of the negotiation of a transaction and the direct provision of information from human resources departments) may cumulatively satisfy the requirements of regulation 11. Careful coordination and management of the information provision process will nonetheless be needed to avoid confusion and dispute.

F. INDIRECT PROVISION

The requisite employee liability information can be provided 'indirectly, through **8.41** a third party'.[50] This delivery option was included to reflect the fact that, where contracts are reassigned or re-tendered, the ultimate client may well be responsible for passing employee liability information to bidders and the successful contractor and indeed may be the only party in direct contact with bidders and an incoming contractor during a tender process or contract reassignment.

Incumbent contractors will wish to ensure that any client wishing to be **8.42** responsible for providing information to bidders as part of a re-tendering process does indeed pass the information on in a timely fashion. On an outsourcing, therefore, whilst a client may wish to include in the relevant contract provisions requiring an initial contractor to provide employee liability information as and when required (and particularly in advance of re-tendering or termination), the contractor itself will want protection from the client with regard to timely provision of information to new contractors (as well as compliance by the client with the protections of DPA 1998). This is especially relevant if the re-tendering is, as can often be the case, a process in which the transferor is not involved, over which it has no control, and of whose precise timing (apart from the ultimate end of its contract with the client) it is ignorant. Incumbent contractors will wish to avoid the situation where, because they have no control over the re-tendering process, they have inadequate information as to when the obligation

---

[49] Regulation 11(7)(a).

[50] Regulation 11(7)(b). The 2001 Consultation had considered making it a requirement to provide the information through the client in a re-tendering situation (ie a service provision change involving the reassignment of a service contract) but this was not adopted since it was considered not always to be appropriate—see 2005 Consultation para 78 and 2001 Consultation para 72.

to provide employee liability information arises (and in respect of what transferee) and consequently inadvertently become exposed to a potentially significant penalty for breach of the requirements of regulation 11.

G. TIMING

8.43 The draft of regulation 11 produced as part of the 2005 Consultation required that the employee information required to be delivered by the transferor to the transferee should be provided in good time before the relevant transfer. Pursuant to regulation 11(6) the requirement actually implemented is to provide the relevant information 'not less than fourteen days before the relevant transfer'. If special circumstances render this not reasonably practicable the information should be disclosed as soon as reasonably practicable. Regulation 11(3) requires disclosure of the information 'as at a specified date not more than 14 days before the date on which the information is notified to the transferee'. If by that time it is out of date, the updating requirement operates.

8.44 A requirement of notification in any event no later than the 'completion' of the relevant transfer was contained in the draft regulation but was omitted from the final version of Regulation 11. Where special circumstances apply, notification can presumably therefore be provided after the transfer as long as this still constitutes disclosure as soon as reasonably practicable.

8.45 The DTI Guidance[51] addressed the issue of the circumstances where it may not be reasonably practicable to provide the information two weeks in advance of the transfer occurring and indicated that:

[t]hese would be various depending on circumstances. But, clearly, it would not be reasonably practicable to provide the information in time, if the transferor did not know the identity of the transferee until very late in the process, as might occur when service contracts are re-assigned from one contractor to another by a client, or, more generally, when the transfer takes place at very short notice.

8.46 The fact that the obligation is to provide the requisite information not less than 14 days before the transfer seriously undermines the value of the obligation to transferees. The delivery of the requisite information is not calibrated by reference to the entry by the commercial parties into a binding contract to effect the transaction which constitutes a TUPE transfer. If (as will very often be the case) the relevant contract giving rise to a transfer of an undertaking is agreed some time before the transfer takes place, the obligation to provide employee liability information, which only has to be complied with by 14 days prior to the actual transfer, will not assist a transferee in terms of ascertaining employment-related liabilities for the purposes of the commercial negotiation of contract terms.

8.47 It is assumed, although TUPE 2006 does not expressly address the point, that

---

[51] At p 24.

the obligation only applies when there is a likely or definite transferee. On this analysis provision of employee information to bidders in a tender process before a final decision is made on the tender would fall outside the scope of regulation 11 and therefore be subject to the data protection considerations described above.

H. REMEDY

1. 2005 Consultation

In terms of the remedy for breach of this information notification obligation, the Government did consider the possibility of the transferee having the ability to seek damages against the transferor from a civil court. The concern about such a remedy was the likely difficulty in many cases of demonstrating a quantifiable financial loss consequent upon a failure to provide the requisite information.[52] Information about employees may not always go to the price paid for a particular business or the value of a contract, either directly or at all. **8.48**

An alternative remedy which was considered[53] was to provide that, if an employee made a claim against the transferee in relation to a liability arising from rights or obligations which had not been notified as required: **8.49**

- the transferee could apply to the court or ET to join the transferor into the proceedings;
- the court or ET could apportion liability on a just and equitable basis having regard to the damage suffered by the employee and the relative responsibility of the parties, subject to a defence that the rights and obligations in question were not ones that the transferor knew or ought to have known about at the time of transfer. Article 3.1 would permit such joint and several liability.[54]

An example quoted of how this second option could have operated in practice was where liability for acts of sex discrimination was inherited by the transferee on transfer but had not been notified to the transferee pursuant to the obligation to supply employee liability information. Had the apportionment of liability approach been adopted, the ET would have been entitled to find that the transferor's level of contribution should be 100 per cent.[55] The disadvantage of this approach was considered to be the fact that the transferee would only have redress if a claim were brought against it by the relevant employee.[56] This would **8.50**

---

[52] 2005 Consultation para 64.   [53] Ibid para 65.

[54] Pursuant to Article 3.1, Member States may provide that, after the date of transfer, the transferor and the transferee shall be jointly and severally liable in respect of obligations which arose before the date of transfer of the contract of employment or an employment relationship existing on the date of transfer.

[55] 2001 Consultation para 66.   [56] Ibid para 67.

have detracted from any incentivising effect which the penalty might have had to encourage compliance with the obligation to provide employee liability information.

8.51 The initial draft of regulation 11 provided that the transferor would be liable to pay a penalty to the transferee for breach of the obligation to provide employee liability information imposed by regulation 11. As originally formulated in the 2005 Consultation, the penalty payable for breach of the obligation to provide employee information was to be 'such as the High Court considers just and equitable in all the circumstances, but may not exceed £75,000'. The claim would have been brought in the High Court rather than the ET.

8.52 Criteria to be taken into account in determining the penalty would have been:

- the extent of the failure to comply with regulation 11;
- the reason for the failure;
- the terms of any contract between the transferor and the transferee relating to the transfer under which the transferor may be liable to pay any sums to the transferee in respect of the failure to notify the transferee of employee liability information;
- the employment protection purposes of the regulations. No specific guidance was provided about what this reference to the employment protection purposes of the legislation would have entailed.

2. TUPE 2006

8.53 Ultimately the decision was to have the ET as the forum to determine disputes and for compensation to be loss based rather than a penalty.[57] The complaint must be presented:

- before the end of the period of three months beginning with the date of the relevant transfer;[58]
- within such further period as the tribunal considers reasonable in a case where it is satisfied that it was not reasonably practicable for the complaint to be presented before the end of that period of three months.[59]

8.54 Where an ET finds a complaint under paragraph (1) well founded, it:

- shall make a declaration to that effect;[60]
- may make an award of compensation to be paid by the transferor to the transferee.[61]

8.55 The amount of the compensation shall be:

---

[57] Regulation 12(1). Regulation 12(7), combined with Employment Tribunals Act 1996, s 18, renders the ET the forum for such complaints.
[58] Regulation 12(2)(a).   [59] Regulation 12(2)(b).   [60] Regulation 12(3)(a).
[61] Regulation 12(3)(b).

such as the tribunal considers just and equitable in all the circumstances, . . . having particular regard to—

(a) any loss sustained by the transferee which is attributable to the matters complained of; and

(b) the terms of any contract between the transferor and the transferee relating to the transfer under which the transferor may be liable to pay any sum to the transferee in respect of a failure to notify the transferee of employee liability information.[62]

3. Principles of Award

This very general power to award compensation based on loss has no statutory **8.56** maximum in contrast to the remedies for breach of the collective information and consultation regimes applying to relevant transfers[63] and redundancy exercises of the requisite scale which are both penal in nature.[64] As it will be adjudicating a loss-based provision, the ET will be called upon to make assessments of the consequences of failure to notify requisite information. This will be a new task for ETs to perform and entails a role materially different to the adjudication of the penalty regime suggested in the 2005 Consultation to be administered by the High Court. This was arguably more similar to the ET's historic jurisdictions than a structure which will entail detailed consideration of causation and loss. The concerns about a loss-based approach aired in the 2005 Consultation[65] do not appear to have deterred the Government.

Whilst loss may be straightforward to identify in relation, for example, to an **8.57** undisclosed discrimination claim which the transferee inherits, the fact that an award for breach of regulation 11 is determined by reference to what is just and equitable in all the circumstances gives ETs considerable flexibility in the awards which they may make. It appears possible that transferees will be able to mount compensation claims analogous to breach of warranty claims. The developing case law on this area will be important but transferees may well seek to base arguments for compensation on what they would have done, the value of what they would have acquired, and what they would have paid for the relevant business had accurate and comprehensive employee liability information been provided. Case law guidance will be needed as to when loss is 'attributable' to a breach of regulation 11, especially where breach occurs after contract execution, where it can be argued that commercial relations between the parties are unaffected.

The complexity of the adjudication which the ET conducts pursuant to regu- **8.58** lation 12 is only increased by regulation 12(4)(b). The terms of a commercial agreement between transferor and transferee will be relevant where that contract provides for the transferor to pay 'any sum' to the transferee 'in respect of a failure to notify the transferee of employee liability information'. Thus if warranty and indemnity provisions in a transfer agreement entail compensation

---

[62] Regulation 12(4)(a) and (b).   [63] Regulations 13–16.   [64] TULRCA 1992, s 188.
[65] See para 8.48 above.

for breach of their full disclosure obligations, they can be taken into account in assessing the loss by reference to which the just and equitable award of compensation for breach of regulation 11. Presumably, *de minimis* provisions can also be taken into account at this stage of the analysis as an integral part of the determination of any contractual compensation payable.

8.59   The relevance of compensation or damages payable by the transferor to the transferee pursuant to their commercial arrangements is defined by reference to the obligation to provide employee liability information. Construed strictly, compensation for breach of warranties relating to wider matters outside the scope of the concept of employee liability information (as defined by regulation 11(2)) is irrelevant to the ET's consideration of the level of award to be made (unless considered to be just and equitable in the circumstances).

4. Minimum Award

8.60   The assessment of the potentially unlimited compensation capable of being awarded by the ET in respect of breach of the regulation 11 obligation is subject to important further provisions.

8.61   First, regulation 11(5) provides that, regardless of the issues of loss described above, the minimum award shall be £500 per employee in respect of whom the transferor has failed to comply with its obligations. This minimum award need not, however, be made if the ET considers it 'just and equitable in all the circumstances, to award a lesser sum'.

8.62   Care will need to be taken to consider the nature of the transferor's breach in determining the number of employees in respect of whom such a minimum award can or should be made by the ET. Unlike regulation 15, which bases compensation on an award of up to 13 weeks' pay per affected employee (as that term is widely defined in regulation 13(1)), regulation 12(5) limits the application of the minimum award to those employees in respect of whom the transferor has breached its regulation 11 obligations. By way of example, strictly construing this provision, if the transferor complied with all its regulation 11 obligations save for the provision to the transferee of the relevant employment particulars of one employee, the regulation 11 breach would only relate to one employee and presumably the £500 minimum award could only be made in respect of that one employee.

8.63   By way of contrast, a failure by the transferor to notify the transferee of a collective agreement covering a workforce of thousands would constitute a breach of the regulation 11 obligation in respect of all those employees in relation to all of whom the £500 minimum award should be made. One senses that the discretion afforded to the ET to award compensation on a just and equitable basis will be central to the operation of this compensatory regime.

8.64   The DTI Guidance[66] also addressed the issue of when the tribunal would not

---

[66] Page 34.

make the minimum award of compensation because to do so would be unjust or inequitable. It indicated that 'it might be fair to assume that trivial or unwitting breaches of the duty may lead to a tribunal waiving what would otherwise be a minimum award of compensation'.

5. Mitigation

Regulation 12(6) provides a further principle for the ET to consider in exercising   **8.65** its jurisdiction to award compensation in respect of breach of regulation 11. The principle of mitigation of loss under common law must also be taken into account in assessing the loss in respect of which (to the extent just and equitable and subject to the parties' commercial terms) an award can be made under regulation 12.

I. DUE DILIGENCE EXERCISES

The parties involved in a relevant transfer will therefore need to consider a   **8.66** variety of issues in relation to employee information provision. Clients awarding contracts will wish to oblige their contractors contractually to provide the requisite information to them as and when requested for onward transmission to potential bidders in order to ensure that subsequent re-tendering processes can be managed effectively and to reassure transferees that an incumbent contractor is bound contractually to provide the information which is required by statute to be disclosed and which they may often wish to see earlier than the statute actually requires to assist in the formulation of bids. Transferors will wish to ensure that they take proper steps, by way of investigation of the liabilities which have arisen in respect of the transferring employees, to comply with the (albeit limited) obligation imposed by regulation 11. Incumbent contractors will wish to ensure that on a re-tendering no dispute arises about the timely provision of information and that the client is contractually required to do all that is reasonably necessary to enable them to comply with their obligations.

Notwithstanding the introduction of the obligation to notify employee liabil-   **8.67** ity information and the availability of compensation in respect of breach, transferees will still wish, where feasible, to ensure that appropriate warranties and indemnities provide more extensive protection when compared with that supplied by regulation 11.

That said, whether or not commercial indemnity protection can be obtained,   **8.68** transferees may often wish to utilise the new TUPE 2006 obligation to provide employee liability information to put pressure on transferors promptly to provide full employee information. Transferees may well wish to make specific and detailed requests and argue that the request simply reflects the transferor's obligations under regulation 11 in any event.

In formulating due diligence requests by reference to the obligation on the   **8.69** transferor to provide employee liability information, it needs to be borne in mind that the obligation imposed by regulation 11 is limited to the specific items referred to in regulation 11(2). Contractual obligations and responsibilities, claims, and debts can be seen clearly to fall within the scope of the employee liability information which is to be notified by the transferor to the transferee. That said, there may well also be information which a transferee will wish to seek, depending upon the nature of the business in question, as part of a due diligence process but which will fall outside the strict scope of the concept of employee liability information for the purposes of regulation 11. By way of example, information about the industrial relations history of the operation in question, whether the Commission for Racial Equality, Equal Opportunities Commission, or Disability Rights Commission have ever investigated the business, staff turnover, and other matters may need to be sought for important commercial reasons but would be outside the scope of regulation 11.

8.70   Whilst space precludes a detailed treatment of all the due diligence issues which can arise when negotiating and documenting relevant transfers, there are a number of crucial categories of information that a transferee will wish wherever possible to obtain.

8.71   A list of all potential employees who might transfer employment following the transaction should be sought including those who have not yet commenced employment. Relevant details about those employees would include, in respect of each employee, the employer, the name of the employee, the date on which the employee's continuous employment for statutory purposes began, the job title, the notice period, salary, any overtime entitlements, and any pay increases awarded.

8.72   Full details should be sought of any share option bonus, profit sharing, or commission arrangements in which the transferring employees participate, including the applicable scheme rules. Not least in order to be able to assess employment costs and the arrangements needing to be replicated post-transfer, details should be sought of all other employment benefits offered or provided to the transferring employees. Examples of the arrangements about which information should be sought include life assurance schemes, private and permanent health insurance arrangements, company car and travel policies, enhanced redundancy arrangements, retirement policies, relocation policies, and long service award schemes.

8.73   Employment documentation itself is of course crucial and copies should be sought of all standard terms and conditions of employment, of all employment contracts with directors and other transferring employees whose employment is terminable on greater than, say, three months' notice, of any employment handbooks and similar policy documents, all applicable disciplinary and grievance procedures, and details of any pension schemes. Pension details sought should extend to early retirement entitlements, eligibility requirements, and which transferring employees are eligible to participate in the scheme.

8.74   An appreciation of the collective and industrial relations framework in which the transferring undertaking operates can be invaluable. Accordingly, details should be sought of all agreements with trade unions, of works councils arrangements and other employee representative structures, of trade union membership, and of the industrial relations history of the business. Full details should also be sought of past, outstanding, and anticipated applications to ETs or courts by any existing or past employees.

J. CONTRACTING OUT

In the first draft of what became TUPE 2006, the prohibition on contracting **8.75** out of the provisions of TUPE established by draft regulation 17 referred to a number of provisions of TUPE 2006 other than regulation 11. The omission of regulation 11 from the scope of the anti-avoidance provisions of draft regulation 17 would presumably have meant that, as between themselves, the transferor and transferee could have agreed to disapply regulation 11. This position was reversed in the final version of TUPE 2006 because, in the DTI's view,[67] it would have disadvantaged the employees. The prohibition of contracting out in regulation 18 applies equally to the obligation imposed upon the transferor to provide employee liability information to the transferee.[68]

---

[67] See DTI Guidance p 25.   [68] See Chap 12, para 12.4.

9

COLLECTIVE INFORMATION
AND CONSULTATION

A. Overview	9.01
B. Affected Employees	9.06
C. Information	9.09
D. Consultation	9.21
E. Representation of Employees	9.35
F. Remedies for Breach	9.65
G. Interaction with Other Consultation Requirements	9.97
H. Planning for Compliance	9.110

A. OVERVIEW

Regulation 13 (as supplemented by regulations 14 and 15) imposes on transferors **9.01** and transferees specific obligations with regard to the provision of information to, and the conduct of consultation with, representatives of those employees who are affected by a relevant transfer.

By way of overview, the Transfer of Undertakings (Protection of Employment) **9.02** Regulations (TUPE) 2006 require that, long enough before a relevant transfer to enable the employer of any affected employees to consult appropriate representatives of those affected employees, the employer shall provide specified information to those representatives[1] and shall consult with them with a view to reaching agreement in relation to any measures proposed.[2] Appropriate representatives for these purposes will be representatives of a recognised trade union or, if there is none, employee representatives, either existing or elected in accordance with the requirements of regulation 14. The penalty for failure to comply with these obligations is potentially significant—an award of up to 13 weeks' pay per affected employee.[3]

---

[1] Regulation 13(2).   [2] Regulation 13(6).   [3] Regulation 15(15).

9.03 These are therefore material obligations which complicate any transfer process and which necessitate careful planning to ensure compliance, given their detailed technical requirements with regard not only to the information and consultation obligations themselves but also the identity and election of the representatives of the affected employees with whom the parties must deal in order to satisfy the requirements of the legislation.

9.04 With regard to these information and consultation obligations, TUPE 2006 largely repeats the provisions of TUPE 1981.[4] As it was put in the 2005 Consultation, other than with regard to the issue of joint and several liability for breach of their requirements, these provisions essentially mirror TUPE 1981, regulations 10 and 11 'with only a couple of minor amendments to reflect more closely the wording of the current Directive'.[5] Accordingly, the previous case law remains relevant.

9.05 The principal amendment which TUPE 2006 made to this information and consultation regime was to provide that the liability for the penalty potentially due for failure to provide information to and consult with employee representatives as required is borne jointly and severally between transferor and transferee. This resolved some previous case law uncertainty as to whether liability for this penalty for non-compliance rested only with the transferor or could transfer to the transferee along with other employment-related liabilities (on the basis that it constituted a liability in connection with an employee's employment).[6]

B. AFFECTED EMPLOYEES

9.06 The information and consultation obligations imposed by regulation 13 apply only in respect of employees affected by the transfer. Whilst those who are not employees in terms of their legal status are irrelevant for these purposes, this is a broader category of person than the transferring employees.[7] As regulation 13(1) makes clear, the references in the information and consultation provisions to 'affected employees' are to:

---

[4] Which were first introduced by the Collective Redundancies and Transfer of Undertakings (Protection of Employment) (Amendment) Regulations 1995 SI 1995/2587. The Collective Redundancies and Transfer of Undertakings (Protection of Employment) (Amendment) Regulations 1999 SI 1999/1925 made further amendments, in particular requiring the employer to deal with a recognised trade union where there is one (rather than being able to choose instead to deal with employee representatives) and establishing the current requirements for election of employee representatives.

[5] At para 81.

[6] See 2005 Consultation paras 82 and 83 as well as *Alamo Group (Europe) Limited v Tucker and another* [2003] IRLR 266, EAT; *TGWU v James McKinnon, JR Haulage Ltd and others* [2001] IRLR 597, EAT; *Kerry Foods Limited v Creber* [2000] IRLR 10, EAT.

[7] The transferring employees are those employees who, pursuant to regulation 4(1), are assigned to the relevant organised grouping of resources or employees and whose employment therefore transfers from transferor to transferee as a result of the relevant transfer.

any employees of the transferor or the transferee (whether or not assigned to the organised grouping of resources or employees that is the subject of a relevant transfer) who may be affected by the transfer or may be affected by measures taken in connection with it; and references to the employer shall be construed accordingly.

Employees of the transferor who do not transfer under TUPE to the transferee **9.07** because they are not assigned to the relevant undertaking or activities may nonetheless be affected by a relevant transfer. For example, redundancies related to a divestment process may ensue that affect the transferor's remaining workforce, perhaps, for example, in relation to a central services function. The transferee's existing workforce may be affected by a harmonisation and rationalisation process conducted in the period after a business acquisition. Careful consideration needs to be given to what effects the transfer may have and therefore whether constituencies of employee wider than just those who fall within the scope of TUPE (such that their employment transfers from the transferor to the transferee) need to be addressed by the transferor or the transferee in an information and consultation process complying with the requirements of regulation 13.

It is also important to appreciate that, however unrealistic it may appear **9.08** where very few employees are affected by a TUPE transfer, these obligations under regulation 13 apply in relation to any transfer of an undertaking regardless of the number of employees involved. This is in contrast to the threshold which applies in relation to collective consultation obligations which arise in relation to redundancies that are only triggered where 20 or more employees are proposed to be made redundant at one establishment in a 90-day period.[8]

C. INFORMATION

1. Required Information

The information which the employer of employees affected or to be affected by a **9.09** relevant transfer is obliged to provide to appropriate representatives of those employees in advance of a relevant transfer is as follows:

- the fact that the relevant transfer is to take place, the date or proposed date of the transfer, and the reasons for it;[9]
- the legal, economic, and social implications of the transfer for any affected employees;[10]
- the measures which the employer envisages it will, in connection with the transfer, take in relation to any affected employees or, if he envisages that no measures will be so taken, that fact;[11]

---

[8] Trade Union and Labour Relations (Consolidation) Act (TULRCA) 1992, s 188.
[9] Regulation 13(2)(a).　　[10] Regulation 13(2)(b).　　[11] Regulation 13(2)(c).

- if the employer is the transferor, the measures, in connection with the transfer, which it (ie the transferor) envisages that the transferee will take in relation to any affected employees who will become employees of the transferee after the transfer by virtue of regulation 4 or, if it envisages that no measures will be so taken, that fact.[12]

9.10 Regulation 13(2)(a), following the amended provisions of the Acquired Rights Directive (ARD) 2001, requires confirmation of 'the date or proposed date of the transfer'. The equivalent provision in TUPE 1981 required a less precise disclosure of 'when, approximately, [the transfer] is to take place'.[13]

2. Legal, Economic and Social Implications

9.11 The concept of the 'legal, economic and social implications' of the transfer for the affected employees of which the appropriate representatives must be informed pursuant to regulation 13(2)(b) is inevitably somewhat open textured but needs to be considered carefully in order to avoid breach of the relevant obligations. The legal consequences of a relevant transfer are usually clear (in terms of the change to the identity of the employer and the retention of statutory and contractual employment rights other than in relation to the occupational pension scheme benefits).

9.12 The economic and social consequences of a relevant transfer (in terms of issues such as the human resources and industrial relations philosophy, working environment, financial stability, and other characteristics of the transferee) may be somewhat more difficult to assess and convey succinctly, objectively, and comprehensively than the legal consequences. These consequences cannot, however, be ignored in formulating the notification to be given to appropriate representatives of the employees affected by a relevant transfer in accordance with regulation 13(2).

3. Timing

9.13 That an anticipated TUPE transfer does not ultimately take place does not avoid the arising of information and consultation obligations.[14] Regulation 13 requires

---

[12] Regulation 13(2)(d).   [13] TUPE 1981, regulation 10(2)(a).

[14] *Banking Insurance and Finance Union v Barclays Bank plc* [1987] ICR 495, EAT per Popplewell J (at para 504H): '[i]t would be quite contrary to the whole spirit of the legislation and to the Directive if there were to be no sanction for failure to consult in relation to a proposed transfer which happened not to take place. It is true that the word "proposed" does not appear as it does, for instance, in section 101 of the Employment Protection Act 1975, but the Regulations are clearly designed to deal with consultation before any transfer has taken place and to give the union the right to complain if they are not informed or consulted about the proposed transfer. The Regulations say nothing as to when the complaint can be presented and industrial common sense dictates that an actual transfer is not an essential part of the bringing of a complaint.'

information and consultation in respect of a potential transfer. Precisely when the obligation to provide information to employee representatives arises will inevitably be a question of fact, given the lack of any more specific prescribed requirement in the legislation than that information be provided 'long enough before' the transfer to enable consultation to take place.[15] Again, this contrasts with the collective redundancy consultation regime established by the Trade Union and Labour Relations (Consolidation) Act (TULRCA) 1992, s 188 with its prescribed minimum 30- and 90-day consultation periods by reference to which the proper time for the provision of the requisite information can be assessed (because the information must be provided before that consultation commences).

What constitutes provision of the required information long enough before **9.14** the transfer to enable consultation is a particularly nebulous concept if no 'measures' are envisaged to be taken in relation to the transfer by either the transferor or transferee. In that scenario there is no consultation required by reference to which the timing of the provision of information can be calibrated. A transfer may occur on completion of a contract or transfer of actual management responsibility so careful assessment needs to be made of when the obligation arises.

4. Delivery

The provision of the requisite information to appropriate representatives is not **9.15** expressly required to be in writing although common sense, good practice, and the clear implication of the wording of regulation 13(5) all suggest that this is the proper method of delivery.

Regulation 13(5) states that the information to be given to the appropriate **9.16** representatives 'shall be given to each of them by being delivered to them, or sent by post to an address notified by them to the employer, or (in the case of representatives of a trade union) sent by post to the union at the address of its head or main office'. As a practical matter, in order to ensure certainty and avoid subsequent disputes, where employee representatives are being dealt with (as opposed to trade union representatives) how and where information is to be delivered needs to be determined (presumably by agreement if possible with the body of employee representatives).

5. Transferee Measures

The transferor is required to inform the appropriate representatives of the **9.17** affected employees whom it employs of the measures (if any) which it, the transferor, envisages that the transferee will take in connection with the transfer

---

[15] Regulation 13(2)—'[l]ong enough before a relevant transfer to enable the employer of any affected employees to consult the appropriate representatives of any affected employees . . .'.

in relation to its employees who will transfer to the transferee. In line with the legislation's objective of ensuring that employees (through their representatives) are adequately informed about the transfer and consulted about related changes, the representatives are to be informed in advance of what (if anything) the transferee plans to do post-transfer in relation to the employment of those affected employees.

9.18 TUPE makes this obligation practicable by requiring the transferee to notify the transferor of such intentions as it may have prior to the transfer with regard to measures which it may take in relation to the transferring employees. Regulation 13(4) requires the transferee to 'give the transferor such information at such a time as will enable the transferor to perform' its duty to inform the appropriate representatives of the measures which the transferee envisages taking in respect of the transferring employees (or, if there are none, of that fact).[16] Compliance with this obligation requires a careful assessment by the transferee of whether it has plans for the workforce which can be construed as being measures and are sufficiently definite to have the status of being envisaged.

9.19 The transferee is incentivised to comply with this obligation to inform the transferor of any measures which it envisages taking by the fact that regulation 15(5) enables the transferor to join the transferee into any proceedings complaining of breach of these obligations. In such circumstances the Employment Tribunal (ET) can award compensation against the transferee rather than transferor where the transferor, for example, failed to inform the appropriate representatives of the transferee's envisaged measures because the transferee did not inform the transferor of its position.[17]

9.20 Regulation 13(2)(d) is formulated differently from the equivalent provision in TUPE 1981,[18] in that it is based on the transferor's anticipation of what the transferee will do, a change to the legislation which went without detailed comment from the Government as to the rationale for its introduction. TUPE 1981 required provision by the transferor of information as the measures which the transferee envisaged taking. Regulation 13(2)(d) refers to what the transferor envisages the transferee will do by way of measures. Whilst, in complying with this duty, the transferor is assisted by the obligation imposed on the transferee by regulation 13(4), and to calibrate the obligation by reference to the transferor's state of mind provides the transferor with greater protection from claims, it appears possible that the reformulated regulation 13(2)(d) requires greater consideration by the transferor of what it considers the transferee might do than reliance only on the transferee's notification by way of compliance with regulation 13(4).

---

[16] The transferor's duty to provide details of the measures anticipated by the transferee is imposed by regulation 13(2)(d). See para 9.09 above.

[17] See para 9.70 below for further discussion.   [18] TUPE 1981, regulation 10(2)(d).

D. CONSULTATION

1. When Consultation is Required

Regulation 13(6) imposes an obligation on the employer of any employees **9.21** affected by a relevant transfer to consult with appropriate representatives if it envisages that it will, in connection with the transfer, be taking measures in relation to any of the affected employees.[19]

That the obligation to consult is framed by reference to the affected employees **9.22** means, as noted above, that the collective consultation obligation under regulation 13 may arise in respect of non-transferring employees of the transferor or the transferee's existing employees as well as those who do transfer. Those of the transferor's workforce whose roles and position may be affected by specific measures to be taken as a consequence of the transfer of the relevant undertaking, and those of the transferee's workforce in relation to whom measures are envisaged connected with or prompted by the transferring employees joining the transferee's operation, can therefore constitute affected employees for these purposes.

The trigger for consultation is therefore the employer envisaging taking measures. **9.23** Only measures to be taken 'in connection with the transfer' fall within the scope of this obligation. There therefore needs to be a causal connection or clear link between the relevant measures and the TUPE transfer in question for these provisions to be engaged such that details of the measures envisaged must be provided to employee representatives under regulation 13(2) and consultation about them conducted pursuant to regulation 13(6). Measures entirely unconnected with the transfer do not trigger these obligations. So, for example, a relocation or changes to benefits not prompted by, connected to, or forming part of the process of a transfer may not trigger the obligation to provide information to and to conduct consultation with appropriate representatives. However, depending on the numbers involved and whether dismissals could potentially result, the collective redundancy consultation obligations of TULRCA 1992, s 188 could nonetheless be triggered.

2. Measures

The term 'measures' is a wide concept and is generally assumed to describe **9.24** dismissals or changes to terms and conditions or other variations in terms of working patterns, working methods, or location which affect the employees in question. The principal judicial guidance on the concepts of 'measures' and

---

[19] Regulation 13(6)—'[a]n employer of any affected employees who envisages that he will take measures in relation to an affected employee, in connection with the relevant transfer, shall consult the appropriate representatives of that employee with a view to seeking their agreement to the intended measures.'

what is meant by their being 'envisaged' was provided by Millett J in *Institution of Professional Civil Servants v Secretary of State for Defence*.[20] He described 'measures' as:

a word of the widest import, and includ[ing] any action, step or arrangement, while 'envisages' simply means 'visualises' or 'foresees'. Despite the width of these words, it is clear that manpower projections may not be measures; though positive steps to achieve planned reductions in manpower levels otherwise than through natural wastage would be.[21]

9.25   It is generally considered that the concept of measures being envisaged does require some relatively clear (if not finalised or definite) plan or proposal to have been formulated or which the employer has in mind to implement. General and unspecific intentions to review the situation post-transfer will arguably not give rise to the obligation to consult (not least since there would then be very little to discuss). The act of entering into a transaction whose consequence is the transfer of employees from the transferor to the transferee in accordance with TUPE is not a measure about which consultation is required as it constitutes a matter of 'business policy'.[22]

9.26   The description of measures for these purposes offered by Millett J also suggests that the steps which an employer can envisage which will fall within the scope of these information and consultation obligations can extend to actions which are lawful and contractually valid. Reliance by an employer on a contractual power, for example, to vary an employee's place of work or bonus entitlements is capable of falling within this concept of measures if the relevant step is connected with the transfer.

9.27   The specific position with regard to pensions is also worth considering. Although the precise scope of regulation 10 is complex,[23] rights in relation to occupational pension schemes, generally speaking, do not transfer to the transferee on a relevant transfer. Subject therefore to the minimum standards of post-transfer pension preservation established by the combined effect of the Pensions Act (PA) 2004 and the Transfer of Employment (Pension Protection) Regulations 2005 (PPR) 2005 and the commercial and human resources imperatives of the situation, the transferee therefore has free rein with regard to the pension arrangements which it puts in place for transferring employees who have previously enjoyed pension benefits falling within the scope of the pensions exclusion.

9.28   It might be thought that the changes to transferring employees' pension rights which a transfer often entails do not constitute 'measures' because they do not affect contractual rights which the transferee inherits. Especially in the light of Millett J's comments, it is clear that pension changes connected with a transfer

---

[20] [1987] IRLR 373, HC.   [21] At para 12.   [22] Ibid per Millett J at para 13.
[23] See Chap 11.

do constitute measures and therefore trigger the consultation obligations of regulation 13, even though the transferring employees' post-transfer rights may be limited to the entitlements conferred by the combined effect of PA 2004 and PPR 2005.

3. Whose Obligation?

The obligation to inform and consult pursuant to regulation 13 is imposed on the employer of affected employees. It is important, if measures are envisaged, to identify upon whom the obligation to consult is imposed. A transferor that is simply disposing of a business in circumstances where it is the transferee that proposes to take measures in relation to those employees whom it inherits will not envisage taking any measures while it is the employer of the affected employees.   **9.29**

Whilst it has an obligation to deliver to the appropriate representatives the requisite information about the measures which it envisages that the transferee will take pursuant to regulation 13(2)(d), the transferor is therefore generally considered not to have a consultation obligation with regard to those measures—that obligation should, it is submitted, fall to the transferee. That said, in practical terms, pre-transfer consultation with regard to measures which the transferee wishes to implement (such as a change of location, redundancies etc) may well need to occur prior to transfer in order that the relevant measures can be implemented at the required point in time. Such consultation therefore, for human resources and industrial relations reasons, as well as to avoid breach of TUPE, may be conducted jointly by the transferor and the transferee.   **9.30**

4. Nature and Timing of Consultation

For these purposes, consultation is expressly required to be conducted 'with a view to seeking . . . agreement'.[24] Regulation 13(7) makes clear the basis upon which this dialogue should be conducted. The employer is required 'in the course of those consultations' to: **9.31**

- consider any representations made by the appropriate representatives;[25]
- reply to those representations;[26]
- if it rejects any of those representations, state its reasons for doing so.[27]

It is important, substantively and evidentially, for employers to engage in and record the consultation conducted in order to reduce the scope for disputes either during the process itself or subsequently by a complaint of breach of regulation 13.   **9.32**

With the introduction by TUPE 2006 of this specific statutory formulation as   **9.33**

---

[24] Regulation 13(6).   [25] Regulation 13(7)(a).   [26] Regulation 13(7)(b).   [27] Ibid.

to the meaning of consultation, there can be little doubt as to the continued relevance in this particular context of the guidance as to the meaning of consultation in *R v British Coal Corporation and Secretary of State for Trade and Industry ex parte Price*:[28]

fair consultation involves giving the body consulted a fair and proper opportunity to understand fully the matters about which it is being consulted and to express its views on those subjects with the consultor thereafter considering those views properly and genuinely.[29]

9.34 Nothing specific is said in regulation 13 about a minimum duration of consultation. As already noted, there are, in contrast to the TULRCA 1992 collective redundancy consultation regime, no prescribed periods for TUPE consultation. The period of time for which consultation should be conducted will therefore be determined by reference to the complexity of the matter, the significance and seriousness of any measures envisaged by the transferor or transferee, and good human resources practice in order to ensure that it cannot be argued that, by failing to engage in the process for long enough or in sufficient detail, the relevant employer has failed to consult as required 'with a view to seeking agreement'. If the TULRCA 1992 collective redundancy consultation obligations also arise because of a redundancy exercise relating to the TUPE transfer, its separate consultation obligations and specific timing requirements will also need to be considered with additional consequences for the timing and detail of the consultation process.

E. REPRESENTATION OF EMPLOYEES

1. Appropriate Representatives

9.35 The obligation imposed on the relevant employer by regulation 13, both with regard to the provision of information and the conduct of consultation concerning measures, is to deal with 'appropriate representatives'. Regulation 13(3) defines appropriate representatives as either:

- representatives of an independent trade union which is recognised by the employer in respect of the relevant employees;[30]

or in any other case at the employer's election:

- employee representatives appointed or elected by the affected employees otherwise than for the purposes of regulation 13, who (having regard to the

---

[28] [1994] IRLR 72, CA, a decision in an entirely different context but which is often cited as providing a useful description of what consultation means in the context of collective employment law more generally.
[29] At para 25.   [30] Regulation 13(3)(a).

purposes for and the method by which they were appointed or elected) have authority from those employees to receive information and to be consulted about the transfer on their behalf;[31] or

- employee representatives elected by any affected employees, for the purposes of regulation 13, in an election satisfying the requirements of regulation 14(1).[32]

In the absence of a recognised independent trade union, the employer can **9.36** choose to deal with either representatives elected in accordance with the specific requirements set out in regulation 14[33] or representatives elected or appointed as representatives on another occasion but who nonetheless have authority to receive information and to be consulted about the transfer on behalf of the relevant employees.

If an independent trade union is recognised in respect of some or all of the **9.37** employees affected by the relevant transfer, the employer is obliged to deal with that trade union in respect of the employees in respect of whom it is recognised. The employer cannot choose to disregard the recognised independent trade union and instead elect to deal with elected employee representatives.[34]

It is immaterial whether all the employees in respect of which the recognised **9.38** trade union is recognised are or are not members of that trade union. What matters in establishing the obligation on the employer to deal with a trade union when complying with regulation 13 is the scope of that trade union's recognition. If the trade union is recognised in respect of a particular undertaking, it constitutes the appropriate representative for all employees within the scope of its recognition whether or not they are members. There is no duty to provide information to or to consult with a trade union which is not recognised.

For the purposes of regulation 13, a trade union representative is defined by **9.39** regulation 2(2) as 'an official or other person authorised to carry on collective bargaining with that employer by that trade union'. A trade union representative for these purposes therefore need not be employed by the transferor nor a transferring employee and can be an external official.

If there is no recognised independent trade union in respect of the affected **9.40** employees or there are affected employees or categories of employee in respect of which there is no independent recognised trade union, then 'employee representatives' of those employees must be dealt with by the employer which is subject to the regulation 13 consultation obligation. Even where the workforce is heavily unionised, the relevant union or unions may not, for example, have recognition in respect of management. In that eventuality appropriate employee representatives will need to be dealt with on behalf of that category of staff in order to ensure compliance with the requirements of regulation 13.

---

[31] Regulation 13(3)(b)(i).   [32] Regulation 13(3)(b)(ii).   [33] See para 9.44 *et seq* below.
[34] The ability of the employer to elect to deal with employee representatives instead of a recognised trade union was removed from TUPE 1981 by the Collective Redundancies and Transfer of Undertakings (Protection of Employment) (Amendment) Regulations 1999 SI 1999/1925.

9.41　　In the absence of a recognised trade union, appropriate representatives of the affected employees will either be specifically elected in accordance with regulation 14 or be existing representatives with appropriate authority. A standing committee of employee representatives or consultative forum will only suffice as a body of employee representatives for the purposes of regulation 13 if, 'having regard to the purposes for and the method by which they were appointed or elected',[35] they have the authority from those employees to receive information and to be consulted about the transfer. In order to constitute appropriate representatives with whom an employer can deal in order to comply with the obligations imposed by regulation 13, an employee consultative forum therefore needs not only to have been constituted by an election or nomination process which gives it representative legitimacy but also for its terms of reference clearly to encompass receipt of information about and consultation in relation to TUPE transfers.

9.42　　Given these fact-sensitive requirements, care needs to be taken in this regard if a staff committee is to be utilised for the purposes of collective TUPE information and consultation. That regulation 15(3) places the burden of proof on the employer (to establish that an employee representative or representatives satisfied the relevant requirements) reinforces the need for care in this regard.

9.43　　Regulation 13(8) requires the employer to provide the appropriate representatives with 'such accommodation and other facilities as may be appropriate'. Office, typing, and meeting facilities may therefore need to be provided. The ACAS Code of Practice on Time Off for Trade Union Duties and Activities refers to facilities which may be appropriate for trade union representatives and which could by analogy be relevant for appropriate representatives.[36]

2. Electing Employee Representatives

9.44　　Regulation 14 sets out the requirements for the election of employee representatives in the absence of a recognised trade union or of existing employee representatives who satisfy the requirements of regulation 13(3)(b)(i). Only if these requirements are complied with do such elected employee representatives qualify as appropriate representatives for the purposes of compliance with regulation 13.

9.45　　The prescribed election requirements pursuant to regulation 14 are that:

- the employer shall make such arrangements as are reasonably practicable to ensure that the election is fair;[37]

- the employer shall determine the number of representatives to be elected so

---

[35] Regulation 13(3)(b)(i).

[36] Para 38 of the ACAS Code on Time off for Trade Union Duties and Activities indicates that, 'where resources permit', facilities would include use of a notice board, email, and intranet/internet facilities, use of a dedicated office space, and accommodation for meetings.

[37] Regulation 14(1)(a).

that there are sufficient representatives to represent the interests of all affected employees having regard to the number and classes of those employees;[38]

- the employer shall determine whether the affected employees should be represented either by representatives of all the affected employees or by representatives of particular classes of those employees;[39]

- before the election the employer shall determine the term of office as employee representatives so that it is of sufficient length to enable information to be given and consultation under regulation 13 to be completed;[40]

- the candidates for election as employee representatives are affected employees on the date of the election;[41]

- no affected employee is unreasonably excluded from standing for election;[42]

- all affected employees on the date of the election shall be entitled to vote for employee representatives;[43]

- the employees entitled to vote shall be entitled to vote for as many candidates as there are representatives to be elected to represent them or, if there are to be representatives for particular classes of employee, may vote for as many candidates as there are representatives to be elected to represent their particular class of employee;[44]

- the election shall be conducted so as to secure, so far as reasonably practicable, that those voting do so in secret[45] and that the votes at the election are accurately counted.[46]

9.46 If one of the representatives elected in accordance with regulation 14 ceases so to act, then the employees should be asked to elect a replacement essentially in the same manner.[47]

9.47 If the employer needs to elect employee representatives for the purposes of a consultation process, then, in timing terms, the employer complies with regulation 13 if it provides the prescribed information as soon as is reasonably practicable after the election of the representatives (provided that the employer has invited the affected employees to elect employee representatives and that information was issued long enough before the time for provision of information to allow for an election).[48] Careful thought therefore needs to be given to the time required to be committed to the election process in order to ensure that the representatives are in place long enough before the transfer for the information to be provided and for adequate consultation, where relevant, to be conducted.

---

[38] Regulation 14(1)(b).   [39] Regulation 14(1)(c).   [40] Regulation 14(1)(d).
[41] Regulation 14(1)(e).   [42] Regulation 14(1)(f).   [43] Regulation 14(1)(g).
[44] Regulation 14(1)(h).   [45] Regulation 14(1)(i)(ii).   [46] Regulation 14(1)(i)(i) and (ii).
[47] Regulation 14(2). The requirements of regulation 14(1)(b), (c), (d), (g), and (h) do not apply in relation to an election for a replacement employee representative.
[48] Regulation 13(10).

9.48   If there is no recognised independent trade union in respect of relevant affected employees, and the employer seeks to arrange an election for employee representatives but the employees fail to elect representatives within a reasonable time, then the employer can comply with its information provision obligation by providing the relevant information directly to each affected employee.[49] In *Howard v Millrise Limited (1) SG Printers (2)*[50] it was confirmed that the employer does have an obligation to initiate an election for representatives and, if an election process fails to produce employee representatives, to inform and consult with employees directly.

3. Protection of Employee Representatives

(a) *Introduction*

9.49   Employee representatives for the purposes of the information and consultation obligations of regulation 13 are afforded specific statutory protections designed to enable employees to become involved in the collective information and consultation aspects of transfers of undertakings without fear or favour.[51] These protections are similar to the protections afforded to trade union representatives in the performance of their duties.

(b) *Detriment*

9.50   The Employment Rights Act 1996 (ERA 1996), s 47(1) provides protection for employees from being subjected by their employer to a 'detriment' as a result of any functions or activities which they perform (or propose to perform) as employee representatives. The right is 'not to be subjected to any detriment by any act, or any deliberate failure to act'.

9.51   The same protection is afforded to candidates standing for election as employee representatives. ERA 1996, s 47(1A) provides protection to employees who participate in the election of employee representatives (for example, by casting their vote in the election). ERA 1996, s 47(1A) differs slightly from ERA 1996, s 47(1), however, in that there is no protection against proposed

---

[49] Regulation 13(11)—'[i]f, after the employer has invited any affected employees to elect appropriate representatives, they fail to do so within a reasonable time, he shall give to any affected employees the information set out in [regulation 13](2)'. This provision derives from Article 7.6 which states that:

'Member States shall provide that, where there are no representatives of the employees in an undertaking or business through no fault of their own, the employees concerned must be informed in advance of:
• the date or proposed date of the transfer,
• the reason for the transfer,
• the legal, economic and social implications of the transfer for the employees,
• any measures envisaged in relation to the employees.'

[50] EAT/0658/04.

[51] See the comments of Otton J in *R v Secretary of State for Trade and Industry ex parte Unison* [1996] IRLR 439 (at para 40) where he indicated that representatives must be 'independent of and not beholden to the employer'.

participation. This could technically prevent an employee from seeking redress where he or she suffered a detriment as a result of his or her proposed (as opposed to actual) participation in an election for employee representatives. It is generally considered[52] that a purposive construction should be applied to the interpretation of this provision and that participation should be widely construed to include proposed participation.

The term 'detriment' is not given a statutory definition. It clearly means **9.52** prejudicial treatment short of actual dismissal. It has been held to mean 'putting under a disadvantage'.[53]

A detriment can therefore arise by way of failure to promote or offer training **9.53** facilities or other unfavourable treatment. In order to attract the statutory protection applicable in this context, the detrimental act or omission must be taken on the ground of the employee's activities as an actual or potential employee representative. This factual issue therefore needs to be addressed by reference to the employer's reason for action. It is not strictly necessary to show an intention to penalise an employee for becoming involved in the representative process.

The compensation to be awarded by the ET (which hears complaints in this **9.54** regard) in relation to an employee being subjected to such a detriment (in addition to a declaration to that effect)[54] is based upon what is just and equitable in all the circumstances, taking into account the nature of the infringement and any loss suffered by the employee.[55] In determining compensation the ET is entitled to take into account whether or not the employee has mitigated his or her loss[56] and the extent to which the employee contributed to the events giving rise to the complaint of detriment.[57] The loss for which compensation is to be awarded can cover expenses incurred as a result of the relevant act or omission and the loss of any benefit otherwise reasonably expected.[58]

Where the detriment in question amounts to dismissal, the provisions of **9.55** ERA, s 47 do not apply.[59] The separate protection against dismissal must then be considered.

(c) *Dismissal*

Where an employee has been dismissed by virtue of involvement in the employee **9.56** representative process, protection is provided by way of a claim for unfair dismissal. ERA 1996, s 103 provides that where an employee has been dismissed (including, for these purposes, selected for redundancy) due to any functions or activities which he performed (or proposed to perform) as an employee representative or candidate, that dismissal will be automatically unfair. If

---

[52] See *Harvey on Industrial Relations and Employment Law*, Division DII Victimisation, para 336.

[53] *Ministry of Defence v Jeremiah* [1979] IRLR 436, CA (at para 637).

[54] ERA 1996, s 49(1)(a).   [55] ERA 1996, s 49(1)(b), (2).   [56] ERA 1996, s 49(4).

[57] ERA 1996, s 49(5).   [58] ERA 1996, s 49(3)(a), (b).   [59] ERA 1996, s 47(2).

the employee is dismissed as a result of his or her involvement in the election of employee representatives, this too will constitute an automatically unfair dismissal pursuant to ERA 1996, s 105.

9.57 The normal qualifying period of one year's service required for an employee to be eligible to claim unfair dismissal does not apply in these circumstances[60] nor does the upper age limit of 65 above which unfair dismissal claims cannot be brought (or, if lower, the normal retiring age for an employee holding such a position).[61] Similarly, the exclusion of unfair dismissal claims in relation to dismissals connected with industrial action does not apply in such circumstances.[62]

9.58 In order to seek to preserve his or her position, an employee dismissed in these circumstances can seek interim relief (pursuant to which the ET may order continuation of the employment contract).[63]

9.59 Whilst the compensatory award for unfair dismissal is assessed on the usual basis, the unfair dismissal basic award in these circumstances will be a minimum of £4,000.[64]

9.60 Protection is also provided to trade union representatives against action short of dismissal or dismissal related to their trade union activities.[65]

(d) Time Off

9.61 ERA 1996, s 61 provides an employee representative with the right to be permitted by his or her employer to take reasonable time off during working hours in order to perform his or her functions as a candidate for election as or as an employee representative or in order to undergo training to perform such functions.[66] There is no statutory obligation on an employer to train employee representatives in relation to what can after all be quite complex issues. This time off is paid.[67] Complaints of unreasonable refusal of time off or failure to make the required payments in respect of such time off to an employee are made to the ET.[68]

9.62 A complaint of breach is to be presented to the ET[69] within three months from the relevant event or, if not reasonably practicable, as soon as possible.[70] If

---

[60] ERA 1996, s 108(3)(f).   [61] ERA 1996, s 109(2)(f).

[62] TULRCA 1992, ss 237(1A), 238(2A).   [63] ERA 1996, s 120.

[64] Employment Rights (Increase of Limits) Order 2005 SI 2005/3352.

[65] TULRCA 1992, ss 146, 152. No period of qualifying service is required for an unfair dismissal claim on these grounds nor does the normal upper age limit apply (TULRCA 1992, s 154).

[66] ERA 1996, s 61(1).

[67] ERA 1996, s 61(2) sets out the detailed provisions establishing the appropriate hourly rate payable to an employee who exercises his or her right to paid time off in those circumstances. The right is only to be paid in respect of hours required to be worked under the employee's contract. Time spent on representative duties outside the employee's contracted hours do not attract the right to be paid (*Hairsine v Kingston upon Hull C.C.* [1992] ICR 212, EAT).

[68] ERA 1996, s 63.

[69] As to permitting time off to be taken or payment in respect of such time off (ERA 1996, s 63(1)(a) and (b).

[70] ERA 1996, s 63(2)(a) and (b).

an employee succeeds in a complaint then the ET must make a declaration to that effect,[71] can order payment to the employee in respect of any time off where the employer has breached its payment obligations[72] and can, in cases where time off has been unreasonably refused, order payment of the amount which would have been payable had the time off been taken.[73]

9.63 TULRCA 1992, s 168 provides that an employee who is an official of a recognised trade union has the right to paid time off during working hours for the purpose of carrying out his or her duties as such an official concerned with the provision of information and the consultation required under TUPE 2006.[74] Detailed provisions[75] address the employee's entitlement to pay in respect of such time off. Time off is also required to be permitted for relevant training approved by the Trades Union Congress or relevant trade union.[76]

9.64 The amount of time which can be taken off and the appropriate occasions for time to be taken off must be reasonable having regard to any relevant ACAS Code.[77] Presumably ACAS guidance in respect of trade union representatives will be relevant by analogy in relation to employee representatives.[78] Factors to be taken into account in determining whether proposed time off is reasonable include potentially the amount of time already taken off, the size of the organisation, the number of workers, the need to maintain safety and security, and the nature (if applicable) of the employer's production process.[79] Employers are also encouraged to consider the issues which arise in the context of ensuring proper representation as a result of factors such as shift and part-time working.[80]

F. REMEDIES FOR BREACH

1. Complaints

(a) *Who Can Complain?*

9.65 Failure to inform or consult as required by regulation 13 can lead to a complaint to the ET pursuant to regulation 15.[81] Regulation 15 identifies which persons can bring a complaint in respect of what nature of default. A complaint may be brought:

- by any of the affected employees employed by him if the failure relates to the

---

[71] ERA 1996, s 63(3).   [72] ERA 1996, s 63(5).   [73] ERA 1996, s 63(4).

[74] TULRCA 1992, s 168(1)(c).   [75] TULRCA 1992, s 169.

[76] TULRCA 1992, s 168(2).   [77] TULRCA 1992, s 168(3).

[78] See ACAS Code of Practice 3; Time Off for Trade Union Duties and Activities (2003).

[79] Ibid paras 25 and 32.   [80] Ibid para 26.

[81] Pursuant to regulation 16(1), ERA 1996, s 205(1) and Employment Tribunals Act 1996, s 18 render a complaint to the ET the sole route by which compensation can be obtained under regulation 15. Pursuant to regulation 16(2), appeals are to the EAT (on questions of law only).

election of employee representatives[82] (for example, a failure to comply with the election requirements of regulation 14);

- by the employee representatives to whom the failure related in relation to any other failure relating to them[83] (such as timely provision of information to or failure properly to consult with the elected representatives);

- by a trade union if the failure relates to trade union representatives[84] (such as failure to provide adequate or timely information to them or to consult with them where required);

- by any of the affected employees employed by the employer in any other case[85] (such as a complete failure to comply with the TUPE information and consultation regime).

(b) Burden of Proof

9.66 Whilst the burden of proof will normally rest with the complainant to show failure to comply with the requirements of regulation 13, the burden of proof is specifically placed on the employer in relation to certain specific issues.

9.67 First, where a question arises as to whether or not it was reasonably practicable for an employer to perform a particular duty or what steps it took towards performing it, it is for the employer to show special circumstances which rendered it not reasonably practicable for it to perform the duty[86] and that it took all such steps towards its performance as were reasonably practicable in those circumstances.[87]

9.68 Second, where a question arises as to whether or not an employee representative constituted an appropriate representative for the purposes of regulation 13, it is for the employer to show that the employee representative had the necessary authority to represent the affected employees.[88] This will be particularly relevant where the employer seeks to deal with an existing staff representative body.

9.69 Third, if there is a complaint with regard to the election of employee representatives (ie that the election of employee representatives was in some way defective), then it is for the employer to demonstrate that the applicable requirements have been satisfied.[89]

(c) Transferee's Breach

9.70 A transferor may breach its information provision obligations under regulation 13 if it is unaware prior to the transfer of the measures which the transferee envisages taking and therefore fails to comply with its obligation to notify the relevant representatives of the transferee's anticipated measures. It should of course be recalled that the transferor's obligation under the reformulated regulation 13(2)(d) is to notify those measures which it envisages that the transferee

---

[82] Regulation 15(1)(a).   [83] Regulation 15(1)(b).   [84] Regulation 15(1)(c).
[85] Regulation 15(1)(d).   [86] Regulation 15(2)(a).   [87] Regulation 15(2)(b).
[88] Regulation 15(3).   [89] Regulation 15(4).

will take. If the transferor fails to comply with its information provision obligations because the transferee does not provide it with the requisite information with regard to its envisaged measures in advance of the transfer,[90] then the transferor may put forward a defence that it was not reasonably practicable for it to perform the duty in question by reason of that failure on the part of the transferee.[91] However, this argument cannot be put forward unless the transferor gives the transferee notice of its intention to show that fact and thereby joins the transferee as a party to the proceedings.[92] Where a complaint is made out in such circumstances, the ET is required to make a declaration to that effect and may order the transferee to pay appropriate compensation 'to such descriptions of affected employees as may be specified in the award'.[93]

(d) Timing of Complaint

A complaint of breach of the information and consultation obligations imposed by regulation 13 must be presented to the ET within three months of the date of the relevant transfer[94] or, in the case of an attempt to enforce against the transferee an order made against the transferor on the basis of joint and several liability, three months from the date of the relevant order.[95] The ET is entitled to permit late lodging of a complaint within such further period as the ET considers reasonable in a case where it is satisfied that it was not reasonably practicable for the complaint to be presented before the end of the three-month period.[96]   **9.71**

2. Compensation

Where a complaint against the transferor is made out, the ET is obliged[97] to make a declaration to that effect and may order the transferor to pay compensation to affected employees.[98]   **9.72**

Regulation 16(3) specifies the compensation to be paid ('appropriate compensation') in relation to failure to comply with the information and consultation obligations imposed by regulation 13. The compensation to be awarded is 'such sum not exceeding thirteen weeks' pay for the employee in question as the tribunal considers just and equitable having regard to the seriousness of the failure of the employer to comply with his duty'. This is payable in respect of 'such descriptions of affected employees as may be specified in the award'.[99] In the light of the width of the definition of an affected employee, it can be appreciated that these liabilities can, depending upon the circumstances, be significant.   **9.73**

A week's pay is calculated by reference to the following dates:[100]   **9.74**

- if an employee is dismissed by reason of redundancy,[101] then a week's pay for

---

[90] As required by regulation 13(4).   [91] Regulation 15(5).   [92] Ibid.
[93] Regulation 15(7).   [94] Regulation 15(12)(a).   [95] Regulation 15(12)(b).
[96] Regulation 15(12).   [97] Regulation 15(8).   [98] Regulation 15(8)(a).   [99] Ibid.
[100] Regulation 16(4).   [101] Within the meaning of ERA 1996, ss 139 and 155.

the purposes of compensation for failure to comply with the TUPE information and consultation regime is calculated by reference to the date by reference to which the statutory redundancy payment is calculated or would have been calculated had the employee been entitled to a redundancy payment;[102]

- if the employee is dismissed for any other reason[103] the effective date of termination of the employment;[104]
- in any other case, the date of the relevant transfer.[105]

9.75 A week's pay is calculated in accordance with the provisions of ERA 1996[106] but does not appear to be[107] subject to the statutory cap (of, at the time of writing, £290[108]) which applies in respect of certain other statutory entitlements such as the weekly wage taken into account when calculating the statutory redundancy payment.

9.76 *Sweetin v Coral Racing*[109] confirmed that the approach to be adopted in assessing compensation for breach of regulation 13 is the same as that to be applied in respect of the collective redundancy consultation regime under TULRCA 1992. Whilst the respondent submitted that the circumstances of a failure to comply with the TUPE consultation obligation would not necessarily fall to be regarded in as serious a light as in the case of failure to conduct collective redundancy consultation, the Employment Appeal Tribunal (EAT) disagreed.

9.77 In the view of the EAT, the respective drafting of TUPE 1981, regulation 11[110] and of TULRCA 1992, s 188 reflect each other and both underline the importance of compliance with the duty to consult. Although it was accepted that the consequences of redundancy (loss of employment) could be more serious than of failure to consult in relation to a TUPE transfer (where employment should be preserved), the imposition of a consultation requirement by the Directive and the use of the same terminology in both statutes displaced the possibility of an inference that the approach to compensation should be any different. Both TUPE and TULRCA 1992 focus on the nature and extent of the employer's default and accordingly it was clear that both awards were 'penal in nature, rather than solely compensatory'.[111]

9.78 The ET's decision in *Sweetin* was therefore flawed as it had focused on what amounted to 'appropriate compensation' rather than recognised the need to focus on the punitive and deterrent nature of the award and any mitigating factors.

9.79 Accordingly, the approach to be adopted in determining compensation for breach of regulation 13 is that applying to breaches of TULRCA 1992. The

---

[102] Regulation 16(4)(a).   [103] Regulation 16(4)(b).
[104] As determined in accordance with ERA 1996, ss 95(1) and (2), 97.
[105] Regulation 16(4)(c).   [106] ERA 1996, ss 220–228 per regulation 16(4).
[107] Despite the statement to this effect in the DTI Guidance on p 33.
[108] Employment Rights Increase of Limits Order 2005 SI 2005/3352.
[109] [2006] IRLR 252, EAT.   [110] Now regulation 15.   [111] *Sweetin*, at para 30.

relevant principles were set out by Peter Gibson LJ in *Susie Radin v GMB and others*[112] as follows:

- the purpose of the award is to provide a sanction for breach not to compensate employees for consequential loss;
- the ET has a wide discretion as to what is just and equitable;
- the employer's default may vary from the technical to a complete failure to inform and consult;
- the deliberateness of the failure and any advice taken may be relevant;
- the proper approach is to start with the maximum award and reduce the award only where mitigating circumstances are judged appropriate to justify a reduction.

Arguments to the effect that consultation would have been futile are viewed as irrelevant as Longmore LJ confirmed in *Radin*:[113]   **9.80**

It may at first sight seem surprising to say that the fact that consultation would have been futile is something which an employment tribunal should not take into account when assessing the length of time for which a protective award should be made. But the argument that took place has convinced me (1) that there is nothing in the statutory wording which requires such futility to be taken into account and (2) that in a collective claim brought by a union it would be impossible to take such futility into account in a fair and practical way.

Transport and General Workers Union v Morgan Platts Ltd (in administration)[114]   **9.81**
also indicates the penal nature of such awards. Again in the context of collective redundancy consultation, the EAT indicated that the maximum 90-day period should be the starting point in calculating an award in respect of breach. The ET should then consider whether it can be argued that a lesser award should be made. In this particular case, the employer's failures had been serious in that there was no consultation at all and there was accordingly no justification for an award lower than the maximum penalty.

The ET nonetheless has a wide discretion to do what is just and equitable as   **9.82**
the EAT confirmed in *Amicus v GBS Tooling Ltd (in administration)*.[115] An appeal was rejected against the ET's decision in determining a protective award to take into account, by way of mitigating circumstances, steps which had been taken to keep the relevant trade union informed of developments. These steps indicated that the employer had not deliberately, recklessly, or negligently failed to comply with its obligations. The ET had not erred in awarding a protective award for a period of 70 days (as opposed to the maximum permissible period of 90 days). Mitigating factors, in terms of previous informal discussions with

---

[112] [2004] ICR 893, CA. See also *Smith and another v Cherry Lewis Limited* [2005] IRLR 86, EAT.
[113] At para 49.   [114] EAT/0646/02.   [115] [2005] IRLR 683, EAT.

the trade union, pre-dating the decision which triggered the consultation obligation, could properly be taken into account in determining the appropriate
penalty.

3. Joint and Several Liability

9.83 Regulation 15(9) renders the transferee jointly and severally liable with the
transferor in respect of any compensation payable as a consequence of breach
of these information and consultation obligations. Regulation 15(9) identifies
the compensation for which liability is joint and several as that payable under
regulation 15(8)(a) (an order against the transferor for breach of its regulation
13 obligations) and regulation 15(11) (an order to pay compensation which has
previously been ordered to be paid by the transferor or transferee but which has
not been satisfied).

9.84 As the 2005 Consultation noted,[116] there had been conflicting case law as to
whether liability for failure to comply with the information and consultation
obligations could be inherited by the transferee. The argument that the transferee
should inherit liability for the transferor's failure to comply with its information and consultation obligations was that the obligations in question and
the associated financial penalties for breach relate to transferring employees'
employment and therefore should be inherited by the transferee on the same
basis that it inherits other pre-transfer obligations and liabilities.

9.85 The counter-argument was that to pass the liability for breach of TUPE's
information and consultation obligations to the transferee would not only be
unfair on a transferee (which would often have no control over the transferor's
conduct) but would also remove any incentive on the transferor to comply with
the obligations imposed upon it. On this analysis, these liabilities should be
an exception to the rule that employment liabilities generally transfer to the
transferee on a relevant transfer.

9.86 The change to the legislation to make the transferor and transferee jointly and
severally liable for the compensation payable for breach of the regulation 13
information and consultation obligations was permitted by Article 3.1 and was
perceived as enabling employee representatives to choose whether to take action
against either or both of the relevant parties.[117] The Government acknowledged
that, in making a choice as to who to sue, the employee representatives would be
strongly influenced by the relative ability to pay of transferor and transferee.
Joint and several liability therefore makes it more likely (particularly in insolvency situations) that employees and their representatives will be able to find
respondents against whom they can bring claims which can economically be
enforced. Issues of apportionment of liability can nonetheless be put before the
ET pursuant to the Civil Liability (Contribution) Act 1978.

9.87 However, where the transferor is insolvent and the transferee has been unable

---

[116] 2005 Consultation paras 83–85. See n 6 above.   [117] 2005 Consultation para 84.

to insist on compliance by the transferor with its obligations or to secure protection against the consequent compensation exposure by way of a worthwhile indemnity or retention, the introduction of joint and several liability in this context will leave the transferee in practice liable for potentially significant compensation awards. In order to facilitate recovery by the affected employees or representatives of the compensation due for breach of regulation 13, the risk is allocated to the transferee in respect of breach of obligations over compliance with which it may have no control or influence.

This change introduced by TUPE 2006 reinforces the need (where possible) **9.88** for transferees to obtain adequate warranty and indemnity protection in respect of those obligations for which it is not directly responsible and to take more proactive steps to ensure that transferors comply with their obligations. Likewise, the transferor will wish to seek reciprocal protection as it is jointly and severally liable for compensation payable by the transferee as a result of its defaults, particularly where it fails to provide information as to the measures which it envisages to the transferor as required by regulation 13(4).

4. Special Circumstances Defence

Regulation 13(9) provides that if there are 'special circumstances which render it **9.89** not reasonably practicable for an employer to perform a duty imposed on him by any of [Regulation 13] paragraphs (2) to (7) he shall take all such steps towards performing that duty as are reasonably practicable in the circumstances'. Regulation 13(9) essentially requires the employer to act to the extent it can as soon as it can.

When it comes to a complaint of breach, the 'special circumstances' defence **9.90** mirrors regulation 13(9). Regulation 15(2) states that, if there is a question of reasonable practicability, the burden of proof is on the employer to show that there were special circumstances which rendered it not reasonably practicable for it to perform the duty[118] and that it took all such steps towards its performance as were reasonably practicable in those circumstances.[119] The matter is one of fact for the ET to assess. The case law on the equivalent provisions in the context of the collective redundancy consultation obligation imposed by TULRCA 1992, s 188 is again of assistance in this regard.

As the ET noted in *Clarks of Hove Limited v Bakers Union*,[120] special circum- **9.91** stances are 'something out of the ordinary run of events' such as a disruption of the plant or withdrawal of supplies suddenly by a major supplier. Insolvency, precipitating a fire sale of assets, may not be sufficient to constitute special circumstances (as the decision in *Re Hartlebury Printers Limited (in liquidation)*[121] demonstrates).

It is also clear that a parent company's decision that results in a transfer **9.92**

---

[118] Regulation 15(2)(a).   [119] Regulation 15(2)(b).
[120] [1978] ICR 1076, CA (at para 10).   [121] [1992] IRLR 516, HC.

triggers the regulation 13 information and consultation obligations. That a parent took the relevant decision is no excuse for failure by the subsidiary transferor or transferee to comply with its obligations under regulation 13. Lack of internal group communication is no excuse for non-compliance. Regulation 13(12) provides that 'the duties imposed on an employer by this regulation shall apply irrespective of whether the decision resulting in the relevant transfer is taken by the employer or a person controlling the employer'.[122] This is a similar provision to TULRCA 1992, s 188(7) which deems a parent's failure to inform an employer of decisions leading to redundancies not to constitute special circumstances rendering compliance with the statutory obligation not reasonably practicable.

9.93 One issue which often concerns parties to transfers of undertakings in the context of employee consultation is confidentiality. This is a particular concern for companies listed on stock exchanges who will be reluctant to elect representatives and provide information to them if the transaction which would then be discussed is price sensitive and accordingly highly confidential. The case law on the collective redundancy consultation obligations of TULRCA 1992 indicates that an argument based on this sort of commercial confidentiality may well receive short shrift from the ET.

9.94 In *MSF v Refuge Assurance plc*[123] the employer contended that the requirement for secrecy in the Takeover Code amounted to special circumstances legitimately preventing disclosure of a potential merger by way of special circumstances until it was completed. The EAT noted that 'in our view it cannot be simply assumed that disclosure to, say, a senior union official on the like terms of confidence as would be applicable to the company's directors would necessarily be so restrictive that it would be completely useless to him and that it would therefore represent a step that need not be taken'.[124] This comment suggests that an ET should be reluctant to allow confidentiality issues unduly to affect a consultation process and that the employer should make every effort to disclose what it can to appropriate representatives and to consider what confidentiality protections will facilitate that disclosure process.

5. Injunctions

9.95 *Amicus v Dynamex Friction Ltd*[125] addressed the potential use of injunctions in the context of the enforcement of a complaint of breach of TUPE's collective information and consultation obligations. The relevant trade union, which had

---

[122] This provision derives from Article 7.4 which states that '[t]he obligations laid down in this Article shall apply irrespective of whether the decision resulting in the transfer is taken by the employer or an undertaking controlling the employer. In considering alleged breaches of information and consultation requirements laid down by this Directive, the argument that such a breach occurred because the information was not provided by an undertaking controlling the employer shall not be accepted as an excuse.'
[123] [2002] IRLR 324, EAT.   [124] At para 55.   [125] [2005] IRLR 724, HC.

commenced ET proceedings alleging breach of what are now the regulation 13 information and consultation requirements, sought an injunction against the two transferees of the business in question ordering them not to dispose of their assets. An injunction was granted prohibiting the disposal of, dealing with, or other diminution of the value of the transferees' assets up to a value of £325,000 pending determination of the ET claims. Such a freezing order is only available in respect of proceedings which exist at the time of the application for the order. A pre-existing cause of action in respect of which ET proceedings had been issued could be protected by such an order to avoid the dissipation of assets and consequent removal of the possibility of enforcement of any compensation awarded by the ET. There was sufficient evidence to support the award of a freezing order in this case.

The TUC proposed during the consultation on the changes which led to **9.96** TUPE 2006 that the legislation should include an ability for those affected to seek an injunction to prevent completion of a relevant transfer until the requisite collective information and consultation obligations have been fulfilled. The Government concluded that the remedy already provided was adequate.[126]

G. INTERACTION WITH OTHER CONSULTATION REQUIREMENTS

1. Collective Redundancy Consultation

A detailed treatment of the collective redundancy consultation requirements of **9.97** TULRCA 1992, s 188 is beyond the scope of this work. Suffice it to say, where an employer proposes to make redundant 20 or more employees in a 90-day period at one establishment, an obligation arises to consult with recognised unions or employee representatives with a view to seeking agreement as does an obligation to provide certain specified information to those representatives in writing as a precursor to that consultation. The protective penalty for breach is an award of up to 90 days' pay per affected employee. The principles with regard to the election of employee representatives and the nature of the consultation to be conducted, as well as the special circumstances defence to claims of breach, are very similar to the TUPE 2006 requirements.

The particular point to note in this context is that the two obligations are **9.98** separate. Complaints of breach lead to separate and therefore potentially cumulative awards of compensation. Whilst there may be some degree of overlap, particularly in relation to redundancy situations arising in connection with a transfer, both sets of obligations need to be considered carefully for compliance where they apply. It may be that collective redundancy and TUPE consultation needs to be conducted in tandem where redundancies are being effected, for

---

[126] Consultation Response para 7.7.

example, on a relocation as part of the transfer process. Conversely, where the TULRCA 1992 collective redundancy consultation requirements do not apply on the basis that fewer than 20 employees are being made redundant during the relevant period, consultation with appropriate representatives will still be required with regard to those redundancies under regulation 13 on the basis that the redundancies constitute 'measures'.

2. Other Statutory Obligations

(a) *Information and Consultation of Employees Regulations 2004*

9.99 Consideration may also need to be given to the relevant employer's obligations under the Information and Consultation of Employees Regulations 2004 (ICE), the penalty for breach of which is an award by the Central Arbitration Committee (CAC) of a penalty up to £75,000.[127]

9.100 Under ICE, an employer may be required to establish information and consultation arrangements in relation to which a variety of information provision and consultation obligations arise. Any specific obligations contained in a negotiated agreement will of course be relevant. Otherwise, under ICE, regulation 20, the 'standard information and consultation provisions' apply and the employer will be required to provide a variety of information to those ICE representatives including information regarding:

- the recent and probable development of the undertaking's activities and economic situation;[128]

- the situation, structure, and probable development of employment within the undertaking;[129]

- decisions likely to lead to substantial changes in work organisation or in contractual relations including those referred to in regulations 10 to 12 TUPE 1981.[130]

9.101 This information must be given at such time, in such fashion, and with such content as is appropriate to enable, in particular, the ICE representatives to conduct an adequate study and, where necessary, to prepare for consultation.[131]

9.102 Consultation is required in relation to the second and third of the categories above. This consultation is, *inter alia*, to be conducted with a view to seeking agreement on decisions within the scope of the employer's power.[132]

9.103 All this would indicate that a separate and additional obligation to consult

---

[127] For detailed discussion see Squire, Healy, and Broadbent, *Informing and Consulting Employees: The New Law* (Oxford, OUP 2005).

[128] ICE, regulation 20(1)(a).   [129] ICE, regulation 20(1)(b).

[130] ICE, regulation 20(1)(c). These are the TUPE provisions with regard to 'measures'. So decisions which could lead to a business sale or other relevant transfer or to measures trigger the obligation to consult with ICE representatives under ICE, regulation 20(1)(c).

[131] ICE, regulation 20(2).   [132] ICE, regulation 20(4)(d).

with ICE representatives would be required in relation to a proposed transfer of an undertaking were it not for ICE, regulation 20(5)(b). ICE, regulation 20(5)(b)[133] brings to an end any obligation to deal with ICE representatives from the point when the collective information and consultation obligations under regulation 13 arise. Provided that the employer notifies the ICE representatives in writing that it is doing so, the employer can then proceed to comply with the TUPE information and consultation obligations without reference to the ICE information and consultation obligations and the ICE representatives. If it does not notify the ICE representatives of a decision only to conduct TUPE consultation, the employer remains bound by the obligations imposed both under ICE and under TUPE. This notification must be 'given on each occasion on which the employer has become or is about to become subject to the [regulation 13] duty'.

If there is a recognised trade union which must be dealt with in accordance with regulation 13, then the ICE process cannot be used to avoid that obligation. Absent a recognised trade union, ICE representatives may constitute appropriate representatives for TUPE 2006 purposes but the employer is free if it chooses, once the TUPE 2006 obligations arise, to cease to deal with the ICE representatives and to elect or deal with a separate body of representatives which satisfies the requirements of regulation 14.   **9.104**

It is worth noting that ICE, regulation 20(5) only permits an employer to cease consultation under ICE and to follow only the TUPE collective consultation route in relation to its ICE, regulation 20(1)(c) obligation, ie as to decisions likely to lead to substantial changes in work organisation or in contractual relations including those referred to in TUPE 1981, regulations 10 to 12. The obligation imposed by ICE, regulation 20(1)(b) (to consult about the situation, structure, and probable development of employment within the undertaking) must still be complied with by way of dealing with the ICE representatives in relation to what is after all a decision-making stage earlier than that which triggers TUPE collective consultation requirements. Considerations as to the general future of the relevant undertaking or activities will therefore still be covered by ICE, regulation 20(1)(b).   **9.105**

This framework applies to standard ICE arrangements implemented under ICE. The interaction between regulation 13 and pre-existing agreements and   **9.106**

---

[133] ICE, regulation 20(5) provides that '[t]he duties in this regulation to inform and consult the information and consultation representatives on decisions falling within paragraph (1)(c) cease to apply once the employer is under a duty under— . . .

(b) regulation 10 of the Regulations referred to in paragraph 1(c)(ii) (duty to inform and consult representatives),

and he has notified the information and consultation representatives in writing that he will be complying with his duty under the legislation referred to in sub-paragraph (a) or (b), as the case may be, instead of under these Regulations, provided that the notification is given on each occasion on which the employer has become or is about to become subject to the duty'.

negotiated agreements for the purposes of ICE will depend on the terms of the relevant agreements.

9.107 What this all means in short is that an employer which has in place a standard information and consultation arrangement under ICE must inform and consult the relevant ICE representatives about matters which may lead to a transfer of an undertaking falling within the scope of TUPE. Once a potential transaction is sufficiently advanced, the employer must deal with a recognised trade union if there is one as required by regulation 13 but otherwise is able to elect to switch to the TUPE 2006 regime, or to deal with the ICE representatives, or indeed to address the issues under both sets of arrangement. This distinction between consideration of matters which may lead to a TUPE transfer and a TUPE transfer process which engages regulation 13 will require careful consideration.

(b) *European Works Council Obligations*

9.108 Whilst the detailed rules and regulations relating to the establishment of European Works Councils (EWCs) is beyond the scope of this work, the domestic legislation[134] implementing into UK law the requirements of the EU Directive on the establishment of European Works Councils[135] should not entirely be ignored in this context. This legislation establishes the requirement with which undertakings or groups of undertakings with at least 1000 employees in EU Member States and at least 150 employees in two of those States can be made to comply.

9.109 While the parties to an EWC arrangement may determine (through the 'Special Negotiating Body') the details of how their EWC mechanism is to work, there is a default model which applies if agreement is not reached. For these purposes it is worth noting that of the matters which must be considered with an EWC and which may be relevant in the TUPE context are the structure, economic, and financial situation of the business, the probable trend of employment, investments and substantial changes affecting the organisation, and closures. Accordingly, developments which may lead to TUPE transfers may in any event fall for consideration in the context of an applicable EWC arrangement if transnational in scope or effect.

H. PLANNING FOR COMPLIANCE

9.110 The fact that liability for failure to comply with the information and consultation regime is now joint and several places transferees in a difficult situation if they lack a commercial or contractual position which enables them to require the transferor to comply with its obligations and/or provide suitable indemnity protection in relation to any liability which may arise in respect of the relevant

---

[134] The Transitional Information and Consultation of Employees Regulations 1999 SI 1999/3323.
[135] Directive 94/45/EC.

requirements. In view of the potentially significant exposure involved, commercial contracts recording outsourcings and other similar arrangements will often need to impose specific obligations on the relevant parties to comply with their obligations and to provide appropriate financial protection by way of reliable indemnities in respect of the liabilities arising on breach.

Assuming that the parties are able and prepared to comply with their obligations, careful planning also needs to take place with regard to what can be a complex process in terms of, for example: **9.111**

- identifying the constituencies from whom employee representatives should be elected;
- conducting an election for employee representatives at a potentially sensitive time;
- identifying what if any measures the transferee envisages taking and whether any plans are sufficiently definite and formulated to constitute proposals which the transferee envisages making;
- analysing whether employees other than those directly transferring are sufficiently affected to need to be drawn into the consultation process;
- whether different categories of employees need to be consulted with separately depending on the nature of their involvement and the effects upon them of the transfer;
- the logistical and practical issues involved in running a fair and secret election, whether or not with the participation of an independent scrutineer;
- potentially conducting a collective redundancy process in parallel with the transfer of undertakings consultation process if a redundancy or relocation programme of the requisite scale is being implemented in conjunction with the transfer;
- assessing whether ICE or EWC obligations are triggered and need to be addressed.

The Department of Trade and Industry (DTI) Guidance[136] offers a gloss on these issues: **9.112**

The legislation does not specify how many representatives must be elected or the process by which they are to be chosen. An employment tribunal may wish to consider, in determining a claim that the employer has not informed or consulted in accordance with the requirements, whether the arrangements were such that the purpose of the legislation could not be met. An employer will therefore need to consider such matters as whether:
- the arrangements adequately cover all the categories of employees who may be affected by the transfer and provide a reasonable balance between the interests of the different groups;

---

[136] At p 27.

- the employees have sufficient time to nominate and consider candidates;
- the employees (including any who are absent from work for any reason) can freely choose who to vote for;
- there is any normal company custom and practice for similar elections and, if so, whether there are good reasons for departing from it.

10

INSOLVENCY SITUATIONS

A. Introduction	10.01
B. Bankruptcy and Analogous Insolvency Proceedings	10.09
C. Transferor's Debts	10.14
D. Contract Variations	10.22
E. Misuse of Insolvency Proceedings	10.53
F. Hiving Down	10.54

A. INTRODUCTION

The Directive permits domestic legislation to make specific variations to its **10.01** application and effect in certain insolvency contexts. The Transfer of Undertakings (Protection of Employment) Regulations (TUPE) 2006 took up the ability to make such variations. In short, TUPE's protection for employees (in terms of transferring their employment to the transferee and deeming transfer-related dismissals potentially automatically unfair) does not apply in relation to transactions entered into in the context of 'terminal insolvencies'. In certain other insolvency situations, TUPE provides that the transferee does not inherit certain debts owed to the transferring employees by the transferor which are met by the Government. The employer may also, in certain insolvency situations, agree changes to the terms and conditions of employment of the transferring employees with appropriate representatives of those employees. The extent to which the Directive's usual application is varied will depend on the nature of the insolvency in question.

Article 5.1 provides that, unless domestic legislation provides to the contrary, **10.02** the Directive's safeguards for employees against transfer-related changes to terms and conditions of employment and transfer-related dismissals do not apply where 'the transferor is the subject of bankruptcy proceedings or any analogous insolvency proceedings which have been instituted with a view to the liquidation of the assets of the transferor and are under the supervision of a competent public authority (which may be an insolvency practitioner authorised by a competent public authority)'.[1] Accordingly, other than in such cases of what has been styled 'terminal insolvency', the transfer legislation will still apply with its full rigour subject to the derogations permitted by Article 5.2.

10.03   Article 5.2 introduced two new options for Member States in certain insolvency contexts. The options introduced by Article 5.2 were to:

- provide that the transferor's pre-existing debts towards the transferring employees do not pass to the transferee where protection is provided in relation to these debts for those employees which is at least equivalent to that provided for by the EC Insolvency Directive;[2]

- permit employers and employee representatives to agree changes to terms and conditions of employment which are made by reason of the transfer itself, provided that these changes are made in accordance with national law and practice and with a view to ensuring the survival of the business and thereby preserving jobs.

10.04   These options apply, pursuant to Article 5.2, in relation to 'insolvency proceedings which have been opened in relation to a transferor whether or not these proceedings have been instituted with a view to the liquidation of the assets of the transferor and provided that such proceedings are under the supervision of a competent public authority'. These variations to the effect of the Directive can therefore be applied to a wider category of insolvency situation than a 'terminal insolvency'.

10.05   In introducing TUPE 2006, the Government determined that it would take up both options provided by Article 5.2 in line with the 'rescue culture' that it aims to promote.[3] The provisions of regulations 8 and 9, which record the modified application of TUPE in the insolvency context, apply to relevant transfers and therefore in relation both to transfers of undertakings for the purposes of regulation 3(1)(a) and service provision changes for the purposes of regulation 3(1)(b).

10.06   As noted already, it is important to distinguish between the different effects on the application of the Directive of different types of insolvency situation. Unless a Member State's implementing legislation provides otherwise, transactions occurring in context of terminal insolvencies (bankruptcies and liquidations) cannot attract the employment protection provisions of the Directive in terms of transfer of employment and prohibition of transfer-related dismissal in the absence of an economic, technical or organisational reason entailing changes in the workforce (ETOR). Other insolvency proceedings (which are not instituted with a view to the liquidation of the transferor's assets) can still attract the application of the Directive and TUPE where transactions falling within their scope occur but their application can be moderated by the limitation of the

---

[1] See 2001 Consultation para 84.   [2] AT/987/EEC.   [3] 2001 Consultation para 87.

debts inherited by the transferee and the ability to agree what TUPE styles in regulation 9 'permitted variations' to the contracts of employment of transferring employees.

In implementing Article 5.1 and adopting the provisions permitted by Article 5.2, TUPE 2006 was not drafted by reference to domestic insolvency law and its various specific forms of insolvency procedure. The Directive's formulations (which are framed by reference to the purpose of the relevant procedure) were adopted instead. The failure in drafting TUPE 2006 precisely to relate its insolvency-related provisions to the specific domestic insolvency regime is potentially unhelpful.   10.07

In the light of this purpose-based approach to distinguishing whether the Directive is disapplied or simply modified in a given insolvency context and the failure to relate the provisions of TUPE 2006 directly to the domestic forms of insolvency procedure, problems may arise. It may not always be clear whether the relevant proceedings are conducted with a view to liquidation of assets (in which case the employment protection provisions of TUPE 2006 are disapplied) or to continue the business (in which case TUPE 2006 applies as modified in the specific ways described in this chapter). This problem may perhaps be most acute in relation to administrations. Whether the insolvency in question entails relevant insolvency proceedings is an essential element of the avoidance of transferring debts and the contract variations permitted by regulation 9 and therefore the issue could be of considerable practical importance.   10.08

B. BANKRUPTCY AND ANALOGOUS INSOLVENCY PROCEEDINGS

Under regulation 8(7), it is specifically provided[4] that the protections of TUPE in terms of the transfer of employees and the ability to claim unfair dismissal in relation to transfer-related dismissals[5] do not apply 'to any relevant transfer where the transferor is the subject of bankruptcy proceedings or any analogous insolvency proceedings which have been instituted with a view to the liquidation of the assets of the transferor and are under the supervision of an insolvency practitioner'. This effectively repeats the exclusion from the scope of the Directive pursuant to Article 5.1 of transactions effected as part of a terminal insolvency. Regulation 8(7) was not intended to change the legal position but rather (according to the 2005 Consultation) to make explicit what was previously implicit.[6]   10.09

---

[4] Reflecting Article 5.1.   [5] Regulations 4 and 7.

[6] 2005 Consultation para 65. The inapplicability of the Directive to terminal insolvencies was established in *Abels* [1987] CMLR 406, ECJ. *Perth & Kinross Council v Donaldson and Others* [2004] IRLR 121, EAT confirmed in the domestic context (by reference, *inter alia*, to *Abels*) that the Directive does not apply to a case of 'irretrievable insolvency'.

10.10   The Insolvency Act (IA) 1986, Part XIII provides the definition of an individual's acting as an insolvency practitioner which applies for the purposes of
regulations 8 and 9. Capacities in which an individual acts as an insolvency
practitioner in respect of companies include those of liquidator, administrative
receiver, administrator, and supervisor of a voluntary arrangement.[7] Other
sections of IA 1986, Part XIII[8] set out the relevant provisions applicable to the
qualifications required for a person to act as an insolvency practitioner.

10.11   The wording of regulation 8(7) adopts the generic description set out in Article 5.1 of the sorts of procedures falling outside the scope of the protection of
the transfer of undertakings legislation. Despite the inevitable uncertainty
which this 'copying out' approach entails, the justification for its adoption was
that it ensures a simple provision, 'future proofs' the provision against subsequent changes in insolvency procedures, and ensures that TUPE 2006 goes
no further in derogating from its normal protections for employees than the
Directive permits.[9]

10.12   In terms of the application of this generic wording to the current domestic
insolvency regime, the Government's view[10] was that regulation 8(7) applies 'in
particular [to] compulsory winding up and bankruptcy' and 'that relevant transfers are most unlikely to occur in these cases in any event, as it is very rare that a
business or part of a business, survives in the wake of such a procedure'. The
2005 Consultation acknowledged[11] a degree of uncertainty with regard to
whether a creditors' voluntary winding up falls within the scope of Article 5.1's
exclusion of the Directive's normal application (as well as whether the exclusion
by Article 5.2 of the transfer to the transferee of the relevant category of debts
applies in such a situation).

10.13   It should be noted that regulation 8(7) only disapplies regulations 4 and 7
from applying to relevant transfers arising in relation to bankruptcy and analogous insolvency proceedings. The regulation 13 collective information and
consultation obligations would still apply to a relevant transfer effected in such a
scenario (even if a relevant transfer is very unlikely in such circumstances).

C. TRANSFEROR'S DEBTS

1. Relevant Insolvency Proceedings

10.14   Pursuant to regulation 8(1) the provisions of TUPE 2006 relating to the transferor's debts to its employees[12] apply in relation to 'relevant insolvency proceedings'. As is the case with regulation 8(7), the approach of TUPE 2006 in defining

---

[7] IA 1986, s 388(1) (a) and (b); IA 1986, s 389 (2) identifies the situations in which a person acts as
a insolvency practitioner in relation to individuals.
[8] IA 1986, ss 390–398.   [9] 2005 Consultation paras 58 and 64.   [10] Ibid para 64.
[11] Para 64 footnote 8.   [12] Regulation 8(2)–(6).

the insolvency proceedings to which the provisions relating to the transferor's debts applies is to repeat the wording of the Directive.[13] Following Article 5.2, relevant insolvency proceedings are defined by regulation 8(6) as 'insolvency proceedings which have been opened in relation to the transferor not with a view to the liquidation of the assets of the transferor and which are under the supervision of an insolvency practitioner'. This reflects the provisions of Article 5.2 and the focus of the relevant European Court of Justice (ECJ) decisions on the purpose of the relevant insolvency regime.[14] Accordingly, where the insolvency is not terminal, then TUPE still applies although modified in its effect.

The 2005 Consultation indicated[15] that administration, company and individual voluntary arrangements, and creditors' voluntary winding up, but not administrative or other receivership or any other voluntary winding up, are covered by these provisions with regard to the transferor's debts. The Department of Trade and Industry (DTI) Guidance[16] described the Government's analysis somewhat differently: **10.15**

It is the Department's view that 'relevant insolvency proceedings' mean any collective insolvency proceedings in which the whole or part of the business or undertaking is transferred to another entity as a going concern. That is to say it covers an insolvency proceeding in which all creditors of the debtor may participate, and in relation to which the insolvency office-holder owes a duty to all creditors. The Department considers that 'relevant insolvency proceedings' does *not* cover winding-up by either creditors or members where there is no such transfer.

2. Affected Employees

Pursuant to regulation 8(2), the 'relevant employees' who are covered by TUPE's specific provisions with regard to the transfer of the transferor's debts in relation to relevant insolvency proceedings are those employees of the transferor: **10.16**

- whose contract of employment transfers to the transferee pursuant to TUPE.[17] Transfer by agreement will not suffice. TUPE must actually operate to transfer (or apply to the transfer of) the relevant employee's employment since regulation 8(2)(a) requires the relevant employee's employment to transfer 'by virtue of these Regulations';

- whose employment with the transferor is terminated 'before the time of the transfer in the circumstances described in regulation 7(1)'.[18] This extends the limitation of the transfer of the transferor's debts to the transferee to those owed to an employee automatically unfairly dismissed prior to the relevant

---

[13] 2005 Consultation para 58.
[14] Cf *D'Urso v Ercole Marelli Elettromeccanica Generale SpA* [1992] IRLR 136, ECJ; *Spano v Fiat Geotech* [1995] ECR 1–4321; *Jules Detlier Equipement v Dassy* [1998] IRLR 266, ECJ.
[15] At para 58.   [16] At p 30.   [17] Regulation 8(2)(a).   [18] Regulation 8(2)(b).

transfer (ie an employee who was unfairly dismissed before or after the transfer due to the transfer itself or a reason connected with the transfer that is not an ETOR).

3. Excluded Debts

10.17 Were it not for the regime established by regulation 8, all the debts owed by the transferor to the transferring employees would transfer to the transferee.[19] Regulation 8(5) provides that regulation 4 'shall not operate to transfer liability for the sums payable to the relevant employee under the relevant statutory schemes'. Regulation 8 therefore excludes from the scope of the liabilities which the transferee inherits under regulation 4 those sums which are payable to relevant employees under the 'relevant statutory schemes'. These schemes are specified in regulation 8(4) and are the schemes for payment from the National Insurance Fund.

10.18 Whilst a detailed treatment of the statutory insolvency payment schemes, and in particular the limitations to which they are subject, is outside the scope of this work, they are:

- the payments to be made by the Secretary of State under the Employment Rights Act 1996 (ERA 1996), ss 166–170.[20] These include statutory redundancy payments and payments in accordance with conciliation or compromise agreements made by way of an agreement to refrain from bringing a claim for the statutory redundancy entitlement;

- the payments to be made by the Secretary of State under ERA 1996, ss 182–190 on the insolvency of an employer where the relevant employee's employment has been terminated.[21] These payments relate to matters such as arrears of pay, notice pay, holiday pay, and guarantee payments, subject to detailed eligibility requirements and limitations.

10.19 It is important to appreciate, as already noted, that this insolvency regime applies not only to employees dismissed in relation to the transfer but also those whose employment has transferred to the transferee by virtue of TUPE (as opposed to a transfer of employment by agreement where the employee falls outside the scope of TUPE).[22] This leads to a variation of the usual position under ERA 1996, s 102(b), which applies the statutory insolvency payment provisions only to those who have actually been dismissed. For these purposes, the date of the relevant transfer is treated as the date of the termination of employment for the purposes of the relevant statutory payments and the transferor is treated as the employer.[23] A transferring employee can therefore claim

---

[19] Under what is now regulation 4—see 2005 Consultation para 59.
[20] Regulation 8(4)(a).   [21] Regulation 8(4)(b).
[22] Regulation 8(2)(b).   [23] Regulation 8(3).

the statutory redundancy payment and other relevant payments from the State at the point of transfer. In response to concerns raised by consultees, the DTI[24] confirmed its view that payment to a transferring employee of the statutory redundancy payment by the Government pursuant to a relevant statutory scheme has the effect of ensuring 'that the transferred workers have to build up their future entitlement to redundancy payments with the new employer from zero'.

10.20 The overall effect of these provisions is therefore that those whose employment by a transferor in relation to which relevant insolvency proceedings are ongoing transfer to the transferee in accordance with TUPE or who are automatically unfairly dismissed in connection with the transfer, are entitled to receive payments from the Secretary of State in respect of the relevant debts in the same way as they would have been had they been dismissed by the insolvent employer. The transferee does not, as would otherwise be the case, inherit liability for those debts for which the Secretary of State is liable.

10.21 It is important to appreciate that the transferee is only excused from liability for the specific debts which the Government meets. Debts not covered by the relevant statutory schemes or the excess of any debts owed by the transferor to the transferring employees over the applicable statutory limits are still inherited by the transferee in the normal course under regulation 4. As the 2005 Consultation noted,[25] liabilities for debts owed to employees other than those who transfer under TUPE to the transferee remain with the transferor. Debts owed to those dismissed prior to transfer for an ETOR remain with the transferor. Also, this modified insolvency regime in relation to relevant insolvency proceedings only deals with debts. Transferees are not excused from liabilities for automatically unfair pre- or post-transfer dismissals under TUPE. Given these constraints, the benefit of this new regime to the 'rescue culture' may be limited.

D. CONTRACT VARIATIONS

1. Introduction

10.22 Utilising the option provided by Article 5.2, where relevant insolvency proceedings are on foot in relation to the transferor, regulation 9 establishes the ability of employers and appropriate representatives of the transferring employees validly to agree changes connected with or caused by a relevant transfer to the terms and conditions of employment of these transferring employees. For such changes to be valid, certain specific requirements must be satisfied.

10.23 The Government considered[26] that the consequences of taking up this option would be entirely positive provided that adequate safeguards were provided for employees. Employers and appropriate representatives of the transferring

---

[24] Consultation Response paras 5.5 and 5.7.   [25] Para 59 footnote 5.
[26] 2001 Consultation para 93.

employees would then have the same freedom to negotiate in transfer scenarios as in other situations where changes to terms and conditions might need to be agreed with a view to securing the survival of an insolvent business and the consequent saving of jobs.

10.24　This ability to change terms not only counters the prohibition on transfer-related contract changes established by cases such as *Daddy's Dance Hall* and *Wilson*[27] but is also less constrained, and therefore wider in scope, than the ability introduced by regulations 4(4) and 4(5) to agree transfer-related contract changes.[28]

10.25　Regulation 9 only applies in relation to 'relevant insolvency proceedings' (ie to the same kinds of proceeding as the provisions as to the transferor's debts).[29]

10.26　If at the time of transfer the transferor is subject to relevant insolvency proceedings, then 'permitted variations' can be agreed pursuant to regulation 9.[30] These changes can be agreed between the transferor or transferee (or an insolvency practitioner) and 'appropriate representatives'. Presumably, although it is not expressly stated, the transferee must agree the changes prior to or at the point of transfer—it can be surmised that the special regime is intended only to operate while the relevant business or undertaking is the subject of the relevant insolvency proceedings in order to facilitate its whole or partial sale as a going concern. Perhaps regrettably, the period during which permitted variations can be agreed is not expressly addressed by regulation 9.

10.27　Regulation 9 also only makes reference to permitted variations being agreed by appropriate representatives of the transferring employees. This implies that employees cannot individually agree contract changes under regulation 9. Consequently, it must be presumed that changes agreed by employees individually which are connected with a relevant transfer must satisfy regulations 4(4) and 4(5) in order to be valid.

2. Which Employees?

10.28　Permitted variations can only be agreed by appropriate representatives of 'assigned employees'. For these purposes 'assigned employees' are 'those employees assigned to the organised grouping of resources or employees that is the subject of a relevant transfer'.[31] Permitted variations therefore can only be

---

[27] See Chap 6.　　[28] Ibid.

[29] See para 10.14 *et seq* above. Regulation 9(7) provides that 'relevant insolvency proceedings' has the meaning given to the expression by regulation 8(6) ie 'insolvency proceedings which have been opened in relation to the transferor not with a view to the liquidation of the assets of the transferor and which are under the supervision of an insolvency practitioner'.

[30] Regulation 9(1): '[i]f at the time of a relevant transfer the transferor is subject to relevant insolvency proceedings these Regulations shall not prevent the transferor or transferee (or an insolvency practitioner) and appropriate representatives of assigned employees agreeing to permitted variations'.

[31] Regulation 9(7).

agreed in relation to those affected directly by the proposed transfer in the sense that they are employees whose employment transfers to the transferee by virtue of TUPE on the relevant transfer in question.

This limitation on the scope of regulation 9 therefore means that those of the transferor's employees who do not transfer to the transferee by virtue of the particular relevant transfer cannot agree permitted variations under this regime. This is perhaps unsurprising as they do not fall to transfer to the transferee as a consequence of the transaction which the ability to agree permitted variations is intended to facilitate. **10.29**

3. Appropriate Representatives

Regulation 9(2) defines (and provides protection for) the 'appropriate represen- **10.30** tatives' of the transferring employees who can act to agree permitted variations in insolvency situations. Regulation 9(2) provides that:

[f]or the purposes of this regulation 'appropriate representatives' are:
(a) if the employees are of a description in respect of which an independent trade union is recognised by their employer, representatives of the trade union; or
(b) in any other case, whichever of the following employee representatives the employer chooses—
   (i) employee representatives appointed or elected by the assigned employees (whether they make the appointment or election alone or with others) otherwise than for the purposes of this regulation, who (having regard to the purposes for, and the method by which they were appointed or elected) have authority from those employees to agree permitted variations to contracts of employment on their behalf;
   (ii) employee representatives elected by assigned employees (whether they make the appointment or election alone or with others) for these particular purposes, in an election satisfying requirements identical to those contained in regulation 14 except those in regulation 14(1)(d).

The provisions of regulation 9 relating to employee representation are in essence **10.31** the same as those applying in relation to the information and consultation provisions of regulation 13.[32] It is essential to note that the appropriateness of representatives is identified by reference to 'assigned' rather than 'affected' employees. As only those who fail to transfer to the transferee can be subjected to permitted variations, only their representatives can agree them.

Accordingly, if a trade union is recognised in respect of the relevant **10.32** employees, it can negotiate valid transfer-related changes on behalf of those

---

[32] See Chap 9. The only difference between regulation 9 and regulations 13–15 in this regard is the omission from regulation 9 of an equivalent of regulation 14(1)(d)—the employer being required to determine the term of office of a representative. This provision was not considered relevant in the (presumably short-term) context of a transaction out of insolvency.

employees in a qualifying insolvency context.[33] It is not clear whether a union is permitted to agree variations only to the extent it is able to do so by virtue of the scope of its recognition or whether regulation 9 confers a potentially wider power. The former analysis is preferable as regulation 9 is permissive, not preventing changes otherwise prohibited. If the latter analysis is correct, however, this ability of a recognised trade union to agree permitted variations could in many cases extend significantly the power and role which the union has outside the insolvency context. Recognised trade unions may not always have the power generally to agree contract changes on behalf of the employees in respect of which they are recognised (whether or not the relevant employees are actually members of the union). Despite suggestions from consultation respondents that a specific provision be enacted confirming the trade union's authority to act, no such provision was included in TUPE 2006. Nor was the Law Society's suggestion taken up that there should be a requirement that agreements with trade unions be notified to the employees concerned in order to allow them to question the changes.[34] Where non-union representatives are involved, such an obligation applies.[35]

10.33   If there is no recognised trade union in respect of the relevant undertaking or activities or there are categories of employee outside the scope of a recognised trade union's recognition, employee representatives can negotiate transfer-related changes provided that they are either elected in accordance with the relevant requirements or have the requisite authority to act.[36] As is the case with the regulation 13 information and consultation regime, if there is a recognised union, only that union is empowered to agree permitted variations with regard to employees falling within the scope of its recognition. Separately elected employee representatives cannot in such circumstances be utilised for these purposes.

10.34   Regulation 9(3) confirms that an individual may be an appropriate representative for the purposes of both the regulation 9 insolvency regime and the regulation 13 information and consultation obligations 'provided that where the representative is not a trade union representative he is either elected by or has authority from assigned employees (within the meaning of this regulation [9]) and affected employees (as described in regulation 13(1)'. Representatives for the purpose of a regulation 13 information and consultation process can perform employee representative functions in relation to permitted variations in the insolvency context but only if also specifically elected for that purpose or if the agreement of permitted variations specifically falls within the competence of the consultative forum or staff body of which they form part in relation to the employees who are the subject of the transfer.

10.35   Specific authority is therefore required for employee representatives to be able validly to agree permitted variations. In this regard, regulation 9(2)(b)(i) provides that, where no election is conducted specifically for the purposes of

---

[33] Regulation 9(2)(a).   [34] See Consultation Response para 5.5.   [35] Regulation 9(5)(b).
[36] Regulation 9(2)(b)(i) and (ii).

appointing employee representatives competent to agree permitted variations, the representatives must '. . . (having regard to the purposes for and the method by which they were appointed or elected) have authority from those employees to agree permitted variations to contracts of employment on their behalf'. It is not possible simply to take representatives elected only for regulation 13 information and consultation purposes or an existing employee forum and agree regulation 9 permitted variations with them.

The speed of completion of many transactions in insolvency situations may make it difficult to utilise this ability to introduce permitted variations if election of employee representatives needs to be conducted. That said, it may well be that, if employee representatives are being elected by employees engaged in a business which is or is likely to be in insolvency, it will be sensible for the employer or relevant insolvency practitioner in arranging the requisite elections specifically to establish the authority of the elected employee representatives to agree regulation 9 permitted variations as well as to participate in regulation 13 information and consultation. **10.36**

TUPE 2006[37] ensures that the protections provided under ERA 1996 for the purposes of the regulation 13 information and consultation obligations similarly apply to employee representatives for the purposes of permitted variations in the insolvency context. **10.37**

Similarly, regulation 9(4) makes consequential amendments to the Trade Union and Labour Relations (Consolidation) Act (TULRCA) 1992, s 168 to ensure that trade union representatives have the rights to time off in this context similar to those which apply in relation to the regulation 13 information and consultation obligations. Time off is specifically permitted in respect of: **10.38**

- negotiations with a view to entering into an agreement for the purposes of regulation 9;
- the performance on behalf of employees of the employer of functions related to or connected with the making of an agreement under that regulation.

4. Agreement of Employee Representatives

For permitted variations to be valid under regulation 9, specific additional requirements must be complied with in situations where the transferring employees are represented by employee representatives as opposed to being represented by a recognised trade union.[38] These additional safeguards are intended to recognise the fact that non-union representatives are not normally involved in negotiating changes to employees' terms and conditions and are therefore less likely to be experienced and knowledgeable than trade union representatives.[39] Variations agreed by union representatives are valid without these requirements **10.39**

---

[37] Sch 2, para 10.   [38] Regulations 9(5)(a) and (b).   [39] 2005 Consultation para 70.

needing to be satisfied. No particular requirements are specified in relation to the agreement by recognised trade unions of permitted variations.

10.40   First, the agreement recording the permitted variations must be in writing and signed by each of the employee representatives who have made it or, where that is not reasonably practicable, by a duly authorised agent of that employee representative.[40]

10.41   Second, the employer must, before the agreement is made available for signature, provide all employees to whom it is intended to apply on the date on which it is to come into effect with copies of the text of the agreement and such guidance as those employees might reasonably require in order to understand it fully.[41] The extent to which detailed guidance will need to be given as to the effects of changes will depend upon their complexity. Nonetheless, this is a potentially open-ended requirement which will need to be addressed with care, especially since failure to comply with it presumably invalidates an otherwise effective permitted variation.

10.42   That the agreement must in these circumstances be signed by the employee representatives or their authorised agent raises two issues. First, it is implicit (but not specifically stated) that the employee representatives must act unanimously (which may provide some further protection for minority groups of employees). Second, what constitutes a duly authorised agent is not specified. Clear, preferably written, evidence of the authorisation of an agent who signs an agreement recording what are intended to be permitted variations for the purposes of regulation 9 (for example, one representative being appointed to act on behalf of the entire body of representatives) will be needed to ensure their validity, assuming all the other requirements are satisfied.

5. The Nature of Permitted Variations

10.43   Regulation 9(6) provides that a permitted variation 'shall take effect as a term or condition of the assigned employee's contract of employment in place, where relevant, of any term or condition which it varies'. It is of immediate effect.

10.44   To be valid, a permitted variation must also be 'designed to safeguard employment opportunities by ensuring the survival of the undertaking, business or part of the undertaking or business that is subject of the relevant transfer'.[42] This is a potentially important requirement necessitating establishment of the purpose of a permitted variation if its validity is challenged subsequently. Contemporaneous evidence on this point may be crucial in this regard.

10.45   Another important element of what can be a valid permitted variation is the requisite reason for it.[43] The sole or principal reason for the permitted variation must be 'the transfer itself or a reason connected with the transfer that is not an

---

[40] Regulation 9(5)(a).   [41] Regulation 9(5)(b).   [42] Regulation 9(7).
[43] Ibid.

economic, technical or organisational reason entailing changes in the work-force'. An example would be a transfer-related pay cut with no attendant workforce changes. If an ETOR applies the permitted variation route cannot be used, although the ability for employees (as distinct from their representatives) to agree ETOR-based contract changes pursuant to regulation 4(4) and 4(5)[44] would then apply and be available. The permitted variation route cannot be used where the changes are not by reason of or related to the transfer. In such a case, pursuant to regulation 4(5)(b), TUPE 2006 does not engage to regulate contractual validity and the common law contractual rules apply.

6. Issues of Interpretation

A number of problems may arise in relation to the operation of this ability on the part of appropriate representatives of transferring employees to agree permitted variations in insolvency situations. The fact that trade union or (in the absence of a recognised trade union) employee representatives are empowered to agree permitted variations appears effectively to enable employees' contractual entitlements to be overridden and to give them no ability, in legal or process terms, individually to object to a change or changes which those representatives agree on their behalf. These changes are deemed contractual by regulation 9(6) if the representatives are appointed and act in accordance with the applicable requirements. **10.46**

TUPE 2006 provides no effective framework for employees to be able to object to the decision of their representatives with regard to the detail of permitted variations or to opt out of the effect of the powers which regulation 9 confers. Accordingly, it appears that an employee's contract can, in contrast to the common law position, be amended without his or her agreement or authority with regard to the particularity of the change. In cases where a recognised union constitutes the appropriate representatives, the employees may not even have given the union authority to agree such changes in the normal course of events but may find it conferred by statute in the insolvency context if a broad interpretation is applied to regulation 9. An employee who does not actually vote for the election of appropriate representatives or is not a member of the relevant recognised trade union may be seen by some as the author of his or her own misfortune by virtue of his or her failure to participate in the process. Nonetheless, a majority would seem able effectively to impose on a minority of the relevant workforce amendments to their contracts of employment without those affected having taken any step to validate the detailed results of the negotiations conducted by their representatives. **10.47**

There is no apparent prohibition on differential treatment of different classes of or particular employees. A provision to this effect would at least have secured **10.48**

---

[44] See Chap 6.

some equity in the application of whatever changes are agreed by appropriate representatives. There therefore appears to be no basis provided explicitly by TUPE 2006 upon which, for example, senior executives with generous salaries and notice periods could avoid their contractual entitlements being reduced by an agreement reached by their employee representatives (or a trade union within the scope of whose recognition they fall) without their consent or agreement, provided that the other applicable requirements of regulation 9 are satisfied.

10.49   Quite apart from the fact that individual contractual entitlements are capable, pursuant to regulation 9, of being overridden by a process which has the apparent aura of democracy, these issues will arguably increase the exposure of employee representatives to the (as yet untested) possibility of claims by employees against their representatives of negligence in the performance of their duties and the negotiation of contract changes. A representative's potential predicament in this regard may be exacerbated by the fact that, despite requests that such an obligation be introduced, nothing in TUPE 2006 requires the disclosure by the employer of any information to the representatives engaged in negotiating permitted variations.[45] These issues are put in even starker relief by the fact that regulation 9 (as is the case with regulation 13) does not expressly require elected employee representatives to be informed of their responsibilities, or indeed potential liabilities, nor does it specify their responsibilities to the employees whom they represent.

10.50   The 2005 Consultation did not address these concerns to any material extent. The role of appropriate representatives was likened to that of similarly elected persons under regulation 13[46] (even though appropriate representatives in relation to the collective information and consultation process do not, by virtue of TUPE, have the power to commit their constituency to legally binding agreements). The requirement, where the appropriate representatives are not union representatives, to circulate the proposed agreement and appropriate guidance was described as being based on the 'established precedent' of the Working Time Regulations 1998 where similarly structured 'workforce agreements' are permitted. Such workforce agreements are, however, limited in scope to a narrow category of working time issues in contrast to permitted variations, which could cover any aspect of the relevant employees' contracts of employment and benefit packages.

10.51   Objecting to transfer does not appear to be a route to compensation for employees whose rights are overridden by the collective permitted variation process. The fact that regulation 4(9) is expressly made subject to regulation 9 means that affected employees cannot exercise the right to terminate their employment by reason of a substantial change to their working conditions to their material detriment where the change has been agreed by their appropriate representatives in an insolvency situation under regulation 9. A traditional

---

[45] See Consultation Response para 5.6.   [46] Para 68.

constructive dismissal claim (preserved by regulation 4(11)) would appear to be unavailable because a permitted variation is deemed contractually valid and effective by regulation 9(6).

Employees who find themselves unhappy with changes which have been **10.52** agreed on their behalf by appropriate representatives may therefore have little room for manoeuvre. In terms of challenge to the validity of a permitted variation, employees would appear to have two particular avenues to consider in terms of arguing that a change is not valid and effective because it does not satisfy the definition of a permitted variation. It may be possible to argue that the change was not designed to safeguard employment opportunities. The purposive aspect of a permitted variation appears to require only an intention or objective of safeguarding employment opportunities. Accordingly, it would appear that a permitted variation should not be capable of being rendered invalid on the basis that it was not objectively required in order to (as opposed to being intended to) safeguard employment. Alternatively, and again this is an open textured issue, it could be argued that inadequate guidance was given to the employees in order to enable them to understand the changes.

E. MISUSE OF INSOLVENCY PROCEEDINGS

Article 5.4 requires Member States to 'take appropriate measures with a view to **10.53** preventing misuse of insolvency proceedings in such a way as to deprive employees of the rights provided for'. The Government considered that the existing safeguards set out in the Insolvency Act 1986 remain adequate for these purposes and therefore that no amendment to TUPE was required in that regard.[47] Essentially, protection against misuse of insolvency proceedings is provided by the limitation of the control and supervision of insolvency proceedings to those authorised to act as insolvency practitioners together with the other regulatory provisions of the Insolvency Act 1986 and the Company Directors' Disqualification Act 1986 establishing the regime of potential investigations and prosecutions following the cases of malpractice.

F. HIVING DOWN

TUPE 1981, regulation 4(1) provided that, where the receiver of property or an **10.54** administrator or liquidator in a creditors' voluntary winding up transferred the company's undertaking or part of the company's undertaking to a wholly owned subsidiary, the relevant transfer should be deemed for the purposes of the legislation not to have been effected until immediately before whichever was first to occur of:

---

[47] 2001 Consultation paras 98–100; 2005 Consultation para 73.

- the transferee company ceasing (otherwise than by reason of its being wound up) to be a wholly owned subsidiary of the transferor company;
- the relevant undertaking being transferred by the transferee company to another person.

10.55 For the purposes of TUPE 1981, the transfer was then taken to have been effected immediately before the final transaction in the process thereby leaving the employees employed by the insolvent company unprotected. This provision addressed what is known as 'hiving down' but was not replicated in TUPE 2006 on the basis that it no longer served any useful purpose.[48] Hiving down was used as a mechanism to seek to avoid the application of TUPE. However, following *Litster*,[49] pre-transfer dismissals can lead to liability on the part of the transferee in any case, thereby rendering the TUPE 1981 provisions redundant.

---

[48] See 2001 Consultation paras 101–103.   [49] [1989] IRLR 161, HL.

11

PENSIONS

A. Overview	11.01
B. The Pensions Exclusion	11.06
C. *Beckmann* and *Martin*	11.17
D. TUPE 2006 Pension Provisions	11.32
E. PA 2004 and PPR 2005	11.38

A. OVERVIEW

11.01 The Directive permits Member States' domestic legislation to exclude membership of and benefits under occupational pension schemes from those rights of transferring employees which are preserved on a transfer falling within its scope.[1] For ease of reference, this can be styled the 'the pensions exclusion'. The Transfer of Undertakings (Protection of Employment) Regulations (TUPE) 1981, regulation 7[2] incorporated into domestic law this permissible exclusion of occupational pension rights from the scope of the entitlements of transferring employees which the transferee inherits and is required to honour after a TUPE transfer. In very general terms, occupational pension schemes for these purposes are defined benefit or defined contribution schemes established and operated by employers (as distinct from obligations to contribute to personal pension arrangements which do transfer to the transferee on a TUPE transfer). However, the detailed operation of the pension exclusion presents more complexities than would first appear.

11.02 The pensions exclusion proved over time to be a particularly controversial aspect of the transfer legislation, particularly in the context of the contracting out of services from the public sector with the consequent potential loss of valuable pension rights more favourable than those generally offered in the private sector.

---

[1] By virtue of Article 4 (whilst also permitting Member States to provide that occupational pension rights do transfer).

[2] Now regulation 10(1).

11.03 To an extent this lack of pension protection has in more recent times been mitigated in the public sector context by Government practice and contracting requirements. More generally, in practical terms, the consequences from the human resources and industrial relations perspectives of failure to provide pension benefits post-transfer often impel transferees to put in place some form of pension benefit in order to avoid potentially disastrous effects on staff morale and retention. However, until 6 April 2005, the only impetus in the private sector to continue any pension provision for those who enjoyed pre-transfer occupational pension arrangements was either the commercial imperative of maintaining staff relations or a requirement on the part of a client awarding a contract that pension provision be maintained for its former employees after transfer to the new contractor.

11.04 The combined effect of the Pensions Act 2004 (PA 2004) and the Transfer of Employment (Pension Protection) Regulations 2005 (PPR 2005) establishes a minimum level of pension provision for transferring employees who enjoyed (or were eligible for) pension benefits in their pre-transfer employment with the transferor. It is important to note that the pension protection (or, perhaps more accurately, preservation) regime established by PA 2004 and PPR 2005 is exactly that. The statutory requirement is only to extend pension benefits to those transferring employees who enjoyed or were eligible (actually or contingently) for pre-transfer pension entitlements. For those who had no pension entitlements prior to transfer, no specific provision is made beyond the general obligation to offer stakeholder pension arrangements. Employment costs may be increased for transferees as a consequence of the requirement to maintain a minimum level of pension benefit for transferring employees, but this pension preservation regime was introduced on the basis of a 'level playing field' for those competing for the award of contracts and a fairly moderate standard of required pension provision.

11.05 However, the resolution of pensions issues in the transfer of undertakings context may not simply consist of complying with PA 2004 and PPR 2005. The European Court of Justice (ECJ) case law on the extent of the pensions exclusion means that the pension-related benefits provided by the transferor which are available to transferring employees may still need to be replicated post-transfer if they fall outside the narrowly construed scope of the pensions exclusion. For example, if a transferee assumes that it can simply offer a money purchase scheme complying with PA 2004 and PPR 2005 but discovers that it is nonetheless, post-transfer, bound by certain aspects of the transferor's final salary scheme which it erroneously assumed to fall within the scope of the pensions exclusion (such as an entitlement to early retirement in certain circumstances), there could be extremely significant cost in replicating those aspects of a pension scheme which, *ex hypothesi*, the transferee will have decided not to continue. Challenging commercial and liability allocation issues can therefore arise.

B. THE PENSIONS EXCLUSION

1. The Directive

Article 4[3] sets out the relevant provisions of the Directive: **11.06**

(a) Paragraphs 1 and 3[4] shall not apply in relation to employees' rights to old age, invalidity or survivors' benefits under supplementary company or intercompany pension schemes outside the statutory social security schemes in Member States.

(b) Member States shall adopt the measures necessary to protect the interests of employees and of persons no longer employed in the transferor's business at the time of the transfer in respect of rights conferring on them immediate or prospective entitlement to old age benefits, including survivors' benefits, under supplementary schemes referred to in sub-paragraph (a).

Put shortly, Article 4(a) excludes occupational pension scheme rights from the **11.07** benefits which the transferee inherits. Article 4(b) requires the Member States to ensure that the accrued pension benefits of the transferring employees are adequately protected but does not require the Member States in their domestic implementing legislation to impose any mandatory obligation on transferees to continue those existing occupational pension benefits after transfer.

That the obligation in the predecessor provision of Article 4(b) to preserve **11.08** pension rights could not be interpreted to require transferees to provide after a relevant transfer occupational pension benefits equivalent to those provided pre-transfer was confirmed in *Walden Engineering Co Limited v Warrener*.[5] In that case it was argued that a scheme operated to replace the State Earnings Related Pension Scheme (SERPS) pension arrangement did not fall within the scope of the pensions exclusion because the relevant company scheme did not fall outside the statutory social security scheme—it was a replacement for it. The Employment Appeal Tribunal (EAT) made clear that the requirement in the Directive that Member States take measures to protect employees' and former employees' interests was simply a requirement to protect pension scheme rights accrued at the point of transfer—the UK has a separate statutory protection regime in this regard.[6]

In *Adams v Lancashire County Council and BET*,[7] the Court of Appeal held **11.09** that a Council which was the transferor of various employees was not in breach of the Directive by failing to secure the ongoing benefit of its occupational

---

[3] The equivalent provision in ARD 1977 was Article 3(3), which did not provide an option for Member States to include (rather than exclude) pension rights as a transferring entitlement.

[4] Which are the operative provisions of the Directive requiring domestic legislation to transfer to the transferee all obligations, rights, powers, and duties in relation to the transferring employees.

[5] [1993] ICR 967, EAT.

[6] The Pension Schemes Act 1993, the Pensions Act 2004, and other protective legislation outside the scope of this work.

[7] [1997] IRLR 436, CA. See also *Eidesund v Stavanger Catering A/S* [1996] IRLR 684 ECJ.

pension scheme when the employees transferred to the transferee. The argument was rejected that TUPE 1981, regulation 7 was of wider scope than permitted by the Directive. It was held that the Directive did not require occupational pension benefits to be continued post-transfer.

2. Occupational Pension Schemes

11.10 There are two principal aspects of the pensions exclusion set out in the Acquired Rights Directive (ARD) 2001. The first is that it is limited in its scope to 'old age, invalidity or survivors' benefits'. Other benefits do transfer to and are inherited by the transferee. As discussed below, this formulation presents some potentially difficult issues. Second, the type of arrangements which the pension exclusion covers are 'supplementary company or inter-company pension schemes'.

11.11 TUPE does not refer to the concept of supplementary company or inter-company pension schemes. Rather, it provides that 'occupational pension schemes' fall outside the scope of the transfer of contractual entitlements to the transferee.[8]

11.12 The Pension Schemes Act 1993 (PSA 1993), s 1 provided the following definition of an occupational pension scheme:

'occupational pension scheme' means any scheme or arrangement which is comprised in one or more instruments or agreements and which has, or is capable of having effect in relation to one or more descriptions of categories of employments so as to provide benefits, in the form of pensions or otherwise, payable on termination of service, or on death or retirement, to or in respect of earners with qualifying service in an employment of any such description or category.

11.13 PA 2004, s 239 introduces a new definition of an occupational pension scheme as follows:

'occupational pension scheme' means a pension scheme:
(a) that:
    (i) for the purpose of providing benefits to, or in respect of, people with service in employments of a description, or
    (ii) for that purpose and also for the purpose of providing benefits to, or in respect of, other people,
is established by, or by persons who include, a person to whom subsection (2) applies when the scheme is established or (as the case may be) to whom that subsection would have applied when the scheme was established had that subsection then been in force, and
(b) that has its main administration in the United Kingdom or outside the Member States,
Or a pension scheme that is prescribed or is of a prescribed description.

11.14 The issue arises of whether there is any practical or other distinction between these two definitions of what constitutes an occupational pension scheme. As

---

[8] Regulation 10.

Pollard[9] notes, the requirement of qualifying service by reference to which benefits must be payable no longer applies but the main administration of the scheme must now be in the United Kingdom or outside the European Union (EU). A pension arrangement which would otherwise constitute an occupational pension scheme would therefore fall outside the PA 2004, s 239 definition (and therefore outside the scope of the pensions exclusion) if administered outside the UK but within the EU.

These definitions of what constitutes an occupational pension scheme are **11.15** considered to cover defined contribution and defined benefit arrangements established and operated by employers (which therefore fall outside the scope of the legislation and need not be continued post-transfer by the transferee) and not to contractual obligations to make a financial contribution to an individual's externally operated and managed personal pension arrangement (which the transferee therefore does inherit). An employer's obligation to make a financial contribution to an employee's own personal pension arrangement simply constitutes a cash contribution and therefore does not fall within the scope of the pensions exclusion—it is preserved on transfer like any other contractual benefit. Similarly, a stakeholder pension[10] arrangement, even if it has been established by the employer, may well not constitute an occupational pension scheme and will be inherited by the transferee on a relevant transfer.

A group personal pension scheme is akin to a personal pension arrangement **11.16** falling outside the scope of pension exclusion because it entails the making of contributions by the employer to be invested on behalf of the employee by a pension provider. The fact that there are now (consequent upon amendments made by PA 2004) separate definitions of occupational pension schemes and personal pension schemes in the PSA 1993, s 1 bolsters this argument. However, the fact that a group personal pension scheme is to an extent operated by the employer does provide some basis for arguing that it is an occupational pension scheme within the meaning of the legislation. The fact that such arrangements can, in administrative terms, be transferred relatively easily to a transferee and entail specific and finite contribution liabilities (as well as the advantage of external administration) means that in practice this debate is rarely relevant. It is, however, generally accepted that group personal pensions do not constitute occupational pension schemes on the basis that they are by their nature akin to a grouping of individual personal pension arrangements.

C. *BECKMANN* AND *MARTIN*

The litigation surrounding the precise scope of the pensions exclusion makes **11.17** clear that transferees cannot simply ignore occupational pension schemes in

---

[9] David Pollard, 'Pensions and TUPE' [2005] 34 ILJ 127.

[10] Established pursuant to the requirements of the Welfare Reform and Pensions Act 1999.

their entirety. The pensions exclusion is expressly confined in its scope to old age, survivors', and invalidity benefits. Therefore, other entitlements which are on occasion provided under occupational pension schemes (such as enhanced redundancy and early retirement entitlements) may fall outside the scope of the pensions exclusion and accordingly constitute benefits to which transferring employees remain entitled post-transfer as against the transferee.

11.18   The first major case addressing the extent of the pensions exclusion was *Frankling v BPS Public Sector Limited*.[11] Employees who had been employed by a National Health Service (NHS) trust, and whose employment transferred to a new employer when their activities were outsourced, had been engaged originally under the Whitley Council terms and conditions of employment. These terms and conditions made special provision for early payment of superannuation and compensation benefits if the employees were made redundant. These entitlements effectively constituted accelerated pension benefits payable in a redundancy situation. The transferee argued that these specific entitlements fell within the scope of the pensions exclusion under TUPE 1981, regulation 7 so that it was accordingly not legally bound to honour them.

11.19   The EAT held that, as the entitlements were payable under legislation, they did not constitute a contractual liability which would transfer under TUPE 1981, regulation 5. More importantly for these purposes, the EAT also took the view that the relevant entitlements constituted benefits for old age, invalidity, or survivors and therefore fell within the scope of the pensions exclusion. The basis for this finding was the characterisation of the relevant benefits as related to retirement, even though the retirement in relation to which they were payable was earlier than normal retirement age. Pension benefits were held not to change their character simply because they were triggered early by redundancy.

11.20   However, this approach to the interpretation of the pensions exclusion was rejected by the ECJ in *Beckmann v Dynamco Whicheloe Macfarlane Limited*.[12] Again, under the Whitley Council rules, employees were entitled to an enhanced lump sum redundancy payment and to early retirement pension entitlements upon dismissal by redundancy after the age of 50. The ECJ applied a strict interpretation of the pensions exclusion which it considered should be construed narrowly. Only benefits which are payable on conclusion of the employee's working life are excluded. Benefits which become due earlier, even if they are provided as part of and are payable in accordance with the rules of a pension scheme, fall outside the scope of the pensions exclusion and are inherited by the transferee. That the relevant entitlements derived from statutory obligations made no difference to this analysis.

11.21   As the ECJ put it:

only benefits paid from the time when an employee reaches the end of his normal working life as laid down by the general structure of the pension scheme in question, and not

---

[11] [1999] IRLR 212, EAT.   [12] [2002] IRLR 578, ECJ.

benefits paid in circumstances such as those in point in the main proceedings (dismissal for redundancy) that can be classified as old-age benefits, even if they are calculated by reference to the rules for calculating normal pension benefits did not fall within the pensions exclusion and therefore were inherited by the transferee.'[13]

Accordingly, rights going beyond the strict ambit of old age, invalidity, and sur- **11.22** vivors' benefits can survive a TUPE transfer and remain part of the employee's contractual entitlements as against the transferee. This analysis can extend not just to items which can easily be characterised as not being pension related (such as enhanced redundancy payments) but also to benefits which are to a degree pension related but which arise earlier than at normal retirement age such as early retirement entitlements.

Martin and others v South Bank University[14] again concerned the issue of **11.23** whether a transferee was bound to honour Whitley Council conditions of service with regard to enhanced retirement pension entitlements and other compensation payable on cessation of work by reason of redundancy, efficiency, or organisational change. The ECJ held that early retirement benefits and benefits intended to enhance the conditions of such retirement are not old age, invalidity, or survivors' benefits within the meaning of the Directive.

The ECJ considered that there was no basis upon which entitlements arising **11.24** on dismissal or early retirement agreed with the employer should be treated differently from entitlements arising after the age of 50 (which in *Beckmann* had been held not to constitute old age benefits and therefore to fall outside the scope of the pensions exclusion). Accordingly, these benefits did fall within the scope of the contractual entitlements passing to the transferee on a relevant transfer. Any consent to an unfavourable alteration of the applicable early retirement terms was accordingly invalid in principle.[15]

It has been suggested that, since both *Beckmann* and *Martin* address NHS **11.25** pension arrangements, it is not certain that the principles they establish apply in the private sector context. It can be argued that there is little apparent support for that view to be found in the decisions themselves. That said, there is little indication in the two decisions as to whether they are of general application. The cases both related to a specific public sector context not normally found in the private sector. The relevant public sector arrangements comprised not only a pension payable from normal retirement but also a pension payable until that point.

It is therefore not absolutely clear whether the ECJ's decisions apply to all **11.26** pension schemes or just to the specific public sector pension payable prior to retirement. No guidance has been given on the issue of whether it makes any difference to the analysis that in a private sector context the pensions obligation may be borne by the trustees of the relevant pension scheme rather than directly by the transferor employer. How the transfer of early retirement and

---

[13] Ibid at para 30.   [14] [2004] IRLR 74, ECJ.   [15] See Chap 6.

redundancy entitlements to the transferee interacts with the relevant employee's extant pension benefits under the transferor's pension scheme has also not been addressed. Without further case law guidance, the scope of the principle which these decisions establish will remain uncertain. For example, it is arguable that ill-health early retirement benefits do still fall within the pensions exclusion on the basis that they constitute invalidity benefits.

11.27   Transferees accordingly need to appreciate the limited scope of the pensions exclusion and the possibility that they will have to honour pension benefits payable earlier than normal retirement.

11.28   Due diligence as to what the transferee will or might arguably inherit in terms of ongoing occupational pension obligations is therefore crucial for those engaging in transfers of undertakings since transferees need to establish what liabilities they do inherit, what pre-transfer entitlements do not transfer, and to what extent new pension arrangements may need to be implemented to comply with PA 2004 and PPR 2005.

11.29   As the potential liabilities arising under the principles established by these cases can be very significant, the transferee may, where the commercial circumstances permit, wish to seek to extract an indemnity from the transferor in respect of any claims made by transferring employees post-transfer to benefits preserved by *Beckmann/Martin*. Employees may seek to rely on the *Beckmann/Martin* decisions a considerable time after the relevant transfer took place. Alternatively, an adjustment may need to be negotiated to the purchase price where a business sale is affected by the issue.

11.30   Quite apart from the need to analyse carefully what the transferor's obligations are and whether they transfer to the transferee on a relevant transfer under the *Beckmann/Martin* decisions, actuarial advice may need to be obtained to assess the potential exposure if the transferee proposes not to continue the relevant benefits and it is arguable that they may nonetheless transfer under TUPE.

11.31   The unpredictability and potential scale of the liabilities which may arise as a result of *Beckmann* and *Martin* may make it unlikely that a transferor will readily agree to an open-ended indemnity liability as may the availability of ways in which the liabilities associated with this issue can be mitigated. If the employer's consent is required to the taking of early retirement pension benefits covered by the *Beckmann/Martin* decisions, then the employer may be able to decline to give this consent. This may of course lead an employee to argue that the decision to withhold the required consent when taken by the transferee is in breach of contract as a capricious or entirely unjustifiable exercise of the discretion.[16] This argument may have particular force if the transferor had a specific practice in relation to the grant of consent in relation to early retirement pensions. Deviation from that practice without good reason may be difficult to

---

[16] Under the principles established in decisions such as *Clarke v Nomura International plc* [2000] IRLR 766, QBD and *Horkulak v Cantor Fitzgerald International* [2004] IRLR 942, CA.

justify as not being capricious. There is also a respectable argument that under regulation 4 the transferee may be bound by the transferor's approach if that can be characterised as effectively contractual by virtue of being a custom and practice.

D. TUPE 2006 PENSION PROVISIONS

Regulation 10 repeats largely unchanged the provisions of TUPE 1981, regula- **11.32** tion 7 with regard to the pensions exclusion and its scope. The Government's view[17] was that *Beckmann* and *Martin* 'merely interpreted the requirements of the Directive, as fully implemented in the existing [TUPE 1981], and were consistent with the Government's own view of the intended effect in this regard'. Accordingly, there was no requirement to make express reference to the effect of those decisions in an updated TUPE.[18] These provisions apply to all relevant transfers and therefore both to transfers of undertakings for the purposes of regulation 3(1)(a) and service provision changes for the purposes of regulation 3(1)(b).

Accordingly, regulation 10(1) provides that regulations 4 and 5 (which provide **11.33** for employees' contractual rights and collective agreements to transfer) shall not apply:

(a) to so much of a contract of employment or collective agreement as relates to an occupational pension scheme within the meaning of the Pensions Schemes Act 1993; or
(b) to any rights, powers, duties or liabilities under or in connection with any such contract or subsisting by virtue of any such agreement relating to such a scheme or otherwise arising in connection with that person's employment and relating to such a scheme.

Regulation 10(2) further confirms that 'any provisions of an occupational pen- **11.34** sion scheme which do not relate to benefits for old age, invalidity or survivors shall be treated as not being part of the scheme'.

One specific pension-related change was made by TUPE 2006. Regulation **11.35** 10(3) provides that:

An employee whose contract of employment is transferred in the circumstances described in regulation 4(1) shall not be entitled to bring a claim against the transferor for—
(a) breach of contract; or
(b) constructive unfair dismissal under Section 95(1)(c) of the 1996 [Employment Rights] Act

---

[17] 2005 Consultation para 75.
[18] See also Consultation Response para 8.4 where it was stated that the Government considered that PA 2004 remained the most appropriate way to deal with the position of occupational pensions when a transfer occurs and that no further changes were required to TUPE.

arising out of a loss or reduction in his rights under an occupational pension scheme in consequence of the transfer, save insofar as the alleged breach of contract or dismissal (as the case may be) occurred prior to the date on which these Regulations took effect.[19]

11.36　Some commentators had argued in relation to TUPE 1981 that a failure by the transferee to confirm that it would continue to make pension provision equivalent to that enjoyed pre-transfer could constitute constructive dismissal on the part of the transferor or at least entitle an employee to terminate his or her employment in accordance with what was TUPE 1981, regulation 5(5)[20] on the basis of a substantial change to his or her detriment in his or her working conditions. Liability for such a claim would remain with the transferor pursuant to the pensions exclusion.[21] The risk of such a claim has now been removed with effect from TUPE 2006 coming into force.

11.37　In the 2001 Consultation[22] the possibility had been raised of legislating specifically to confirm the preservation by TUPE of exactly the sort of age-related payments arising on redundancy as were addressed in *Beckmann*. An express provision reversing *Frankling* was anticipated regardless of the ECJ judgment in *Beckmann* which had not yet at that time been given. By 2005, when the first draft of what became TUPE 2006 was issued, the ECJ had given its guidance and the specific provision anticipated in 2001 was considered no longer to be necessary.

E.　PA 2004 AND PPR 2005

1. Introduction

11.38　The debate with regard to the protection of employees' occupational pension rights following a TUPE transfer has in recent years been particularly acute with regard to public sector pension provision. In its reforms of the transfer of undertakings legislation, the Government proceeded to require all transferees, whether in the private or the public sector, and regardless of whether the transferor operated a defined benefit, defined contribution, or stakeholder occupational pension scheme, to make a minimum level of pension provision for transferring employees who were active members of occupational pension schemes when employed by the transferor to which the employer made a

---

[19] Breaches prior to the commencement of TUPE 2006 are not 'saved' by this new provision.

[20] Now regulation 4(9).

[21] Following the analysis, confirmed in *Hagen v ICI Chemicals and Polymers Ltd* [2002] IRLR 31 EAT, that occupational pension scheme-related liabilities do not transfer to the transferee and *Humphreys* (discussed in Chap 4 at para 4.78 *et seq*), pursuant to which the transferor is liable in respect of the termination of the employee's employment in these circumstances even though it is caused by the transferee's actions.

[22] At paras 60–61.

contribution, were eligible to become active members of such schemes, or would have become eligible to do so had they been employed for a longer period of time.[23]

The obligation on transferees to preserve some level of pension benefits **11.39** post-transfer for transferring employees is imposed by the combined effect of PA 2004, ss 257 and 258 and of PPR 2005. These pension provisions operate independently from and in addition to TUPE 2006 and therefore do not affect its exclusion of the transferor's pre-transfer provision of old age, invalidity, and survivors' benefits under occupational pension schemes from those contractual rights which are inherited by the transferee.

PA 2004 and PPR 2005 establish a minimum level of pension benefits to be **11.40** provided by the transferee to transferring employees for or in respect of whom an occupational pension scheme was provided prior to transfer. This may of course constitute a reduction (or even, although perhaps less likely, an increase) to the pre-transfer level of pension benefits enjoyed by transferring employees whilst they were employed by the transferor. Whilst pensions law more generally, which is outside the scope of this work, establishes a detailed regulatory regime, PA 2004 and PPR 2005 do not prescribe in detail the rules and other administrative provisions of the pension arrangements to be put in place and do not require continuation of early retirement or ill health aspects of the transferor's pension arrangements (to which the *Beckmann/Martin* decisions described above may nonetheless apply). Put simply, the transferee can elect, without regard to the nature and value of the pension benefits which the transferor afforded to the transferring employees, to provide defined contribution or defined benefit arrangements of its choosing to those employees who enjoyed pre-transfer pension benefits provided that they comply with the basic standards required by PA 2004 and PPR 2005.

It has to be said that PA 2004 and PPR 2005 were not greeted with unanimous **11.41** approval. That the new regime requires a basic level of pension provision for transferring employees does nothing to protect valuable defined benefit pension arrangements which employees enjoy prior to a TUPE transfer. It has also been argued that employees with low earnings are particularly prejudiced by PA 2004 and PPR 2005 because the employer's obligation to make pension contributions is parasitic upon the employee's contributions which low earners will find more difficult to make than higher earners.

In passing it is worth noting that, whilst PA 2004 and PPR 2005 only afford **11.42** their protections to those employees who actually do transfer under TUPE 2006 to the transferee, the pensions protection regime will presumably also be relevant to dismissal claims related to a transfer. An employee who enjoyed pension benefits with the transferor and who succeeds in a claim of automatically unfair dismissal against the transferee on the basis that he or she was dismissed in

---

[23] See 2001 Consultation paras 36–59 for detailed discussion of the options considered for pension protection both in the public sector context and otherwise.

connection with the relevant transfer will presumably be able to recover compensation incorporating a pension element based on the requirements of PA 2004 and PPR 2005. After all, those regulations prescribe the minimum level of pensions benefits which the employee should have enjoyed with the transferee had he or she not been unfairly dismissed which thereby form a potential head of loss in an unfair dismissal (and potentially a wrongful dismissal) claim.

2. Eligibility Requirements

(a) Transfer

11.43   A number of requirements need to be satisfied for the protective regime of PA 2004 and PPR 2005 to apply:

- there must be a relevant transfer to which TUPE applies;[24]

- as a result of this TUPE transfer, the employee in question must cease to be employed by the transferor of the relevant business/undertaking and become employed by the transferee;[25]

- the transferor must have been the employer for the purposes of an occupational pension scheme.[26]

There therefore appears to be nothing to prevent PA 2004 and PPR 2005 from applying to an intra-group transfer falling within the scope of TUPE.

(b) Eligible Employees

11.44   The following categories of employee qualify for the protection of the pensions protection regime established by PA 2004 and PPR 2005:

- employees who immediately before the transfer were active members of the transferor's occupational pension scheme;[27]

- employees who immediately before transfer were not members but were eligible to become members of the transferor's occupational pension scheme[28]—those who had not taken up pension scheme membership but are still entitled to do so at the point of transfer are therefore protected. There is no definition

---

[24] PA 2004, s 257(1)(a).

[25] PA 2004, s 257(1)(b). Under PA 2004, s 257(8) this includes employment with an associate of the transferor.

[26] PA 2004, s 257(1)(c)(i). The relevant occupational pension scheme of which a transferring employee was an actual or potential member must be one for the purpose of which the transferor was the employer—this must presumably be taken, in a group context, to cover occupational pension schemes in respect of which the transferor is one of several participating employers.

[27] PA 2004, s 257(2)(a). An active member for the purposes of PA 2004 is an employee in pensionable service for the purposes of pension benefits under the relevant scheme. PA 2004, s 318(1) cross-refers to this definition in the Pensions Act 1995, s 124(1). A deferred member or pensioner is therefore not within the scope of these provisions.

[28] PA 2004, s 257(3)(a).

of eligibility, raising therefore the issue of whether an employee whose participation in the transferor's occupational pension scheme is at the employer's discretion qualifies for the protection afforded by PA 2004 and PPR 2005;[29]

- employees who immediately before the transfer would have been active members or eligible to be active members of an occupational scheme had they been employed for a longer period.[30] Those who as at the date of transfer had yet to complete a waiting period of employment required before they could become members of the relevant pension scheme therefore also enjoy the entitlements conferred by PA 2004 and PPR 2005.

In relation to all these categories of protected employee, the employee's actual **11.45** or potential entitlement to occupational pension benefits is to be assessed immediately before the relevant transfer. Employees' contractual rights and the eligibility rules of the relevant pension scheme therefore need to be considered as at the point of transfer to determine whether the regime established by PA 2004 and PPR 2005 applies in each particular case.

In relation to defined contribution arrangements operated by a transferor **11.46** prior to a TUPE transfer, an employee will not qualify for the pensions entitlements conferred by PA 2004 and PPR 2005 unless the transferor employer either did or was required to make contributions for that employee (or would have been so required had the otherwise eligible employee joined the relevant scheme).[31]

3. The Minimum Standard of Pension Provision

(a) *The Entitlement*

The pensions preservation regime established by PA 2004 and PPR 2005 **11.47** incorporates into protected employees' contracts of employment a contractual entitlement[32] either:

- to become a member of an occupational pension scheme provided by the transferee employer[33] which satisfies the specific requirements prescribed by PA 2004 and PPR 2005; or
- to 'relevant contributions'[34] by the transferee to a stakeholder pension scheme of which the employee is a member.[35]

---

[29] See Pollard n 9 above at p 132: '[t]he better view seems to be that such an employee is not "eligible" for this purpose. But it is not as clear as it might be.'

[30] PA 2004, s 257(4)(a).

[31] PA 2004, ss 257(2)(b), (3)(b), (4)(b). Pursuant to PA 2004, s 257(7) minimum payments required to be made pursuant to PSA 1993 do not satisfy this requirement. These minimum payments arise in relation to schemes which are contracted out of the state second pension.

[32] PA 2004, s 258(1).   [33] PA 2004, s 258(1) and (2).   [34] PA 2004, s 258(7).

[35] PA 2004, s 258(1) and (3). A stakeholder pension scheme for these purposes is, pursuant to PA 2004 s 258(7), a pension scheme registered under the Welfare Reform and Pensions Act 1999, s 2.

11.48   The obligation to provide the prescribed level of pension provision commences with immediate effect from the employee's employment transferring from the transferor to the transferee or (if later) the date on which the employee would have become eligible to join the transferor's pension scheme had he or she remained with the transferee.[36] Accordingly, transferring employees must still complete any waiting period for pension benefits which applied to them in relation to the transferor's pension scheme before being able to insist on their entitlements under PA 2004 and PPR 2005 being provided to them by the transferee. Even though the pension benefit which the transferee provides by way of compliance with PA 2004 and PPR 2005 may, depending upon the circumstances, constitute an inferior level of pension provision than that afforded by the transferor, PA 2004 and PPR 2005 do not, by virtue of the relevant employees transferring to the transferee, accelerate or vary the existing eligibility requirements under the arrangements operated by the transferor.

11.49   As the application of PA 2004 and PPR 2005 is based on eligibility (as opposed to actual membership), it would also appear that the transferee must make pension provision for those who did not take it up whilst employed by the transferor (even though entitled to do so) but who choose to exercise their eligibility rights post-transfer. There appears to be no time limit to that obligation. Accordingly, employees who were eligible to join the transferor's occupational pension scheme but did not do so will have the right to insist on the minimum standard of provision required by PA 2004 and PPR 2005 as and when they elect to insist on that right.

11.50   The eligibility rules of the transferor's occupational pension scheme may well repay careful attention to determine if such a contingent entitlement needs to be catered for effectively in perpetuity. It may be the case, depending on the particular scheme rules, that if an employee does not exercise his or her right to join a pension scheme within a certain time after he or she becomes eligible to participate in it, participation is at the employer's discretion. In this situation, as noted above, it may be doubtful whether the employee qualifies for the protection afforded by PA 2004 and PPR 2005.

(b) *Level of Benefit*

11.51   It is for the transferee to decide what sort of occupational pension benefit to provide post-transfer (ie a defined benefit or defined contribution or stakeholder arrangement). The statutory criteria governing the value of the arrangement which the transferee is required to provide depend on what type of scheme is offered.

11.52   If the scheme which the transferee offers is a defined contribution or stakeholder scheme, then the transferee employer must, in respect of each period for which the employee is paid, at least match the employee's contributions up to a

---

[36] PA 2004, s 258(7) (definition of 'the relevant time').

maximum contribution of 6 per cent of remuneration (regardless of the level of pre-transfer contribution).[37] Remuneration for these purposes only includes the employee's basic rate of pay and excludes bonuses, commissions, overtime, and any similar payments or deductions in respect of tax, national insurance, or pension contributions.[38] No guidance is provided by the legislation with regard to how relevant contributions are to be fixed.[39] Employees therefore appear able to increase and vary contributions. There is no express provision limiting the number and amount of such changes.

If the transferee does not offer a defined contribution, money purchase, or **11.53** stakeholder scheme, then the benefits which it provides must satisfy one of the following requirements. The transferee's scheme must satisfy either the 'reference scheme' test or 'such other test as may be prescribed in regulations'.[40]

The reference scheme test is satisfied if the relevant pension scheme meets the **11.54** statutory standard referred to in PSA 1993, s 12A. The reference scheme test is the test that applies if a pension scheme is to be contracted out of the second state pension. Its key elements[41] are, *inter alia*:

- a normal pension age of 65 for both men and women;
- a pension payable from normal retirement age in respect of each year of pensionable service of 1/80 of average qualifying earnings calculated over the last three tax years;
- specified spouse's pension entitlements;
- prescribed annual pension increases;
- revaluation of deferred pension.

PPR 2005 establishes the alternative basis on which a defined benefit scheme **11.55** which does not satisfy the reference scheme test will nonetheless comply with the obligation to provide post-transfer pension benefits to those who enjoyed them prior to a relevant transfer. Pension arrangements will satisfy PPR 2005 if the employer establishes an arrangement which satisfies either of the following:

- the arrangement provides a value of benefits of at least 6 per cent of pensionable pay for each year of employment[42] together with the total amount of any contributions made by the employee (which employee contributions may not

---

[37] PPR 2005, regulation 3(1)(a) and (b).

[38] PPR 2005, regulation 3(2)(a) and (b). The minimum payments required to be made in respect of money purchase schemes which are contracted out of the state second pension are also ignored pursuant to PA 2004, s 257(7) and PPR 2005, regulation 3(3).

[39] See Pollard n 9 above at p 133.   [40] PA 2004, s 258(2)(c).

[41] See Occupational Pension Schemes (Contracting-Out) Regulations 1996 SI 1996/1172.

[42] 'Pensionable pay' is defined (PPR 2005, regulation 2(2)) as that part of the remuneration payable to a member of a scheme by reference to which the amount of contributions and benefits are determined under the rules of the scheme.

exceed 6 per cent of pensionable pay)[43]—there is no prescribed mechanism for calculating this value;

- the employer makes 'relevant contributions' which match the employee's contributions up to a maximum of 6 per cent of basic pay in respect of each period in relation to which the employee is paid.[44]

4. Enforcement

(a) *Contractual Status*

11.56 PA 2004 renders the prescribed minimum level of pension benefits a contractual right for employees.[45] This arguably places transferring employees in a better position than those of the transferee's employees who participate in its existing pension arrangements. Those employees may well not have a contractual right to a specific level of benefit which cannot be varied without the employee's consent. The pension benefits of the transferee's existing employees may be capable of being changed or even discontinued unilaterally by the employer if the rules of the relevant pension arrangements so permit (subject of course to the ability to vary entitlements being contractually valid and subject to any challenge to the exercise of that power on grounds of irrationality, perversity, or breach by the employer of the implied duty to maintain trust and confidence). It therefore may well be desirable for the transferee to seek, if feasible, to agree with transferring employees[46] that their post-transfer pension provision is specifically subject to and in accordance with the rules of the relevant scheme, thereby incorporating an ability to change or discontinue pension arrangements in the future.

(b) *Pensions Regulator*

11.57 Failure to provide pension benefits of the required standard not only leaves employees with direct claims against the transferee. The Pensions Regulator has the following powers in respect of breaches of PA 2004 (which extends therefore to breaches of these minimum pension obligations) which could be used to penalise employers who fail to comply with their obligations:

- fines of up to £5,000 can be imposed on individuals or £50,000 otherwise;[47]
- where an employer contribution to an occupational pension scheme is not paid, the Pensions Regulator has the power to exercise such powers as the trustees or manager of the scheme has to recover the contribution.[48]

---

[43] PPR 2005, regulation 2(1)(a).   [44] PPR 2005, regulation 2(1)(b).
[45] PA 2004, s 258(1).
[46] But only after transfer, as permitted by PA 2004, s 258(b)—see para 11.59 below. Presumably such an agreement is more likely to be achievable if the benefits offered exceed the minimum level prescribed by PA 2004 and PPR 2005.
[47] PA 2004, ss 7 and 10.   [48] PA 2004, s 17.

(c) *Anti-avoidance*

PA 2004, s 257(5) makes clear that an employee who is an active, eligible, or **11.58** contingent member of an occupational pension scheme will still qualify for the protection of PA 2004 and PPR 2005 where the relevant requirement 'would have been satisfied but for any action taken by the transferor by reason of the transfer'. Steps taken by an employer to terminate a pension scheme or amend eligibility or other conditions prior to transfer in order to remove or limit the obligations which a transferee will inherit will therefore be open to challenge, subject to the ability on the part of the affected employees to demonstrate (in terms of causation) that the relevant action was taken by reason of the transfer.

(d) *Changing Benefits*

It is open to transferring employees and the transferee to agree that the entitle- **11.59** ments established by PA 2004 and PPR 2005 be varied or disapplied[49] but this appears[50] only to be permitted post-transfer. In contrast to other transfer-related changes to employees' contractual terms and conditions, a change to the basic entitlements established by PA 2004 and PPR 2005 appears not to require satis-faction of any specific criteria or requirements. An otherwise contractually valid change to pension entitlements derived from PA 2004 and PPR 2005, provided that it is effected post-transfer, is therefore permissible and effective.

5. Consultation

Amendment to the pension entitlements of transferring employees, even if this **11.60** simply entails the replacement of pre-transfer occupational pension entitlements with the minimum level of pension provision required by PA 2004 and PPR 2005, will engage the information and consultation requirements of regulation 13. Occupational pension matters are not excluded from the scope of those information and consultation requirements in the way that they are by regula-tion 10 from the provisions relating to transfer of individual and collective obligations under regulations 4 and 5. Consultation obligations in this regard will presumably fall primarily on the transferee as it will be the party which will be implementing 'measures' by way of pension changes. However, the transferor may also need to consider what steps it needs to take and what consultations are thereby necessitated with regard to the pension scheme in which the transferring (or its remaining) employees participate, for example if the scheme is to be terminated as a consequence of or in connection with a relevant transfer.[51]

---

[49] PA 2004, s 256(b).   [50] From PA 2004, s 257(5).

[51] Subject to compliance if applicable with the Occupational and Personal Pension Schemes (Consultation by Employers and Miscellaneous Amendment) Regulations 2006 SI 2006/349.

12

MISCELLANEOUS

A. Contracting Out	12.01
B. Territoriality	12.12
C. Drafting and Commercial Points	12.33
D. Assertion of Statutory Rights	12.47

A. CONTRACTING OUT

1. Prohibition

Any attempt to contract out of the effect of and protections provided by the transfer legislation is unlawful. Regulation 18 provides that: **12.01**

Section 203 of the 1996 [Employment Rights] Act (restrictions on contracting out) shall apply in relation to these Regulations as if they were contained in that Act, save for that section shall not apply in so far as these Regulations provide for an agreement (whether a contract of employment or not) to exclude or limit the operation of these Regulations.

The Employment Rights Act 1996 (ERA 1996), s 203 provides that: **12.02**

Any provision in an agreement (whether a contract of employment or not) is void insofar as it purports:
(a) to exclude or limit the operation of any provision of this Act; or
(b) to preclude a person from any proceedings under this Act before an [employment tribunal].

There are limited circumstances in which the prohibition against contracting out in ERA 1996 does not apply.[1] These include agreements where an ACAS conciliation officer has taken action under the Employment Tribunals Act 1996, s 18[2] and compromise agreements satisfying the relevant statutory requirements.[3] **12.03**

---

[1] ERA 1996, s 203(2).   [2] ERA 1996, s 203(2)(d).

[3] ERA 1996, s 203(2)(e) and equivalent provisions in the Sex Discrimination Act 1975, s 77, Race Relations Act 1976, s 72, Trade Union and Labour Relations (Consolidation) Act (TULRCA) 1992, s 288, Disability Discrimination Act 1995, s 9, Working Time Regulations 1998 (SI 1998/1833), regulation 35, National Minimum Wage Act 1998, s 49(3), Transnational Information and Consultation of Employees Regulations 1999 (SI 1999/3323), regulation 41, Part-time Workers (Prevention

12.04   Regulation 18 provides a more general and comprehensive prohibition on contracting out than the suggested provision in the initial draft of what became the Transfer of Undertakings (Protection of Employment) Regulations (TUPE) 2006. It only permits agreements modifying the effect of the legislation where specifically legitimised by TUPE 2006—an example would be a permitted variation agreement pursuant to regulation 9. The original draft of what became regulation 18 focused on rendering void any attempt to exclude or limit the operation of specified regulations. The absence of reference in that draft provision to the obligation to provide employee liability information raised concerns that commercial parties were to be permitted to contract out of that obligation. That is clearly not possible under the reformulated TUPE 2006 provision.[4]

2. Compromise Agreements

12.05   In the transfer of undertakings context, compromise agreements are relevant to more than just the settlement of actual or potential unfair dismissal claims. Such agreements have regularly been deployed in relation to transfer-related changes to employees' terms and conditions of employment in order to avoid associated unfair dismissal claims. The *Wilson* and *Meade* decisions established that transfer-related contract changes to employees' terms and conditions of employment, even if agreed by the affected employees, are invalid. Accordingly, the only way in which employees could validly agree to the amendment of their terms and conditions of employment would be by agreeing new contracts after a dismissal. Dismissal and re-engagement would not invalidate the new terms and conditions of employment whereas a simple agreement during continued employment would be void.

12.06   Since to adopt this route, when seeking to implement valid transfer-related changes, would entail a dismissal upon which an unfair dismissal claim could be based, the practice arose of employers seeking to agree compromise agreements with individuals where transfer-related changes were being implemented. On this basis, the employer could argue that the transfer-related change was valid because it was introduced in a new employment following a dismissal and could take comfort from the fact that the compromise agreement, provided it was otherwise valid, would sign away any employment-related claims arising from

---

of Less Favourable Treatment) Regulations 2000 (SI 2000/1551), regulation 9, Information & Consultation of Employees Regulations 2004 (SI 2004/3426), regulation 9, Fixed-Term Employees (Prevention of Less Favourable Treatment) Regulations 2002 (SI 2002/2034), regulation 10, Employment Equality (Sexual Orientation) Regulations 2003 (SI 2003/1661), regulation 35 and Employment Equality (Religion or Belief) Regulations 2003 (SI 2003/1660), regulation 35.

[4] See Consultation Response paras 6.11 and 6.12 where it was noted that contracting out of the obligation to provide employee liability information, which would be 'likely to be used most frequently where the transferee is a smaller contractor who could be coerced into accepting this requirement by a large client/transferor', would not be permitted.

the dismissal. The concern inevitably arose as to whether such an arrangement would constitute contracting out of the effect or operation of TUPE and therefore be invalid.

To an extent this problem has diminished in importance given the ability **12.07** introduced by regulations 4(4) and 4(5) for employees to agree transfer-related changes and for appropriate representatives of transferring employees to agree permitted variations in certain insolvency situations. That said, as a result of the potential narrow scope of the ability to change terms under regulation 4, employers may still seek to utilise the compromise agreement route but need to appreciate that its efficacy remains doubtful.

The Employment Appeal Tribunal (EAT) decision in *Solectron Scotland* **12.08** *Limited v Roper & Others*[5] dealt with a slightly different point—the extent to which a compromise agreement can be valid in relation to the settlement of termination-related claims based on TUPE. The employees had signed compromise agreements when made redundant. They subsequently argued that they were nonetheless entitled to enhanced redundancy terms which they had enjoyed in a previous employment from which they had transferred pursuant to the transfer legislation to the employer by whom they were dismissed. The Employment Tribunal (ET) held that the employees were entitled to the enhanced redundancy terms. *Inter alia*, the ET relied on the then applicable prohibition on contracting out, TUPE 1981, regulation 12, which provided that 'any provision of any agreement (whether a contract of employment or not) shall be void insofar as it purports to exclude or limit the operation of regulation 5 . . .'.[6]

The EAT held that the ET was wrong to find that the compromise agreement **12.09** was invalidated by TUPE 1981, regulation 12. The compromise agreement did not arise solely or even mainly by reason of the transfer. It compromised the claims which the employees had on termination of their employment. This was not an agreement varying the employment contract (or, for that matter, the effect of TUPE) but one settling a dispute with regard to the consequences of its termination. The compromise agreement did not therefore fall foul of the prohibition on contracting out. The implicit risk nonetheless remains that a termination coupled with a compromise agreement designed to validate otherwise void transfer-related contract changes may fall foul of the prohibition on contracting out.

Two other issues are worth noting in passing in relation to TUPE-related **12.10** compromise agreements. First, *Thompson and others v Walton Car Delivery and BRS Automotive*[7] demonstrates an important point of privity of contract in the context of compromise agreements. An agreement entered into by an employee with the transferor did not operate to protect the transferee from claims under TUPE. A tripartite agreement between employee, transferor, and transferee may

---

[5] [2004] IRLR 4, EAT.   [6] Regulation 18 has the equivalent effect.
[7] [1997] IRLR 343, EAT.

therefore be necessary. Alternatively, the benefit of the compromise agreement could be extended to the desired persons by use of the Contracts (Rights of Third Parties) Act 1999.

12.11   Second, it should also be noted that claims for compensation for breach of the regulation 13 information and consultation obligations fall within the scope of the prohibition on contracting out provided by regulation 18. Such claims are matters in respect of which an ACAS Conciliation Officer can act to effect a binding settlement. Regulation 16(1) provides that the Employment Tribunals Act 1996, s 18 applies to proceedings bringing complaints in this regard, thereby enabling an ACAS Conciliation Officer to act to effect a binding settlement between the parties. The incorporation by reference of ERA 1996, s 203 in TUPE 2006 raises for the first time the possibility of compromise agreements waiving claims for breach of regulation 13.

B. TERRITORIALITY

1. Introduction

12.12   The Acquired Rights Directive (ARD) 2001 contains territorial limitations even if the interaction between domestic Member States' implementing legislation is unclear. Article 1.2 provides that the Directive applies 'where and insofar as the undertaking, business or part of the undertaking or business to be transferred is situated within the territorial scope of the Treaty [of Rome]'. The key to the application of the Directive is physical location of the relevant operations as opposed to their ownership, company registration, or overall control and direction.

12.13   However, the Directive provides no further guidance on or assistance in relation to transfer of undertakings issues as between Member States. The Directive cannot of course straightforwardly be relied on *per se*. It is the Member States' implementing legislation that confers rights on employees. Regard therefore needs to be had to that domestic legislation with regard to the territorial scope of each Member State's transfer protections.

12.14   TUPE 1981 contained specific provisions as to its territorial scope. TUPE 1981, regulation 13(1) provided that its principal provisions did not apply to an employment in respect of which the employee ordinarily worked outside the United Kingdom. Thus, the protection against dismissal because of a relevant transfer,[8] the obligation to inform and consult representatives,[9] and the ability to bring claims for compensation for breach of those information and consultation obligations[10] did not extend to those ordinarily working outside the United Kingdom. Also, TUPE 1981, regulation 13(2) deemed a person working on board a ship registered in the United Kingdom to be ordinarily working in the

---

[8] TUPE 1981, regulation 8.   [9] TUPE 1981, regulation 10.
[10] TUPE 1981, regulation 11.

United Kingdom unless the employment was wholly outside the United Kingdom or the employee was not ordinarily resident in the United Kingdom.

TUPE 2006 contains no such territoriality provisions. As the 2005 Consultation noted,[11] similar territoriality provisions were removed from other employment rights legislation in 1999. Whether an employee working abroad is able to bring a claim under TUPE 2006 depends in part on the principles of international law, particularly where the employee seeks to claim unfair dismissal.[12]   **12.15**

2. TUPE 2006

TUPE 2006 does nonetheless contain some provisions addressing certain specific aspects of its territorial application with regard to the undertakings and activities which it covers. The service provision concept established by regulation 3(1)(b) does not apply in Northern Ireland pursuant to Schedule 1.[13] The definitions of a relevant transfer under regulations 3(1)(a) and 3(1)(b) apply only where the relevant undertaking is or activities are situated in the United Kingdom immediately before the transfer.[14] The requirement of a domestic location immediately before the transfer is therefore essential to the application of the legislation. TUPE therefore does not engage and provide protection to employees of an undertaking situated outside the United Kingdom immediately before the transfer even if the transaction in question entails a transfer of the relevant undertaking from outside into the United Kingdom.   **12.16**

The Department of Trade and Industry (DTI) Guidance provides[15] a useful example in the context of a service provision change: **12.17**

the test is whether there is an organised grouping of employees situated in the UK (immediately before the service provision change). For example, where a contract to provide website maintenance comes to an end and the client wants someone else to take over the contract, if in the organised grouping of employees that has performed the contract, one of the IT technicians works from home, which is outside the UK, that should not prevent the Regulations applying to the transfer of the business. However if the whole team of IT technicians worked from home which was outside the UK, then a transfer of the business for which they work would not fall within the Regulations as there would be no organised grouping of employees situated in the United Kingdom.

One potential consequence of the requirement that the undertaking or activities   **12.18**

---

[11] Paras 92 and 93.

[12] The litigation leading to *Lawson v Serco Ltd* [2006] IRLR 289, 42 demonstrates the issues in this context. *Serco*, detailed discussion of which falls outside the scope of this work, makes clear that those working outside Great Britain may in exceptional circumstances enjoy domestic unfair dismissal rights.

[13] Regulation 2(3).

[14] Regulations 3(1)(a)—Great Britain in the case of a service provision change—regulation 3(3)(a)(i).

[15] At p 12.

in question be situated in the United Kingdom immediately before the transfer is that an employee based in the United Kingdom who works in relation to an undertaking based outside the United Kingdom is not protected by TUPE if that business is disposed of unless either he or she falls within the protective scope of the transfer legislation of the Member State in which the relevant undertaking or activity is located, or the UK operation of itself can constitute an undertaking or part thereof, or its transfer is a service provision change falling within the scope of TUPE. For sole representatives, it is feasible (if perhaps unlikely) that in such circumstances neither regulation 3(1)(a) nor regulation 3(1)(b) would be engaged. Accordingly, if TUPE is not engaged, a dismissal of the relevant employee could only avoid being unfair in such circumstances by way of a fairly conducted redundancy process.

12.19   It is also specifically confirmed in regulation 3(4)(b) that a transfer of an undertaking or service provision change falls within the scope of TUPE 2006 regardless of certain international aspects.

12.20   That the transfer or service provision change is governed or effected by the law of a country or territory outside the United Kingdom does not disapply TUPE.[16] That a business sale or outsourcing contract may be governed by foreign law (for example, because one of the relevant contracting parties is overseas and demands a foreign governing law) makes no difference to the application of TUPE.

12.21   Similarly, that the persons employed in the undertaking, business, or part transferred or in relation to the activities which are the subject of a service provision change ordinarily work outside the United Kingdom is not relevant.[17] Employees assigned to a business located in the United Kingdom but who work outside that jurisdiction can still be covered by TUPE. To quote from the DTI Guidance,[18]

the Regulations may still apply notwithstanding that persons employed in the undertaking ordinarily work outside the United Kingdom. For example, if there is a transfer of a UK exporting business, the fact that the sales force spends the majority of its working week outside the UK will not prevent the Regulations applying to the transfer, so long as the undertaking itself (comprising, amongst other things, premises, assets, fixtures & fittings, goodwill as well as employees) is situated in the UK.

12.22   Finally, TUPE can apply to employees otherwise qualifying for its protection even if their employment is governed by the law of a country or territory outside the United Kingdom.[19] By way of example, employees who have been transferred from overseas to a business or undertaking situated in the United Kingdom can still be covered by TUPE even if they themselves have contracts governed by foreign law which they signed when they first joined the employer outside the United Kingdom.

---

[16]   Regulation 3(4)(b((i) (Great Britain in the case of a service provision change).
[17]   Regulation 3(4)(c).   [18]   At p 12.   [19]   Regulation 3(4)(b)(ii).

3. Continental Shelf

Whether TUPE applies to the United Kingdom sector of the continental shelf **12.23** has been a moot point. In *Addison & others v Denholm Ship Management (UK) Limited*,[20] the EAT held that the phrase 'in the United Kingdom'[21] did not include the United Kingdom sector of the continental shelf. The Government's own view[22] was that *Addison* was wrongly decided and that TUPE applies in cases where the transferor's business is situated in the United Kingdom sector of the continental shelf. The combination of this view and the provisions of the TUPE 2006 described above relating to the geographical location of the relevant undertaking or service provision activity made it unnecessary in the Government's opinion for there to be any explicit provision in TUPE 2006 addressing the application of the legislation to the continental shelf.

4. International Transfers

(a) *Introduction*

Two issues which have not to date expressly or adequately been addressed in the **12.24** jurisprudence on the Directive and TUPE is how the various Member States' domestic transfer of undertakings regimes interact and how the legislation operates in relation to transfers which entail the relevant operation being operated after the transfer outside the European Union (EU). These issues have gained increased prominence over recent years as a consequence of the trend towards international outsourcing, particularly in the fields of information technology support and call centre operations. A detailed treatment of this issue is outside the scope of this book. Whilst it is perhaps unfortunate that TUPE 2006 did not make any clearer the application of the legislation to international outsourcing issues, the following tentative thoughts are offered in relation to the various scenarios which may arise.

(b) *Domestic Undertaking—Overseas Employees*

If a business located in the United Kingdom is acquired and is not moved from **12.25** the jurisdiction in which it operates as part of the transaction in question, then TUPE may potentially apply not just to its United Kingdom-based employees but also to those working elsewhere who are assigned to its business, regardless of the governing law of the business transfer or of the contracts of employment of the relevant employees.

It is a moot point whether, in light of the territorial limitation of the Directive, **12.26** this protection can only apply to employees working outside the United

---

[20] [1997] IRLR 389, EAT.
[21] Required of the relevant individual's employment under TUPE 1981, regulation 13 for TUPE to apply to that person.
[22] 2005 Consultation para 93.

Kingdom but within the EU. However, the introduction of TUPE 2006 by way of the Employment Relations Act 1999 (ERA 1999), s 38 as well as the European Communities Act 1972 makes it arguable that TUPE's protection can extend outside the EU.

(c) *Retention of Identity*

12.27 TUPE will not apply to protect employees working abroad or to the transfer of an undertaking or activities from a domestic base to outside the United Kingdom if the change of responsibility for the activities or undertaking based prior to the putative transfer in the United Kingdom does not constitute a transfer of an undertaking under regulation 3(1)(a) or a service provision change for the purposes of regulation 3(1)(b). Whilst a change of location will not necessarily cause the legislation not to apply, it may be arguable that the relocated activity does not retain its identity so that the relevant tests are not satisfied. This argument (of lack of retention of identity on transfer) can be deployed in relation to the regulation 3(1)(a) test establishing a transfer of an undertaking but will be far less easy to mount successfully in relation to the service provision change concept deployed in regulation 3(1)(b) (which is particularly likely to apply to the sorts of activities often outsourced internationally).

12.28 Therefore, while it could be argued in relation to TUPE 1981 that the outsourcing of call centre and other similar labour-intensive activities fell outside its scope on the basis of loss of identity, TUPE 2006 renders it more likely that the legislation will apply by virtue of regulation 3(1)(b). Provided that the dedicated team of staff required under regulation 3(1)(b) can be shown to exist in the United Kingdom prior to the putative transfer, TUPE may well apply to an outsourcing where no assets transfer. That location, equipment, facilities, and working methods may change (all of which, combined with lack of asset transfer, militate against the application of regulation 3(1)(a)) may well not disqualify regulation 3(1)(b) from applying in these problem cases.

(d) *Transfers Abroad from the United Kingdom*

12.29 In the context of the transfer of an operation which is based in the United Kingdom to another jurisdiction, it has to be said that, in practice, the process is often dealt with by the transferor (often in conjunction with the transferee) as a redundancy scenario whether for commercial, human resources, or other reasons. This approach can also be justified if, as discussed above, it can be argued that there is no relevant transfer (for example on the basis that the relevant undertaking does not retain its identity after transfer). The risk of disputes involving the new operator outside the jurisdiction can then be reduced.

12.30 However, the proper legal analysis is less clearly established. At the very least, it can be argued that those aspects of TUPE which apply up until the point where the relevant operation leaves the United Kingdom should still engage. Thus, on an outsourcing of a domestic operation from the United Kingdom to an offshore contractor, TUPE's collective information and consultation regime under regulation 13 and the obligation to provide employee liability information to the transferee under regulation 11 should still apply.

Whilst acknowledging that the fact that the issue appears not to have been tested in litigation presumably indicates that treatment of international outsourcing as a redundancy scenario is the practical way of handling the consequences for employees, the question remains of the possibility of claims for unfair dismissal by those employees. Were their notice periods not honoured, questions of wrongful dismissal would also arise. If the transferor does not actually dismiss an employee engaged in relation to the outsourced activity, then the refusal of the transferee to engage the employee will amount to an actual or constructive dismissal. Such a dismissal (and indeed a dismissal by the transferor prior to transfer) will be transfer related and therefore automatically unfair (unless it can be shown to be for an economic, technical or organisational reason entailing changes in the workforce (ETOR) and is otherwise fair). The relocation occasioned by an offshoring may constitute an ETOR (by virtue of a place of work redundancy). A claim of transfer-related unfair dismissal could then lie against the transferee but this would present potential practical enforcement difficulties given that, *ex hypothesi*, the transferee will not be based, and therefore may have no presence (or assets against which an order or judgment could be enforced) in the United Kingdom.   **12.31**

The other complication which may arise is the issue of jurisdiction in terms of where an employee can prosecute claims arising from TUPE. Regulation 16(1) makes clear that the ET is the only forum to which a complaint of breach of the regulation 13 information and consultation obligations can be presented. Similarly, the ET will be the forum to which unfair dismissal claims under ERA 1996 will be presented if the employee can establish its jurisdiction in relation to unfair dismissal claims brought by those employed abroad. Where other claims, such as for breach of contract, are to be brought will depend on conflict of law principles more generally.   **12.32**

C. DRAFTING AND COMMERCIAL POINTS

1. Introduction

The myriad forms of contractual arrangements to which the transfer of undertakings legislation can apply and the focus of this work on the amendments effected by TUPE 2006 mean that a detailed study of the drafting of all the varieties of commercial contract affected by the transfer legislation is outside its scope and scale. However, in this section a brief review is offered of some of the drafting and other issues which can arise when documenting a TUPE transfer. The level of complexity, scale of potential employment problems, commercial imperatives, and relative bargaining strengths of the parties will vary depending on the particular transaction in question, all of which makes generalisation   **12.33** relatively unhelpful, but there are certain key issues that transferors and transferees and indeed those awarding contracts by way of outsourcing and retendering need to bear in mind.

2. Due Diligence

12.34 The issue of due diligence is often important for both parties. A purchaser of a business or potential contractor will need to understand the terms upon which employees are engaged and the potential liabilities which it may inherit for a variety of reasons. Principal amongst these are the pricing of the contract, the extent to which the transferee will wish to pass back to the transferor liability in respect of particular issues and liabilities which already exist, and the extent to which the transferee may be able to introduce cost savings, flexible working practices, and other changes in order to extract greater value from the relevant business.

12.35 The obligation introduced by TUPE 2006 requiring transferors to provide employee liability information to transferees is of some assistance in bolstering the ability of a transferee to insist on disclosure from the transferor. The compensation payable for breach is intended to incentivise transferors to comply with an obligation which smaller business contractors might not be able to extract by commercial negotiation from a powerful transferor. However, the lateness of the required delivery and the limited scope of the information to be provided means that the obligation may be of limited value. Accordingly, transferees will still seek, where appropriate and possible, full due diligence from transferees and to have these reinforced by warranties.

12.36 In any case, issues which a due diligence request should consider potentially go wider than the scope of the employee liability notification obligation imposed by regulation 11. Information may be sought about those who are not (or may not be) employees such as consultants and agency workers in order to be able to assess their status, whether they automatically transfer, and if not what steps need to be taken to secure their continued involvement in the business if they are key.

3. Warranties

(a) *Commercial Context*

12.37 The issues arising in relation to warranties concerning employment matters in business sale and similar arrangements often interrelate with wider commercial considerations with regard to qualifications and limitations on warranties in the relevant contract generally. The ultimate value to a transferee of an employment warranty may be affected by issues such as thresholds for the aggregate value of liabilities arising by reason of breach of warranty and qualifications to the warranties themselves based on knowledge (for example, by reference to the belief of the warrantors as opposed to objective fact).

Whilst the employee notification obligation imposed by regulation 11 does **12.38** require updating of details which change between initial provision and the actual transfer, it will be important to ensure warranties are accurate at all material times, especially with regard to ongoing issues to be addressed in the lead up to transfer (in particular, compliance with the collective information and consultation obligations).

(b) *Transferor Warranties*

By way of brief summary, the warranties which a transferee will expect from a **12.39** transferor will (in addition to any specific concerns which arise from the due diligence process) address issues such as confirmation that:

- the disclosed employees are the only employees who will transfer to the transferee by virtue of TUPE 2006 as a consequence of the transfer;
- all disclosed employee details are accurate and complete;
- full details of all actual or potential employment-related disputes and claims (both collective and individual) have been disclosed;
- all trade union, recognition, and other employee representation details have been fully disclosed and all such collective agreements and related obligations have been fully complied with;
- save as disclosed, no contract changes or pay rises have been agreed of contracted for;
- the transferor has complied with its obligations under regulation 11 with regard to collective information and consultation obligations;
- full details have been disclosed of all agency workers and all employees on maternity terms or absent by reason of sickness;
- no agreements exist for specific payments on termination of employment to transferring employees;
- full disclosure has been made of benefits such as sick pay entitlements, private medical insurance, company car benefits, relocation benefits, enhanced maternity leave and pay entitlements, and mortgage subsidies;
- full disclosure has been made of disciplinary rules and procedures (whose precise contractual status may be a separate issue);
- there have been no dismissals in connection with the transfer;
- the transferor has complied with all obligations (including orders and awards) to which it is subject in respect of the transferring employees;
- no investigations or enquiries have been threatened, or have been or are being indicated by the Commission for Racial Equality, Equal Opportunities Commission, or Disability Rights Commission under their respective statutory powers;

- all dismissals and grievances have been dealt with in accordance with the statutory minimum disciplinary and grievance procedures detailed by the 2004 Regulations.

(c) *Transferee Warranties*

12.40 In terms of the warranties which the transferor may seek to extract from the transferee, these will often be driven by commercial, industrial relations, or human resource management imperatives to maintain employee morale and loyalty, especially where there is an ongoing relationship between transferor and transferee (for example, on an outsourcing or by continued commercial supply of goods or services). It may be necessary to seek the transferee's commitment to continue the transferor's level of pension benefits or redundancy terms or to seek an undertaking that redundancies in respect of the transferring employees will not be effected for a period after the transfer.

12.41 In terms of the legal liabilities which can arise under TUPE, the transferor may wish to seek warranties from the transferee that it does not propose any changes to terms and conditions of employment or working conditions. Undisclosed intentions in this regard could give rise to liabilities for breach of regulation 13 as well as individual claims based on *University of Oxford v Humphreys*.[23]

4. Indemnities

12.42 Provided that the relevant party has the wherewithal to satisfy its obligations, indemnities are crucial in allocating economic responsibility between the parties in relation to employment liabilities. There may be a variety of qualifications to indemnities based on thresholds for the value of qualifying claims, the time period to which an indemnity extends, and with regard to whether the indemnity covers the entirety of the liability in question or a percentage of it. The types of liability which indemnities will seek to address will include claims in respect of:

- wrongful dismissal;
- unfair dismissal;
- unlawful discrimination under the Sex Discrimination Act 1975, the Race Relations Act 1976, the Disability Discrimination Act 1995, the Employment Equality (Religion or Belief) Regulations 2003 and the Employment Equality (Sexual Orientation) Regulations 2003, and the age discrimination legislation scheduled to come into force in October 2006;
- liabilities under the Working Time Regulations 1998;
- personal injury liabilities;
- unlawful deductions from wages pursuant to ERA 1996;

---

[23] See Chap 4, para 4.78.

- claims against the transferor based on the *Humphreys* decision or regulation 4(9);
- failure to comply with the collective redundancy consultation requirements of the Trade Union and Labour Relations (Consolidation) Act (TULRCA) 1992, s 188;
- failure to comply with regulation 13's information and consultation obligations. This is particularly important following the introduction by TUPE 2006 of the provision that liability for any penalty payable for breach of the regulation 13 requirements is now borne by the transferor and the transferee jointly and severally;
- any fines arising (for example, any penalty payable for failure to notify the DTI of redundancies as required by TULRCA 1992);
- liabilities arising under TUPE 2006 generally;
- legal and other costs incurred in dealing with the above liabilities.

One starting point in drafting indemnities is that the transferor is responsible for **12.43** liabilities arising up to the point of transfer and the transferee responsible for liabilities thereafter. Exceptions to that approach may arise. For example, if a transferor is required by the transferee to effect dismissals prior to dismissal, the transferee may agree to indemnify the transferor for any liability which the transferor inherits (even if as a matter of law, that liability may well transfer to the transferee).

Such indemnities may need to distinguish between fixed termination costs **12.44** (such as notice payments and statutory redundancy payments) and those costs and liabilities which can be avoided, minimised, or mitigated, such as unfair dismissal liabilities and awards for failure to comply with applicable information and consultation obligations under TUPE or in relation to collective redundancies. These latter costs may be allocated on a fault basis (for example, if the transferor simply makes an error in the handling of a dismissal or the transferee fails to provide adequate information to ensure compliance with the applicable collective obligations).

A transfer agreement may also need to address the situation where employees **12.45** other than those disclosed actually do transfer under the legislation to the transferee. In such circumstances it may be that it is commercially agreed that the transferor bears the liability for the dismissal of this employee. However, in order to mitigate its liabilities in that regard, the transferor may wish first to be informed of the situation and to be afforded the opportunity to offer continued employment to the affected employee. Alternatively, an adjustment may need to be made to the pricing of the contract—this will be particularly relevant in those outsourcings where employment costs are an explicit factor in contracting pricing.

5. Outsourcing

12.46 Many of the provisions used in business transfer agreements will be relevant to the commencement and cessation of outsourcing arrangements. Some specific issues which may arise in that context are as follows:

- the client will wish a contractor to be contractually obliged to provide employee information on request in order to facilitate any subsequent retendering process since bidders will expect and, if successful, be entitled to such information;

- contractors will wish the client to be required contractually to do all that is reasonably possible on a retendering or on termination of the contract more generally to ensure that the contractor can comply with its obligation to provide the prescribed employee liability information under regulation 11 to a replacement contractor;

- controls may need to be in place where the pricing of the contracting depends on staffing levels and related employment costs—these would require control on the part of the client over salary levels and terms and conditions of employment;

- the contractor may be required to comply with the client's employment policies;

- on termination of the contract the allocation of liability for employment costs needs to be considered if a new contractor will take on staff. The contractor may wish the client to ensure that a new contractor takes on staff falling within the scope of the transfer legislation on their existing terms or for an indemnity in this regard to be provided. The client may consider these liabilities to be the contractor's responsibility;

- notwithstanding the assignment test deployed in regulation 4(1) to identify which employees transfer on a relevant transfer, controls may be needed on staff allocation to avoid 'social dumping';

- an incoming contractor will often have no contractual or commercial relationship with the incumbent. The party awarding the contract may impose under the initial outsourcing agreement an obligation on the initial contractor to indemnify a new contractor in relation to compliance with its regulation 13 obligations and employment liabilities arising whilst the relevant employees are employed by the initial contractor.

D. ASSERTION OF STATUTORY RIGHTS

12.47 Regulation 19 amends ERA 1996, s 104 so that the rights conferred by TUPE 2006 are rights assertion of which can lead to unfair dismissal claims pursuant to that provision.

STATUTORY INSTRUMENTS

2006 No. 246
Terms and Conditions of Employment

THE TRANSFER OF UNDERTAKINGS (PROTECTION OF EMPLOYMENT)
REGULATIONS 2006

Made	*6th February 2006*
Laid before Parliament	*7th February 2006*
Coming into force	*6th April 2006*

The Secretary of State makes the following Regulations in exercise of the powers conferred upon him by section 2(2) of the European Communities Act 1972[1] (being a Minister designated for the purposes of that section in relation to rights and obligations relating to employers and employees on the transfer or merger of undertakings, businesses or parts of businesses[2]) and section 38 of the Employment Relations Act 1999[3].

Citation, commencement and extent

1.—(1) These Regulations may be cited as the Transfer of Undertakings (Protection of Employment) Regulations 2006.

(2) These Regulations shall come into force on 6 April 2006.

(3) These Regulations shall extend to Northern Ireland, except where otherwise provided.

Interpretation

2.—(1) In these Regulations—

"assigned" means assigned other than on a temporary basis;

"collective agreement", "collective bargaining" and "trade union" have the same meanings respectively as in the 1992 Act;

"contract of employment" means any agreement between an employee and his employer determining the terms and conditions of his employment;

references to "contractor" in regulation 3 shall include a sub-contractor;

"employee" means any individual who works for another person whether under a contract of service or apprenticeship or otherwise but does not include anyone who provides services under a contract for services and references to a person's employer shall be construed accordingly;

"insolvency practitioner" has the meaning given to the expression by Part XIII of the Insolvency Act 1986[4];

references to "organised grouping of employees" shall include a single employee;

227

"recognised" has the meaning given to the expression by section 178(3) of the 1992 Act;

"relevant transfer" means a transfer or a service provision change to which these Regulations apply in accordance with regulation 3 and "transferor" and "transferee" shall be construed accordingly and in the case of a service provision change falling within regulation 3(1)(b), "the transferor" means the person who carried out the activities prior to the service provision change and "the transferee" means the person who carries out the activities as a result of the service provision change;

"the 1992 Act" means the Trade Union and Labour Relations (Consolidation) Act 1992[5];

"the 1996 Act" means the Employment Rights Act 1996[6];

"the 1996 Tribunals Act" means the Employment Tribunals Act 1996[7];

"the 1981 Regulations" means the Transfer of Undertakings (Protection of Employment) Regulations 1981[8].

(2) For the purposes of these Regulations the representative of a trade union recognised by an employer is an official or other person authorised to carry on collective bargaining with that employer by that trade union.

(3) In the application of these Regulations to Northern Ireland the Regulations shall have effect as set out in Schedule 1.

A relevant transfer

3.—(1) These Regulations apply to—

    (a) a transfer of an undertaking, business or part of an undertaking or business situated immediately before the transfer in the United Kingdom to another person where there is a transfer of an economic entity which retains its identity;

    (b) a service provision change, that is a situation in which—

        (i) activities cease to be carried out by a person ("a client") on his own behalf and are carried out instead by another person on the client's behalf ("a contractor");

        (ii) activities cease to be carried out by a contractor on a client's behalf (whether or not those activities had previously been carried out by the client on his own behalf) and are carried out instead by another person ("a subsequent contractor") on the client's behalf; or

        (iii) activities cease to be carried out by a contractor or a subsequent contractor on a client's behalf (whether or not those activities had previously been carried out by the client on his own behalf) and are carried out instead by the client on his own behalf,

    and in which the conditions set out in paragraph (3) are satisfied.

(2) In this regulation "economic entity" means an organised grouping of resources which has the objective of pursuing an economic activity, whether or not that activity is central or ancillary.

(3) The conditions referred to in paragraph (1)(b) are that—

    (a) immediately before the service provision change—

        (i) there is an organised grouping of employees situated in Great Britain which has as its principal purpose the carrying out of the activities concerned on behalf of the client;

       (ii) the client intends that the activities will, following the service provision change, be carried out by the transferee other than in connection with a single specific event or task of short-term duration; and

    (b) the activities concerned do not consist wholly or mainly of the supply of goods for the client's use.

(4) Subject to paragraph (1), these Regulations apply to—

    (a) public and private undertakings engaged in economic activities whether or not they are operating for gain;

    (b) a transfer or service provision change howsoever effected notwithstanding—

       (i) that the transfer of an undertaking, business or part of an undertaking or business is governed or effected by the law of a country or territory outside the United Kingdom or that the service provision change is governed or effected by the law of a country or territory outside Great Britain;

       (ii) that the employment of persons employed in the undertaking, business or part transferred or, in the case of a service provision change, persons employed in the organised grouping of employees, is governed by any such law;

    (c) a transfer of an undertaking, business or part of an undertaking or business (which may also be a service provision change) where persons employed in the undertaking, business or part transferred ordinarily work outside the United Kingdom.

(5) An administrative reorganisation of public administrative authorities or the transfer of administrative functions between public administrative authorities is not a relevant transfer.

(6) A relevant transfer—

    (a) may be effected by a series of two or more transactions; and

    (b) may take place whether or not any property is transferred to the transferee by the transferor.

(7) Where, in consequence (whether directly or indirectly) of the transfer of an undertaking, business or part of an undertaking or business which was situated immediately before the transfer in the United Kingdom, a ship within the meaning of the Merchant Shipping Act 1995[9] registered in the United Kingdom ceases to be so registered, these Regulations shall not affect the right conferred by section 29 of that Act (right of seamen to be discharged when ship ceases to be registered in the United Kingdom) on a seaman employed in the ship.

Effect of relevant transfer on contracts of employment

4.—(1) Except where objection is made under paragraph (7), a relevant transfer shall not operate so as to terminate the contract of employment of any person employed by the transferor and assigned to the organised grouping of resources or employees that is subject to the relevant transfer, which would otherwise be terminated by the transfer, but any such contract shall have effect after the transfer as if originally made between the person so employed and the transferee.

(2) Without prejudice to paragraph (1), but subject to paragraph (6), and regulations 8 and 15(9), on the completion of a relevant transfer—

    (a) all the transferor's rights, powers, duties and liabilities under or in connection with any such contract shall be transferred by virtue of this regulation to the transferee; and

(b) any act or omission before the transfer is completed, of or in relation to the transferor in respect of that contract or a person assigned to that organised grouping of resources or employees, shall be deemed to have been an act or omission of or in relation to the transferee.

(3) Any reference in paragraph (1) to a person employed by the transferor and assigned to the organised grouping of resources or employees that is subject to a relevant transfer, is a reference to a person so employed immediately before the transfer, or who would have been so employed if he had not been dismissed in the circumstances described in regulation 7(1), including, where the transfer is effected by a series of two or more transactions, a person so employed and assigned or who would have been so employed and assigned immediately before any of those transactions.

(4) Subject to regulation 9, in respect of a contract of employment that is, or will be, transferred by paragraph (1), any purported variation of the contract shall be void if the sole or principal reason for the variation is—

(a) the transfer itself; or

(b) a reason connected with the transfer that is not an economic, technical or organisational reason entailing changes in the workforce.

(5) Paragraph (4) shall not prevent the employer and his employee, whose contract of employment is, or will be, transferred by paragraph (1), from agreeing a variation of that contract if the sole or principal reason for the variation is—

(a) a reason connected with the transfer that is an economic, technical or organisational reason entailing changes in the workforce; or

(b) a reason unconnected with the transfer.

(6) Paragraph (2) shall not transfer or otherwise affect the liability of any person to be prosecuted for, convicted of and sentenced for any offence.

(7) Paragraphs (1) and (2) shall not operate to transfer the contract of employment and the rights, powers, duties and liabilities under or in connection with it of an employee who informs the transferor or the transferee that he objects to becoming employed by the transferee.

(8) Subject to paragraphs (9) and (11), where an employee so objects, the relevant transfer shall operate so as to terminate his contract of employment with the transferor but he shall not be treated, for any purpose, as having been dismissed by the transferor.

(9) Subject to regulation 9, where a relevant transfer involves or would involve a substantial change in working conditions to the material detriment of a person whose contract of employment is or would be transferred under paragraph (1), such an employee may treat the contract of employment as having been terminated, and the employee shall be treated for any purpose as having been dismissed by the employer.

(10) No damages shall be payable by an employer as a result of a dismissal falling within paragraph (9) in respect of any failure by the employer to pay wages to an employee in respect of a notice period which the employee has failed to work.

(11) Paragraphs (1), (7), (8) and (9) are without prejudice to any right of an employee arising apart from these Regulations to terminate his contract of

employment without notice in acceptance of a repudiatory breach of contract by his employer.

Effect of relevant transfer on collective agreements

5. Where at the time of a relevant transfer there exists a collective agreement made by or on behalf of the transferor with a trade union recognised by the transferor in respect of any employee whose contract of employment is preserved by regulation 4(1) above, then—
    (a) without prejudice to sections 179 and 180 of the 1992 Act (collective agreements presumed to be unenforceable in specified circumstances) that agreement, in its application in relation to the employee, shall, after the transfer, have effect as if made by or on behalf of the transferee with that trade union, and accordingly anything done under or in connection with it, in its application in relation to the employee, by or in relation to the transferor before the transfer, shall, after the transfer, be deemed to have been done by or in relation to the transferee; and
    (b) any order made in respect of that agreement, in its application in relation to the employee, shall, after the transfer, have effect as if the transferee were a party to the agreement.

Effect of relevant transfer on trade union recognition

6.—(1) This regulation applies where after a relevant transfer the transferred organised grouping of resources or employees maintains an identity distinct from the remainder of the transferee's undertaking.
    (2) Where before such a transfer an independent trade union is recognised to any extent by the transferor in respect of employees of any description who in consequence of the transfer become employees of the transferee, then, after the transfer—
    (a) the trade union shall be deemed to have been recognised by the transferee to the same extent in respect of employees of that description so employed; and
    (b) any agreement for recognition may be varied or rescinded accordingly.

Dismissal of employee because of relevant transfer

7.—(1) Where either before or after a relevant transfer, any employee of the transferor or transferee is dismissed, that employee shall be treated for the purposes of Part X of the 1996 Act (unfair dismissal) as unfairly dismissed if the sole or principal reason for his dismissal is—
    (a) the transfer itself; or
    (b) a reason connected with the transfer that is not an economic, technical or organisational reason entailing changes in the workforce.
    (2) This paragraph applies where the sole or principal reason for the dismissal is a reason connected with the transfer that is an economic, technical or organisational reason entailing changes in the workforce of either the transferor or the transferee before or after a relevant transfer.
    (3) Where paragraph (2) applies—
    (a) paragraph (1) shall not apply;
    (b) without prejudice to the application of section 98(4) of the 1996 Act (test of fair dismissal), the dismissal shall, for the purposes of sections 98(1) and 135 of that Act (reason for dismissal), be regarded as having been for

redundancy where section 98(2)(c) of that Act applies, or otherwise for a substantial reason of a kind such as to justify the dismissal of an employee holding the position which that employee held.

(4) The provisions of this regulation apply irrespective of whether the employee in question is assigned to the organised grouping of resources or employees that is, or will be, transferred.

(5) Paragraph (1) shall not apply in relation to the dismissal of any employee which was required by reason of the application of section 5 of the Aliens Restriction (Amendment) Act 1919[10] to his employment.

(6) Paragraph (1) shall not apply in relation to a dismissal of an employee if the application of section 94 of the 1996 Act to the dismissal of the employee is excluded by or under any provision of the 1996 Act, the 1996 Tribunals Act or the 1992 Act.

Insolvency

8.—(1) If at the time of a relevant transfer the transferor is subject to relevant insolvency proceedings paragraphs (2) to (6) apply.

(2) In this regulation "relevant employee" means an employee of the transferor—

(a) whose contract of employment transfers to the transferee by virtue of the operation of these Regulations; or

(b) whose employment with the transferor is terminated before the time of the relevant transfer in the circumstances described in regulation 7(1).

(3) The relevant statutory scheme specified in paragraph (4)(b) (including that sub-paragraph as applied by paragraph 5 of Schedule 1) shall apply in the case of a relevant employee irrespective of the fact that the qualifying requirement that the employee's employment has been terminated is not met and for those purposes the date of the transfer shall be treated as the date of the termination and the transferor shall be treated as the employer.

(4) In this regulation the "relevant statutory schemes" are—

(a) Chapter VI of Part XI of the 1996 Act;

(b) Part XII of the 1996 Act.

(5) Regulation 4 shall not operate to transfer liability for the sums payable to the relevant employee under the relevant statutory schemes.

(6) In this regulation "relevant insolvency proceedings" means insolvency proceedings which have been opened in relation to the transferor not with a view to the liquidation of the assets of the transferor and which are under the supervision of an insolvency practitioner.

(7) Regulations 4 and 7 do not apply to any relevant transfer where the transferor is the subject of bankruptcy proceedings or any analogous insolvency proceedings which have been instituted with a view to the liquidation of the assets of the transferor and are under the supervision of an insolvency practitioner.

Variations of contract where transferors are subject to relevant insolvency proceedings

9.—(1) If at the time of a relevant transfer the transferor is subject to relevant insolvency proceedings these Regulations shall not prevent the transferor or transferee (or an insolvency practitioner) and appropriate representatives of assigned employees agreeing to permitted variations.

(2) For the purposes of this regulation "appropriate representatives" are—

    (a) if the employees are of a description in respect of which an independent trade union is recognised by their employer, representatives of the trade union; or

    (b) in any other case, whichever of the following employee representatives the employer chooses—

        (i) employee representatives appointed or elected by the assigned employees (whether they make the appointment or election alone or with others) otherwise than for the purposes of this regulation, who (having regard to the purposes for, and the method by which they were appointed or elected) have authority from those employees to agree permitted variations to contracts of employment on their behalf;

        (ii) employee representatives elected by assigned employees (whether they make the appointment or election alone or with others) for these particular purposes, in an election satisfying requirements identical to those contained in regulation 14 except those in regulation 14(1)(d).

(3) An individual may be an appropriate representative for the purposes of both this regulation and regulation 13 provided that where the representative is not a trade union representative he is either elected by or has authority from assigned employees (within the meaning of this regulation) and affected employees (as described in regulation 13(1)).

(4) In section 168 of the 1992 Act (time off for carrying out trade union duties) in subsection (1), after paragraph (c) there is inserted—

    ", or

    (d) negotiations with a view to entering into an agreement under regulation 9 of the Transfer of Undertakings (Protection of Employment) Regulations 2006 that applies to employees of the employer, or

    (e) the performance on behalf of employees of the employer of functions related to or connected with the making of an agreement under that regulation.".

(5) Where assigned employees are represented by non-trade union representatives—

    (a) the agreement recording a permitted variation must be in writing and signed by each of the representatives who have made it or, where that is not reasonably practicable, by a duly authorised agent of that representative; and

    (b) the employer must, before the agreement is made available for signature, provide all employees to whom it is intended to apply on the date on which it is to come into effect with copies of the text of the agreement and such guidance as those employees might reasonably require in order to understand it fully.

(6) A permitted variation shall take effect as a term or condition of the assigned employee's contract of employment in place, where relevant, of any term or condition which it varies.

(7) In this regulation—

    "assigned employees" means those employees assigned to the organised grouping of resources or employees that is the subject of a relevant transfer;

    "permitted variation" is a variation to the contract of employment of an assigned employee where—

(a) the sole or principal reason for it is the transfer itself or a reason connected with the transfer that is not an economic, technical or organisational reason entailing changes in the workforce; and

(b) it is designed to safeguard employment opportunities by ensuring the survival of the undertaking, business or part of the undertaking or business that is the subject of the relevant transfer;

"relevant insolvency proceedings" has the meaning given to the expression by regulation 8(6).

Pensions

10.—(1) Regulations 4 and 5 shall not apply—

(a) to so much of a contract of employment or collective agreement as relates to an occupational pension scheme within the meaning of the Pension Schemes Act 1993[11]; or

(b) to any rights, powers, duties or liabilities under or in connection with any such contract or subsisting by virtue of any such agreement and relating to such a scheme or otherwise arising in connection with that person's employment and relating to such a scheme.

(2) For the purposes of paragraphs (1) and (3), any provisions of an occupational pension scheme which do not relate to benefits for old age, invalidity or survivors shall not be treated as being part of the scheme.

(3) An employee whose contract of employment is transferred in the circumstances described in regulation 4(1) shall not be entitled to bring a claim against the transferor for—

(a) breach of contract; or

(b) constructive unfair dismissal under section 95(1)(c) of the 1996 Act,

arising out of a loss or reduction in his rights under an occupational pension scheme in consequence of the transfer, save insofar as the alleged breach of contract or dismissal (as the case may be) occurred prior to the date on which these Regulations took effect.

Notification of Employee Liability Information

11.—(1) The transferor shall notify to the transferee the employee liability information of any person employed by him who is assigned to the organised grouping of resources or employees that is the subject of a relevant transfer—

(a) in writing; or

(b) by making it available to him in a readily accessible form.

(2) In this regulation and in regulation 12 "employee liability information" means—

(a) the identity and age of the employee;

(b) those particulars of employment that an employer is obliged to give to an employee pursuant to section 1 of the 1996 Act;

(c) information of any—

(i) disciplinary procedure taken against an employee;

(ii) grievance procedure taken by an employee,

within the previous two years, in circumstances where the Employment Act 2002 (Dispute Resolution) Regulations 2004[12] apply;

(d) information of any court or tribunal case, claim or action—

       (i)   brought by an employee against the transferor, within the previous two years;

      (ii)   that the transferor has reasonable grounds to believe that an employee may bring against the transferee, arising out of the employee's employment with the transferor; and

   (e)   information of any collective agreement which will have effect after the transfer, in its application in relation to the employee, pursuant to regulation 5(a).

(3)   Employee liability information shall contain information as at a specified date not more than fourteen days before the date on which the information is notified to the transferee.

(4)   The duty to provide employee liability information in paragraph (1) shall include a duty to provide employee liability information of any person who would have been employed by the transferor and assigned to the organised grouping of resources or employees that is the subject of a relevant transfer immediately before the transfer if he had not been dismissed in the circumstances described in regulation 7(1), including, where the transfer is effected by a series of two or more transactions, a person so employed and assigned or who would have been so employed and assigned immediately before any of those transactions.

(5)   Following notification of the employee liability information in accordance with this regulation, the transferor shall notify the transferee in writing of any change in the employee liability information.

(6)   A notification under this regulation shall be given not less than fourteen days before the relevant transfer or, if special circumstances make this not reasonably practicable, as soon as reasonably practicable thereafter.

(7)   A notification under this regulation may be given—

   (a) in more than one instalment;

   (b) indirectly, through a third party.

Remedy for failure to notify employee liability information

12.—(1)   On or after a relevant transfer, the transferee may present a complaint to an employment tribunal that the transferor has failed to comply with any provision of regulation 11.

(2)   An employment tribunal shall not consider a complaint under this regulation unless it is presented—

   (a) before the end of the period of three months beginning with the date of the relevant transfer;

   (b) within such further period as the tribunal considers reasonable in a case where it is satisfied that it was not reasonably practicable for the complaint to be presented before the end of that period of three months.

(3)   Where an employment tribunal finds a complaint under paragraph (1) well-founded, the tribunal—

   (a) shall make a declaration to that effect; and

   (b) may make an award of compensation to be paid by the transferor to the transferee.

(4)   The amount of the compensation shall be such as the tribunal considers just and equitable in all the circumstances, subject to paragraph (5), having particular regard to—

    (a) any loss sustained by the transferee which is attributable to the matters complained of; and

    (b) the terms of any contract between the transferor and the transferee relating to the transfer under which the transferor may be liable to pay any sum to the transferee in respect of a failure to notify the transferee of employee liability information.

(5) Subject to paragraph (6), the amount of compensation awarded under paragraph (3) shall be not less than £500 per employee in respect of whom the transferor has failed to comply with a provision of regulation 11, unless the tribunal considers it just and equitable, in all the circumstances, to award a lesser sum.

(6) In ascertaining the loss referred to in paragraph (4)(a) the tribunal shall apply the same rule concerning the duty of a person to mitigate his loss as applies to any damages recoverable under the common law of England and Wales, Northern Ireland or Scotland, as applicable.

(7) Section 18 of the 1996 Tribunals Act (conciliation) shall apply to the right conferred by this regulation and to proceedings under this regulation as it applies to the rights conferred by that Act and the employment tribunal proceedings mentioned in that Act.

Duty to inform and consult representatives

13.—(1) In this regulation and regulations 14 and 15 references to affected employees, in relation to a relevant transfer, are to any employees of the transferor or the transferee (whether or not assigned to the organised grouping of resources or employees that is the subject of a relevant transfer) who may be affected by the transfer or may be affected by measures taken in connection with it; and references to the employer shall be construed accordingly.

(2) Long enough before a relevant transfer to enable the employer of any affected employees to consult the appropriate representatives of any affected employees, the employer shall inform those representatives of—

    (a) the fact that the transfer is to take place, the date or proposed date of the transfer and the reasons for it;

    (b) the legal, economic and social implications of the transfer for any affected employees;

    (c) the measures which he envisages he will, in connection with the transfer, take in relation to any affected employees or, if he envisages that no measures will be so taken, that fact; and

    (d) if the employer is the transferor, the measures, in connection with the transfer, which he envisages the transferee will take in relation to any affected employees who will become employees of the transferee after the transfer by virtue of regulation 4 or, if he envisages that no measures will be so taken, that fact.

(3) For the purposes of this regulation the appropriate representatives of any affected employees are—

    (a) if the employees are of a description in respect of which an independent trade union is recognised by their employer, representatives of the trade union; or

    (b) in any other case, whichever of the following employee representatives the employer chooses—

      (i)   employee representatives appointed or elected by the affected employees otherwise than for the purposes of this regulation, who (having regard to the purposes for, and the method by which they were appointed or elected) have authority from those employees to receive information and to be consulted about the transfer on their behalf;

     (ii)   employee representatives elected by any affected employees, for the purposes of this regulation, in an election satisfying the requirements of regulation 14(1).

(4) The transferee shall give the transferor such information at such a time as will enable the transferor to perform the duty imposed on him by virtue of paragraph (2)(d).

(5) The information which is to be given to the appropriate representatives shall be given to each of them by being delivered to them, or sent by post to an address notified by them to the employer, or (in the case of representatives of a trade union) sent by post to the trade union at the address of its head or main office.

(6) An employer of an affected employee who envisages that he will take measures in relation to an affected employee, in connection with the relevant transfer, shall consult the appropriate representatives of that employee with a view to seeking their agreement to the intended measures.

(7) In the course of those consultations the employer shall—

    (a) consider any representations made by the appropriate representatives; and

    (b) reply to those representations and, if he rejects any of those representations, state his reasons.

(8) The employer shall allow the appropriate representatives access to any affected employees and shall afford to those representatives such accommodation and other facilities as may be appropriate.

(9) If in any case there are special circumstances which render it not reasonably practicable for an employer to perform a duty imposed on him by any of paragraphs (2) to (7), he shall take all such steps towards performing that duty as are reasonably practicable in the circumstances.

(10) Where—

    (a) the employer has invited any of the affected employee[s] to elect employee representatives; and

    (b) the invitation was issued long enough before the time when the employer is required to give information under paragraph (2) to allow them to elect representatives by that time,

the employer shall be treated as complying with the requirements of this regulation in relation to those employees if he complies with those requirements as soon as is reasonably practicable after the election of the representatives.

(11) If, after the employer has invited any affected employees to elect representatives, they fail to do so within a reasonable time, he shall give to any affected employees the information set out in paragraph (2).

(12) The duties imposed on an employer by this regulation shall apply irrespective of whether the decision resulting in the relevant transfer is taken by the employer or a person controlling the employer.

Election of employee representatives

14.—(1) The requirements for the election of employee representatives under regulation 13(3) are that—

(a) the employer shall make such arrangements as are reasonably practicable to ensure that the election is fair;

(b) the employer shall determine the number of representatives to be elected so that there are sufficient representatives to represent the interests of all affected employees having regard to the number and classes of those employees;

(c) the employer shall determine whether the affected employees should be represented either by representatives of all the affected employees or by representatives of particular classes of those employees;

(d) before the election the employer shall determine the term of office as employee representatives so that it is of sufficient length to enable information to be given and consultations under regulation 13 to be completed;

(e) the candidates for election as employee representatives are affected employees on the date of the election;

(f) no affected employee is unreasonably excluded from standing for election;

(g) all affected employees on the date of the election are entitled to vote for employee representatives;

(h) the employees entitled to vote may vote for as many candidates as there are representatives to be elected to represent them or, if there are to be representatives for particular classes of employees, may vote for as many candidates as there are representatives to be elected to represent their particular class of employee;

(i) the election is conducted so as to secure that—

(i) so far as is reasonably practicable, those voting do so in secret; and

(ii) the votes given at the election are accurately counted.

(2) Where, after an election of employee representatives satisfying the requirements of paragraph (1) has been held, one of those elected ceases to act as an employee representative and as a result any affected employees are no longer represented, those employees shall elect another representative by an election satisfying the requirements of paragraph (1)(a), (e), (f) and (i).

Failure to inform or consult

15.—(1) Where an employer has failed to comply with a requirement of regulation 13 or regulation 14, a complaint may be presented to an employment tribunal on that ground—

(a) in the case of a failure relating to the election of employee representatives, by any of his employees who are affected employees;

(b) in the case of any other failure relating to employee representatives, by any of the employee representatives to whom the failure related;

(c) in the case of [a] failure relating to representatives of a trade union, by the trade union; and

(d) in any other case, by any of his employees who are affected employees.

(2) If on a complaint under paragraph (1) a question arises whether or not it was reasonably practicable for an employer to perform a particular duty or as to what steps he took towards performing it, it shall be for him to show—

(a) that there were special circumstances which rendered it not reasonably practicable for him to perform the duty; and

(b) that he took all such steps towards its performance as were reasonably practicable in those circumstances.

(3) If on a complaint under paragraph (1) a question arises as to whether or not an employee representative was an appropriate representative for the purposes of regulation 13, it shall be for the employer to show that the employee representative had the necessary authority to represent the affected employees.

(4) On a complaint under paragraph (1)(a) it shall be for the employer to show that the requirements in regulation 14 have been satisfied.

(5) On a complaint against a transferor that he had failed to perform the duty imposed upon him by virtue of regulation 13(2)(d) or, so far as relating thereto, regulation 13(9), he may not show that it was not reasonably practicable for him to perform the duty in question for the reason that the transferee had failed to give him the requisite information at the requisite time in accordance with regulation 13(4) unless he gives the transferee notice of his intention to show that fact; and the giving of the notice shall make the transferee a party to the proceedings.

(6) In relation to any complaint under paragraph (1), a failure on the part of a person controlling (directly or indirectly) the employer to provide information to the employer shall not constitute special circumstances rendering it not reasonably practicable for the employer to comply with such a requirement.

(7) Where the tribunal finds a complaint against a transferee under paragraph (1) well-founded it shall make a declaration to that effect and may order the transferee to pay appropriate compensation to such descriptions of affected employees as may be specified in the award.

(8) Where the tribunal finds a complaint against a transferor under paragraph (1) well-founded it shall make a declaration to that effect and may—

(a) order the transferor, subject to paragraph (9), to pay appropriate compensation to such descriptions of affected employees as may be specified in the award; or

(b) if the complaint is that the transferor did not perform the duty mentioned in paragraph (5) and the transferor (after giving due notice) shows the facts so mentioned, order the transferee to pay appropriate compensation to such descriptions of affected employees as may be specified in the award.

(9) The transferee shall be jointly and severally liable with the transferor in respect of compensation payable under sub-paragraph (8)(a) or paragraph (11).

(10) An employee may present a complaint to an employment tribunal on the ground that he is an employee of a description to which an order under paragraph (7) or (8) relates and that—

(a) in respect of an order under paragraph (7), the transferee has failed, wholly or in part, to pay him compensation in pursuance of the order;

(b) in respect of an order under paragraph (8), the transferor or transferee, as applicable, has failed, wholly or in part, to pay him compensation in pursuance of the order.

(11) Where the tribunal finds a complaint under paragraph (10) well-founded it shall order the transferor or transferee as applicable to pay the complainant the amount of compensation which it finds is due to him.

(12) An employment tribunal shall not consider a complaint under paragraph (1) or (10) unless it is presented to the tribunal before the end of the period of three months beginning with—

   (a) in respect of a complaint under paragraph (1), the date on which the relevant transfer is completed; or

   (b) in respect of a complaint under paragraph (10), the date of the tribunal's order under paragraph (7) or (8),

   or within such further period as the tribunal considers reasonable in a case where it is satisfied that it was not reasonably practicable for the complaint to be presented before the end of the period of three months.

Failure to inform or consult: supplemental

16.—(1) Section 205(1) of the 1996 Act (complaint to be sole remedy for breach of relevant rights) and section 18 of the 1996 Tribunals Act (conciliation) shall apply to the rights conferred by regulation 15 and to proceedings under this regulation as they apply to the rights conferred by those Acts and the employment tribunal proceedings mentioned in those Acts.

(2) An appeal shall lie and shall lie only to the Employment Appeal Tribunal on a question of law arising from any decision of, or arising in any proceedings before, an employment tribunal under or by virtue of these Regulations; and section 11(1) of the Tribunals and Inquiries Act 1992[13] (appeals from certain tribunals to the High Court) shall not apply in relation to any such proceedings.

(3) "Appropriate compensation" in regulation 15 means such sum not exceeding thirteen weeks' pay for the employee in question as the tribunal considers just and equitable having regard to the seriousness of the failure of the employer to comply with his duty.

(4) Sections 220 to 228 of the 1996 Act shall apply for calculating the amount of a week's pay for any employee for the purposes of paragraph (3) and, for the purposes of that calculation, the calculation date shall be—

   (a) in the case of an employee who is dismissed by reason of redundancy (within the meaning of sections 139 and 155 of the 1996 Act) the date which is the calculation date for the purposes of any entitlement of his to a redundancy payment (within the meaning of those sections) or which would be that calculation date if he were so entitled;

   (b) in the case of an employee who is dismissed for any other reason, the effective date of termination (within the meaning of sections 95(1) and (2) and 97 of the 1996 Act) of his contract of employment;

   (c) in any other case, the date of the relevant transfer.

Employers' Liability Compulsory Insurance

17.—(1) Paragraph (2) applies where—

   (a) by virtue of section 3(1)(a) or (b) of the Employers' Liability (Compulsory Insurance) Act 1969[14] ("the 1969 Act"), the transferor is not required by that Act to effect any insurance; or

   (b) by virtue of section 3(1)(c) of the 1969 Act, the transferor is exempted from the requirement of that Act to effect insurance.

(2) Where this paragraph applies, on completion of a relevant transfer the transferor and the transferee shall be jointly and severally liable in respect of any

liability referred to in section 1(1) of the 1969 Act, in so far as such liability relates to the employee's employment with the transferor.

Restriction on contracting out

18. Section 203 of the 1996 Act (restrictions on contracting out) shall apply in relation to these Regulations as if they were contained in that Act, save for that section shall not apply in so far as these Regulations provide for an agreement (whether a contract of employment or not) to exclude or limit the operation of these Regulations.

Amendment to the 1996 Act

19. In section 104 of the 1996 Act (assertion of statutory right) in subsection (4)—
  (a) the word "and" at the end of paragraph (c) is omitted; and
  (b) after paragraph (d), there is inserted—
      ", and
    (e) the rights conferred by the Transfer of Undertakings (Protection of Employment) Regulations 2006.".

Repeals, revocations and amendments

20.—(1) Subject to regulation 21, the 1981 Regulations are revoked.
  (2) Section 33 of, and paragraph 4 of Schedule 9 to, the Trade Union Reform and Employment Rights Act 1993[15] are repealed.
  (3) Schedule 2 (consequential amendments) shall have effect.

Transitional provisions and savings

21.—(1) These Regulations shall apply in relation to—
  (a) a relevant transfer that takes place on or after 6 April 2006;
  (b) a transfer or service provision change, not falling within sub-paragraph (a), that takes place on or after 6 April 2006 and is regarded by virtue of any enactment as a relevant transfer.
  (2) The 1981 Regulations shall continue to apply in relation to—
  (a) a relevant transfer (within the meaning of the 1981 Regulations) that took place before 6 April 2006;
  (b) a transfer, not falling within sub-paragraph (a), that took place before 6 April 2006 and is regarded by virtue of any enactment as a relevant transfer (within the meaning of the 1981 Regulations).
  (3) In respect of a relevant transfer that takes place on or after 6 April 2006, any action taken by a transferor or transferee to discharge a duty that applied to them under regulation 10 or 10A of the 1981 Regulations shall be deemed to satisfy the corresponding obligation imposed by regulations 13 and 14 of these Regulations, in so far as that action would have discharged those obligations had the action taken place on or after 6 April 2006.
  (4) The duty on a transferor to provide a transferee with employee liability information shall not apply in the case of a relevant transfer that takes place on or before 19 April 2006.
  (5) Regulations 13, 14, 15 and 16 shall not apply in the case of a service provision change that is not also a transfer of an undertaking, business or part of an undertaking or business that takes place on or before 4 May 2006.
  (6) The repeal of paragraph 4 of Schedule 9 to the Trade Union Reform and

Employment Rights Act 1993 does not affect the continued operation of that paragraph so far as it remains capable of having effect.

Gerry Sutcliffe

Parliamentary Under Secretary of State for Employment Relations and Consumer Affairs, Department of Trade and Industry

6th February 2006

SCHEDULE 1

Regulation 2

APPLICATION OF THE REGULATIONS TO NORTHERN IRELAND

1. These Regulations shall apply to Northern Ireland, subject to the modifications in this Schedule.

2. Sub-paragraph (1)(b) of regulation 3 and any other provision of these Regulations insofar as it relates to that sub-paragraph shall not apply to Northern Ireland.

3. Any reference in these Regulations—

   (a) to an employment tribunal shall be construed as a reference to an Industrial Tribunal; and

   (b) to the Employment Appeal Tribunal shall be construed as a reference to the Court of Appeal.

4. For the words from "Paragraph (1)" to "the 1992 Act" in regulation 7(6) there is substituted—

   "Paragraph (1) shall not apply in relation to a dismissal of an employee if the application of Article 126 of the Employment Rights (Northern Ireland) Order 1996[16] to the dismissal of the employee is excluded by or under any provision of that Order, the Industrial Tribunals (Northern Ireland) Order 1996[17] or the 1992 Act insofar as it extends to Northern Ireland, the Industrial Relations (Northern Ireland) Order 1992[18] or the Trade Union and Labour Relations (Northern Ireland) Order 1995[19]".

5. For the words from "In this Regulation" to "Part XII of the 1996 Act" in regulation 8(4) there is substituted—

   "In this Regulation the 'relevant statutory schemes' are—

   (a) Chapter VI of Part XII of the Employment Rights (Northern Ireland) Order 1996 ('the 1996 Order');

   (b) Part XIV of the 1996 Order".

6. For paragraph (4) of regulation 9 there is substituted—

   "In article 92 of the 1996 Order (time off for carrying out trade union duties) in paragraph (1), for the full stop at the end of sub-subparagraph (c) there is inserted—

'(d) negotiations with a view to entering into an agreement under regulation 9 of the Transfer of Undertakings (Protection of Employment) Regulations 2006 that applies to employees of the employer, or

(e) the performance on behalf of employees of the employer of functions related to or connected with the making of an agreement under that regulation.'."

7. For the words from "Paragraph (2)" to "the employee's employment with the transferor" in regulation 17 there is substituted—

"Paragraph (2) applies where—

(a) by virtue of article 7(a), 7(aa) or 7(b) of the Employers' Liability (Defective Equipment and Compulsory Insurance) (Northern Ireland) Order 1972[20] ('the 1972 Order'), the transferor is not required by that Order to effect any insurance; or

(b) by virtue of article 7(c) of the 1972 Order, the transferor is exempted from the requirement of that Order to effect insurance.

(2) Where this paragraph applies, on completion of a relevant transfer the transferor and the transferee shall be jointly and severally liable in respect of any liability referred to in article 5(1) of the 1972 Order, in so far as such liability relates to the employee's employment with the transferor".

8. In regulation 2 for "the 1992 Act" there is substituted "the Industrial Relations (Northern Ireland) Order 1992" and for "Part XIII of the Insolvency Act 1986" there is substituted "Part XII of the Insolvency (NI) Order 1989[21]".

9. In regulation 5 for "sections 179 and 180 of the 1992 Act" there is substituted "Article 26 of the Industrial Relations (NI) Order 1992 No.807 (N.I. 5)".

10.—(1) In regulation 10 for "the Pensions Schemes Act 1993" there is substituted "the Social Security Pensions (Northern Ireland) Order 1975[22]".

(2) In regulation 11 for "the Employment Act 2002 (Dispute Resolution) Regulations 2004" there is substituted "the Employment (Northern Ireland) Order 2003 (Dispute Resolution) Regulations (NI) 2004[23]".

(3) In regulation 12 for "Section 18 of the 1996 Tribunals Act" there is substituted "Article 20 of the Industrial Tribunals (NI) Order 1996 No.1921 (NI 18)".

(4) In regulation 16—

(a) for "Section 18 of the 1996 Tribunals Act" there is substituted "Article 20 of the Industrial Tribunals (NI) Order 1996 No.1921 (NI 18)"; and

(b) for any reference to "those Acts" there is substituted a reference to "those Orders".

11. For a reference to a provision of the 1996 Act in column one of Table 1 there is substituted the corresponding reference to the Employment Rights (Northern Ireland) Order 1996 in column two of Table 1—

Table 1

Column 1	Column 2
Provision of the Employment Rights Act 1996	*Equivalent Provision in the Employment Rights (Northern Ireland) Order 1996*
Part X	Part XI
Section 98(4)	Article 130(4)
Section 98(1)	Article 130(1)
Section 135	Article 170(I)
Section 98(2)(c)	Article 130(2)(c)
Section 95(1)(c)	Article 127(1)(c)
Section 1	Article 33
Section 205(1)	Article 247(I)
Sections 220–228	Articles 16–24
Section 139	Article 174
Section 155	Article 190
Section 95(1)	Article 127(1)
Section 95(2)	Article 127(2)
Section 97	Article 129
Section 203	Article 245
Section 104	Article 135

12. Any expression used in this Schedule which is defined in the Interpretation Act (Northern Ireland) 1954[24] shall have the meaning assigned by that Act.

APPENDIX 2

Pensions Act 2004

Pension protection on transfer of employment

257. Conditions for pension protection

(1) This section applies in relation to a person ("the employee") where—
   (a) there is a relevant transfer within the meaning of[1] of the TUPE Regulations,
   (b) by virtue of the transfer the employee ceases to be employed by the transferor and becomes employed by the transferee, and
   (c) at the time immediately before the employee becomes employed by the transferee—
      (i) there is an occupational pension scheme ("the scheme") in relation to which the transferor is the employer, and
      (ii) one of subsections (2), (3) and (4) applies.

(2) This subsection applies where—
   (a) the employee is an active member of the scheme, and
   (b) if any of the benefits that may be provided under the scheme are money purchase benefits—
      (i) the transferor is required to make contributions to the scheme in respect of the employee, or
      (ii) the transferor is not so required but has made one or more such contributions.

(3) This subsection applies where—
   (a) the employee is not an active member of the scheme but is eligible to be such a member, and
   (b) if any of the benefits that may be provided under the scheme are money purchase benefits, the transferor would have been required to make contributions to the scheme in respect of the employee if the employee had been an active member of it.

(4) This subsection applies where—
   (a) the employee is not an active member of the scheme, nor eligible to be such a member, but would have been an active member of the scheme or eligible to be such a member if, after the date on which he became employed by the transferor, he had been employed by the transferor for a longer period, and
   (b) if any of the benefits that may be provided under the scheme are money purchase benefits, the transferor would have been required to make contributions to the scheme in respect of the employee if the employee had been an active member of it.

---

[1] Amended by TUPE 2006, Schedule 2, paragraph 13(2).

(5) For the purposes of this section, the condition in subsection (1)(c) is to be regarded as satisfied in any case where it would have been satisfied but for any action taken by the transferor by reason of the transfer.

[ ]²

(7) In the case of a scheme which is contracted-out by virtue of section 9 of the Pension Schemes Act 1993 (c. 48), the references in subsections (2)(b), (3)(b) and (4)(b) to contributions mean contributions other than minimum payments (within the meaning of that Act).

(8) In this section—

the "TUPE Regulations" means the Transfer of Undertakings (Protection of Employment) Regulations 2006;³

references to the transferor include any associate of the transferor, and section 435 of the Insolvency Act 1986 (c. 45) applies for the purposes of this section as it applies for the purposes of that Act.

258. Form of protection

(1) In a case where section 257 applies, it is a condition of the employee's contract of employment with the transferee that the requirements in subsection (2) or the requirement in subsection (3) are complied with.

(2) The requirements in this subsection are that—
    (a) the transferee secures that, as from the relevant time, the employee is, or is eligible to be, an active member of an occupational pension scheme in relation to which the transferee is the employer, and
    (b) in a case where the scheme is a money purchase scheme, as from the relevant time—
        (i) the transferee makes relevant contributions to the scheme in respect of the employee, or
        (ii) if the employee is not an active member of the scheme but is eligible to be such a member, the transferee would be required to make such contributions if the employee were an active member, and
    (c) in a case where the scheme is not a money purchase scheme, as from the relevant time the scheme—
        (i) satisfies the statutory standard referred to in section 12A of the Pension Schemes Act 1993 (c. 48), or
        (ii) if regulations so provide, complies with such other requirements as may be prescribed.

(3) The requirement in this subsection is that, as from the relevant time, the transferee makes relevant contributions to a stakeholder pension scheme of which the employee is a member.

(4) The requirement in subsection (3) is for the purposes of this section to be regarded as complied with by the transferee during any period in relation to which the condition in subsection (5) is satisfied.

(5) The condition in this subsection is that the transferee has offered to make relevant

² Amended by TUPE 2006, Schedule 2, paragraph 13(3).
³ Amended by TUPE 2006, Schedule 2, paragraph 13(3).

246

contributions to a stakeholder pension scheme of which the employee is eligible to be a member (and the transferee has not withdrawn the offer).

(6) Subsection (1) does not apply in relation to a contract if or to the extent that the employee and the transferee so agree at any time after the time when the employee becomes employed by the transferee.

(7) In this section—

"the relevant time" means—

(a) in a case where section 257 applies by virtue of the application of subsection (2) or (3) of that section, the time when the employee becomes employed by the transferee;

(b) in a case where that section applies by virtue of the application of subsection (4) of that section, the time at which the employee would have been a member of the scheme referred to in subsection (1)(c)(i) of that section or (if earlier) would have been eligible to be such a member;

"relevant contributions" means such contributions in respect of such period or periods as may be prescribed;

"stakeholder pension scheme" means a pension scheme which is registered under section 2 of the Welfare Reform and Pensions Act 1999 (c. 30).

STATUTORY INSTRUMENTS

2005 No. 649

PENSIONS

THE TRANSFER OF EMPLOYMENT (PENSION PROTECTION) REGULATIONS 2005

Made	*10th March 2005*
Laid before Parliament	*16th March 2005*
Coming into force	*6th April 2005*

The Secretary of State for Work and Pensions, in exercise of the powers conferred upon him by sections 258(2)(c)(ii) and (7), 315(2) and 318(1) of the Pensions Act 2004[1] and all other powers enabling him in that behalf, by this instrument, which contains regulations made before the end of the period of six months beginning with the coming into force of the provisions by virtue of which they are made[2], hereby makes the following Regulations:

Citation, commencement, application and interpretation

1.—(1) These Regulations may be cited as the Transfer of Employment (Pension Protection) Regulations 2005 and shall come into force on 6th April 2005.

(2) These Regulations apply in the case of a person ("the employee") in relation to whom section 257 of the Act (conditions for pension protection) applies, that is to say a person who, in the circumstances described in subsection (1) of that section, ceases to be employed by the transferor of an undertaking or part of an undertaking and becomes employed by the transferee.

(3) In these Regulations "the Act" means the Pensions Act 2004.

Requirements concerning a transferee's pension scheme

2.—(1) In a case where these Regulations apply, and the transferee is the employer in relation to a pension scheme which is not a money purchase scheme, that scheme complies with section 258(2)(c)(ii) of the Act (alternative standard for a scheme which is not a money purchase scheme) if it provides either—

(a) for members to be entitled to benefits the value of which equals or exceeds 6 per cent. of pensionable pay for each year of employment together with the total amount of any contributions made by them, and, where members are required to make contributions to the scheme, for them to contribute at a rate which does not exceed 6 per cent. of their pensionable pay; or

(b) for the transferee to make relevant contributions to the scheme on behalf of each employee of his who is an active member of it.

(2) In this regulation—

"pensionable pay" means that part of the remuneration payable to a member of a scheme by reference to which the amount of contributions and benefits are determined under the rules of the scheme.

Requirements concerning a transferee's pension contributions

3.—(1) In a case where these Regulations apply, the transferee's pension contributions are relevant contributions for the purposes of section 258(2)(b) of the Act in the case of a money purchase scheme, section 258(3) to (5) of the Act in the case of a stakeholder pension scheme, and regulation 2(1)(b) above in the case of a scheme which is not a money purchase scheme, if—

    (a) the contributions are made in respect of each period for which the employee is paid remuneration, provided that the employee also contributes to the scheme in respect of that period, and

    (b) the amount contributed in respect of each such period is—

        (i) in a case where the employee's contribution in respect of that period is less than 6 per cent. of the remuneration paid to him, an amount at least equal to the amount of the employee's contribution;

        (ii) in a case where the employee's contribution in respect of that period equals or exceeds 6 per cent. of the remuneration paid to him, an amount at least equal to 6 per cent. of that remuneration.

(2) In calculating the amount of an employee's remuneration for the purposes of paragraph (1)—

    (a) only payments made in respect of basic pay shall be taken into account, and bonus, commission, overtime and similar payments shall be disregarded, and

    (b) no account shall be taken of any deductions which are made in respect of tax, national insurance or pension contributions.

(3) In calculating the amount of a transferee's pension contributions for the purposes of paragraph (1) in the case of a scheme which is contracted-out by virtue of section 9 of the Pension Schemes Act 1993[3], minimum payments within the meaning of that Act shall be disregarded.

Signed by authority of the Secretary of State for Work and Pensions.

Malcolm Wicks

Minister of State, Department for Work and Pensions

10th March 2005

EXPLANATORY NOTE
(This note is not part of the Regulations)

These Regulations concern the obligations of an employer under section 258 of the Pensions Act 2004 (c. 35) towards a person in relation to whom section 257 of that Act applies.

Section 257 applies to a person ("the employee") who becomes the employee of a new employer ("the transferee") by virtue of a transfer to which the Transfer of Undertakings (Protection of Employment) Regulations 1981 (S.I. 1981/1794) apply, and who had actual or contingent rights in relation to an occupational pension scheme immediately before the transfer.

Under section 258, the transferee is required to secure that the employee is, or is eligible to become, an active member of an occupational pension scheme (as defined in section 1 of the Pension Schemes Act 1993 (c. 48) as substituted by section 239 of the 2004 Act) in relation to which the transferee is the employer and, if it is a money purchase scheme, to make "relevant contributions" to it. Alternatively, the transferee must make such contributions to a stakeholder pension scheme of which the employee is a member (or offer to contribute to a stakeholder scheme of which he is eligible to be a member).

Section 258(2)(c) provides that a scheme in relation to which the transferee is the employer, if it is not a money purchase scheme, must satisfy a standard provided for in the Pension Schemes Act 1993, or, if regulations so provide, comply with prescribed requirements. For the purposes of this provision, regulation 2 requires that either the value of the benefits provided for by the transferee's scheme must be at least 6% of pensionable pay for each year of employment in addition to any contributions made by him or that the scheme must provide for the employer to make relevant contributions on behalf of his employees.

Section 258(7) provides for "relevant contributions" to be defined in regulations. Regulation 3 provides that such contributions must be made in respect of each period for which the employee contributes to the pension scheme, and that the amount contributed must equal the employee's contribution subject to an upper limit of 6% of basic pay.

As these Regulations are made before the expiry of the period of six months beginning with the coming into force of the provisions of the Pensions Act 2004 by virtue of which they are made, the requirement for the Secretary of State to consult such persons as he considers appropriate does not apply.

An assessment of the impact on business, charities and the voluntary sector of the provisions in these Regulations is included in the Regulatory Impact Assessment that accompanied the Pensions Act 2004. A copy of that assessment has been placed in the libraries of both Houses of Parliament. Copies may be obtained from the Department for Work and Pensions, Regulatory Impact Unit, Adelphi, 1–11 John Adam Street, London WC2N 6HT.

Notes:

[1] 2004 c.35; section 318(1) is cited for the definitions of "prescribed" and "regulations".

[2] See section 317(2)(c) of the Pensions Act 2004 which provides that the Secretary of State must consult such persons as he considers appropriate before making regulations by virtue of the provisions of that Act (other than Part 8). This duty does not apply where regulations are made before the end of six months beginning with the coming into force of the provisions of that Act by virtue of which the regulations are made.

[3] 1993 c.48; section 9 was amended by the Pensions Act 1995 (c.26), section 136(3), and the Pensions Act 2004, section 283.

Index

References are to Paragraph Numbers

References to the Appendices are in Italics

ACAS Code of Practice on Time Off for Trade Union Activities 9.43
ACAS conciliation officers 12.03, 12.11
Acquired Rights Directives
1977 Directive 1.02, 1.04, 1.13, 1.16–1.17, 4.01
1998 Directive 1.16
2001 Directive 1.13, 1.16
assignment 4.16
collective agreements 5.42
collective information and consultation 9.10
constructive dismissal 4.68
consultation 1.16
continuity of employment 1.04
dismissals 7.01–7.02, 7.08
economic, technical or organisational reasons entailing change in the workforce (ETOR) 6.29–6.32, 6.39
electing not to transfer 4.47–4.48
employees, definition of 4.01
employment by transferor 4.08
employment contracts 4.01
European Court of Justice 1.16
implementation 1.01
individual rights, transfer of 5.03
information and consultation arrangements 1.17, 8.01–8.02
insolvency 10.01–10.04, 10.06–10.12, 10.22
interpretation 1.02, 1.04
one-off contracts 3.07
pensions 11.01, 11.06–11.10, 11.23
revision 1.16–1.17
service provision changes 3.02–3.04, 3.07
terms and conditions, variations to 6.05, 6.12, 6.14–6.15, 6.29
territoriality 12.12–12.13, 12.24
trade unions, recognised 5.56–5.57, 5.63–5.64
TUPE 1981 and 1.01
working conditions, changes to 4.68
administrative functions 1.40–1.47
agencies 2.23, 4.04
apportionment of liability 8.49–8.50, 9.86
ARD *see* **Acquired Rights Directives**
assets, transfer of
customers, continuity of 2.57

economic entity 2.20
employees, transfer of 2.47–2.52, 2.54
identity of economic activity, retention of 2.36, 2.47–2.59
labour-intensive activities 2.58–2.59
multifactorial test 2.50, 2.52, 2.59
part of assets, sale of 1.03
re-tendering 2.51
service provision change 2.59, 3.11–3.12
ships 2.51–2.52
Spijkers factors 2.48, 2.58
transfers of undertakings 2.10, 2.47–2.59
TUPE 2006 and 2.47–2.59
assignment
2005 Consultation 4.15
Acquired Rights Directive 4.16
assignment test 3.9, 4.15–4.31, 12.46
EC law 4.15–4.16
employee liability information 8.09
employees, definition of 4.14–4.31
employees, organised grouping of 3.19, 4.15
employment contracts 4.15
human stock approach 4.17
insolvency 10.28
labour-intensive factors 2.58–2.59, 2.61, 2.64–2.65, 2.68, 2.74
outsourcing 12.46
permitted variations 10.28–10.31
relevant transfer, definition of 4.14
resources, organised grouping of 4.15
temporary 4.26–4.31
TUPE 2006 and 4.14–4.16

benefits *see* **bonuses and benefits**
best value 3.06
bonuses and benefits
continuation of benefits 5.20
individual rights, transfer of 5.20, 5.22–5.24
parts of undertakings 5.22
substantial equivalence test 5.23–5.24
terms and conditions, changes to 5.22
TUPE 2006 and 5.22
break in activities
identity, retention of 2.45–2.46
service provision changes 3.51
Spijkers factor 2.45

break in activities (*cont.*):
  TUPE 2006 and 2.45–2.46

Central Arbitration Committee 1.30, 5.66, 9.99
changes to contracts *see* **variation to employees'**
  terms and conditions
changes to the operation
  identity of economic activity 2.41–2.44
  integration 2.44
  location 2.41–2.42
  methods of work 2.41–2.42
  TUPE 2006 and 2.41–2.44
changes to working conditions
  2005 Consultation 4.66
  Acquired Rights Directive 4.68
  consequences 4.69–4.72
  constructive dismissal 4.59, 4.64, 4.67–4.69,
    4.76
  detriment 4.57–4.64, 4.69, 4.73, 4.75, 6.15
  dismissals 4.64–4.67, 4.70–4.71
  DTI Guidance 4.62, 4.70
  electing not to transfer 4.48, 4.57–4.76, 4.78
  individual rights, transfer of 5.03, 5.09
  insolvency 4.75, 10.51
  material changes 4.63, 4.73, 4.75–4.76
  notice period 4.65–4.66, 4.73
  relocation 4.62, 4.69
  repudiatory breach of contract 4.59, 4.64,
    4.69, 4.76
  resignation 4.48, 4.57–4.76, 4.78
  substantial changes 4.57–4.64, 4.70, 4.73,
    4.75–4.76
  timing of changes 4.74
  trade unions, recognised 5.61
  trust and confidence, breach of 4.80
  TUPE 1981 and 4.57–4.59, 4.64, 4.73
  TUPE 2006 and 4.60–4.76
  unfair dismissal 4.66–4.67, 4.70–4.71
  variations to employment contracts 4.75,
    6.15
  warranties 12.41
  wrongful dismissal 4.65–4.66
collective agreements 5.42–5.55
  Acquired Rights Directive 5.42
  collective information and consultation
    5.48
  compensation 8.63
  definition 5.49–5.50
  employee liability information 8.13
  employment contracts, incorporation into
    5.55
  individual rights, transfer of 5.08, 5.15
  industry-wide 5.47
  knowledge of transfer 4.45
  legal enforceability 5.44, 5.46, 5.52–5.55
  minimum obligations 5.43
  statutory test 5.50
  termination before transfer 5.48

trade unions, recognised 5.42, 5.46–5.49,
  5.52, 5.54, 5.61
transfer 5.42–5.52
TUPE 2006 and 5.42–5.46, 5.52
collective information and consultation
  9.01–9.112 *see also* **employee liability**
  information, information and
  consultation arrangements
  2005 Consultation 9.04, 9.84
  Acquired Rights Directive 9.10
  affected employees 9.06–9.08, 9.22, 9.65
  apportionment of liability 9.86
  breach by transferee 9.70
  burden of proof 9.66–9.69, 9.90
  claims 9.65
  collective agreements 5.48
  compensation 9.05, 9.19, 9.72–9.82,
    9.95
    amount 9.02, 9.73–9.79
    cap 9.75
    collective redundancy consultation
      9.97–9.98
    joint and several liability 9.83–9.88
    mitigation 9.82
  complaints 8.65–9.71
    burden of proof 9.66–9.69
    persons who can make 9.65
    timing of 9.71
  compliance, planning for 9.110–9.112
  confidentiality 9.93–9.94
  contribution 9.86
  date of transfer 9.10, 9.74
  delivery 9.15–9.16, 9.30
  DTI Guidance 9.112
  due diligence 8.06, 8.40, 8.66–8.74
  duration of consultation 9.34
  employee representatives 9.02–9.03,
    9.35–9.64, 9.68–9.69
    complaints 9.65
    compliance, planning for 9.111
    delivery 9.15–9.16
    liability for failure to provide information
      and consult with 9.05
  employment tribunals 9.65, 9.70–9.82,
    9.95–9.96
  failure to provide information and consult,
    liability for 9.05, 9.65–9.96
  former employees 8.31–8.36
  freezing orders 9.95
  indemnities 9.87–9.88, 9.110
  indirect provision 8.41–8.42
  injunctions 9.95–9.96
  insolvency 9.87, 9.91
  instalments 1.32, 8.40
  joint and several liability 9.05, 9.71,
    9.83–9.88, 9.110
  legal, social and economic implications 9.09,
    9.11–9.12

measures in connection with transfer
9.23–9.29, 9.98, 9.111
minimum award 8.60–8.64
mitigation 9.82
nature and timing of consultation 9.31–9.34
parent companies, decisions of 9.92
pensions 9.27–9.28
principles of award 8.56–8.59
rationalisation and harmonisation 9.07
records 9.32
redundancies 6.03, 9.07–9.08, 9.13, 9.34,
9.111
compensation 9.97–9.98
interaction with collective redundancy
consultation 9.97–9.98
payments 9.74, 9.76–9.77, 9.81
special circumstances defence 9.90,
9.92–9.93
remedies 9.65–9.96
required consultation 9.21–9.23
required information 9.09–9.10
service provision changes 1.39
special circumstances defence 9.89–9.94
terms and conditions, variations to 6.03
territoriality 12.30
timing 9.13–9.14, 9.31–9.34
trade unions 9.02–9.03, 9.65
transferee measures 9.17–9.20
triggers 9.23
TUPE 1981 and 9.04, 9.20, 9.77
TUPE 2006 and 1.39, 9.01–9.112
updating 1.31, 8.37–8.39
warranties 9.87–9.88
when consultation is required 9.31–9.34
whose obligation 9.29–9.30
commission arrangements 8.72
commodity services 3.07
compensation
collective agreements 8.63
compromise agreements 12.11
employee liability information 1.32, 8.48,
8.54–8.65, 8.67
employee representatives 9.54, 9.59
failure to inform and consult
collective information and consultation
9.02, 9.05, 9.19, 9.72–9.88, 9.95,
9.97–9.98
redundancy 9.97–9.98
information and consultation arrangements
9.99
insolvency 10.51
minimum award 8.60–8.64
mitigation 8.65, 9.82
redundancy 9.97–9.98
territoriality 12.14
unfair dismissal 9.59
compromise agreements
ACAS conciliation officers 12.11

compensation 12.11
contracting out 12.05–12.11
enforceability 12.08–12.09
information and consultation 12.11
insolvency 12.07
privity of contract 12.10
redundancy 12.08
settlement of termination-related claims
12.08–12.09
terms and conditions, changes to 6.17–6.20,
12.05–12.07
TUPE 1981 and 12.08–12.09
TUPE 2006 and 12.06–12.11
unfair dismissal 6.17–6.21, 12.05–12.06
confidentiality 8.31, 9.93–9.94
constructive dismissal
economic, technical or organisational
reasons entailing change in the
workforce (ETOR) 7.38–7.39
electing not to transfer 4.48, 4.77–4.78,
4.80
objection to transfer 4.79
pensions 1.37
pre-transfer conduct 4.80
repudiatory breach of contract 4.59, 4.64,
4.76–4.77
terms and conditions, changes to 4.79
trust and confidence, breach of 4.80
TUPE 2006 and 4.77, 7.13
working conditions, changes to 4.59, 4.64,
4.67–4.69, 4.76
consultation see collective information and
consultation, information and
consultation arrangements
continental shelf 12.23
continuity of employment
Acquired Rights Directive 1.04
EC law 1.04, 5.38
individual rights, transfer of 5.36–5.41
objection to transfer 5.40
redundancy payments 5.40–5.41
re-engagement 6.21
single contract undertakings 2.30
terms and conditions, variations to 6.21
timing of transfers 2.80
TUPE 1981 and 5.40
TUPE 2006 and 5.36, 5.38–5.41
contracting out see contracting out of TUPE,
outsourcing
contracting out of TUPE 12.01–12.11
ACAS conciliation officers 12.03
compromise agreements 12.05–12.11
employee liability information 8.75, 12.04
permitted variations 12.04
prohibition 12.01–12.04
terms and conditions, variations to
6.17–6.20
TUPE 2006 and 12.01, 12.04

contract would otherwise terminate, where
4.32–4.36
contracts of employment *see* **employment contracts**
court or tribunal claims *see* **employment tribunals**
claims information 8.23
DTI Guidance 8.25
employee liability information 1.32, 8.13,
8.21–8.25, 8.50
TUPE 2006 and 1.32, 8.13, 8.21–8.25, 8.50
covenants *see* **restrictive covenants**
criminal liabilities 5.09, 8.14

damages *see* **compensation**
data protection
accuracy 8.32
anonymised lists of employees 8.27
confidentiality 8.31
data processing 8.27
data protection principles 8.32
due diligence 8.27, 8.30
employee liability information 8.26–8.33
personal data 8.27–8.33
sensitive personal data 8.29–8.30, 8.33
transfer of personal data outside EEA
8.32
date of transfer 2.82, 9.10, 9.79
definition of relevant transfers *see* **relevant transfers, definition and identification of**
Department of Trade and Industry
2001 Consultation 1.14
2005 Consultation 1.14
Consultation response to 1.14
Guidance 1.14
TUPE 2006 and 1.14, 1.46
disciplinary and grievance procedures 8.13,
8.18–8.21
dismissals 7.01–7.44; *see also* **constructive dismissal, unfair dismissal**
Acquired Rights Directive 7.01–7.02,
7.08
categories of 7.05–7.08
common law 1.05
costs of 1.38
economic, technical or organisational
reasons entailing change in the
workforce (ETOR) 1.27, 6.29, 7.02,
7.04–7.07, 7.10, 7.30–7.42
employee representatives 9.55–9.60
indemnities 12.42–12.43
individual rights, transfer of 5.07
objections to transfer 4.50, 4.56
pensions 11.42
pre-transfer employment 4.39–4.43
reasons 7.42
redundancies 7.05, 7.09, 7.42
relocation 7.05

sole or principal reason test 7.05
terms and conditions, variations to
6.02–6.03, 6.05, 6.08, 6.10, 6.17,
6.21
territoriality 12.18
transfer-related 1.27
TUPE 1981 and 7.06
TUPE 2006 and 1.27, 1.38, 7.01, 7.03–7.09
working conditions, changes to 4.64–4.67,
4.70–4.71
wrongful dismissal 4.48, 4.65–4.66
drafting 12.33, 12.43
DTI *see* **Department of Trade and Industry**
due diligence 12.34–12.36
data protection 8.27, 8.30
employee liability information 8.06, 8.40,
8.66–8.74, 12.35–12.36
pensions 11.28
pricing 12.34
TUPE 2006 and 12.35
warranties 12.35

EC law; *see also* **Acquired Rights Directive**
assignment 4.15–4.16
continuity of employment 5.38
European Works Council 5.68, 9.108–9.109
insolvency 10.03
objections to transfer 4.50
terms and conditions, variations to
6.29–6.31
TUPE 1981 and 1.01
TUPE 2006 and 1.15
economic activities
break in 2.45–2.46
definition 1.42, 2.17–2.24, 3.13, 3.47
economic entity 2.17–2.18
non-commercial activities 2.18
one-person undertakings 2.25
primary purpose test 2.18
public sector 1.41–1.42
reorganisations 1.43–1.45
service provision changes 3.62
single contract undertakings 2.27–2.31
subcontractors 3.62
economic entity; *see also* **retention of identity of economic entity**
assets, transfer of 2.20
autonomy 2.19–2.20
definition 2.17–2.24
distinct cost centre, use of term 2.21
economic activities 2.17–2.18
employment agencies, transfer of
employment to 2.23
non-commercial activities 2.18
one-person undertakings 2.25–2.26
primary purpose of organisation 2.18
resources, organised group of 2.18–2.19
retention of identity 2.20, 2.22–2.23

stability and structure, importance of
2.19–2.24
TUPE 2006 and 2.17–2.24
**economic, technical and organisational reasons
entailing changes in the workforce
(ETOR)**
Acquired Rights Directive 6.29–6.32,
6.39
Consultation Response 6.40
constructive dismissal 7.38–7.39
definition 7.36–7.37
dismissals 1.27, 6.29, 7.02, 7.04–7.07, 7.10,
7.30–7.42
DTI Guidance 6.38, 7.36
former employees 8.35
harmonisation of terms and conditions
6.38–6.40
insolvency 10.06, 10.45
job functions, change in 7.38–7.39
pensions 6.43
permitted variations 10.45
redundancy 7.34–7.35, 7.40
re-engagement 6.29
sole or principal reason test 6.32
terms and conditions, variations to 6.24,
6.26–6.40
territoriality 12.31
TUPE 1981 and 1.07
TUPE 2006 and 6.30, 6.32, 6.35–6.40,
7.31–7.41
unfair dismissal 6.36, 7.04, 7.10, 7.12–7.13,
7.17, 7.30–7.42
variation to terms and conditions, connection
of transfer to 6.29–6.33
waiver of rights 6.30
workforce, changes in 6.35–6.37, 7.38–7.39
electing not to transfer 4.47–4.80
2005 Consultation 4.47
Acquired Rights Directive 4.47–4.48
conduct towards employees before transfer
4.80
constructive dismissal 4.48, 4.77–4.78,
4.80
objection to transfer 4.48–4.56, 4.78–4.80
repudiatory breach of contract, resignation
in 4.48
resignation 4.48, 4.57–4.76
terms and conditions, changes to
4.78–4.79
timing of transfer 4.79
transferor, claims against the 4.78–4.80
trust and confidence, breach of 4.80
TUPE 1981 and 4.78–4.79
TUPE 2006 and 4.47–4.48, 4.78–4.79
unfair dismissal 4.48
working conditions, resignation due to
changes in 4.48, 4.57–4.76, 4.78, 4.80
wrongful dismissal 4.48

employee liability information;
see also **collective information and
consultation, information and
consultation arrangements**
2005 Consultation 8.06, 8.43, 8.48–8.52,
8.56
apportionment of liability 8.49–8.50
assignment 8.09
changes in 8.38
collective agreements 8.13
commission arrangements 8.72
compensation 1.32, 8.54–8.65,
8.67
amount of 8.55–8.64
minimum award 8.60–8.64
mitigation 8.65
principles of award 8.56–8.59
complaints 1.32, 8.48–8.55
contracting out 8.75, 12.04
copy documentation 8.37
costs of 1.38
court or tribunal claims 1.32, 8.13,
8.21–8.25, 8.50
criminal liabilities 8.14
damages 8.48, 8.59
data protection 8.26–8.33
declarations 8.54
definition 1.31, 8.10
delivery 8.37–8.39
disciplinary and grievance procedures 8.13,
8.18–8.21
DTI Guidance 8.45, 8.64
due diligence 8.06, 8.40, 8.66–8.74,
12.35–12.36
electronic data room, access to 8.37
employee status 8.08–8.09
employment documentation 8.73
employment particulars, written 8.13,
8.14–8.17
employment tribunals 1.32, 8.13, 8.21–8.25,
8.50, 8.53–8.65
financial penalties 8.51–8.52
former employees 8.31–8.36
indemnities 8.67–8.68
indirect provision 8.41–8.42
industrial relations 8.74
instalments 1.32, 8.40
joint and several liability 8.49
list of employees and their details 8.71
notification of 1.31–1.32, 1.38–1.39,
8.04–8.05, 8.11, 8.37–8.38, 8.48–8.49,
8.56
outsourcing 8.42, 12.46
pensions 8.73
prescribed information 8.12–8.14
profit sharing 8.72
remedies 1.32, 8.48–8.55
resources, organised grouping of 8.09

employee liability information (*cont.*):
re-tendering 8.42, 8.66
service provision changes 3.05
share options 8.72
small businesses 8.05
special circumstances defence 1.31
tenders 8.39, 8.42, 8.46
terms and conditions 8.73
territoriality 12.30
third parties, provision by 1.32, 8.41–8.42
timing 1.31, 8.43–8.47, 8.66
transparency 8.03
TUPE 2006 and 1.31–1.32, 1.38, 1.39,
8.03–8.75
updates 1.31, 8.37–8.39
warranties 8.59, 8.67, 12.38
writing, information in 8.37
written particulars of employment 8.13,
8.14

employee representatives
ACAS Code of Practice on Time Off for
Trade Union Activities 9.43
accommodation and facilities, provision of
9.43
appointment 9.35, 9.41
appropriate representatives 9.35–9.44,
10.26–10.27, 10.30–10.39, 10.46–10.52
collective information and consultation
9.02–9.03, 9.35–9.64, 9.68–9.69
complaints 9.65
compliance, planning for 9.111
delivery 9.15–9.16
failure to carry out 1.29
liability for failure to provide information
and consult with 9.05
compensation 9.54, 9.59
detriment, protection from suffering a
9.50–9.55
dismissals 9.55–9.60
election 9.35, 9.41, 9.44–9.48, 9.51, 9.56
ICE representatives 9.100–9.107
information and consultation 1.29, 5.67,
9.100–9.107
insolvency 1.17, 10.30–10.39, 10.46
agreement 10.39–10.42
appropriate 10.26–10.27, 10.30–10.39,
10.46–10.52
elections 10.36
permitted variations 10.26–10.27,
10.30–10.42, 10.46–10.52
terms and conditions, negotiation of 1.17
interim relief 9.58
knowledge of transfer 4.45
nomination 9.41
number of 9.45
permitted variations 10.26–10.27, 10,
30–10.42, 10.46–10.52
protection of 9.49–9.71

selection 9.36, 9.41
staff committees 9.42
term of office 9.45
terms and conditions
negotiation of changes to 1.17
permitted variations 10.26–10.27,
10.30–10.42, 10.46–10.52
time off 9.43, 9.61–9.63, 10.38
timing of election of 9.47
trade unions, recognised 9.35, 9.37–9.40,
9.43, 9.60, 10.31–10.33, 10.39
TUPE 2006 and 5.67, 9.35–9.43
unfair dismissal 9.56–9.60

employees; *see also* **employee liability
information, employee representatives,
terms and conditions of employment,
organised grouping of employees,
transfer of**
assignment 4.14–4.28
definition of 1.26, 4.01–4.31
electing not to transfer 4.47–4.80
former 8.31–8.36
knowledge of transfer 4.45–4.46
pre-transfer employment 4.37–4.44
quality of workforce 2.73–2.75, 4.26–4.28
status of employees 8.08–8.09
terminate, contract would otherwise
4.32–4.36
transfer 2.47–2.52, 2.54

employees, definition of
Acquired Rights Directive 4.01
agency workers 4.04
assignment 4.14–4.31
transferor, employment by 4.05–4.13
TUPE 2006 and 1.26, 4.02–4.04

employees, transfer of organised grouping of
1.22, 1.26
2005 Consultation 3.15–3.16
assignment 3.19, 4.15
autonomy 3.17
Consultation Response 3.19
division of activities between contractors
3.55
DTI Guidance 3.17
duration 3.46
identity of economic entity, retention of
3.19
labour-intensive activities 2.76
one-off short-term service contracts 3.22
one-person undertakings 3.52
outsourcing 3.18
pre-transfer activities 3.18–3.19, 3.56
principal purpose test 3.15, 3.20–3.21, 3.57
professional services 3.42, 3.44
public sector 1.46
resources, organised grouping of 3.17
service provision changes 1.22, 2.05, 3.11,
3.14–3.21, 3.46, 3.52, 3.55–3.57, 3.59

stability and structure 3.17, 3.52
subcontractors 3.14
supply of goods 3.34
trade unions, recognised 5.58
TUPE 2006 and 3.11, 3.14–3.21, 3.59
employer's liability compulsory insurance
2001 Consultation 5.18
individual rights, transfer of 5.16–5.19
industrial diseases 5.16
joint and several liability 5.18–5.19
personal injuries 5.16
privity of contract 5.16
public sector 1.25, 5.18–5.19
TUPE 2006 and 1.25, 5.16, 5.18
employment agencies 2.23
employment by transferor
Acquired Rights Directive 4.08
groups of companies 4.09–4.12
management services companies 4.09, 4.12
relevant transfer, definition of 4.06, 4.08
service provision change 4.07, 4.13
transferor, definition of 4.08
TUPE 2006 and 4.05–4.13
veil of incorporation, lifting the 4.11
employment contracts; *see also* **terms and**
conditions of employment, variation to
employees' terms and conditions
Acquired Rights Directive 4.01
assignment 4.15
collective agreements, incorporation of
5.55
equality clauses 5.02, 5.05, 5.09, 5.29
insolvency 10.16
mobility clauses 4.30
national laws 4.01
objections to transfer 4.49
pre-transfer employment 4.37–4.44
restrictive covenants 4.52
share-based transactions 1.09, 5.25
transfer at common law 1.05
transferor, employment by 4.05–4.13
TUPE 1981 and 1.07
TUPE 2006 and 1.24, 4.02, 4.37–4.44
employment tribunals
collective information and consultation
9.65, 8.70–9.82, 9.95–9.96
employee liability information 1.32, 8.13,
8.21–8.25, 8.50, 8.53–8.65
injunctions 9.95–9.96
territoriality 12.32
TUPE 2006 and 1.32, 8.13, 8.21–8.25, 8.50
equal pay claims 5.29
ETOR *see* **economic, technical and**
organisational reasons entailing changes
in the workforce
European Works Council 5.68, 9.108–9.109
external service providers, awards of contracts
to 1.03

failure to inform and consult
compensation 9.02, 9.05, 9.19, 9.72–9.88,
9.95, 9.97–9.98
employee representatives 1.29
joint and several liability 1.29
liability for 1.29, 9.05, 9.65–9.96
special circumstances defence 9.89–9.94
TUPE 2006 and 1.29
Fairness at Work **White Paper** 1.12
foreign law, contract covered by 12.22
former employees
collective information and consultation
8.31–8.36
economic, technical or organisational
reasons entailing change in the
workforce (ETOR) 8.35
employee liability information 8.31–8.36
TUPE 2006 and 8.34–8.36

groups of companies 4.09–4.12, 11.16,
11.43

hiving down 10.54–10.55

identification of relevant transfer *see* **relevant**
transfers, definition and identification of
identity of economic entity *see* **retention of**
identity of economic entity
indemnities 12.42–12.45
collective information and consultation
9.87–9.88, 9.110
dismissals 12.42–12.43
drafting 12.43
employee liability information 8.67–8.68
fixed termination costs 12.44
information and consultation 12.44
pensions 11.29, 11.31
pricing 12.45
transfer agreements 12.45
TUPE 2006 and 12.44
types of liability 12.42
independent contractors 4.03
individual rights, transfer of 5.01–5.41;
see also **occupational pensions**
2005 Consultation 5.03–5.04, 5.12
Acquired Rights Directive 5.03
benefits, continuation of 5.20
bonuses and benefits 5.22–5.24
collective agreements 5.08, 5.15
consultation 5.12
continuity of employment 5.36–5.41
criminal liabilities, transfer of 5.11
custom and practice 5.09
discrimination 5.05
dismissals 5.07
employers' liability compulsory insurance
5.16–5.19
employment contracts 5.02, 5.05, 5.09

individual rights, transfer of (*cont.*):
  health and safety rules, pre-transfer breach
    of 5.11
  information and consultation 5.12, 5.15
  notice 5.07
  occupational pensions 5.10
  powers, rights, duties and liabilities, transfer
    of 5.05–5.15
  restrictive covenants 5.21
  retirement 5.30–5.35
  share options 5.25–5.29
  trade unions, consultation with recognised
    5.12
  TUPE 1981 and 5.04
  TUPE 2006 and 5.01–5.41
  unfair dismissal 5.30–5.35
  what is not transferred 5.10–5.12
  what is transferred 5.05–5.09
  working conditions, detrimental changes to
    5.09
information and consultation arrangements
    8.01–8.75, 9.99–9.107; *see also* **collective
    information and consultation, employee
    liability information**
  2001 Consultation 8.03
  Acquired Rights Directive 2001 1.17,
    8.01–8.02
  Central Arbitration Committee 9.99
  common law 1.06
  compensation 9.99
  compromise agreements 12.11
  costs of 1.38
  employee representatives 5.67
  ICE representatives 9.100–9.107
  indemnities 12.44
  individual rights, transfer of 5.12, 5.15
  insolvency 10.31, 10.34–10.38
  pensions 11.60
  territoriality 12.14, 12.32
  trade unions, recognised 5.12, 9.104
  TUPE 2006 and 1.38, 5.67–5.68, 8.02–8.07,
    9.103–9.107
in-housing 1.03
  labour-intensive activities 2.60
  relevant transfers, definition and
    identification 1.22
  service provision changes 1.22, 2.05, 3.03,
    3.06, 3.09, 3.59
injunctions 9.95–9.96
innovative bids
  level playing field 3.37
  new methods of working 3.36
  service provision changes 3.35–3.38, 3.49
  TUPE 2006 and 3.35–3.38
insolvency 10.01–10.55
  2005 Consultation 10.15, 10.21, 10.50
  Acquired Rights Directive 10.01–10.04,
    10.06–10.12, 10.22

affected employees 10.16
appropriate representatives 10.30–10.39
assigned employees 10.28
bankruptcy and analogous insolvency
  10.02, 10.09–10.13
collective information and consultation
  9.87, 9.91
compensation 10.51
compromise agreements 12.10
costs of 1.38
debts, transfer of 1.17, 10.17–10.21
DTI Guidance 10.15
economic, technical or organisational
  resources entailing change in the
  workforce (ETOR) 10.06, 10.45
employee representatives 1.17, 10.30–10.39,
  10.46
  agreement of 10.39–10.42
  appropriate 10.26–10.27, 10.30–10.39,
    10.46–10.52
  elections 10.36
  permitted variations 10.26–10.27,
    10.30–10.42, 10.46–10.52
employment contracts, transfer of 10.16
excluded debts 10.17–10.21
hiving down 10.54–10.55
information and consultation 10.31,
  10.34–10.38
Insolvency Directive 10.03
insolvency practitioners 10.10, 10.53
interpretation 10.46–10.52
misuse of 10.53
National Insolvency Fund 1.33
objections to transfer 10.51
permitted variations 10.06, 10.26–10.52
  appropriate representatives 10.26–10.27,
    10.30–10.39, 10.46–10.52
  assigned employees 10.28–10.31
  economic, technical or organisational
    resources entailing change in the
    workforce (ETOR) 10.45
  employee representatives 10.26–10.27,
    10.30–10.42, 10.46–10.52
  interpretation 10.46–10.52
  nature of 10.43–10.45
  objection to transfer 10.51
  requirements for 10.22
  safeguards 10.23
  signatures 10.40–10.42
  trade unions, recognised 10.32–10.33,
    10.39, 10.47, 10.50
  writing 10.40–10.41
proceedings 10.06–10.07, 10.11,
  10.14–10.16, 10.21, 10.25
redundancy 10.18–10.19
relevant insolvency proceedings
  10.14–10.15, 10.25
rescue culture 10.05

resources, organised grouping of 10.28
statutory schemes 10.18, 10.21
terminal insolvencies 10.01–10.02, 10.06
terms and conditions 1.17
  negotiation of 1.17
  variations to 1.33, 6.05, 10.03, 10.06,
    10.22–10.53
time off 10.38
trade unions, recognised 1.17, 10.31–10.32,
  10.38–10.39, 10.47
transferor's debts 10.14–10.20
TUPE 1981 and 10.54–10.55
TUPE 2006 and 1.33, 1.38, 10.01,
  10.05–10.55
unfair dismissal 7.25, 7.43–7.44, 10.09
workforce agreements 10.50
working conditions, changes detrimental to
  4.75, 10.51
insurance, employers' liability compulsory 1.25,
  5.16, 5.18–5.19
international transfers 12.24–12.32
interpretation
  Acquired Rights Directive 1.02, 1.04
  insolvency 10.46–10.52
  permitted variations 10.46–10.52
  restrictive covenants 5.21
  service provision changes 3.45–3.59
interruptions *see* **break in activities**

knowledge of transfer
  collective information and consultation
    4.45
  employee representatives, consultation of
    4.45
  notification 4.45
  TUPE 1981 and 4.45
  TUPE 2006 and 4.45–4.46

labour-intensive activities
  assets, transfer of 2.58–2.59, 2.61, 2.64–2.65,
    2.68, 2.74
  avoiding TUPE, motive of 2.67–2.75
  employees, organised grouping of 2.76
  employees, transfer of 2.62, 2.64–2.76
  identity, retention of 2.36, 2.62, 2.72
  in-housing 2.60
  motive of parties 2.67–2.76
  multifactorial test 2.69
  outsourcing 2.60, 2.72
  poor performance of staff 2.73–2.75
  relevant transfers, definition and
    identification 1.22
  re-tendering 2.60, 2.65
  retention of identity of economic entity
    2.62, 2.72
  service contracts, transfer of 2.63
  service provision change 2.59–2.60, 2.76,
    3.59

Spijkers principles 2.61–2.62
  TUPE 2006 and 2.60–2.76, 2.64
location
  changes to the operation 2.41–2.42
  dismissals 7.05
  working conditions, changes to 4.62, 4.69

mobility clauses 4.30

notice period
  objection to transfer 4.53, 4.56
  pre-transfer employment 4.44
  working conditions, changes to 4.65–4.66,
    4.73

objection to transfer
  communication of 4.54
  constructive dismissal 4.79
  continuity of employment 5.40
  dismissals 4.50, 4.56
  EU law 4.50
  electing not to transfer 4.48–4.56, 4.78–4.80
  employment contracts and liabilities,
    transfer of 4.49
  genuine objections 4.55
  insolvency 10.51
  justification for 4.53
  notice period 4.53, 4.56
  permitted variations 10.51
  reasonableness of 4.53
  remain with transferor, agreement to 4.51
  reorganisation 4.53
  restrictive covenants 4.52
  terminate, contract would otherwise 4.35
  termination of employment, resulting in
    4.51–4.53
  TUPE 1981 and 4.49
  TUPE 2006 and 4.49–4.57
  understanding of consequences of 4.54, 4.56
  unfair dismissal 4.56
occupational pensions 11.01–11.60
  2001 Consultation 11.37
  Acquired Rights Directive 11.01,
    11.06–11.10, 11.23
  anti-avoidance 11.58
  Beckman and *Martin* decisions 11.17–11.32,
    11.37
  changing benefits 11.59
  collective information and consultation
    9.27–9.28
  constructive dismissal 1.37
  contractual status 11.56
  contributions 1.36, 11.16, 11.41,
    11.46–11.47, 11.52–11.57
  defined benefit schemes 1.36, 11.05, 11.15,
    11.40, 11.53, 11.55
  defined contribution schemes 1.36, 11.01,
    11.15, 11.40, 11.46, 11.52–11.53

occupational pensions (*cont.*):
  definition of occupational pensions
    11.12–11.15
  dismissals 11.42
  due diligence 11.28
  economic, technical or organisational
    reasons entailing change in the
    workforce (ETOR) 6.43
  employee liability information
    8.73
  exclusion 11.01–11.31, 11.36
  fines 11.57
  group personal pensions 11.16
  groups, transfers between 11.43
  indemnities 11.29, 11.31
  individual rights, transfer of 5.10
  information and consultation 11.60
  level of benefit 11.51–11.52
  level playing field 11.04
  minimum level of pension provision
    post-transfer 1.14, 1.35, 11.38–11.42,
    11.47–11.56
  misrepresentation, detrimental reliance on
    5.27–5.28
  negligent misrepresentation 5.27
  occupational pension schemes 1.35, 1.49,
    6.41–6.42, 9.27, 11.01, 11.07–11.31
  Pensions Act 2004 and 1.14, 1.20, 1.35,
    6.41–6.44, 11.04–11.05, 11.38–11.60
    categories of employee 11.44–11.46
    changing benefits 11.59
    collective information and consultation
      9.27–9.28
    eligibility 11.43–11.50
    enforcement 11.56–11.59
    minimum level of pension provision 1.14,
      1.35, 11.38–11.42, 11.47–11.56
    ss. 257–8 text *App 2*
  Pensions Protection Regulations (PPR)
    2005 1.14, 1.20, 1.35, 6.41–6.44,
    11.04–11.05, 11.38–11.60
    categories of employee 11.44–11.46
    changing benefits 11.59
    collective information and consultation
      9.27–9.28
    eligibility 11.43–11.50
    minimum level of pension provision 1.14,
      1.35, 11.38–11.42, 11.47–11.55
    text of *App 3*
  Pensions Regulator 11.57
  public sector 1.49, 11.02–11.03,
    11.17–11.31, 11.38
  reference scheme test 1.36, 11.54
  second state pension, contracting out of
    11.54
  SERPS 11.08
  stakeholder pensions 1.36, 11.04, 11.47,
    11.52

  supplementary or inter-company schemes
    11.10–11.11
  terms and conditions, variations to
    6.41–6.44
  TUPE 1981 and 11.01, 11.09, 11.18–11.19,
    11.32, 11.36
  TUPE 2006 and 1.14, 1.35–1.37, 6.41–6.43,
    11.32–11.42
  waiting period 11.48
one-off short-term service contracts
  2005 Consultation 3.22
  Acquired Rights Directive 3.02–3.04,
    3.07
  anti-avoidance 3.28
  assignment 4.27
  Consultation Response 3.26, 3.30
  DTI Guidance 3.24, 3.27
  employees, organised grouping of 3.22
  evidence 3.28
  large projects 3.25–3.226
  retrospective claims 3.29
  series of engagements 3.23
  service provision changes 1.22–1.23, 2.05,
    3.07, 3.13, 3.22–3.30, 3.47, 3.59
  successive contracts 3.28–3.29
  TUPE 2006 and 3.22–3.30
one-person undertakings
  autonomy 2.26
  economic activities 2.25
  economic entity, as 2.25–2.26
  employees, organised grouping of 3.52
  service provision changes 3.52–3.54
  Spijkers principles 2.25
  structure 2.26
  TUPE 2006 and 2.25–2.26
operation, changes to *see* **changes to the**
  operation
organised grouping of employees see **employees,**
  transfer of organised grouping of
organised grouping of resources *see* **resources,**
  organised grouping of
outsourcing 1.03, 12.46
  assignment test 12.46
  costs 12.46
  employee liability information 8.42,
    12.46
  employees, organised grouping of
    3.18–13.19
  labour-intensive activities 2.60, 2.72
  pricing 12.46
  public sector 1.40, 1.49
  relevant transfers, definition and
    identification 1.22
  re-tendering 1.03, 12.46
  service provision changes 1.22, 1.38, 2.05,
    3.03, 3.06, 3.09, 3.59
  share-based transactions 1.11
  territoriality 12.24, 12.28, 12.31

part of undertaking, transfer of
  bonuses and benefits 5.22
  identity of economic activity, retention of
    2.39
  re-tendering 2.39–2.40
  stability 2.39
particulars of employment 8.13, 8.14–8.17
pensions *see* **occupational pensions**
period of time, transfers over a 2.79–2.82
permitted variations, insolvency and 10.06,
    10.26–10.52
  appropriate representatives 10.26–10.27,
    10.30–10.39, 10.46–10.52
  assigned employees 10.28–10.31
  economic, technical or organisational
    resources entailing change in the
    workforce (ETOR) 10.45
  employee representatives 10.26–10.27,
    10.30–10.42, 10.46–10.52
  interpretation 10.46–10.52
  nature of 10.43–10.45
  objections to transfer 10.51
  requirements for 10.22
  safeguards 10.23
  signatures 10.40–10.42
  trade unions, recognised 10.32–10.33, 10.39,
    10.47, 10.50
  writing 10.40–10.41
pre-transfer employment
  2005 Consultation 4.38, 4.43
  breaks in employment 4.44
  dismissal 4.39–4.43
  employment contracts and liabilities,
    transfer of 4.37–4.44
  notice period, serving a 4.44
  series of transactions 4.42
  service provision changes 3.56
  TUPE 1981 and 4.38–4.40
  TUPE 2006 and 4.37–4.44
  unfair dismissal 4.40
professional business services, exemption for
  2005 Consultation 3.41–3.43
  dedicated teams of employees 3.42–3.44
  employees, organised grouping of 3.42, 3.44
  public sector 3.41
  service provision changes 3.08, 3.39–3.44
  TUPE 2006 and 3.39–3.44
public sector
  2001 Consultation 1.46
  administration 1.40–1.47
  best value 3.06
  codes of practice 1.49–1.51
  economic activities 1.41–1.42
  employees, organised grouping of 1.46
  employers' liability compulsory insurance
    1.25, 5.18–5.19
  Employment Relations Act 1999 section 38
    1.52–1.53

  exclusion zones 1.43–1.46, 1.49
  external contracting out 1.49
  government codes of practice 1.49–1.51
  guidance 1.50–1.51
  internal transfers 1.48, 1.50
  outsourcing 1.40, 1.49
  pensions 1.49, 11.02–11.03, 11.38
  professional services 3.41
  reorganisation 1.43–1.45, 1.49
  service provision changes 1.50, 3.06
  transfers in and out of 1.40
  TUPE 2006 and 1.46–1.48
  TUPE-equivalent protection 1.48, 1.53
purpose of transfer legislation 1.01–1.07

reasons for dismissal 7.42
recognised trade unions 5.56–5.66
  2001 Consultation 5.63
  2005 Consultation 5.57, 5.63
  Acquired Rights Directive 5.56–5.57,
    5.63–5.64
  Central Arbitration Committee (CAC) 1.30,
    5.66
  collective agreements 5.42, 5.46–5.49, 5.52,
    5.54, 5.61
  collective bargaining 5.59
  continuation of recognition 5.61–5.65
  employee representatives 9.35, 9.37–9.40,
    9.43, 9.60, 10.31–10.33, 10.39
  employees organised grouping of 5.58
  identity of economic entity, retention of
    5.57, 5.62–5.63, 5.65
  individual rights, transfer of 5.12
  information and consultation 5.12, 5.64,
    9.104
  permitted variations 10.32–10.33, 10.39,
    10.47, 10.50
  pre-transfer recognition 5.60
  resources, organised grouping of 5.58,
    5.65
  statutory recognition 1.30, 5.66
  transfer of recognition 5.59
  TUPE 1981 and 5.57
  TUPE 2006 and 1.30, 5.57–5.64, 5.66
  working conditions, detrimental changes to
    5.61
redundancy; *see also* **redundancy payments**
  collective information and consultation
    9.07–9.08, 9.13, 9.34, 9.111
    compensation 9.97–9.98
    interaction with collective redundancy
      consultation 9.97–9.98
    special circumstances defence 9.90,
      9.92–9.93
  compensation 9.97–9.98
  compromise agreements 12.08
  continuity of employment 5.40–5.41
  dismissals 7.05, 7.42

redundancy (*cont.*):
  economic, technical or organisational
    reasons entailing change in the
    workforce (ETOR) 7.40
  insolvency 10.18–10.19
  special circumstances defence 9.90,
    9.92–9.93
  terms and conditions, variations to 6.03
  territoriality 12.31
redundancy payments 7.34–7.35
  collective information and consultation
    9.74, 9.76–9.77, 9.81
  dismissals 7.09
  economic, technical or organisational
    reasons entailing change in the
    workforce (ETOR) 7.34–7.35
  regulation 7(3)(b) 7.34–7.35
  TUPE 1981 and 7.34
  TUPE 2006 and 7.34–7.35
re-engagement
  continuity of employment 6.21
  economic, technical or organisational
    reasons entailing change in the
    workforce (ETOR) 6.29
  terms and conditions, variations to 6.02,
    6.08, 6.10, 6.17, 6.21
relevant insolvency proceedings 10.14–10.15,
  10.25
relevant transfers, definition and identification
  of 1.21–1.23, 2.01–2.84
  2005 Consultation 2.01
  assignment of 4.14
  definition of transfer of undertaking 2.04,
    2.07–2.59
  economic entity retaining its identity 1.21,
    2.06
  employees, organised grouping of
    1.22
  employment by transferor 4.06, 4.08
  in-housing 1.22
  labour-intensive activities 2.60–2.76
  outsourcing 1.22
  re-tendering 1.22
  service provision change 1.22–1.23, 2.03,
    2.05
  transfer of undertakings 2.03–2.04,
    2.08–2.59
  TUPE 2006 and 1.21–1.23, 1.39
relocation *see* **location**
reorganisation
  administrative functions 1.43–1.45
  economic activity 1.43–1.45
  internal 1.03
  objections to transfer 4.53
  public sector 1.43–1.45, 1.49
  share-based transactions 1.11
repudiatory breach of contract 4.48, 4.59, 4.64,
  4.69, 4.76–4.77

resignation
  electing not to transfer 4.48, 4.56–4.76
  repudiatory breach 4.48
  working conditions, changes to 4.48,
    4.57–4.76, 4.78
resources, organised grouping of
  assignment 4.15
  economic entity 2.18–2.19
  employees, organised grouping of 3.17
  insolvency 10.28
  trade unions, recognised 5.58, 5.65
  unfair dismissal 7.14
restrictive covenants
  employment contracts 4.52
  individual rights, transfer of 5.21
  interpretation 5.21
  objections to transfer 4.52
  terms and conditions, variations to 6.22
  TUPE 2006 and 5.21
re-tendering
  assets, transfer of 2.51
  employee liability information 8.42, 8.66
  identity of economic activity, retention of
    2.39–2.40
  labour-intensive factors 2.60, 2.65
  outsourcing 1.03, 12.46
  parts of undertakings 2.39–2.40
  relevant transfers, definition and
    identification 1.22
  service provision changes 1.22, 2.05, 3.03,
    3.05, 3.09, 3.14, 3.59
retention of identity of economic entity 2.20,
  2.22–2.23
  assets, transfer of 2.36, 2.47–2.59
  break in activities 2.45–2.46
  changes to the operation 2.41–2.44
  employees, organised grouping of 3.19
  labour-intensive activities 2.36, 2.62, 2.72
  parts of undertakings 2.39
  re-tendering 2.39–2.40
  service provision changes 3.47, 3.49–3.50
  Spijkers factors 2.33–2.36, 2.45
  stability 2.39
  territoriality 12.27–12.29
  trade unions, recognised 5.57, 5.62–5.63,
    5.65
  TUPE 2006 and 2.32–2.36
retirement
  age 5.31–5.34
  individual rights, transfer of 5.30–5.35
  normal retirement age 5.32–5.34
  TUPE 1981 and 5.34
  TUPE 2006 and 5.30–5.35
  unfair dismissal, retirement age and
    5.32–5.35
retrospective claims
  one-off short-term service contracts
    3.28–3.29

terms and conditions, variations to 6.26,
6.32

sale of assets *see* **assets, transfer of**
series of transactions 2.27, 2.82, 4.42
service companies 4.09, 4.12
service contracts, transfer of 2.63;
see also **one-off short-term service
contracts**
service provision changes 3.01–3.62
2001 Consultation 3.04, 3.07
Acquired Rights Directive 3.02–3.04, 3.07
activities, definition of 3.13
assets, transfer of 2.59, 3.11–3.12
best value 3.06
break in activities 3.51
collective information and consultation 1.39
commodity services 3.07
Consultation Response 3.02, 3.14, 3.49, 3.53
dedicated teams of employees 3.47
definition 1.22, 3.09–3.14
delivery, change in the nature of service 3.48
division of activities between contractors
3.55–3.56
DTI Guidance 3.02–3.03, 3.54, 3.56–3.57
economic entities 3.47, 3.62
employees, organised grouping of 2.05, 3.11,
3.14–3.21, 3.59
division of activities between contractors
3.55
duration of 3.46
one-person undertakings 3.52
pre-transfer activities 3.56
principal purpose 3.20–3.21, 3.57
stability 3.52
subcontractors 3.14
transfer of 1.22, 2.05, 3.11, 3.14–3.21,
3.59
employment by transferor 4.07, 4.13
geographical division of activities 3.55
identity of economic entity, retention of
3.47, 3.49–3.50
information to employees 3.05
in-housing 1.22, 2.05, 3.03, 3.06, 3.09,
3.59
innovative bids 3.35–3.38, 3.49
interpretation 3.45–3.59
labour-intensive contracts 2.59–2.60, 2.76,
3.59
level playing field 3.05–3.06
motives 3.11
one-off awards of short duration 1.22–1.23,
2.05, 3.07, 3.13, 3.22–3.30, 3.47, 3.59
one-person activities 3.52–3.54
outsourcing 1.22, 1.38, 2.05, 3.03, 3.06, 3.09,
3.59
pre-transfer activities 3.56
principal purpose 1.22, 3.20–3.21, 3.57

professional business services, proposal of
exemption for 3.08, 3.39–3.44
public sector 3.06
relevant transfers, definition and
identification 1.22–1.23, 2.03, 2.05
re-tendering 1.22, 2.05, 3.03, 3.06, 3.09,
3.14, 3.59
service, definition of 3.13
single contract undertakings 2.31
Spijkers principles 3.05
stability and structure 3.07, 3.10, 3.52
subcontractors 3.14, 3.62
supply of goods 1.23, 3.31–3.34, 3.47, 3.58
terminate, contract would otherwise 4.36
territoriality 12.19–12.20, 12.27
test for 2.31
TUPE 1981 and 3.03, 3.61
TUPE 2006 and 1.22, 1.38, 1.39, 1.50, 2.31,
3.01–3.62
share-based transactions 1.08–1.113
see also **share options**
employment contracts 1.09
outsourcing 1.11
reorganisation 1.11
transfers 1.08–1.11
share options
employee liability information 8.72
employment contracts 5.25
lapse of 5.26
substantial equivalence test 5.26
TUPE 2006 and 5.25
ships
2005 Consultation 2.83
assets, transfer of 2.51–2.52
crew, transfer of 2.83
registration, change in 2.84
transfer of ships 2.83–2.84
TUPE 2006 and 2.83–2.84
short-term service contracts *see* **one-off
short-term service contracts**
single contract undertakings
autonomy 2.28
continuity of employment 2.30
economic activities 2.27–2.31
service provision change 2.31
stability 2.27–2.28
TUPE 2006 and 2.27–2.31
single persons *see* **one-person undertakings**
special circumstances defence
employee liability information 1.31
failure to inform and consult 9.89–9.94
Spijkers **principles**
assets, transfer of 2.48, 2.58
break in activities 2.45
identity of economic activity, retention of
2.33–2.36, 2.45
one-person undertakings 2.25
service provision changes 3.05

stability and structure
  economic entity 2.19–2.24
  employees, organised grouping of 3.17, 3.52
  identity of economic activity, retention of
    2.39
  parts of undertakings 2.39
  service provision changes 3.07, 3.10, 3.52
  single contract undertakings 2.27–2.28
subcontractors 3.14, 3.62
substantial equivalence test 5.23–5.24
supply of goods
  2005 Consultation 3.31
  outsourcing of procurement 3.34
  procurement 3.34
  service provision changes 1.23, 3.31–3.34,
    3.47, 3.58
  TUPE 2006 and 3.31, 3.34
  wholly or mainly test 3.33, 3.58

temporary assignment 4.26–4.31
  2005 Consultation 4.29
  assignment test 4.26
  human stock approach 4.17
  mobility clauses 4.30
  one-off contracts 4.27
  quality of workforce 4.26–4.28
  terms and conditions 4.30
  TUPE 2006 and 4.26–4.31
temporary cessation *see* **break in activities**
tenders 8.39, 8.42, 8.46; *see also* **re-tendering**
terminate, contracts would otherwise
  Consultation Response 4.35
  objection to transfer 4.35
  service provision changes 4.36
  TUPE 1981 and 4.32–4.34
  TUPE 2006 and 4.33–4.36
terms and conditions of employment;
    see also **variation to employees' terms**
    and conditions
  assignment 4.30
  common law 1.06
  employee liability information 8.73
  harmonisation 6.14, 6.38–6.40
  insolvency, negotiation of changes on
    1.17
  TUPE 2006 and 1.28
  written particulars 8.13, 8.14–8.17
territoriality 12.12–12.32
  abroad from the UK, transfers 12.29–12.32
  abroad, working 1.34, 12.14, 12.16,
    12.20–12.22, 12.26–12.28
  Acquired Rights Directive 12.12–12.13,
    12.24
  collective information and consultation
    12.30
  compensation 12.14
  continental shelf 12.23
  dismissal 12.18

  domestic undertakings with overseas
    employees 12.25–12.26
  DTI Guidance 12.17, 12.21
  economic, technical or organisational
    reasons entailing change in the
    workforce (ETOR) 12.31
  employee liability information 12.30
  employment tribunal claims 12.32
  foreign law, contract covered by 12.22
  identity of economic entity, retention of
    12.27–12.29
  information and consultation 12.14, 12.32
  international transfers 12.24–12.32
  outsourcing 12.24, 12.28, 12.31
  overseas employees, domestic undertakings
    with 12.25–12.26
  redundancy 12.31
  service provision change 12.19–12.20, 12.27
  transfer of undertakings 12.19–12.20, 12.27
  TUPE 1981 and 12.14
  TUPE 2006 and 1.34, 12.15–12.32
  UK, work outside the 1.34, 12.14, 12.16,
    12.20–12.22, 12.26–12.28
  unfair dismissal 12.31–12.32
time off
  ACAS Code of Practice on Time Off for
    Trade Union Activities 9.43
  employee representatives 9.43, 9.61–9.63,
    10.38
  employment tribunals 9.61–9.62
  insolvency 10.38
timing of transfers
  continuity of employment 2.80
  date of transfer 2.82
  importance of 2.78–2.82
  period of time, transfers over a 2.79–2.82
  TUPE 2006 and 2.78–2.82
trade unions; *see also* **recognised trade unions**
  ACAS Code of Practice on Time Off for
    Trade Union Activities 9.43
  collective information and consultation
    9.02–9.03, 9.65
  insolvency 1.17
  terms and conditions, negotiation of
    changes to 1.17
transfers of undertakings
  assets, transfer of 2.10, 2.47–2.59
  break in activities 2.45–2.46
  connected transactions 2.77
  change to the operation 2.41–2.44
  components of 2.09–2.10
  definition 2.04, 2.07–2.59
  economic entities, definition of 2.17–2.24
  legal agreements or relationships 2.14
  one-person undertakings 2.25–2.26
  part of undertaking, transfer of 2.37–40
  relevant transfers, definition and
    identification 2.03–2.04, 2.08–2.59

responsibility test 2.13–2.15
retention of identity 2.32–2.36
retention of control, effect of 2.15
series of transactions 2.77, 2.82
single contract undertakings 2.27–2.31
territoriality 12.19–12.20, 12.27
timing of transfers 2.78–2.82
TUPE 2006 and 2.04, 2.07–2.59
Transfer of Undertakings Regulations
    see **TUPE 1981, TUPE 2006**
transitional provisions 1.39
tribunals *see* **employment tribunals**
TUPE 1981
2001 Consultation 1.14
Acquired Rights Directive, implementation
    of 1.01
amendments 1.12–1.14, 1.20–1.37
application of 1.03–1.07
consultation on amendment of 1.14
draft regulations 1.14
EU law 1.01
economic, technical and organisational
    reasons entailing change in the
    workforce (ETOR) 1.07
effects of 1.07
employment contracts 1.07
Fairness at Work White Paper 1.12
purpose 1.01–1.07
unfair dismissal 7.22
TUPE 2006
2001 Consultation 1.46
administrative functions 1.43–1.45
collective information and consultation 1.39
consultation process 1.14
dismissals 1.27, 1.38
EU law 1.15
employee liability information, notification
    of 1.31–1.32, 1.38, 1.39
employees, definition of 1.26
employers' liability insurance 1.25
employment contracts and liabilities,
    transfer of 1.24
employment contracts, changes to 1.38
Employment Relations Act 1999 1.15
employment tribunals 1.32
failure to inform and consult, liability for
    1.29
guidance 1.14
insolvency 1.33, 1.38
objectives of 1.18–1.20
pensions 1.35–1.37
regulatory impact assessment 1.38
relevant transfer, definition of 1.21–1.23,
    1.39
terms and conditions 1.28, 1.38
territoriality 1.34
text of *App 1*
trade union, recognition of 1.30

transitional provisions 1.39
unfair dismissal 1.27, 7.01, 7.03, 7.12–7.24,
    7.43–7.44
who transfers 1.26

unfair dismissal
automatic 1.27, 7.03–7.05, 7.12–7.21,
    7.43–7.44
compensation 9.59
compromise agreements 6.17–6.21,
    12.05–12.06
connection with the transfer 7.22–7.29
economic, technical or organisational
    reasons entailing change in the
    workforce (ETOR) 6.36, 7.04, 7.10,
    7.12–7.13, 7.17, 7.30–7.42
electing not to transfer 4.48
exceptions 7.18–7.21
fairness 7.43–7.44
insolvency 7.25, 7.43–7.44, 10.09
objections to transfer 4.56
pre-transfer dismissals 4.40, 7.44
protected persons 7.14–7.17
qualifying period 9.59
reasonable responses, range of 7.44
resources, organised grouping of 7.14
retirement age 5.32–5.35
sole or principal reason test 7.22–7.24
terms and conditions, variations to
    6.02–6.03, 6.17–6.21
territoriality 12.31–12.32
timing 7.23–7.24
TUPE 1981 and 7.22
TUPE 2006 and 1.27, 7.01, 7.03, 7.12–7.24,
    7.43–7.44, 9.56–9.60
uncertain transactions 7.25–7.29
waiver 6.17–6.21
working conditions, changes to 4.66–4.67,
    4.70–4.71

variation to employees' terms and conditions
    6.01–6.44; *see also* **permitted variations,**
    insolvency and
2001 Consultation 6.24
2005 Consultation 6.25, 6.29
Acquired Rights Directive 6.05, 6.12,
    6.14–6.15, 6.29
bonuses and benefits 5.22
breach of contract 6.04
case law background 6.01–6.23
categories of variation 6.26–6.28
collective consultation and information 6.03
compromise agreements 6.17–6.20,
    12.05–12.07
consent 6.01–6.02, 6.05, 6.16
constructive dismissal 4.79
continuity of employment 6.21
contracting out 6.17–6.20, 12.04

variation to employees' terms and conditions (*cont.*):
dismissals 6.02–6.03, 6.05, 6.08, 6.10, 6.17, 6.21
distancing change from the transfer 6.23
DTI Guidance 6.23, 6.26–6.27
EU law 6.29–6.31
economic, technical and organisational reasons entailing changes in the workforce (ETOR) 6.24, 6.26–6.40
electing not to transfer 4.78–4.79
employee representatives 1.17
harmonisation of terms and conditions 6.14
insolvency 1.33, 6.05, 10.03, 10.06, 10.22–10.53
negotiation of changes 1.17
notice 6.02, 6.05
pensions 6.41–6.44
redundancy 6.03
re-engagement, offers of 6.02, 6.08, 6.10, 6.17, 6.21
reform 6.24–6.25
restrictive covenants 6.22
retrospective claims 6.16
sole or principal reason test 6.26, 6.32
trade unions 1.17
transfer as reason for 6.07–6.16, 6.18–6.23, 6.26–6.30
TUPE 1981 and 6.05, 6.11
TUPE 2006 and 1.38, 6.16, 6.18–6.20, 6.24–6.44
unfair dismissal 6.02–6.03, 6.17–6.21
waiver of rights 6.04, 6.06–6.07, 6.17–6.21
warranties 12.41
working conditions, detrimental changes to 4.75, 6.15

waiver of rights 6.04, 6.06–6.07, 6.17–6.21
warranties 12.37–12.41
collective information and consultation 9.87–9.88
commercial context 12.37, 12.40
due diligence 12.35
employee liability information 8.59, 8.67, 12.38
terms and conditions, variation to 12.41
transferee warranties 12.40–12.41
transferor warranties 12.39
TUPE 2006 and 12.39, 12.41
types of 12.39
working conditions, changes to 12.41
working conditions *see* **changes to working conditions**
written particulars of employment 8.13, 8.14–8.17
wrongful dismissal
electing not to transfer 4.48
working conditions, changes to 4.65–4.66

NATIONAL POLICE LIBRARY